Transnational Crime, Crime Control and Security

Series Editors
James Sheptycki, Social Science, York University, Toronto, ON, Canada
Anastassia Tsoukala, Sport Sciences, University of Paris XI Sport Sciences, Orsay, France

Transnational crime and security are key modalities of governance in a globalizing world. World-wide, there is a tendency to treat every imaginable source of harm as a potential source of insecurity, and therefore as a crime. The catastrophic imagination is fueled by the precautionary logics of a world system troubled by systemic risk. As these logics become pervasive, security measures are invoked in an effort to control the imagined sources of harm, and the consequences are not always clear-cut. Further, the terminology of transnational crime, threat, risk and (in)security (and the phenomena to which they refer) is substantively deterritorialized, raising further theoretical and practical difficulties. Research and scholarship concerning these issues touches upon crucial features of the world system. This series offers wide inter-disciplinary scope for scholarship exploring these central aspects of global governance and governance globally.

Elizabeth A. Faulkner

The Trafficking of Children

International Law, Modern Slavery, and the Anti-Trafficking Machine

Elizabeth A. Faulkner
Keele University
Keele, UK

ISSN 2947-4264   ISSN 2947-4272 (electronic)
Transnational Crime, Crime Control and Security
ISBN 978-3-031-23568-9   ISBN 978-3-031-23566-5 (eBook)
https://doi.org/10.1007/978-3-031-23566-5

© The Editor(s) (if applicable) and The Author(s), under exclusive license to Springer Nature Switzerland AG 2023
This work is subject to copyright. All rights are solely and exclusively licensed by the Publisher, whether the whole or part of the material is concerned, specifically the rights of translation, reprinting, reuse of illustrations, recitation, broadcasting, reproduction on microfilms or in any other physical way, and transmission or information storage and retrieval, electronic adaptation, computer software, or by similar or dissimilar methodology now known or hereafter developed.
The use of general descriptive names, registered names, trademarks, service marks, etc. in this publication does not imply, even in the absence of a specific statement, that such names are exempt from the relevant protective laws and regulations and therefore free for general use.
The publisher, the authors, and the editors are safe to assume that the advice and information in this book are believed to be true and accurate at the date of publication. Neither the publisher nor the authors or the editors give a warranty, expressed or implied, with respect to the material contained herein or for any errors or omissions that may have been made. The publisher remains neutral with regard to jurisdictional claims in published maps and institutional affiliations.

This Palgrave Macmillan imprint is published by the registered company Springer Nature Switzerland AG
The registered company address is: Gewerbestrasse 11, 6330 Cham, Switzerland

For Cathal, Orlaith, Niamh, Baby Bean and Méabh

Foreword

When the United Nations adopted a new international treaty in 2000 defining the crime of 'trafficking in persons' (the UN Protocol to Prevent, Suppress and Punish Trafficking in Persons, Especially Women and Children, supplementing the UN Convention against Transnational Organized Crime), it was hailed in many countries as a major initiative to stop 'modern day slavery'. It was regarded by some as a significant step forward in protecting human rights, particularly the rights of women and girls. However, as is so often the case, the devil was in the detail.

The treaty only defined the cases in which children were trafficked in an oblique way, creating the potential for ambiguity and for all sorts of situations involving young people aged under 18 to be labelled as 'child trafficking', and those supporting or employing them to be accused of being traffickers. Whereas the crime of trafficking adults was defined to involve some sort of coercion or trickery in recruiting them or arranging their travel, in the case of anyone aged under 18 this aspect was not deemed necessary, meaning that helping adolescents to migrate could potentially be regarded as a trafficking offence if they ended up being exploited in one of the ways mentioned in the treaty.

To create further confusion, the same year the UN adopted a separate treaty labelling similar situations in which young people were exploited as 'sale of children', whilst the previous year the International Labour Organization (ILO) had decided to use the term 'worst forms of child labour'. When it comes to applying them in 'real word' situations, a great deal of imprecision still surrounds all these terms. Nevertheless, the scene was set for an explosion of interest in human trafficking in general and child trafficking in particular, especially in the United States. This interest was fuelled by exaggerated portrayals of the scale of the problem, often eclipsing cases involving children who were genuinely suffering dreadful abuse. During the first decade of the twenty-first century 'child trafficking' became a *cause célèbre* that Hollywood stars queued up to denounce. Estimates of the numbers of child victims increased from year to year, with one part of the UN misquoting statistics published by another. The total numbers of trafficking victims around the world counted by UN institutions climbed from an initial 12.5 million (in 2005) to almost 50 million by 2022—the result of ever-changing methods for counting cases rather than evidence that the scale of abuse was increasing. Legislators and policymakers claimed credit for 'saving' countless adults and children from harm (including irregular migrants who were promptly deported). Equally troubling, some children who sought to work away from home were labelled 'trafficking victims' and the United States Department of State exerted pressure on the countries involved to keep such children at home—even when this meant girls as young as 13 and 14 were obliged to marry instead.

When abuses of human rights are reported in such an inaccurate, emotive, and politicised way, the subject matter requires careful analysis by disinterested parties—analysis of what activities are being labelled as abuse (in this case, 'child trafficking'), by whom and for what purpose, including what advantages it brings to those using the label and what the implications are for those being labelled (as 'victims' or even 'slaves'). An understanding of the historical background is especially helpful, for it shows how the treaty adopted in 2000 was developed on the basis of almost a century of international 'concern' (and often misunderstanding) of cases in which children exercise their independence by embarking on life away from their family or school—and are sometimes (but only sometimes) subjected to exploitation and abuse.

Two decades after the UN Protocol on trafficking in persons was adopted, Elizabeth A. Faulkner provides many of the insights necessary to understand how the term 'child trafficking' was developed, how it has been manipulated, and what the implications are. Whether the confusion and mess that has been created will ever be sorted out remains to be seen. Like so many miscarriages of justice, at the moment the institutions responsible are in denial and unwilling to remedy their mistakes. It is even more of a cliché, but the road to hell remains paved with good intentions.

Author in 2003 of '*Kids as commodities? Child trafficking and what to do about it*'

United Kingdom   Mike Dottridge
November 2022

Mike Dottridge has worked in the human rights field for 45 years. He worked for two human rights non-governmental organisations (Amnesty International and Anti-Slavery International, where he was director until 2002). His work for Amnesty concerned sub-Saharan Africa. Since 1995 he has focused on the rights of adults and children who experience economic or sexual exploitation. Since 2002 he has worked independently, undertaking evaluations and institutional learning exercises for both international organisations and NGOs. He is the author of numerous articles and handbooks commenting on aspects of international law concerning slavery, servitude, forced labour, child labour and human trafficking or suggesting ways to prevent such exploitation and how to protect and assist the victims.

Acknowledgements

I would like to start by thanking former tutors, some of whom are now colleagues at Keele Law School, Jane Krishnadas, Ambreena Manji, Zoe Pearson, Mario Prost, and Dania Thomas for their roles in developing my interests in international law, human rights, and social justice and to the realisation that being an academic was a career option. To Mario for his unforgettable first 'International Law' lecture featuring family guy and to Jane from our first encounter in Law in Action, to the exchange programme with the TATA Institute of Social Sciences, Mumbai as part of my MA programme shaped my intellectual curiosity. To my Grandad who flew to Goa on a holiday during my exchange, who used to swell with pride talking about me as I was "book smart" and made it to university.

Trevor Buck and Alisdair Gillespie for selecting me from the interviewees as the 'International Child Law Ph.D. Scholarship' student at De Montfort University, UK almost ten years ago. My supervision team aided my struggles with confidence and transitioning to doctoral research, in addition to two periods of maternity leave the unwavering support from Trevor despite delaying his retirement plans. To my examiners Gavin Dingwall and Jessica Elliott, which felt like a surreal and pleasant experience after the VIVA preparation with Vanessa Bettinson.

Without meeting Joel Quirk in London in 2018, this book would not have materialised, and I am forever indebted to Joel and his mentorship and guidance over the last few years. I felt so inspired after hearing your guest lecture at Kings College London and the coffee afterwards, I started to write the proposal on the train ride home. Joel, you opened my eyes to so many opportunities which have influenced my plans and continue to encourage and nurture despite how busy you are. Thank you to Joel for reviewing the full draft, to Laura Lammasniemi, Neil Howard, Hila Shamir, and colleagues from the TraffLab, Mario Prost, and John Cotter for their comments on sections of the book.

The archival research would not have been possible without a chance meeting with Celine Tan at the University of Leicester conference 'Neglected methodologies of international law' organised by Rossana Deplano. Thanks to Celine and her networks, she put me in contact with Stéphanie De Moerloose (University of Geneva) who arranged with her brother Benedicte Moerloose for me to stay in Geneva free of charge. This generosity sparked this entire book and the reformulation of my research ideas. To Jacques Oberson of the League of Nations archives, whose patience and kindness for an archive novice was fantastic.

To colleagues both current and former, Lorena Arocha, my friend and confidant, Jean Allain who kindly shared his digitised archival research to supplement my own and particularly John Oldfield for offering the Lectureship in Contemporary Slavery at the Wilberforce Institute and supporting my plans to organise the 2019 conference *Critical Perspectives on Modern Slavery: Law Policy and Society*. To all those who presented and attended creating a forum to develop ideas to the inspiring final keynote from the legend that is Julia O'Connell Davidson.

From a chance meeting at the Law and Society Association Conference, Mexico City 2017 to everything we've worked on together since and hopefully in the future, Laura Lammasniemi. Someone who has had faith in me, challenged me, encouraged me, and shared some laughs, tears, and frustrations with me thank you for your continued friendship. A thank you to Hila Shamir and colleagues of the TraffLab for

Acknowledgements   xiii

allowing me to present a draft chapter of this book in June 2022. Your feedback and thoughtful insights were greatly appreciated. To others who have either inspired me, or allowed me to discuss, or present and exchange ideas to those who have encouraged and supported me. Thanks to Julia O'Connell Davidson, Conrad Nyamutata, Rajnaara Akhtar, Alex Balch, Lennon Mhishi, Patricia Hynes, Fiona de Londras, Ella Cockbain, Ayushman Bhagat, Hannah Lewis, Mike Dottridge, Nandita Sharma, Laura Higson-Bliss, Yossi Nehushtan, and numerous authors of Beyond Trafficking Beyond Slavery and finally to members of the 'Critical Modern Slavery Studies Group'.

I have a few special mentions, firstly to Annie Bunting and Benjamin Lawrence, who following my own personal tragedy in 2019 nurtured and re-sparked my passion for academia whilst patiently holding my hands as I drafted a book chapter. A chapter that almost did not come to fruition as after a period of reflection I had led to the decision to leave and pursue a different career. Secondly, to Laura Lundy, Helen Stalford, and Leona Vaughn who dried my tears in December 2019, encouraging me not to quit. Thank you for unknowingly keeping me within academia and rediscovering the passion that I have for it. Thirdly, to my third year 'Child Law' undergraduate students during the 2022–2023 academic year at Keele University. Thank you for allowing me to test, develop, and finalise some of the points covered within this monograph during the module. Your patience, support, and enthusiasm has been remarkable.

Finally, thanks to my family and most importantly to my rock of support and my biggest champion Cathal. I will be forever grateful to you for your unwavering support and the integral role you have in nurturing our girls when I am burning the midnight oil or hopping onto a witch's broom to another conference. You also sacrificed your own career aspirations in academia, completing your Ph.D. corrections evenings and weekends whilst working full-time so that I could complete my own doctoral research part-time. Sharing the highs and lows of parenthood together, I think we've juggled it all rather well.

Thank you.

Contents

1	**Introduction—The Tale of Children and the Anti-trafficking Machine**	1
1.1	Introduction	1
1.2	The Neglected Histories of Child Trafficking	5
1.3	Child Trafficking Globally—A Brief Overview	8
1.4	Defining the Trafficking of Children	11
1.5	Contemporary Anti-trafficking	16
	1.5.1 The Trafficked Child: Prostitution, "Sex Trafficking", and Victim Pornography	19
1.6	Methods and Theoretical Framework	29
	1.6.1 The League of Nations Archival Research	30
	1.6.2 The Theoretical Frameworks: Introducing the "Anti-trafficking Machine"	33
1.7	Structure of the Book	37
	References	40

2	**Protecting Children: Childhood, Rights, and the Trafficked Child**		51
	2.1 Introduction		51
	2.2 Childhood, Children's Rights, and International Law		52
		2.2.1 Childhood	52
		2.2.2 Human Rights, Children's Rights, and International Law	56
		2.2.3 The United Nations Convention on the Rights of the Child 1989	64
	2.3 International Law and "Children on the Move"		78
		2.3.1 The Global Compacts (2018)	83
		2.3.2 The Clash: Fears of Migration and the Anti-Trafficking Machine	86
	2.4 Summary		93
	References		95
3	**The Emergence of Child Trafficking (1900–1946)**		105
	3.1 Introduction		105
	3.2 Human Trafficking in the Twentieth Century—A Brief History		107
		3.2.1 The International Instruments 1904–1933	108
	3.3 The League of Nations (1919–1945) and Human Trafficking		114
		3.3.1 The League of Nations: Anti-Trafficking	116
		3.3.2 The Advisory Committee on the Traffic in Women and Children	125
		3.3.3 The Summary of Annual Reports: 1922–1945	127
	3.4 Empire, Race, and White Slavery		134
	3.5 Summary		137
	References		138

4	**Child Trafficking, Children's Rights, and Modern Slavery: International Law in the Twentieth and Twenty-First Centuries**		143
	4.1	Introduction	143
	4.2	The Conflict of Definitions: Trafficking, Slavery, and Modern Slavery	144
	4.3	The International Legal Framework of the Twentieth and Twenty-First Centuries: Slavery and Trafficking	149
		4.3.1 The Slavery Convention 1926	153
		4.3.2 The Supplementary Convention on the Abolition of Slavery, the Slave Trade, and Institutions and Practices Similar to Slavery 1956	162
	4.4	The United Nations (1945–Present Day)	168
		4.4.1 Universal Declaration of Human Rights (UDHR), 1948	168
		4.4.2 UN Convention for the Suppression of the Traffic in Persons and of the Exploitation of the Prostitution of Others, 1949	172
		4.4.3 The UN Protocol to Prevent, Suppress, and Punish Trafficking in Persons, Especially Women and Children 2000	176
		4.4.4 The Convention on the Rights of the Child (CRC) 1989	186
	4.5	Summary	196
	References		197
5	**Child Trafficking: Contemporary Action in the Twenty-First Century**		205
	5.1	Introduction	205
		5.1.1 The Contemporary Anti-Trafficking Crusaders	206
	5.2	Global Sustainable Development Goals (SDGs)	208
	5.3	The International Labour Organization (ILO)	213

		5.3.1	International Programme on the Elimination of Child Labour (IPEC)	216
	5.4		The Special Rapporteurs of the United Nations	217
		5.4.1	Special Rapporteur on the Sale and Sexual Exploitation of Children, Including Child Prostitution, Child Pornography, and Other Child Sexual Abuse Material	219
		5.4.2	Special Rapporteur on Trafficking in Persons, Especially Women and Children	222
		5.4.3	Special Rapporteur on Contemporary Forms of Slavery, Including Its Causes and Consequences	222
	5.5	Unicef		223
	5.6		The Anti-Trafficking Giant—Understanding the Role of the USA, (TIP)	224
	5.7		The International Criminal Court (ICC)	230
	5.8		The Inter-American Court of Human Rights (IACtHR): 'Hacienda Brasil Verde Workers V. Brazil' 2016	234
	5.9		The United Nations Office on Drugs and Crime: Human Trafficking Case Law Database	236
		5.9.1	Labour Exploitation Case, Malawi, 2005	236
		5.9.2	Illegal Adoption Case, Guatemala, 2009	237
		5.9.3	Sexual Exploitation Case, The Philippines, 2011	238
		5.9.4	Begging and Labour Exploitation Case, Bosnia and Herzegovina, 2017	238
	5.10	Summary		239
	References			240
6	**Child Trafficking in Europe: Nationalism, Vulnerability, and Protection**			**247**
	6.1	Introduction		247
	6.2		The Anti-Trafficking Legal Regime of Europe	249
		6.2.1	The Council of Europe	252
		6.2.2	The European Union	262

6.3	The European Court of Human Rights	274
6.4	Case Study: The UK of Great Britain and Northern Ireland	276
	6.4.1 The Rise of Modern Slavery in the UK	277
	6.4.2 The Modern Slavery Act 2015	282
	6.4.3 Children: Slavery, Trafficking, and Exploitation	287
	6.4.4 "Categorical Fetishism" and Children in the UK	292
	6.4.5 The UK and the European Court of Human Rights	298
6.5	Summary	310
	References	311

7 Conclusion: A Tale of Child Trafficking and the Shift to Modern Slavery — 321
References — 329

Appendix A: The White Slavery Agreement of 1904 and Convention of 1910 — 331

Appendix B: The Questions of the Summary of Reports (1921–1938) — 341

Index — 347

Abbreviations

ASEAN	Association of Southeast Asian Nations
AU	African Union
CAHTEH Ad Hoc	Committee on Action against Trafficking in Human Beings (Council of Europe)
CEDAW	Convention on the Elimination of All Forms of Discrimination against Women
CoE	Council of Europe
CRC	Convention on the Rights of the Child
ECHR	European Court of Human Rights
ECOSOC	Economic and Social Council
EU	European Union
EUROSTAT	Eurostat Statistical Office of the European Union
GEMS	Global Estimates of Modern Slavery
GRETA	Group of Experts on Action against Trafficking in Human Beings
HRC	Human Rights Committee
HTCLD	Human Trafficking Case Law Database
ICC	International Criminal Court
ICCPR	International Covenant on Civil and Political Rights
ICESCR	International Covenant on Economic, Social and Cultural Rights

ICJ	International Court of Justice
IDAC	International Data Alliance on Children on the Move
IDMC	Internal Displacement Monitoring Centre
IGO	International governmental organisation
ILO	International Labour Organization
IOM	International Organization for Migration
LNTWC	League's Traffic in Women and Children Committee
LoN	League of Nations
MSA	Modern Slavery Act
NCA	National Crime Agency
NGO	Non-governmental organisation
OCSE	Organization for Security and Co-operation in Europe
OECD	Organisation for Economic Cooperation and Development
OPAC	Optional Protocol to the Convention on the Rights of the Child on the Involvement of Children in Armed Conflict
OPIC	Optional Protocol to the Convention on the Rights of the Child on a Communication Procedure
OPSC	Optional Protocol to the Convention on the Rights of the Child on the Sale of Children, child prostitution and child pornography
SAARC	South Asian Association for Regional Cooperation
TIP	Trafficking in Persons
TIP report	The US Trafficking in Persons Report
TSC	League of Nations Temporary Slavery Commission
TVPA	Trafficking Victims Protection Act
TWAIL	Third World Approaches to International Law
UDHR	Universal Declaration of Human Rights
UN	United Nations
UNHCR	United Nations High Commissioner for Refugees
UNCTOC	United Nations Convention against Transnational Organised Crime
UNDESA	UN Department of Social and Economic Affairs
UNHCR	United Nations High Commissioner for Refugees
UNICEF	United Nations Children's Fund
UNODC	United Nations Office on Drugs and Crime
VCLT	Vienna Convention on the Law of Treaties
WFCL	Worst Forms of Child Labour Convention no. 182

List of Figures

Fig. 1.1	Article 3 the Trafficking Protocol	13
Fig. 1.2	Overview of the Trafficking Protocol definition of human trafficking, 2000 (*Source* The author)	14
Fig. 2.1	The Declaration of the Rights of the Child, drafted by the Save the Children Fund International in 1922–1923 and adopted by the Assembly of the League of Nations in 1924 (*Source* Save the Children Fund, London, Weardale Press, 1931)	59
Fig. 2.2	The general principles of the Convention on the Rights of the Child	70
Fig. 4.1	Article 1 of the 1926 Slavery Convention	154
Fig. 4.2	1956 Supplementary Slavery Convention	165
Fig. 4.3	Article 34 of the Convention of the Rights of the Child 1989	190
Fig. 4.4	Article 3 optional protocol on the sale of children, child prostitution, and child pornography	196
Fig. 5.1	Article 3 worst forms child labour convention (C182)	215
Fig. 5.2	TVPA definition of severe forms of human trafficking	225
Fig. 6.1	Article 13–16 EU Directive 2011/36	270

Fig. 6.2	The Non-punishment provision of the Council of Europe Trafficking Convention 2005	299
Graph 6.1	National Referral Mechanism (NRM) referrals (2009–2021) (*Source* Author. Data extracted from the quarterly statistics available via National Referral Mechanism statistics—GOV.UK [www.gov.uk]. Accessed February 2023)	288
Graph 6.2	NRM annual referrals: Children and 'age not known' (2009–2021) (*Source* Author. Data extracted from the quarterly statistics available via National Referral Mechanism statistics—GOV.UK [www.gov.uk]. Accessed February 2023)	288
Graph 6.3	Unaccompanied asylum-seeking children and NRM Referrals (2009–2021) (*Source* Author. Data extracted from the quarterly statistics available via National Referral Mechanism statistics—GOV.UK [www.gov.uk]. Accessed February 2023 and Statistics: looked-after children—GOV.UK [www.gov.uk]. Accessed February 2023)	294

List of Tables

Table 3.1	International convention for the suppression of traffic in women and children 1921	122
Table 3.2	Explicit references to Trafficking: 1922–1938	129

1

Introduction—The Tale of Children and the Anti-trafficking Machine

1.1 Introduction

Child trafficking conjures images of poor, innocent children, trapped, brutalised by evil traffickers, and forced to exist as the slaves of the twenty-first century. The emergence of child trafficking as an issue of contemporary concern was highlighted as a shift from concerns focusing upon child sexual exploitation to child trafficking (Howard, 2017). The phenomenon of child trafficking holds a unique position as an issue of significant contemporary relevance, occupying a principal place in debates about human rights today. Campaigns to eradicate child trafficking and or slavery receive a plethora of support from public figures at all levels of society from celebrities to politicians and religious leaders. What makes child trafficking distinctive within the broader pantheon of human trafficking? This links to the fear and moral outrage that is attached to the commercial sexual exploitation of children. Proponents of children's rights[1] and radical feminists (Barry, 1981, 1994) conceptualise prostitution as sexual exploitation and abuse, reflecting unequal power relations between adults and children, and men and women (Charnley & Nkhoma, 2020). This understanding underpins interventions to 'rescue' children from prostitution, with little appreciation of the complex realities of children's lives and circumstances (Melrose, 2010) Undoubtedly the abuse of a child is abhorrent and this text does not seek to detract from that but seeks to question why children and in turn childhood are constructed within a protectionist discourse, that seeks to protect children with one hand but often with the other conflicts with the rights of those it purports to protect and their voices or agency.

The trafficking of children re-emerged to social prominence in the mid–late 1990s (Howard, 2017, 3) and remains an issue of tantamount importance, but what constitutes and does not constitute child trafficking remains a contested space. With the onslaught of the global pandemic of COVID-19 in 2020 identified by the former Special Rapporteur Maria Grazia Giammatinaro as 'exacerbating the vulnerabilities of children to sexual exploitation'.[2] With ongoing linkages between trafficking and the sexual exploitation effectively capturing popular imagination, child trafficking appears to be an issue that is destined to remain. Evidenced by the increasing number of non-governmental and international non-governmental organisations established, or through the shift in focus of towards eradicating the contemporary evil of social ill of child trafficking and enslavement, to the continued presence of stories of trafficking in the media. One illustrative example can be seen through Save the Children, which proclaims that 'child trafficking is a crime and represents the tragic end to childhood'.[3] A further one through the revelations in July 2022 that a national treasure of the UK and winner of

---

[1] See further the UN Convention on the Rights of the Child 1989; UN Optional Protocols to the Convention on the Rights of the Child; ECPAT (End Child Prostitution and Trafficking) International, *Global Monitoring Report on the Status of Action Against Commercial Sexual Exploitation of Children: Thailand* (Bangkok: ECPAT International; Melrose, M. & Pearce, J., *Critical perspectives on child sexual exploitation and related trafficking*. [Online] (London: Palgrave Macmillan, 2013).

[2] https://www.ohchr.org/Documents/Issues/Trafficking/COVID-19-Impact-trafficking.pdf. Accessed September 2020.

[3] The Fight Against Child Trafficking | Save the Children. Accessed October 2022.

four Olympic Gold medals for long distance running Sir Mo Farah was trafficked at the age of nine into the UK for domestic servitude.[4] You may wonder why I have referenced Mo Farah and his recent (at the time of writing) disclosure?

The context here is important, with successive political support being built upon fears of immigration and the establishment and maintenance of the 'hostile environment' within the UK. This links to research that has illustrated the silences surrounding the issues. For example, a 2009 report commissioned by the National Society for the Prevention of Cruelty to Children highlighted that identifying trafficking can be hindered by silence and that disclosure of abuse is gradual and incremental. The specific story of Mo Farah in the UK raises some difficult questions, such as who deserves to be viewed as a victim and how they are subsequently treated by the legal system (England and Wales in this instance). The difference between the outcomes for Mo Farah and children that have been trafficked into the UK for exploitation such as cannabis cultivation can be illustrated by the recent case V.C.L and A.N. v United Kingdom (2021) European Court of Human Rights.

The potential threat of the legal ramifications of Farah's admission provides an insight into why the topic of child trafficking continues to capture contemporary imagination. The Home Office within the UK has subsequently confirmed that no action will be taken against Farah, but what if he was not an Olympic hero? How might he have been treated by the law and policy frameworks implemented to crack down on illegal immigration and take back control of our borders. The UK's immigration policies have focused on deterrence and are doing little to enable children and adolescents to feel safe enough to disclose that they have been trafficked and or exploited. The fact that Farah said he was "relieved" that the Home Office would not act against him, further indicates the fears and threat of hostile immigration policy and the rhetoric

---

[4] See further 'My name is not Mo Farah, it's Hussein': British Olympic hero reveals he was trafficked into UK | *Daily Mail Online* (2022). Accessed September 2022; The Real Mo Farah review–a beautiful, heart-breaking story that exposes cruel Tory policy | Mo Farah | *The Guardian* (2022). Accessed September 2022.

that surrounds it. This point is acutely noted by Hynes that 'others who are not national sports heroes may not receive the same assurance'.[5]

This leads to a discussion as to how and why the law and society both view and distinguish between different categories of human beings. I appreciate that this text focuses exclusively upon children, but that focus is driven by my intellectual curiosity upon how the law responds to children and demarcates between different categories or statuses of privilege attached to individuals. The perception that children are a concrete and discrete category or measurable category is one that is grappled within the body of this book. The classification of children under legal frameworks marks them as different, as 'other' and in the context of laws implemented to address trafficking, slavery, and children on the move more generally this distinction is complicated. The issue nurtures and fosters the global aspirations to save children. This idea of saving children links into conflicts over victims and victimhood—how do you demarcate between a deserving and underserving victim? These aspirations to save children are prima facie broad and inclusive but the reality is that not all children are deemed worthy of "saving".

Within the broader context of 'children on the move' the responses of the British media to child migrants for example indicate the contentious nature of determining who is and who is not a child.[6] Linking racist and anti-immigrant fears together with the need to protect our own white populations.[7] This need to protect some children, but not all children again are rather neatly illustrated by fears of "Asian sex gangs". The idea of protecting youth, purity, and the innocence of "our own" i.e., white underage British girls from the evil others, i.e., Brown Asian men is not a new fear (Cockbain, 2018). These fears of the exploitation and corruption of young white women and children can be dated back to the fears of "White Slavery" at the turn of the twentieth century. This book seeks

---

[5] Mo Farah: here's why it is so difficult for trafficking victims to disclose their experiences (theconversation.com) Hynes 2022. Accessed September.
[6] See further More than two-thirds of so-called 'child refugees' who had their ages assessed were found to actually be adults, official figures show | *The Sun* (2016). Accessed September 2022; More fears over real age of 'child migrants' arriving from Calais | *Daily Mail Online* (2016). Accessed September 2022.
[7] See further "Britons never will be slaves": the rise of nationalism and 'modern slavery' | openDemocracy. Accessed December 2022.

to navigate how law and policy responses to the issue of child trafficking remain shaped and informed by racial biases and imperial connotations within the anti-trafficking agenda.

1.2 The Neglected Histories of Child Trafficking

This book charts the emergence, decline, and re-emergence of child trafficking law and policy during the twentieth and twenty-first centuries. However, this focus cannot be done without references to the power and influence of the humanitarian industry, this is important also in the historical context as it was the charitable organisations that pushed forward the agendas of children's rights and saving children from exploitation for immoral purposes. This is a book that seeks to begin to critique the entanglements of children's rights and colonialism in relation to the mobility and exploitation of children. Through centralising the legacy of colonialism[8] and the undercurrents of race, white supremacy, patriarchy, and their ongoing influence upon contemporary anti-trafficking legal and policy responses.

Through assessing how moral panics emerge, sustain, and are ultimately replaced or forgotten only to re-emerge like a phoenix from the ashes, this book attempts to offer an alternative perspective upon child trafficking and the law and policy adopted to address the phenomena. The laws that have been implemented to address child trafficking, 'confirm a primary function of moral panics: the reaffirmation of society's

---

[8] The author recognises that referencing the 'legacy' of colonialism implies that it is extinct. However, the continued impact of colonialism continues to influence and control law, policy, politics, and society globally. The references to 'Benin' within theis book are all to the Republic of Benin in West Africa and not to the city of Benin in neighbouring Nigeria. A place which according to Dottridge is a 'place of origin of substantial numbers of trafficked women as well as girls'. See further Bridget Anderson (2007) Motherhood, Apple Pie and Slavery: Reflections on trafficking debates; Kyunghee Kook Kook, K., '"I want to be trafficked so I can migrate!": Cross-border movement of North Koreans into China through brokerage and smuggling networks', *The ANNALS of the American Academy of Political and Social Science*, 676(1) (2018), 114–134. https://doi.org/10.1177/0002716217748591.

moral boundaries'.[9] The trafficking of children has re-emerged as a new pressing issue of international concern and this book will interrogate the trafficking of children from the turn of the twentieth century, to the era of the League of Nations and to the current United Nations (hereafter the UN) system. A series of questions emerge, such as the power of moral panics, what constitutes a social problem and the anti-child trafficking discourse contestations over what does and does not classify as child trafficking.

You may wonder what is the point in analysing the history of child trafficking and international law? The trafficking of children has received extensive attention in recent years, and in the early twenty-first century the issue 'came to dominate the field of international child protection' (Howard, 2017, 1). However, fears of child trafficking are not new to the twenty-first century. Through research in the League of Nations archives in Geneva, this book will track the evolution of child trafficking, demonstrating parallels with the legal and societal fears of "White Slavery" from the early twentieth century.[10]

Through cataloguing the emergence of child trafficking at the start of the twentieth century (preceding the formation of the League of Nations in 1919) and the subsequent development of the international legal, political and policy framework implemented under the auspices of the League and later the United Nations to address the issue. Drawing upon the League of Nations archives in Geneva, this research undertook an archival excavation of the largest and most systematic study of trafficking of the League of Nations era (1919–1946). With the aim of highlighting the power of moral panic and the legacies of race, empire and colonialism that have seeped into the contemporary legal landscape. Moreover, the book looks to critique how child trafficking

---

[9] Chas Critcher, Moral Panics, Criminology and criminal justice, Oxford Research Encyclopedias, 2012.

[10] See further Allain, J., 'White Slave Traffic in International Law,' *Journal of Trafficking and Human Exploitation*. [Online] 1 (1) (2017), 1–40; Laite, J., 'Traffickers and pimps in the era of white slavery,' *Past & Present*. [Online] 237 (1) (2017), 237–269; Lammasniemi, L., 'Anti-White slavery legislation and its legacies in England,' *Anti-Trafficking Review*. [Online] (9) (2017), 64–76; Knepper, P., 'International criminals: The League of Nations, the traffic in women and the press,' *Media History*. [Online] 20 (4) (2014), 400–415 on "White Slavery".

is constructed and identified, with the focus of the League upon trafficking for "immoral purposes" resonating with the contemporary focus upon the trafficking of children for sexual exploitation. Although the sexual exploitation of children does not explicitly appear within the activities of the League, the language focuses upon the trafficking of children for immoral purposes, the legal age of marriage and the production of obscene publications, i.e., pornography (Faulkner, 2019).

The aim is to tease out how the predominant focus on trafficking for the purposes of sexual exploitation as predominant in the work of the Committee on the Rights of the Child, as set up under the Convention on the Rights of the Child (hereafter, the CRC) has been sustained. The focus on 'women and children' across both the 1921 International Convention to Suppress the Traffic in Women and Children and contemporary usage within the 2000 Protocol to Prevent, Suppress and Punish Trafficking in Persons, especially Women and Children will be explored. Interrogating how the image of a 'trafficked child' has been constructed within a 'powerful protectionist discourse' that dominates discussions around children, inadvertently stripping children of the autonomy contained within, for example, the CRC. A focus on prevention of migration and 'rescue' serves as 'a deflection from the complicity of states allowing factors that drive migration to flourish and … mirrored through today's response to human trafficking' (Faulkner, 2019, 16).

This book seeks to challenge the removal of the agency of children within the context of the legal and policy responses to the phenomenon, and to illustrate the Western bias and glorification of the pornographies of pain and human misery. Furthermore, the book will seek to illustrate the Eurocentric nature of international law and policy, and how the relationship between colonial legacies and the construction of knowledge upon human trafficking have been built. The international human rights agenda is not immune to criticism, and indeed as will be demonstrated the contemporary international legal instrument that was adopted in 2000 explicitly framed human trafficking as a criminal issue rather than a human rights issue. With competition mounting for funding, resources, and space within the child trafficking narrative as the "anti-trafficking machine" takes hold. This theoretical framework has been adopted to illustrate or navigate a central hypothesis of this book—that the contemporary anti-trafficking agenda is both imperialist and a continuity of colonial attitudes. The chapters will offer evidence to support this, through charting the international law and policy frameworks of trafficking and slavery spanning more than a century. Although, this book focuses upon child trafficking, it is important to illustrate that the issue is situated within the wider framework of human trafficking, modern slavery, and what I refer to as the "anti-trafficking machine". The anti-trafficking machine is a key organising framework of the book and will be introduced as a theoretical framework throughout the introduction.

1.3 Child Trafficking Globally—A Brief Overview

The former Special Rapporteur on the Sale of Child Maud de Boer-Buqicchio in her 2016 report stated that there is 'no reliable data on the number of children who have been or are being adopted as a result of being sold, trafficked, or subjected to other illegal acts and illicit practices'.[11] The trafficking of children has been identified globally as an issue, evidenced through the UNODC's Global Reports on Trafficking in Persons, to the annually produced (by the US Department of State) Trafficking in Persons Reports (TIP) and Global Estimates of Modern Slavery for example. The UNODC's Global Report deliberately refrains from providing absolute numbers but focuses upon proportions. For example, during 2010–2012 period 33% of the reported trafficked persons globally were children below the age of 18, about twice as many girls as boys and with huge regional differences: children accounted for 62% of the total of reported cases in the Africa/Middle East region in contrast to 18% in Europe/Central Asia.[12] Whilst a 2015 EUROSTAT

---

[11] Maud de Boer-Buquicchio, Report of the Special Rapporteur of the Human Rights Council on the Sale of Children, Child Prostitution and Child Pornography, HRC Res 7/13 and 25/6, UN HRC, 34th sess, agenda item 2, UN Doc A/HRC/34/55 (22 December 2016) 8.
[12] UNODC's Global Reports on Trafficking in Persons (2014) 29 and 31.

Report, however, revealed that simply by adding the age group 18–24 years, the majority of cases (some 55%) of trafficked persons in the EU would be below the age of 25. Additionally, the report highlighted the scarcity of disaggregated data, with only 17 Member States (out of 28) being able to produce figures along age groups; only 13 had data on trafficked children and citizenship; and seven offered information on age-related assistance services provided.[13]

The classification of 'certain phenomena as child trafficking depends on the naming actions of certain actors and on the social acceptance of that naming' (Howard, 2017, 15). This in turn feeds into the 'process of ranking harms' which coincides with 'our concern for children as a separate and special group' (O'Connell Davidson, 2005, 1). A contestation over the label of child trafficking exists, and within the context of the UK for example a shift in the discourse towards the more elastic term of 'modern slavery' has been evidenced in recent years.[14] The elasticity of modern slavery can be noted through the Modern Slavery Act (2018) enacted in Australia, within which trafficking for the purposes of adoption is recognised as a form of modern slavery (Van Doore, 2021). So where does child trafficking happen? If no reliable data exists, then how do we know that child trafficking is a thing? Research conducted has identified child trafficking in a multiplicity of geographical locations and legal jurisdictions globally, for example children identified as trafficked in the USA for sexual and labour exploitation (Gozdziak, 2008). Another example can be located within research identifying the trafficking of children for the purposes of adoption in Nepal (Bott, 2021; Van Doore, 2016). The recognition of this form of trafficking led to Nepal becoming the first nation state to have 'orphanage trafficking' included as a form of child trafficking in the Trafficking in Persons Report 2018. Orphanage tourism was subsequently classified by the UN General Assembly Rights of the Child in 2019 as a driver for 'human trafficking'. Research has identified the trafficking of Central American minors for criminal

---

[13] EUROSTAT, Trafficking in Human Beings–2015 Edition (EUROSTAT Statistical Working Papers).

[14] See further the expansion of the language of 'modern slavery' to incorporate the county lines phenomena within the UK.

activity in the USA (Soltis & Taylor Diaz, 2021) and children trafficked for exploitation in criminal activities in the Netherlands (Oude Breuil, 2021). The use of the term 'minor's is objectionable but is the preferred categorisation for some, notably the Anti-Trafficking reviews edition which focused solely upon the 'trafficking of minors' published in 2021. Through this text I will demonstrate my preference for language, using children, adolescents or children and adolescents interchangeably throughout. The term minors for me creates the perception that they (i.e., the children) are viewed as lesser than adults, something similar to adults but not quite the same as they are lesser, distinct, or are not full adults. This perception in turn has implications from a human rights perspective, as eloquently articulated by Baroness Hale 'are children something else, *sui generis* human beings, having some of the rights peculiar to childhood and some of the rights which all human beings have?'[15] For me, the classification or labelling of children and adolescents from a human rights perspective as minors demarcates them as lesser than adults or others. This is the reality of children's rights; they endorse this separation of children from adults and are granted through a specific treaty through the creation of the CRC.

Yet, significant challenges arise in studying the issue of child trafficking at all (Oude Breuil & Gerasimov, 2021, 1). For example, Hynes (2010) explored the trafficking of children and young people into, within, and out of the UK. A key finding was that this type of forced migration is often viewed as a one-off, often nationally bounded, 'event' by those who have a duty to care for children and young people, but what was required was a broader sociological and international process to provide a greater understanding of the backgrounds of individual children, the human rights contexts within countries of origin and individual migration trajectories undertaken (Hynes, 2021, 155). Moreover, Hynes (2015) suggests that for identification of children as having been trafficked, there is a role for migrant and refugee community-based organisations to participate in formal referral processes. Another example

---

[15] Foreword in 'rewriting Children's Rights Judgments: From Academic Vision to New Practice' Stalford et al. (2017). Accessed September 2022.

in the UK is the work of Cockbain and Wortley (2015) which analysed domestic or internal sex trafficking of British children using data from police investigations. Whilst in the USA, Fedina et al. (2019) and Sapiro et al. (2016) advocated that despite increased efforts to respond to human trafficking at both national and state levels extraordinarily little empirical research has been conducted upon what they classify as 'domestic sex trafficking'. Whilst the works of Okyere critiques the dominant anti-trafficking literature and activism within Ghana by interrogating the role of external forces in influencing the conditions underpinning child labour, mobility and the underlying hardships of the phenomenon today (2017, 2021). Another example is found through the work of Howard which focuses upon Benin and Nigeria, identifying the issues of Western childhood, neoliberalism, and the ideal state as the three core ideologies that set the limits of the child trafficking discourse. Howard's intricate research advocates that 'the child trafficking star is on the wane, and eventually will die out', an interesting perspective that mirrors the emergence and decline of fears of child trafficking that drove international action during the early twentieth century.

This emerging body of research on child trafficking highlights that the law and policies implemented to address the issues need to prioritise measures that address the underlying socio-economic and political root causes of the phenomenon. Furthermore, those related to development, access to education, healthcare, decent work, and migration regimes providing accurate numbers have proven extremely difficult (Oude de Breuil & Gerasimov, 2021).

1.4 Defining the Trafficking of Children

We cannot state with certainty how many children are trafficked or sex trafficked … but it can be stated with certainty that the Gothic narrative of child trafficking does not capture the experience of the majority of child migrants.[16]

---

[16] O'Connell Davidson (2013a, 2013b).

The phenomenon of child trafficking was identified as a pressing issue of concern prior to the arrival of fears of "modern slavery". In the 'early 1990s, nobody knew trafficking was a 'thing' … by the start of the 2000s, it was well on its way to becoming a major transnational issue' (Howard, 2017, 1). This is further evidenced through the observations that 'Since the late 1990s, children's charities and child rights agencies from the United Nations Children's Fund (UNICEF) to small non-governmental organizations (NGOs) have lobbied hard to get child trafficking recognized as a pressing global problem' (O'Connell Davidson, 2013a, 2013b). The child trafficking field emerged from concerns of child labour and collided with the anti-sex trafficking field to create a toxic cocktail of concern and hysteria about child trafficking. Questions arise such as what is child trafficking? Who will decide? And what difference does this make? This series of questions provide an insight into the controversies around defining the phenomenon, and the 'study of the definition of trafficking is, in many senses, also a study of the history of trafficking in international law' (Gallagher, 2012, 13). However, when it comes to the specific issue of child trafficking the existing body of literature is predominately ahistorical in nature, neglecting the hidden histories of child trafficking and how they have shaped and informed contemporary international, regional, and domestic law and policy.

The starting point to any discussion of child trafficking is the international legal definition, created through the Protocol to Prevent, Suppress and Punish Trafficking in Persons Especially Women and Children (hereafter, the Trafficking Protocol) supplementing the United Nations Convention against Transnational Organized Crime in 2000. Prior to the adoption of the Trafficking Protocol, the term "trafficking" was not defined in international law, despite its incorporation in several international legal agreements (Gallagher, 2012, 12). Recognition of this issue is alluded to through the preamble which identified that 'despite the existence of a variety of international instruments containing rules and practical measures to combat the exploitation of persons, especially women and children, there is no universal instrument that addresses all aspects of trafficking in persons' (Fig. 1.1).

Article 3

Use of terms

For the purposes of this Protocol:

(a) "Trafficking in persons" shall mean the recruitment, transportation, transfer, harbouring or receipt of persons, by means of the threat or use of force or other forms of coercion, of abduction, of fraud, of deception, of the abuse of power or of a position of vulnerability or of the giving or receiving of payments or benefits to achieve the consent of a person having control over another person, for the purpose of exploitation. Exploitation shall include, at a minimum, the exploitation of the prostitution of others or other forms of sexual exploitation, forced labour or services, slavery or practices similar to slavery, servitude or the removal of organs;

(b) The consent of a victim of trafficking in persons to the intended exploitation set forth in subparagraph (a) of this article shall be irrelevant where any of the means set forth in subparagraph (a) have been used;

(c) The recruitment, transportation, transfer, harbouring or receipt of a child for the purpose of exploitation shall be considered "trafficking in persons" even if this does not involve any of the means set forth in subparagraph (a) of this article;

(d) "Child" shall mean any person under eighteen years of age.

Fig. 1.1 Article 3 the Trafficking Protocol

Article 3 (a) therefore establishes the three separate elements to the definition, (i) the action, (ii) the means,[17] and (iii) the purpose or exploitation.[18] Human trafficking therefore does not refer to a single, unitary act leading to one specific outcome, but is rather to cover a process (recruitment, transportation, and control) that can be organised in a variety of ways and involve a range of different actions and outcomes (Fig. 1.2).

---

[17] The omission of the means element in regard to children has also been implemented through the Trafficking Victim and Protection Act (TVPA) of the USA which has significant influence through the production of its annual Trafficking in Persons Reports. Child sex trafficking is identified as 'In cases where an individual engages in any of the specified "acts" with a child (under the age of 18), the means element is irrelevant regardless of whether evidence of force, fraud, or coercion exists. The use of children in commercial sex is prohibited by law in the United States and most countries around the world'. See further https://www.state.gov/what-is-trafficking-in-persons/. Accessed October 8, 2021.

[18] For those familiar with the contemporary definition of human trafficking, the terms 'abuse of authority', 'fraud', 'threats', and 'violence' will stand out, as they have been maintained throughout the process from 1902 to the contemporary definition of the twenty-first century. Jean Allain *White Slave Traffic in International Law*. Available from: https://www.researchgate.net/publication/307937864_White_Slave_Traffic_in_International_Law. Accessed May 5, 2021.

Trafficking in persons	Action (i)	Means (ii)	Purpose (iii)
	Recruitment	Threat or use of force	Exploitation, including
	Transport	Coercion	Prostitution of others
	Harboring	Abduction	Sexual Exploitation
	Receipt of Persons	Fraud	Forced Labour
		Deception	Slavery or similar practices
		Abuse of power or vulnerability	Removal of organs
		Giving payments or benefits	Other types of exploitation

Fig. 1.2 Overview of the Trafficking Protocol definition of human trafficking, 2000 (*Source* The author)

The trafficking of children is a crime distinct from the trafficking of adults since it is not necessary to establish the means used; with people under the age of eighteen, it is only necessary to establish the act and the purpose of trafficking the child. The question that follows, is what does this mean in practice? This should clearly convey that it is not necessary to establish that abusive means have been used for the case for it to be categorised as trafficking. Through articulating that there is no need for abusive means to be used, for example when recruiting a child, for it to be considered a 'trafficking offence' was a modification of the way the crime is defined (Dottridge, 2021, 13). This is not a new distinction, and highlights why the histories of child trafficking are of central importance to contemporary debates upon the issue. For example, a link can be drawn between the International Convention for the Suppression of the White Slave Traffic 1910 (hereafter, the 1910 Convention) and the Trafficking Protocol of 2000. The 1910 Convention established a distinction between adults and children through the omission of the means element. This distinction between young victims ('in relation to whom the "means" by which they were procured were irrelevant') and adult victims (in relation to whom some evidence of compulsion as required) has survived through the omission of the means element in relation to children under the Trafficking Protocol of 2000.

Although the Trafficking Protocol has defined "child trafficking", that does not mark the end of the definitional controversies that exist, as fierce competition exists within what I identify as the "anti-trafficking machine" in defining child trafficking. The anti-trafficking machine through projects and debates continually confronts the difficulty of defining the phenomena, and how and whether child trafficking is distinguishable from other closely related activities, such as child marriage, child soldiering, and child labour (Engle Merry, 2016, 271). The first issue that arises is that of the terminology used, what is child trafficking?

The International Labour Organization[19] (hereafter, the ILO) asserts that 'child trafficking is about taking children out of their protective environment and preying on their vulnerability for the purpose of exploitation'. Additionally, the ILO Convention No. 182 (1999) on the Worst Forms of Child Labour (hereafter, WFCL) classifies trafficking amongst "forms of slavery or practices similar to slavery" and that subsequently the WFCL should be 'eliminated as a matter of urgency, irrespective of the country's level of development'. The role of the USA is also significant regarding defining trafficking, as it has had the greatest single impact upon the evolution of the international consensus on the definition of trafficking (Gallagher, 2012, 22).

Legal and policy definitions aside, a simple google internet search of "child trafficking" generates 114,000,000 results in less than 0.52 seconds.[20] A screenshot of some of the first images generated display similar themes, of children bound, gagged, or caged, curled up in foetal positions, silenced (with some physically silenced), wide eyed, sad, and frightened expressions visible. The significance of images or the culture of images surrounding human trafficking and slavery are often excluded from traditional doctrinal analysis of the legal framework. The importance of imagery is not to be neglected, as this powerful imagery continues to play a dominant role within our socio-legal understanding of human trafficking and slavery, providing a simplistic narrative for a

---

[19] As part of larger initiatives to combat the worst forms of child labour, the ILO's International Programme on the Elimination of Child Labour (IPEC) works with governments, workers, and employers' organisations and NGOs to fight child trafficking. See further https://www.ilo.org/ipec/lang--en/index.htm. Accessed October 8, 2021.
[20] Search conducted on 10/06/2021 via google.

complex phenomenon. The ethical and political issues associated with the creation and dissemination of unsettling images and videos for child trafficking and human trafficking abolitionist campaigns alike in Ghana for example have been intricately critiqued by the works of Okyere et al. (2021). With critiques of the portrayal of ideal victims through poverty porn, the media and societal perceptions emerging in Canada (Durisin & van der Meulen, 2021) the UK (Cockbain, 2018; Krsmanovic, 2021) the Netherlands (Ouede de Breuil, 2021) and globally as stressed through the influential works of O'Connell Davidson (2005, 2013a, 2013b). The undercurrent of race, class, gender, colonialism, and patriarchy clash with the toxic cocktail of shock, horror, and outrage that is wielded unforgivingly and unashamedly by the anti-trafficking machine. This construction of the "trafficked child" is shaped and informed by this imagery and the notion of child trafficking will be explored in subsequent chapters.

1.5 Contemporary Anti-trafficking

The deep-rooted and widely shared appeal of anti-trafficking is easy to understand, given that it is an emotive issue that can clearly be identified as 'bad', with the feel-good endorphins generated by being vocally anti-slavery coupled with the fact that it is a vehicle for de-politicisation. This emotive appeal 'subsequently creates a level of unwavering sympathy, moral outrage and intrinsic need to rescue victims from the private actors who steal both their time and labor' (Faulkner, and Bunting, forthcoming 2022). This appeal of anti-trafficking is illustrated through a number of actors such as the former President of the USA,[21] Donald Trump proclaiming in 2019 that 'My Administration is committed to leveraging every resource we have to confront this threat, to support the victims and

---

[21] Note the USA and the stance against sex trafficking for example Tim Ballard: I've fought sex trafficking at the border. This is why we need a wall see further https://trumpwhitehouse.archives.gov/briefings-statements/timothy-ballard-ive-fought-sex-trafficking-dhs-special-agent-need-build-wall-children/. Accessed July 2021.

survivors, and to hold traffickers accountable for their heinous crimes'.[22] The former Prime Minister of the UK Theresa May MP in her 2019 address at the Centenary of the International Labour Organization (ILO) stated that '… modern slavery is immoral. No leader worthy of the name can look the other way while men, women and children are held against their will, forced to work for a pittance or no pay at all, routinely beaten, raped and tortured'.[23] With another former Prime Minister of the UK emphasising in 2020 the Conservative government's commitment to combatting modern slavery, proclaiming that 'those behind such crimes, these traders in human misery, must and will be ruthlessly hunted down and brought to justice'.[24] Indeed, with the revelation that a national treasure of the UK, Olympic Champion Mo Farah was in fact trafficked into the UK as a child and exploited as a domestic worker indicates how concerns of the evils of trafficking have not diminished.[25] This appeal is not limited to politicians with religious figures such as Pope Francis stating in early 2020 that 'the money from their dirty, underhanded business is blood money. I'm not exaggerating: its blood money'.[26] The 'celebrification of anti-trafficking' (Haynes, 2014) further illuminates that child trafficking is a grave issue of concern, one that should unite us all in efforts to eradicate as indicated by Ashton Kutcher 'Today you can go online and buy a child for sex. It's as easy as ordering a pizza'.[27] If there is one 'topic in the anti-trafficking discourse that evokes particularly emotional outrage and a passionate, oftentimes moralistic 'call to arms', it is child trafficking' (Oude Breuil & Gerasimov, 2021). This is not only due to the exceptionality of human trafficking as a criminal act, but that the magnitude of the act is much graver when the victim is a child. This is not isolated to trafficking, the linkage between child and any social ill,

---

[22] https://trumpwhitehouse.archives.gov/briefings-statements/president-donald-J-trump-made-priority-combat-heinous-crime-human-trafficking/. Accessed July 2021.
[23] https://www.gov.uk/government/speeches/pm-speech-at-ilo-centenary-conference-11-june-2019/. Accessed September 2020.
[24] United Kingdom Government, UK Government Modern Slavery Statement, London: HM Government, 2020, I.
[25] See further Sir Mo Farah reveals he was trafficked to the UK as a child–BBC News (https://www.bbc.co.uk/news/uk-62123886). Accessed July 2022.
[26] https://popefrancisdaily.com/pope-money-from-human-trafficking-stained-with-blood. Accessed September 2020.
[27] See further https://fightthenewdrug.org/celebrities-doing-their-part-to-end-exploitation/. Accessed October 2021.

such as murder, rape, or abduction invokes a strong repugnant response but when it is the murder of the child, the rape of the child, or child abduction it adds an additional level of outrage and revulsion.

The emergence of the language of "modern slavery" has engulfed a broad range of exploitative practices due to its elasticity, absorbing everything related to it from forced marriage to child pornography into a meta-category. Advocacy against "modern slavery" was once on the periphery, sidelined by the fascination of human trafficking for sexual exploitation, and now 'it has risen to the fore as the 'catch-all' for a broad range of exploitative practices (Chuang, 2014; O'Connell Davidson, 2015; Segrave et al., 2018). This is highlighted by the following statement from the UN Office of the High Commissioner for Human Rights.

> *The word "slavery" today covers a variety of human rights violations. In addition to traditional slavery and the slave trade, these abuses include the sale of children, child prostitution, child pornography, the exploitation of child labour, the sexual mutilation of female children, the use of children in armed conflicts, debt bondage, the traffic in persons and in the sale of human organs, the exploitation of prostitution, and certain practices under apartheid and colonial régimes.*[28]

The inclusion of abuses such as the sale of children, child prostitution, child pornography, and the sexual mutilation of children (amongst others) highlights the elasticity of the term of 'slavery' and the lack of definitional clarity within the international law of some of the issues identified such as child labour complicates their inclusion under the rubric of modern slavery. The use of "modern slavery" is predominant in the UK and Australia, which have both. Implemented Modern Slavery Acts in 2015 and 2018, respectively. Within the geographical region of Europe human trafficking is the preferred term (Skrivankova, 2018) whilst in the USA the term human trafficking is often used interchangeably with trafficking in persons and modern slavery.[29] For some

---

[28] OHCHR, Fact Sheet No.14 Contemporary Forms of Slavery. http://www.ohchr.org/documents/publications/factsheet14en.pdf. Accessed April 2018.
[29] Trafficking in Persons Report, 2022, 31.

commentators the continued conflation between trafficking and slavery has been done to acknowledge other forms of exploitation that were excluded or missed by efforts of the international legal framework and international counter-trafficking policy regime (Allain, 2017, 61). On the other hand, commentators have advocated that the emergence of modern slavery serves as a distraction: 'in the midst of handwringing over myriad forms of exploitation, attention is not being paid to the factors that contribute to and sustain such exploitation' (Segrave et al., 2018, 9). The crucifixion of the legal inaccuracies of interchangeable terms is expertly highlighted through the works of Janie Chuang (2014), who proclaimed that:

> *Each of modern-day slavery's purported component practices – slavery, trafficking and forced labour – is separately defined under international law, subject to separate legal frameworks and overseen by separate international institutions. Conflating trafficking and forced labour with the far more narrowly defined (and extreme) practice of 'slavery' – however rhetorically effective – is not only legally inaccurate, but it also risks undermining effective application of the relevant legal regimes.*[30]

1.5.1 The Trafficked Child: Prostitution, "Sex Trafficking", and Victim Pornography

The focus of the book is children, and it is important to situate the discussion within the broader framework of contemporary anti-trafficking. The predominant focus of anti-trafficking around the drafting time of the UN Trafficking Protocol was upon sex work, shifting to address extreme exploitation in a range of labour activities. However, it has been advocated that the 'recent discursive shifts to 'modern slavery', and 'forced labour', the anti-trafficking transnational legal order itself reinforces, rather than diffuses cultures of sex work exceptionalism' (Kotiswaran, 2021, 43). The point to highlight here is discussions concerning children in the sex industry are complicated and fraught with

---

[30] Janie A. Chuang, 'Exploitation Creep and the Unmaking of Human Trafficking Law,' *The American Journal of International Law*, 108 (4) (2014), 609–649.

difficulty. Concerns or fears of child prostitution are not new and played a key role in driving fears of 'white slavery' at the turn of the twentieth century. The elevation of concerns of child prostitution and pornography are neatly illustrated by the activities of the United Nations, from hosting World Congresses, the creation of the Special Rapporteurs[31] and adopting a plethora of law and policies to tackle the issues. The repugnance of child sexual abuse is clear, what is less clear is why this form of child suffering is unique and deserving of more attention than structural inequalities such as poverty, education, and malnourishment facing children around the world.

Fears of child prostitution have been well documented, with contestation over the term being advocated by Muntarbhorn in the 1990s. The focus of attention in the 1990s upon Asia and child prostitution, failed to notice that child prostitution also exists in 'enlightened Western societies that are formally committed to 'ideals of democracy and equality'. This account implicitly reproduces the imagined opposition between pre-modern and modern, barbarous, and civilised, 'oriental' and 'occidental' societies (O'Connell Davidson, 2005, 31). Children's involvement in prostitution is a controversial area within academic debate influenced by ideologically informed value positions (Charnley & Nkhoma, 2020; Green, 2016). The term 'child prostitution' has been widely replaced, particularly in the Global North, by 'child sexual exploitation', reflecting the moral status of children (Charnley & Nkhoma, 2020; Furedi, 2015) and stressing the unequal power relations between adults and children (Sanders et al., 2017).

The "trafficked child" immediately conjures images of a young child, kidnapped, tortured, and sold into sexual slavery.[32] The visual and narrative representations of the ideal victim of child trafficking receive limited critique, consider for a moment why do we not recognise "victim pornographies"? The narrative of trafficking involves three key actors,

---

[31] Such as the Special Rapporteur on the sale and sexual exploitation of children, the Special Rapporteur on trafficking in persons, especially women and children and the Special Rapporteur on contemporary forms of slavery, including its causes and consequences.

[32] Jail for 'sexual predators' who led Asian gang that abused girls as young 12 | Daily Mail Online (https://www.dailymail.co.uk/news/article-1345084/Jail-sexual-predators-led-Asian-gang-abused-girls-young-12.html). Accessed July 2022.

namely the victim, villain, and the rescuer/heroes (Faulkner, 2018; O'Brien, 2021). This preconception dates to the late nineteenth century and the emergence of the anti-trafficking movement under the guise of "white slavery". The complexities of trafficking or the process of trafficking can disrupt notions of victims, and how we should effectively distinguish between deserving and undeserving victims. Children are perceived as inherently vulnerable, lacking agentic qualities, and in need of rescue and protection. Ideal constructions of children, childhood, and deserving victims are not isolated to the contemporary world. Moreover, the role of gender, class, and race cannot be removed from the artificial construction of victims. The phrase "trafficked child" has been alluded to throughout this book. It is a powerful image that often drives the anti-trafficking legal and policy responses, but who is a trafficked child? How are they identified? Perceived? And constructed? The following quote perfectly summarises the construct of the child trafficking victim:

> *Selling human misery and suffering is one of the primary currency earners for humanitarian organisations*[33] *… In the child trafficking context, it is justified as a means of speaking for victims who supposedly lack the voice, agency, and capacity to speak for themselves.*[34] (Okyere et al., 2021, 49)

The exploitation of misery and use of victim pornography is rife within the anti-trafficking machine and the emotive power of that image drives contemporary fears of child trafficking and or slavery. This ideal image is not isolated to humanitarian organisations operating in Ghana, research from Canada highlights that 'She is the perfect victim–voiceless, vulnerable and easily manipulated. Her subjectivity is appropriated in the name of trafficking, and legislative changes are justified in the name

---

[33] D. Kennedy, 'Selling the Distant Other: Humanitarianism and imagery-ethical dilemmas of humanitarian action', *The Journal of Humanitarian Assistance*, 28 (2009), 1–25, https://sites.tufts.edu/jha/archives/411.

[34] 'Trade of Innocents: Film captures reality of child trafficking for sexual exploitation', United Nations Office on Drugs and Crime, 28 September 2012, https://www.unodc.org/unodc/en/frontpage/2012/September/trade-of-innocents_-film-captures-reality-of-child-trafficking-for-sexual-exploitation.html; H. R. Evans, 'From the voices of domestic sex trafficking survivors: Experiences of complex trauma & posttraumatic growth', Doctorate in Social Work Dissertations, University of Pennsylvania, 2019, https://repository.upenn.edu/edissertations_sp2/126.

of protecting her innocence' (Durisin & van der Meulen, 2021, 149). Furthermore, this ideal victim is not exclusive to Canada, with research identifying the gender bias amongst frontline workers, with girls being more readily perceived as victims than boys, and interventions in the girls' cases geared towards protection, whereas boys were seen as 'little rascals that should be punished' in the Netherlands (Oude Breuil, 2021, 86). 'The perfect youth victim, who has been evoked in both federal and provincial policy as well as public debates, thus serves to legitimise the development of new or modified legislation that imposes greater restrictions on women's bodily autonomy, freedom of movement, and income generating activities in a context where anti-sex work laws have been found to be harmful'(Durisin & van der Meulen, 2021, 146) Moreover, Nkhoma and Charnley (2018) identified from their empirical research of a participatory study with girls and young women in Malawi who first exchanged sex for material reward as children that most of the participants viewed their involvement as a means of income. Therefore, the legislation and policy enacted to protect and promote their safety remained largely ineffective. Furthermore, evidence from the survivors of trafficking being discriminated against and categorised based on their country of origin, skin colour, gender, experiences, appearance, and behavioural patterns is global in scope and abundant in quantity (Burland, 2018; Krsmanovic, 2021, 70). The 'basic principles of the rule of law are that it should not be administered arbitrarily, it should be consistently applied by actors of the state and everyone within its jurisdiction should have recourse to protection under the law' (Skrivankova, 2018, 250). A prime example of this can be identified through the illustrative case below, involving 2 young Vietnamese nationals in the UK and their journey for justice from first being arrested by police in 2009, to the European Court of Human Rights in 2021.

Trafficking has been a contested category from the start (Doezema, 2010) Part of the issue is that exploitation, like force is a moveable and relative concept (Moravcsik, 1998) and remains undefined in the UN Trafficking Protocol. For those under the age of eighteen (defined as children under both the CRC and Trafficking Protocol), this is particularly problematic. The UNTP stipulates that a child's consent to movement is irrelevant as they still only qualify as victims of trafficking is they are recruited and transported 'for the purposes of exploitation'. Drawing a line between children who are and who are not victims of trafficking therefore also revives a series of judgements about what types and degrees of exploitation are acceptable for working children, in which context and how there remains no consensus on such matters (Bastia, 2005; Howard & Okyere, 2022; Martins & O'Connell-Davidson, 2022; O'Connell Davidson & Howard, 2015).

The issue of who qualifies as a victim of trafficking links in with the emerging trend of fears of child sex trafficking. Although, "sex trafficking" has not found a home in the international legal framework, it has successfully infiltrated contemporary policy, societal or popular perceptions of the issue. As illustrated by the works of Cockbain (2013, 2018) a 'new form of sex trafficking shot to the forefront of media, political and public debate in the UK'. The shift in perceptions of child trafficking in the UK, indicated a shift to the belief that explicitly framed this crime as an attack by hostile outsiders on the white British mainstream, its culture, and values (Cockbain, 2018, 2). The extensive work of Cockbain on child sex trafficking in the UK, highlighted how the agency and choices of the adolescent girls involved were 'overlooked in portrayals that cast them as passive playthings manipulated in offenders' games'. This links to the one-dimensional portrayals of victims that are identified within human trafficking literature as problematic (Andrees & Van der Linden, 2005; O'Connell Davidson, 2015). The issue of 'domestic child sex trafficking' has not only been raised as a pressing issue of concern in the UK, but also in the Netherlands and the USA.

The Netherlands was one of the first European countries to recognise the issue of domestic child sex trafficking with the Dutch research base on the issue dating back to the mid-1990s (Bovenkerk & Pronk, 2007; Horn et al., 2001; Dutch National Rapporteur, 2002, 2009). According to Dutch criminal law, sex trafficking necessarily involves commercial exploitation (Dutch National Rapporteur, 2012). Running in tandem with the UK, the issue is 'often framed in both gendered and racialised terms: the standard trope in the Netherlands is that of a young male trafficker of Moroccan or Antillean heritage who abuses underage female victims also of non-Dutch heritage' (Cockbain, 2018, 7). Whilst in the

USA, measures were initially focused upon international trafficking but in 2006 the US government committed to an increased focus on tackling domestic trafficking (US Department of State, 2006). The key driver for this development was the heightened concern around domestic sex trafficking (Cockbain, 2018, 7). Again, as in the Netherlands sexual exploitation must involve a commercial element to be considered trafficking and the way in which US anti-trafficking law is constructed means that all commercial sex acts involving minors can be effectively classed as sex trafficking (Reid, 2010). Research has illustrated several issues in the USA, such as the enduring tendency to treat victims as juvenile prostitutes rather than sexually exploited children (Clawson & Dutch, 2008; Cockbain, 2018; Hanna, 2002; Kortla, 2010; Reid, 2010). The conceptualisation of child prostitution as sexual exploitation and abuse, underpins interventions to 'rescue' children from prostitution, with little appreciation of the complex realities of children's lives and circumstances (Melrose, 2010). A 17-year-old selling sex in Los Angeles, California, USA may have a completely separate set of reasons or logic behind this decision from a 15-year-old in Malawi for example. With empirical research conducted in Malawi noting that some of the participants spoke of marriage as offering a false hope of security and saw prostitution as a preferable choice offering independence as the housewife has to rely on her husband for her support, despite playing almost the same role (Charnley & Nkhoma, 2020).

The consequence of contemporary fears of child trafficking is a moral panic response, but what does this moral panic mean? The Oxford English Dictionary defines moral panic as 'an instance of public anxiety or alarm in response to a problem regarded as threatening moral standards of society'.[35] The levels of anxiety or alarm with regard to human trafficking are clearly identifiable. The volume of literature published, coupled with the number of organisations established to fight human trafficking (Gozdziak & Bump, 2008) are a response to the moral panic that the phenomenon creates. Whilst Cohen articulated that societies appear to be subject to periods of moral panic (2011, 1) and human trafficking is no exception to this. Whether the moral panic that is driving

---

[35] Oxford dictionary, 7th edition, 2012, Franklin Watts.

the response to the trafficking is detrimental to the rights of the child has been critiqued within this book.

The current understanding of the trafficking of children is hindered by the various misconceptions and generalisations that dominate discussions with regard to human trafficking generally. These misconceptions underline and inform the development of policy actions and legal responses to the phenomenon of human trafficking. The impact of this upon children is significant in many ways. The law draws a basic distinction between an adult and a child but in the context of human trafficking the consequences of this are stark. This underlying drive towards the eradication of human trafficking, or understanding what human trafficking is, serves to deflect from the structural factors that drive and perpetuate migration. Structural factors such as poverty, social exclusion, discrimination, lack of education, and lack of opportunities all play a significant role as do the factors driving migration, whether they are legal, illegal, voluntary, or forced. It has been advocated that links between human trafficking and vulnerability factors, such as poverty, unequal development, and gender-based violence, are however generally well documented and accepted within both the literature and policies on human trafficking (Yea, 2017, 5).

Children are continually infantilised and victimised, and subsequently forced into a strict compartmentalisation as victims with no agency or capacity to make decisions about themselves or what is in their best interests as autonomous individuals. A further conceptualisation draws on structuration theory, linking individual agency with wider structures that enable or constrain individuals' decision-making in particular circumstances (O'Connell Davidson, 2005; Montgomery, 2014; Orchard, 2007; Phoenix, 2007, 2012) A distinction between children and adolescents needs to be considered with regard to labour, migration, and the capacity of every individual to make decisions about their own well-being.

Consider the scenario of a child, or perhaps better phrased an adolescent, who has a choice between a tough situation and a less tough situation. The question is should that individual be allowed that choice? The current discourse does not accept or allow for these choices to be made, instead it pursues a course of 'child rescue', restricting their rights and classifying them as a weak commodity in need of saving. For example, Howard's research findings indicated that community members in Southern Benin regarded the transnational movement of under-18s to Abeokuta, Nigeria[36] for artisal mining[37] as a normative practice that demonstrate the capability of adolescents as able members of their families (Howard, 2017). Further illustrating due to the depiction of youth labour migration by the anti-trafficking community as trafficking, it misses the experiences of the youth migrants themselves and how they perceive their mobility (Howard, 2017).

The question remains, what of research conducted that involves exploited children? A point advocated by Lundy and Stalford (2020) that exploitative research practices undermine trust and have the potential to reduce children to objects in pursuit of empirical data, which is turn is a form of exploitation. Studies such as Okyere (2013), Hashim and Thorsen (2011) and Howard and Morganti (2015) that do neither 'reduce their research subjects to abject victims and suffering bodies, nor romanticise them as 'heroic subalterns' (Brown, 2009, 1235) but instead work with a model of agency, or will, as inalienable; a model of 'agency as the capacity to act–differential, context specific, and always, in some fashion extant', as Svati Shah (2014, 199) puts it' (O'Connell Davidson, 2015, 80) are models of good practice in this context.

This concept is cemented into the Palermo Protocol,[38] which is the lead international legal instrument with regard to human trafficking. The notion of consent has presented problems which currently the international law is unable to address (Elliott, 2015). Consent is widely accepted

---

[36] The research conducted by Howard utilises a case study of adolescent labour migrants from Benin to the artisanal quarries of Abeokuta, Nigeria. Highlighting the inaccurate discourse and how related policy is failing.

[37] Artisanal and Small-Scale Mining occurs in approximately 80 countries worldwide and accounts for 80% of global sapphire, 20% of gold mining and up to 20% of diamond mining. It is widespread in developing countries in Africa, Asia, Oceania, and Central and South America. Though the informal nature and on the whole un-mechanised operation generally results in low productivity, the sector represents an important livelihood and income source for the poverty affected local population. It ensures the existence for millions of families in rural areas of developing countries. See further Artisanal and Small-Scale Mining (https://www.worldbank.org/en/topic/extractiveindustries/brief/artisanal-and-small-scale-mining).

[38] Through Article 3, which specifically removes the consent aspect with regard to children that was drawn from the 1910 White Slave Traffic Convention.

as an exercise of autonomy and freedom necessary to enter an agreement (Jones, 2012). The omission of the means element is the most significant provision established by the Trafficking Protocol that aims at ensuring greater protection for trafficked children. No element of coercion is required as children are perceived as vulnerable and incapable to provide informed consent to be trafficked. Drawing a concrete distinction between the conceptual point where a voluntary action can morph in a situation of human trafficking is difficult.[39] Trafficking is seen by many as an inherently coercive environment and therefore it is incredibly difficult to determine true agency or consent.

Consent is an issue which is rife with conflict over its precise meaning and how distinctions should be drawn in relation to children and sexual activity, the sexual encounters between teenagers and the role of childhoods and sexual relationships. For example, in some jurisdictions there is the requirement of 'dual criminality' which essentially means that the crime must be illegal in both the country that is to try the offence (i.e., the State exercising extraterritorial jurisdiction) and the country where the act took place. In many instances this may well be appropriate, but in the context of commercial sexual exploitation, particularly in respect of sex tourism, this can be problematic. In some countries the age of consent remains extremely low, and the principle of dual criminality would therefore permit a sex tourist the right to go to this country for the sole purpose of sexually exploiting a child. An example of the controversy around children and sex, can be found in a study on childhoods and sexual relationships which found that adolescent girls were considered as adults in sexual relationships, and described as '*willing participants*' even though sexual relationships with adolescent girls is criminalised in the Caribbean (Pasura et al., 2013).[40]

---

[39] See further Jones (2012) Human Trafficking Victim Identification: Should Consent Matter, 45 Ind, L, Rev. 483 discussing the justification under the gendered approach (which essentially trivialises the role of voluntary undertakings in human transactions or characterises consent as irrelevant, suffers from several conceptual and empirical realities) for interfering with or ignoring an individual's voluntary actions in certain circumstances, and cannot be based on the absence of or tainted nature of the actor's consent. Jones also indicates that despite objections to paternalism that some choices are so bad that we do not care if they were voluntary.
[40] D. Pasura, A. D. Jones, J. A. Hafner, P. E. Maharaj, K. N. DeCaires and E. J. Johnson, 'Competing meanings of childhood and the social construction of child sexual abuse in the

It is generally accepted that due to the child's unique position, dependence on family members and society, their vulnerability, naivety, and numerous other factors make children easy targets for manipulation and subsequently they fall into the hands of traffickers.[41] The dominant discourse on child trafficking, like the discursive construction of child prostitution as 'forced labour' and 'modern slavery' serves to support the perception of children as passive objects and eternal victims, consequently deflecting attention from the structural factors that underpin and perpetuate the phenomenon (O'Connell Davidson, 2005, 65). Moreover, through constraining trafficking to 'abusive acts committed by boys and men in the context of sex work, the harms girls face from the children welfare system, in the family, and from police and other authorities' are neglected (Durisin & van der Meulen, 2021, 148). This erasure of experiences is important, as the anti-trafficking machine focuses upon a law-and-order response which targets traffickers but deflects from other harms perpetrated against children by the State in addition to private actors.

Another point to consider when discussing the trafficking of children is whether all forms of child movement should be classified as trafficking and is it detrimental to the child to assume that their consent is irrelevant? This assumption feeds into the construction of the "trafficked child". This image is something that will fall under scrutiny throughout this book. The purpose of identifying how the image of the "trafficked child" has been developed is to raise the questions of how and why this image has successfully established itself as a driving force behind both legal and policy responses to child labour, exploitation, and migration. The trafficking of children immediately evokes an emotive response with each person having their own understanding and perception of what the trafficking of children entails. The ability of the discourse to establish itself as such an abhorrent crime, framing itself as the worst of the worst human rights violations feeds into how the

---

Caribbean', *Childhood*, 20(2) (2013), 200–214, https://chd.sagepub.com/doi/10.1177/0907568212462255.
[41] Vinkovic (2010, 96).

trafficking of human beings has been, and is being, constructed. Anti-trafficking measures such as border controls and law enforcement are being used to implement migration control measures under the guise of human rights protection, begging the question of whose interests are being served through these measures.

The superficial construction of human rights violations with human trafficking ranked primarily, is in part due to the unilateral condemnation and levels of bipartisan support it receives. The reason for the universal acceptance of trafficking, as an egregious human rights violation is due in part to the way the discourse has been framed, interpreted, and constructed as modern slavery. With regard to children, is trafficking to be deemed as one of the worst forms of child labour and granted a position of exceptionality, or should the trafficking of children be viewed as one of the worst approaches to young migrants?[42]

1.6 Methods and Theoretical Framework

In recent years it has 'become increasingly self-evident that the research methodologies of international law can no longer be confined to pure normative and doctrinal analysis'.[43] This perspective sits well within the context of this book, which utilises archival research to interrogate the history of child trafficking law and policy implemented since the early twentieth century. Child trafficking is not a phenomenon that exists on the periphery of contemporary human rights concerns but forms an integral piece of the jigsaw puzzle of issues that fall under the rubric of "modern slavery". The issue of "modern slavery" is one that creates tension, in relation to its definition but also the way it is increasingly being used and framed in a way that exploits the legacies of slavery. This

---

[42] Note the Independent Inquiry into Child Sexual Abuse (IICSA) that commenced on February 27, 2017. This is in relation to a deliberate policy of the British Government to send children to commonwealth countries such as Australia and Canada to provide "good white stock". Many of the children were subjected to cruelty, forced labour, and sexual abuse. The programme was essentially state-sponsored child trafficking. https://www.iicsa.org.uk/. Accessed April 2017.

[43] Rossana Deplano (Ed.), Pluralising International Legal Scholarship: The Promise and Perils of Non-Doctrinal Research Methods, Elgar, 2019, 1.

book seeks to centralise child trafficking within the theoretical framework that the author identifies as the "anti-trafficking machine", utilising Third World Approaches to International Law (TWAIL) as a lens to examine and illuminate how child trafficking law and policy is rooted in a set of racialised, gendered, and imperial considerations.

1.6.1 The League of Nations Archival Research

The lengthy legal and political history of human trafficking has been well documented (Allain, 2017; Gallagher, 2012) but a specific focus upon children has been neglected and this research seeks to address that fact. The purpose of the research was to uncover the untold stories of child trafficking and related exploitation, trying to locate whether an evidentiary base of child trafficking existed to justify the adoption of international law and policy on the phenomenon. Additionally, the archival research sought to identify any parallels that existed between the historical and contemporary responses to child trafficking.

My research took me to the League of Nations archives in Geneva, on a mission to arrive and see what I could find. I pre-ordered the materials to read utilising the online database search and asked to view all the relevant documents upon "white slavery" and "human trafficking" that were available. Non-doctrinal methods in international law, broadly speaking are empirical and this book contains both empirical and critical methods. Although, the normative and doctrinal analysis does form part of the background of the archival research conducted.[44] This book has emerged from my doctoral research upon child trafficking and international law, which left me with unanswered questions upon the historical context of child trafficking. This intellectual curiosity led to the archival research that was conducted in 2017 and 2018 in the League of Nations archives, Geneva. The League's archives are a rich resource to utilise and provide insights into the ideology behind the creation and implementation of international law during the era of the League. This research has subsequently been complimented through the generosity of

---

[44] See further Faulkner (2019), Gentile and Lonardo (2019) and Ostřanský (2019).

League of Nations' archivist Jacques Oberson and Professor Jean Allain, the latter of whom shared his extensive archival photograph research to enrich my own, covering 1902–1956 focusing primarily upon "white slavery", slavery, and trafficking. Jacques has shared additional files upon the 'Summary of Annual Reports' when they became available in digitised form as part of the ongoing 'Total Digital Access to the League of Nations Archives Project'[45] (hereafter, LONTAD) which will digitise the complete collection of archives.

The plan prior to the start of the research was a simple one, what are the secret histories of child trafficking, and can I find anything worthwhile, the plan evolved as I reviewed the documents and finally found a focus within the 'Summary of Annual Reports'. The archival inquiry examined a range of primary and secondary sources, primarily from the League of Nations archives, Geneva.[46] The materials include international voluntary association and League of Nations publications, country specific reports, notes from the organisations meeting and conferences, newsletters, minutes of meetings, and correspondences within and between voluntary organisations, the International Bureau, International Abolitionist Federation, and the League of Nations between 1902 and 1945. The focal point of the archival research is upon the 'Summary of Annual Reports',[47] submitted to the League's Traffic in Women and Children Committee (hereafter, LNTWC) between 1922 and 1938. The accidental discovery of the 'Summary of Annual Reports for 1927' by the author ensured that I could undertake an uninterrupted analysis of the reports, which represent the most systematic and comprehensive review of trafficking conducted during the period (1922–1945) Neither the 1925 nor 1927 Reports were mentioned within the repertoire of the League of Nations Serial documents, therefore they were understood not

---

[45] In 2017, the UN Library & Archives Geneva launched the Total Digital Access to the League of Nations Archives Project (LONTAD) that will ensure state-of-the-art free online access and the digital and physical preservation of the entirety of the archives of the League of Nations (1919–1946), containing approximately 15 million pages. See further https://libraryresources.unog.ch/leagueofnationsarchives/Digitized/LeagueArchives. Accessed October 7, 2021.

[46] Archives Consulted; The League of Nations Archives, Geneva, Switzerland; The National Archives, London, United Kingdom and The Women's Library Archive, London School of Economics (LSE), United Kingdom.

[47] Refer to Appendix 2–The Summary of Annual Reports.

to exist. Such is the inherent value and intrigue of archival research, as it leads you to pause and wonder what else does not exist?

The Reports were not analysed in isolation, drawing upon a range of primary and secondary sources to situate the extracted information. A full analysis of the research conducted is located in Chapter 3, with the findings of over 400 written responses between 1922 and 1938 to the question (of the annual questionnaire produced) which specifically focused upon children. The year 1938 marked a notable change in the composition of the questionnaires analysed, with the question that specifically focused upon children being removed and the important that the Committee attached to receiving full information on new legislative or administrative measures implemented.[48]

The international legal argumentative style of the 'experiment narrative' is often afforded as the best lens to analyse the League of Nations through and presents a threefold criterion. Firstly, that a defined period with a beginning and an end can be identified, secondly the idea of failure and thirdly that 'We've learnt something'.[49] This idea of the failure of the League of Nations is a continual theme presented, that we have learned from this failure. Under the so-called 'experiment narrative', its often presumed that the League provided a first attempt at solving the issue of human trafficking, an attempt that failed but is one that we nevertheless 'learnt something' from. Against this narrative, this book will show that the work of the League upon trafficking, and the trafficking of children more specifically built upon the racialised, gendered and exclusionary White Slavery Instruments of 1904 and 1910, the impact of which can still be demonstrated in the contemporary legal and policy responses adopted under the auspices of the United Nations. It is against this context that this book will contest the idea that we have 'learnt something' and that racism, colonialism, nationalism, and patriarchy continue to have a profound influence upon the contemporary law and policy implemented to address child trafficking.

---

[48] League of Nations, Advisory Committee on Social Questions, Summary of Annual Reports for 1937/38 prepared by the Secretariat C.68.M.30. 1939. IV (page 1).

[49] Jean d'Aspremont, 'The League of Nations in Historical Narratives about International Law' paper presented at the conference The Legacy of the League of Nations, University of Leicester, 31 January 2019 (unpublished).

1.6.2 The Theoretical Frameworks: Introducing the "Anti-trafficking Machine"

This book utilises the "anti-trafficking machine" as the primary tool for theoretical analysis, drawing upon aspects of TWAIL and the experiment narrative of the League of Nations to challenge the dominance of the machine. The phenomena of child trafficking cannot be evaluated without being situated within the broader context of what I classify as the "anti-trafficking machine" and it is here that I will introduce you to the machine.

Human trafficking is an emotive and heavily politicised issue. From the international instruments adopted, calls for action from several humanitarian celebrities, politicians, activists alike contribute to the growth of the anti-trafficking industry globally. The "anti-trafficking machine" is distinct from the "new abolitionist movement" as coined by Julia O'Connell Davidson which is used to depict the business of contemporary anti-trafficking and anti-slavery. Both ideas are situated within the critical modern slavery studies school of thought (Bunting & Quirk, 2017; Chuang, 2014; Kempadoo et al., 2012; Kotiswaran, 2017, 2021; O'Connell Davidson, 2015, 2016; Quirk, 2012) The anti-trafficking machine sounds like a futuristic threat extracted from the latest apocalyptic offering from Netflix and it is here I will explain what I mean by the machine.

The Oxford Dictionary offers the definition of machine as.

1. A piece of equipment with many parts that work together to do a particular task. The power used to work a machine may be electricity, steam, gas, etc. or human power;
2. A computer;
3. A particular machine, for example in the home, when you do not refer to it by its full name;

4. An organized system for achieving something and the people who control it.[50]

It is from this last point that the framework emerged and hopefully illustrates how I came to view contemporary efforts to address trafficking and slavery. A 'concept as morally and politically loaded as 'child trafficking' will always generate a backlash' (Howard, 2017, 16) However, prior to exploring the phenomena of child trafficking, a broader introduction to the terms human trafficking and modern slavery is required. This context is pivotal as it helps to situate 'child trafficking' within what Quirk identifies as the 'classificatory conundrums' of the contemporary anti-trafficking machine. The purpose of the machine is purely theoretical, a useful illustrative concept of the manifestation of efforts (legal, policy, political, social, and moral) that have been created to tackle and confront child trafficking and slavery. This idea draws inspiration from the works of Hoffman (2011) with the intention of utilising the anti-trafficking machine framework theoretically to make a specific set of arguments about how child trafficking and in turn modern slavery creates its own self producing logic and technologies. This idea is a distinct mechanism to analyse anti-trafficking and the way that it is, constructed and shaped by a powerful ideology that has been self-created.

This business does not refer to a legal or legitimate business operation, but the "machine" that has emerged from the explosion in interest in the phenomena. The concept of a machine is also understandable as concrete institutions that are united through working upon a shared set of goals, such as the eradication of child trafficking or "modern slavery", with shared funding flows competing for space in a growing industry. This is evidenced through the significant increase in organisations dedicated to the anti-trafficking fight increased from a few to a few thousand (Kempadoo et al., 2005, xxiv). 'Anti-trafficking literature proliferated; national policy frameworks spread worldwide (Cho, 2011); and funding rose from paltry to billions' (Howard, 2017, 4).

---

[50] Oxford Learner's Dictionary accessed via machine_1 noun - Definition, pictures, pronunciation and usage notes | Oxford Advanced Learner's Dictionary at OxfordLearnersDictionaries.com (https://www.oxfordlearnersdictionaries.com/definition/english/machine_1?q=machine). Accessed July 15, 2022.

The 'discourse of modern slavery is all about uncovering, acknowledging and confronting the 'scourge' of modern slavery' (Brace, 2018, 11). This juggernaut enjoys bipartisan support globally from politicians, the United Nations system, celebrities, charities, non-governmental organisations, and businesses.[51] How has "the anti-trafficking machine" been able to successfully garner support from such a diverse range of actors? Two propositions can be offered here, firstly the 'logical observation is that slavery is an abhorrent crime, something from which every individual in the world should be protected and a fundamental human right'. Secondly, and arguably the more cynical approach 'would identify the coupling of anti-immigration rhetoric with anti-trafficking narratives or the inevitable feel-good factor of identifying oneself as a contemporary William Wilberforce or mandated by Kipling's 'White Man's Burden'.

The aim of international law is to create a better society; this is no less so when it comes to children's rights law (Faulkner & Nyamutata, 2020a, 2020b). However, this perception of international law is not universally accepted; for some, international law is a product of European expansion through Empire and colonialism (Allain, 2012) which in turn has subordinated non-European peoples and societies to European conquest and domination (Mutua, 2000, 31). Third world approaches to international law (hereafter, TWAIL) centre upon legal concerns from a 'Third World' perspective. TWAIL begins from the position that international law is a 'predatory system that legitimises, reproduces and sustains plunder and subordination of the Third World by the West' (Mutua, 2000, 31). As asserted by Anghie (2008) the very establishment of international law as an international legal framework went together with colonial enterprise. European colonialism in the fifteenth and nineteenth centuries formed the background for the emergence of international law that we know today. The purpose was to rationalise and regulate the subjugation of non-European lands and peoples. TWAIL is entrenched with movements for decolonisation and is viewed by many as being inaugurated at the

---

[51] Such as former Prime Minister of the UK Theresa May, current PM Boris Johnson and the former President of the USA Donald Trump. Celebrities such as Ashton Kutcher and Emma Thompson, see further Dina Haynes 'Celebrification of Human Trafficking' for commentary. Organisations such as Minderoo, Walk Free Foundation, and International Justice Mission are just a few examples of the explosion in anti-trafficking organisations globally.

1955 Asian-African Conference in Bandung, Indonesia (Kanwar, 2015) Although TWAIL is a wide-ranging intellectual and political project, the TWAIL agenda) has three foci:

1. 'To understand, deconstruct, and unpack the uses of international law as a medium for the creation and perpetuation of a racialized hierarchy of international norms and institutions that subordinate non-Europeans to Europeans';
2. 'To construct and present alternative normative legal edifice for international governance';
3. 'Through scholarship, policy and politics to eradicate the conditions of underdevelopment in the Third World' (Mutua, 2000. 31).

What relevance does TWAIL have to the issue of child trafficking? And why is it an important lens for analysis? Children are victims of some of the most devastating examples of state sanctioned and private human rights abuse, within the context of international law Western constructs of childhood coupled with the adult centric lens adopted have significantly impacted upon the legal and policy responses to "children on the move" (Pobjoy, 2017). 'International law is the principal language in which domination is coming to be expressed in the era of globalization' (Chimni, 2006, 3) and part of the potential (as yet unfulfilled) of TWAIL 'is the promotion of the equal mobility of human beings' (Mayblin & Turner, 2021, 21). A TWAIL perspective 'draws attention to the ways in which international law does not necessarily offer universal justice precisely because unequal power relations following the patterns of the colonial era are maintained through international law today' (Mayblin & Turner, 2021, 21). This is true in relation to children's rights and the international legal and policy responses to the mobility of children.

This book utilises TWAIL as a lens for analysis in tracking the development of child trafficking within international law from the early twentieth century to today, drawing upon a wider critique of the universality of children's rights as enshrined through the much-celebrated CRC. This approach centralises the role of Western perspectives of mobility, vulnerability, and the 'other'. Through addressing the ahistorical nature of contemporary research upon child trafficking and related exploitation this book serves as a unique tool to centralise the historical context and highlight the continuing legacies of colonialism, race, patriarchy, and white supremacy in relation to "children on the move".

1.7 Structure of the Book

The following discussion is split into 5 analytical chapters, with Chapter 7 as a Conclusion. Chapter 2, '*Protecting Children: Childhood, Rights and the Trafficked Child*' will introduce the concepts of childhood, children, and children's rights and the international legal framework that has been adopted to protect and empower them. Understanding the broader context of children's rights serves as an important framing for critiquing the anti-trafficking machine, with the chapter serving as a theoretical hook framing the subsequent critiques. The origins of children's rights can be found in the activities of the League of Nations (1919–1945), which sought to protect children in wake of the first world war (1914–1918). However, for some this move towards protection can be seen as reflective of white supremacy and the need to protect white populations from fears of exploitation and abuse. The legacy of the colonial contours of the new world order are often excluded within the context of children's rights, this chapter seeks to re-centralise kaleidoscope of undercurrent themes within discussions of children's rights and the anti-trafficking movement and indicate towards the lessons of the past for contemporary law and policy.

Chapter 3 '*The Emergence of Child Trafficking 1900–1946*' seeks to address the ahistorical nature of contemporary research upon the phenomena, or what I perceive as a silence of history. The history of human trafficking can be divided into three periods, firstly pre-League of Nations, secondly the League of Nations era 1919–1945, and finally the era of the United Nations from 1945–today (Allain, 2017, 1). This chapter transcends the first two periods, looking at child trafficking through the emergence of the international instruments to address the "White Slave Traffic" during the early twentieth century. Although many authors have investigated the 'White Slave Traffic' and the contemporary parallels with anti-trafficking, the same cannot be said in relation to children. This chapter highlights what we can learn from examining the historical responses to child trafficking or to use the language of the time the traffic of children for immoral purposes. Drawing upon a range of primary and secondary materials from the League of Nations archives in Geneva, Switzerland, the focal point of the research is upon the 'Summary of Annual Reports' submitted to the League's Traffic in Women and Children Committee between 1922 and 1938. You may wonder, why the focus upon the 'Summary of Annual Reports'? They represent the most systematic and comprehensive review of trafficking conducted during that period and are not examined in isolation. The aim of analysis is to critique to roles of race and empire as race served as a central organising framework that underpinned the spectacular success of slavery and colonialism. Tracking whether the rhetoric of the "other" continued from the instruments of the early twentieth century, into anti-trafficking responses globally and the subsequent impact upon children. Moreover, through addressing the apparent racial biases and preoccupation upon "trafficking for immoral purposes" and the impact that this had upon children, the chapter seeks to deconstruct fears of sexual slavery, highlighting other forms of exploitation identified within the archives and charting the application of ideas of childhood and exploitation within a diverse cultural melting pot of subjugated populations. Through challenging the evidential base behind fears of 'trafficking of children for immoral purposes' of the era, the chapter seeks to centralise the role of moral panics and impact that they can have upon the development and subsequent adoption of law and policy mechanisms to eradicate harm.

Chapter 4, '*Child Trafficking, Children's Rights, and Modern Slavery: International Law in the in the Twentieth and Twenty-First Centuries*' provides an overview of the discourse of "modern slavery" and the international legal instruments adopted in the twentieth and twenty-first centuries to address the issues. Defining the phenomenon has proven difficult in the contemporary world, with fierce debates over the parameters of the term and critiques of its elasticity. The chapter begins with a focus upon the League of Nations, as it established a foundation upon which the most recent jurisprudence concerning slavery was built (Quirk, 2012, 257). From the Slavery Convention of 1926 to the United

Nations Protocol to Prevent, Suppress and Punish Trafficking in Persons especially women and children adopted in 2000 and the Convention on the Rights of the Child 1989 and its Optional Protocols this chapter focuses upon the definitional conflicts and uncertainties of each instrument. Drawing upon the archival research from Chapter 3, this chapter will enrich contemporary analysis of child trafficking in international law by highlighting the synergies between instruments adopted decades apart.

Chapter 5 '*Child Trafficking and Contemporary Action in the Twenty-First Century*' serves as a bridge between the international law and policy actions of the International Labour Organization (ILO), UNICEF, the Special Rapporteurs, the Sustainable Development Goals (SDGs), and the Courts looking to the International Criminal Court (ICC), Inter-American Court of Human Rights, and four selected cases from the e Human Trafficking Case Law Database (HTCLD) created by the UN Office on Drugs and Crime (UNODC). An intricate analysis of all the contemporary actions falls outside the scope of this book, however, the broader context is of importance in illustrating the power and presence of the anti-trafficking machine. The chapter also considers the role of the USA as the self-styled international police upon human trafficking. However, the contemporary action to eradicate child trafficking is important. The international action encapsulates a core component of the theoretical framework of the anti-trafficking machine that this book has sought to use as a tool to critique child trafficking law and policy. Utilising research within the HTCLD, the chapter draws upon five case law examples from Malawi, Guatemala, the Philippines, Canada, and Bosnia and Herzegovina that have dealt with child trafficking between 2005 and 2017. Each of the cases selected has been chosen due to what I classify as interesting factors. Each case is unique, concerning children and/adolescents exploited for distinct reasons such as begging, illegal adoption, labour, and sexual exploitation.

Chapter 6 '*Child Trafficking in Europe: Nationalism, Vulnerability and Protection*' captures a slight shift in focus from the international law to the regional law and policy of Europe and domestic activities of the UK to eradicate modern slavery and human trafficking. The term "modern slavery" is not one that is commonly used at the regional level, with a clear preference for the use of 'trafficking in human beings' existing in Europe (Skrivankova, 2018, 243) The anti-trafficking legal machine manifests under two organisations, namely the European Union and the Council of Europe with the case study of the UK selected due to the constant grandstanding or positioning of the UK as the leading nation in the fight against the 'traders of human misery' (Johnson, 2020). The chapter is divided into two sections, the first which evaluates the anti-trafficking legal mechanisms implemented under the auspices of the European Union and Council of Europe respectively, prior to the second half which interrogates the hypocrisy of modern slavery law and policy efforts in the UK immediately preceding the adoption of the Modern Slavery Act 2015 to today. In both Europe and the UK particular attention is paid to fears of "child sex trafficking", with the racialised coding of victims and perpetrators heightening with the apparent shift from outsiders. This renewed focus in the UK upon Britons as victims marks a departure from the established convention of focusing upon 'outsiders' as both the victims and perpetrators, such as foreign nationals working in nail bars, car washes, and other foreign nationals forcing them to do so. The implied racism of a codified suspicion towards those with low local language ability insinuates or hints how modern slavery is increasingly caught up in growing ideas of nationalism. Focusing upon the case of V.C.L and A.N. v United Kingdom, recently decided by the European Court of Human Rights in February 2021 as an illuminating insight into the reality of the jigsaw puzzle of ideals attached to modern slavery, victims, criminality, and children in the UK.

References

Allain, J. (2012). *The legal understanding of slavery: from the historical to the contemporary*. Oxford: Oxford University Press.

Allain, J. (2017). White Slave Traffic in International Law. *Journal of Trafficking and Human Exploitation*, *1*(1), 1–40.

Anderson, B. (2007). Motherhood, Apple Pie and Slavery: Reflections on trafficking debates.

Andrees, B., & Van der Linden, M. N. (2005). Designing trafficking research from a labour market perspective: The ILO experience. *International Migration, 43*, 55–73.

Anghie, A. (2005). *Imperialism, Sovereignty and the Making of International Law* (Vol. 37). Cambridge University Press.

Anghie, A. (2008). TWAIL: Past and future. *International Community Law Review; ICLR, 10*(4), 479–481.

Ballard, T. (2019). Timothy Ballard: "i've fought sex trafficking as a DHS special agent–we need to build the wall for the children".

Barry, K. (1981). Female sexual slavery: Understanding the international dimensions of women's oppression. *Human Rights Quarterly*, [Online]. *3*(2), 44–52.

Barry, K. (1994). *The prostitution of sexuality*. [Online]. New York University Press.

Bastia, T. (2005). Child trafficking or teenage migration? Bolivian Migrants in Argentina. *International Migration, 43*(4), 58–89.

Bernstein, H. et al. (2007). *XXX original articles a global alliance against forced labour? Jens Lerche a global alliance against forced labour? Unfree labour, Neo-Liberal Globalization and the International Labour Organization* (Vol. 7).

Bhabha, J. (2014). *Child migration & human rights in a global age.* Human Rights and Crimes against Humanity Princeton: Princeton University Press. http://portal.igpublish.com/iglibrary/search/PUPB0002246.html

Bott, E. (2021). 'My dark heaven': Hidden voices in orphanage tourism. *Annals of Tourism Research, 87*, 103110.

Bovenkerk, F., & Pronk, G. J. (2007). Fighting loverboy methods. (English) ::: Over de bestrijding van loverboymethoden. *Justitiële verkenningen, 5*(7).

Brace, L. (2018). *The politics of slavery.* Edinburgh University Press.

Brace, L., & O'Connell Davidson, J. (Eds.). (2018). *Revisiting slavery and antislavery: Towards a critical analysis*. Palgrave Macmillan.

Breuil, B. O. (2021). 'Little Rascals' or not-so-ideal victims: Dealing with minors trafficked for exploitation in criminal activities in the Netherlands. *Anti-Trafficking Review, 16*, 86–103.

Brown, V. (2009). Social death and political life in the study of slavery. *The American Historical Review, 114*(5), 1231–1249.

Bunting, A., & Quirk, J. (2017). *Contemporary slavery; The rhetoric of global human rights campaigns.* Cornell University Press. https://doi.org/10.7591/j.ctt1w1vjxf

Burland, P. (2018). Still punishing the wrong people: The criminalisation of potential trafficked cannabis gardeners. In G. Craig et al. (Eds.), *The modern slavery agenda: Policy, politics and practice in the UK*.

Charnley, H., & Nkhoma, P. (2020). Moving beyond contemporary discourses: Children, prostitution, modern slavery and human trafficking. *Critical and Radical Social Work, 2*(8), 205–221.

Chimni. (2006). Third World Approaches to International Law: A Manifesto. *International Community Law Review; ICLR, 8*(1), 3–27.

Cho, S. (2011). The spread of anti-trafficking policies–evidence from a new index. *SSRN Electronic Journal* (3376).

Chuang, J. A. (2014). Exploitation Creep and the Unmaking of Human Trafficking Law. *The American Journal of International Law, 108*(4), 609–649.

Clawson, H. J., & Dutch, N. (2008). Identifying victims of human trafficking: Inherent challenges and promising strategies from the field.

Cockbain, E. (2013). Grooming and the 'Asian sex gang predator': The construction of a racial crime threat. *Race & Class; Race and Class, 54*(4), 22–32.

Cockbain, E. (2018). *Offender and victim networks in human trafficking*. Routledge.

Cockbain, E., & Wortley, R. (2015). Everyday atrocities: Does internal (domestic) sex trafficking of British children satisfy the expectations of opportunity theories of crime? *Crime Science, 4*(1), 1.

Cohen, S. (2011). *Folk devils and moral panics*. Routledge.

Craig, G., Balch, A., Lewis, H., & Waite, L. (2018). Still punishing the wrong people: The criminalisation of potential trafficked cannabis gardeners. In Anonymous *The modern slavery agenda: Policy, politics and practice in the UK*. Polity Press.

Craig, G., et al. (Eds.). (2019). *The modern slavery agenda: Policy, politics and practice in the UK*. Policy Press.

Crépeau, F. (2013). *Children on the move*. International Organization for Migration (IOM). http://publications.iom.int/bookstore/free/Children_on_the_Move_15May.pdf

d'Aspremont, J. (2019, January 31). The League of Nations in Historical Narratives about International Law. In Conference Paper, Univeristy of Leicester.

Davidson, O. (2005). *Children in the global sex trade*. Polity Press.

Deplano, R. (Ed.). (2019). *Pluralising international legal scholarship: The promise and perils of non-doctrinal research methods*. Elgar.

Doezema, J. (2010). *Sex slaves and discourse masters: The construction of trafficking*. Zed Book.
Dottridge, M. (2021). Between theory and reality: The challenge of distinguishing between trafficked children and independent child migrants. *Anti-Trafficking Review, 16*, 11–27.
Durisin, E. M., & van der Meulen, E. (2021). The perfect victim: 'Young girls', domestic trafficking, and anti-prostitution politics in Canada. *Anti-Trafficking Review, 16*, 145–149.
Dutch National Rapporteur. (2002). *Trafficking in human beings. First report of the Dutch National Rapporteur.*
Dutch Rapporteur on Trafficking in Human Beings and Sexual Violence against Children. (2009). *Seventh report of the Dutch National Rapporteur on Trafficking in Human Beings.*
Dutch Rapporteur on Trafficking in Human Beings and Sexual Violence against Children. (2013). *Case Law on Trafficking in Human Beings 2009–2012. An analysis.*
Elliott, J. (2015). *The role of consent in human trafficking*. Routledge.
Engle Merry, S. (2016). *The seductions of quantification: Measuring human rights, gender violence, and sex trafficking*. Chicago University Press.
Eurostat. (2015). Trafficking in human beings-2015 edition, Statistical Working Paper, *KS-TC-14–008-EN-1*.
Evans, H. R. (2019). *From the voices of domestic sex trafficking survivors: Experiences of complex trauma & posttraumatic growth*. University of Pennsylvania.
Faulkner, E. (2018). *"Britons never will be slaves": The rise of nationalism and 'modern slavery'*. https://www.opendemocracy.net/en/beyond-trafficking-and-slavery/britons-never-will-be-slaves-rise-of-nationalism-and-modern-slavery/
Faulkner, E. A. (2019). Historical evolution of the international legal responses to the trafficking of children–a critique. In J. Winterdyk & J. Jones (Eds.), *The Palgrave International Handbook of Human Trafficking*. Palgrave.
Faulkner, E. A., & Bunting, A. (2023). Trafficking and the Law. In B. Lawrence (Ed.), *A cultural history of slavery and human trafficking*. Bloomsbury Academic Press.
Faulkner, E. A., & Nyamutata, C. (2020a). The Decolonisation of children's rights and the colonial contours of the convention on the rights of the child. *The International Journal of Children's Rights, 28*(1), 66–88.
Faulkner, E. A., & Nyamutata, C. (2020b). The decolonisation of children's rights and the colonial contours of the convention on the rights of the child. *The International Journal of Children's Rights, 28*(1), 66–88.

Fedina, L., Williamson, C., & Perdue, T. (2019). Risk factors for domestic child sex trafficking in the United States. *Journal of Interpersonal Violence, 34*(13), 2653–2673.

Feneyrol, O. (2011). *Quelle protection pour les enfants concernés par la mobilité en Afrique de l'Ouest? Nos positions et recommandations.* Accessible via https://resourcecentre.savethechildren.net/document/quelle-protection-pour-les-enfants-concernes-par-la-mobilite-en-afrique-de-louest-rapport/

Fight the New Drug. *10 celebrities who use their platforms to help end sex trafficking.* Accessible via https://fightthenewdrug.org/celebrities-doing-their-part-to-end-exploitation/

Francis, P. (2019). Pope: Money from human trafficking stained with blood.

Furedi, F. (2015). The moral crusade against paedophilia. In V. E. Cree et al. (Eds.), *Revisiting moral panics.* Bristol University Press.

Gallagher, A. T. (2012). *The international law of human trafficking.* Cambridge University Press.

Giammarinaro, M. G. (2018). The role of the UN Special Rapporteur on trafficking in persons, especially women and children. In Anonymous, *Routledge Handbook of Human Trafficking* (1st ed). Routledge. https://doi.org/10.4324/9781315709352-34

Gill, M. (2021). Online child sexual exploitation in the Philippines: Moving beyond the current discourse and approach. *Anti-Trafficking Review, 16*, 150–155.

Global Movement for Children. (2010). *International Conference on Children on the Move-Executive Summary, Barcelona, Spain.*

Global Movement for Children. (2010). *Leaving home: Voices of children on the move* Accessed via https://resourcecentre.savethechildren.net/document/leaving-home-voices-children-move/

Gozdziak, E. M. (2008). On challenges, dilemmas, and opportunities in studying trafficked children. *Anthropological Quarterly,* [Online] *81*(4), 903–923.

Goździak, E. M. (2021). Human trafficking as a security threat. In Anonymous, *Human trafficking as a new (in)security threat.* Springer International Publishing. https://doi.org/10.1007/978-3-030-62873-4_3

Gozdziak, E., & Bump, M. N. (2008). *Victims no longer: Research on child survivors of trafficking for sexual and labor exploitation in the United States.* American Psychological Association (APA).

Green, S. P. (2016). What counts as prostitution? *Bergen Journal of Criminal Law & Criminal Justice, 4*(1).

Hashim, I., & Thorsen, D. (2011). *Child migration in Africa.*

Haynes, D. F. (2014). The celebritization of human trafficking. *The Annals of the American Academy of Political and Social Science, 653*(1), 25–45.
Hoffman, D. (2011). *The war machines*
Horn, J. E. et al. (2001). *Aard en omvang seksueel misbruik en prostitutie allochtone minderjarige jongens.* FORA; VU.
Howard, N. (2013). Promoting 'healthy childhoods' and keeping children 'at home': Beninese anti-trafficking policy in times of neoliberalism. *International Migration, 51*(4), 87–102.
Howard, N. (2015). Accountable to whom? Accountable for what? Understanding anti-child trafficking discourse and policy in southern Benin. *Anti-Trafficking Review, 4,* 43.
Howard, N. (2017). *Child trafficking, youth labour mobility and the politics of protection.* Palgrave Studies on Children and Development London: Palgrave Macmillan UK. https://doi.org/10.1057/978-1-137-47818-4
Howard, N., & Morganti, S. (2015). (Not!) child trafficking in Benin. In M. Dragiewicz (Ed.), *Global human trafficking.* Routledge.
Howard, N., & Okyere, S. (Eds.). (2022). *International child protection: Towards politics and participation.* Palgrave Studies on Children and Development. Palgrave.
Hynes, P. (2010). Global points of 'vulnerability': Understanding processes of the trafficking of children and young people into, within and out of the UK. *The International Journal of Human Rights, 14*(6), 952–970.
Hynes, P. (2015). No 'magic bullets': Children, young people, trafficking and child protection in the UK. *International Migration, 53*(4), 62–76.
Hynes, P. (2021). *Introducing forced migration* (1st ed.). Routledge.
Hynes, P. *Mo Farah: Here's why it is so difficult for trafficking victims to disclose their experiences.* https://theconversation.com/mo-farah-heres-why-it-is-so-difficult-for-trafficking-victims-to-disclose-their-experiences-186967
Jail for 'sexual predators' who led Asian gang that abused girls as young as 12 in 'reign of terror'. 2011.
Jeffries, Stuart *The Real Mo Farah review–a beautiful, heartbreaking story that exposes cruel Tory policy.* https://www.theguardian.com/tv-and-radio/2022/jul/13/the-real-mo-farah-review-a-beautiful-heartbreaking-story-that-exposes-cruel-tory-policy
Kanwar, V. (2015). Not a place, but a project: Bandung, Twail, and the aesthetics of third-ness. In L. Eslava, M. Fakhri, & V. Nesiah (Eds.), *Bandung, Global History and International Law: Critical pasts and pending futures.* Cambridge University Press.

Kempadoo, K., & Shih, E. (2022). *White supremacy, racism and the coloniality of anti-trafficking* (Vol. 1, 1st ed.). Routledge, Taylor & Francis Group.

Kempadoo, K. et al. (Ed.). (2005). *Trafficking and prostitution reconsidered: New perspectives on migration, sex work, and human rights* (1st ed.). Paradigm Publishers.

Kempadoo, K. et al. (Eds.). (2012). *Trafficking and prostitution reconsidered: New perspectives on migration, sex work, and human rights* (2nd ed.). Paradigm Publishers.

Kennedy, D. (2009). Selling the distant other: Humanitarianism and imagery-ethical dilemmas of humanitarian action. *The Journal of Humanitarian Assistance*, 1–25.

Kipling, R. (1998). The white man's burden. *Peace Review (Palo Alto, Calif.), 10*(3), 311–312.

Knepper, P. (2014). International criminals: The league of nations, the traffic in women and the press. *Media History, 20*(4), 400–415.

Knepper, P. (2016). The Investigation into the traffic in women by the league of nations: Sociological Jurisprudence as an international social project.

Koomson, B., & Abdulai, D. (2021). Putting childhood in its place: Rethinking popular discourses on the conceptualisation of child trafficking in Ghana. *Anti-Trafficking Review, 16*, 28–46.

Kotiswaran, P. (2017). *Revisiting the law and governance of trafficking, forced labor and modern slavery*. Cambridge, Cambridge University Press.

Kotiswaran, P. (2021). The sexual politics of anti-trafficking discourse. *Feminist Legal Studies, 29*(1), 43–65.

Krsmanovic, E. (2021). Child trafficking vs. child sexual exploitation: Critical reflection on the UK media reports. *Anti-Trafficking Review, 16*, 69–85.

Lammasniemi, L. (2017). Anti-white slavery legislation and its legacies in England. *Anti-Trafficking Review, 9*, 64–76.

League of Nations. (1939). Summary of annual reports.

Lebaron, G. et al. (Eds.). (2021). *Fighting modern slavery and human trafficking: history and contemporary policy.* Slaveries Since Emancipation. Cambridge University Press.

Limoncelli, S. A. (2010). *The politics of trafficking: The first international movement to combat the sexual exploitation of women.* Stanford University Press.

Lundy, L., & Stalford, H. (2020). Editorial. *The International Journal of Children's Rights, 28*(2), 219–220.

Martin, Arthur, Drury, Ian and Greenhill, Sam. (2016). *Mature beyond their years: More fears over real age of 'child migrants' coming from Calais as facial recognition analysis shows one may be as old as THIRTY-EIGHT.* https:// www.dailymail.co.uk/news/article-3849646/Mature-years-fears-real-age-child-migrants-arriving-Calais.html

Martins Junior, A., & O'Connell Davidson, J. (2021). Tacking towards freedom? Bringing journeys out of slavery into dialogue with contemporary migration. *Journal of Ethnic and Migration Studies, 48*(7), 1479–1495.

Martins, A., & O'Connell-Davidson, J. (2022). Crossing the binaries of mobility control: Agency, force and freedom. *Social Sciences (Basel), 11*(6), 243.

May, T. (2019). PM speech at ILO centenary conference: 11 June 2019.

Mayblin, L., & Turner, J. (2021). *Migration studies and colonialism.* Polity Press.

Melrose, M. (2010). What's love got to do with It? Theorising young people's involvement in prostitution. *Youth and Policy, 104*(104), 12–31.

Melrose, M., & Pearce, J. (2013). *Critical perspectives on child sexual exploitation and related trafficking* (1st ed.). Palgrave Macmillan UK.

Montgomery, H. (2014). Child prostitution as filial duty? The morality of child-rearing in a slum community in Thailand. *Journal of Moral Education, 43*(2), 169–182.

Moravcsik, J. (1998). Slavery and the ties that do not bind. In T. L. Lott (Ed.), *Subjugation and bondage: Critical essays on slavery and social philosophy.* Rowman & Littlefield.

Mutua, M. (2000). What is TWAIL? *American Society of International Law. Proceedings of the Annual Meeting, 94*, 31–38.

Nkhoma, P., & Charnley, H. (2018). Child protection and social inequality: Understanding child prostitution in Malawi. *Special Issue Child Protection and Social Inequality.*

O'Brien, E. (2021). *Challenging the human trafficking narrative: Victims, villains, and heroes (Victims, Culture and Society).* Routledge.

O'Connell Davidson, J. (2013a). Telling tales: Child migration and child trafficking: Stories of trafficking obscure the realities for migrant children. *Child Abuse & Neglect, 37*(12), 1069–1079.

O'Connell Davidson, J. (2013b). Troubling freedom: Migration, debt, and modern slavery. *Migration Studies, 1*(2), 176–195.

O'Connell Davidson, J. (2015). *Modern slavery: The margins of freedom.* Palgrave Macmillan.

O'Connell Davidson, J., & Howard, N. (2015). *Migration and mobility, beyond trafficking and slavery short course.*

OHCHR. (1991). *Fact sheet no. 14: Contemporary forms of slavery (archive)*. https://www.ohchr.org/en/publications/fact-sheets/fact-sheet-no-14-contemporary-forms-slavery-archive

Okyere, S. (2013). Are working children's rights and child labour abolition complementary or opposing realms? *International Social Work, 56*(1), 80–91.

Okyere, S. (2017). 'Shock and awe': A critique of the Ghana-centric child trafficking discourse. *Anti-Trafficking Review, 9*, 92–105.

Okyere, S., Agyeman, N., & Saboro, E. (2021). 'Why was he videoing us?': The ethics and politics of audio-visual propaganda in child trafficking and human trafficking campaigns. *Anti-Trafficking Review, 16*, 47–68.

Orchard, T. R. (2007). Girl, woman, lover, mother: Towards a new understanding of child prostitution among young Devadasis in rural Karnataka, India. *Social Science & Medicine, 64*(12), 2379–2390.

Oude Breuil, B. (2021). 'Little rascals' or not-so-ideal victims: Dealing with minors trafficked for exploitation in criminal activities in the Netherlands. *Anti-Trafficking Review, 16*, 86–103.

Oude Breuil, B., & Gerasimov, B. (2021). Editorial: trafficking in minors: Confronting complex realities, structural inequalities, and agency. *Anti-Trafficking Review, 16*, 1–9.

Pasura, D., Jones, A. D., Hafner, J. A. H., Maharaj, P. E., Nathaniel-DeCaires, K., & Johnson, E. J. (2013). Competing meanings of childhood and the social construction of child sexual abuse in the Caribbean. *Childhood (copenhagen, Denmark), 20*(2), 200–214.

Phoenix, J. (2007). Governing prostitution: New formations, old agendas. *Canadian Journal of Law and Society/la Revue Canadienne Droit Et Société, 22*(2), 73–94.

Phoenix, J. (2012). Violence and prostitution: Beyond the notion of a 'continuum of sexual violence'. In J. Brown, J. & S. L. Walklate (Eds.), *Handbook on sexual violence*. Routledge.

Pobjoy, J. (2017). *The Child in International Refugee Law*. Cambridge Asylum and Migration Studies. Cambridge University Press.

Quirk, J. (2006). The anti-slavery project: Linking the historical and contemporary. *Human Rights Quarterly, 28*(3), 565–598.

Quirk, J. (2012). Defining slavery in all its forms: Historical inquiry as contemporary instruction. In J. Allain (Ed.), *The legal understanding of slavery*. Oxford University Press.

Reid, J. A. (2010). Doors wide shut: Barriers to the successful delivery of victim services for domestically trafficked minors in a southern US metropolitan area. *Women & Criminal Justice, 20*(1–2), 147–166.

Report of the Special Rapporteur on the sale of children, child prostitution and child pornography. (2016). *UN Doc A.HRC.34.55.*

Robinson, Martin and Revoir, Paul. *Home Office tells Mo Farah he will not be deported after Britain's Olympic hero revealed he was TRAFFICKED into UK as a child from Somalia with stolen identity and forced into slavery in London.* https://www.dailymail.co.uk/news/article-11004813/Team-GB-hero-Mo-Farah-reveals-treated-like-slave.html

Sanders, T., O'Neill, M., & Pitcher, J. (2017). *Prostitution: Sex work.* Sage.

Sapiro, B., Johnson, L., Postmus, J. L., & Simmel, C. (2016). Supporting youth involved in domestic minor sex trafficking: Divergent perspectives on youth agency. *Child Abuse & Neglect, 58,* 99–110.

Save the Children. *The fight against child trafficking.* https://www.savethechildren.org/us/charity-stories/child-trafficking-awareness. Accessed 9 Dec 2022.

Segrave, M., Milivojevic, S., & Pickering, S. (2018). *Sex trafficking and modern slavery: The absence of evidence* (2nd ed.). Routledge.

Shah, S. (2014). *Street corner secrets: Sex, work and migration in the city of Mumbai.* Duke University Press.

Skrivankova, K. (2018). The UK's approach to tackling modern slavery in the European context. In G. Craig et al. (Eds.), *The modern slavery agenda: Policy, politics and practice in the UK.*

Soltis, K., & Diaz, M. T. (2021). Ganged up on: How the US immigration system penalises and fails to protect Central American minors who are trafficked for criminal activity by gangs. *Anti-Trafficking Review, 16,* 104–122.

Spangler, K. et al. *Acknowledgements.*

Stalford, H., Hollingsworth, K., & Gilmore, S. (2017). *Rewriting children's rights judgments: From academic vision to new practice* (1st ed.). Hart Publishing.

Taylor, J. S., & Davidson, J. O. (2022). Missing, presumed trafficked: Towards non-binary understandings of 'wayward' youth in Jamaica. *Anti-Trafficking Review, 19,* 9–27.

Tolhurst, Alain. *'WE MUST NOT BE NAIVE' As third load of 'child refugees' arrives from Calais as official figures reveal TWO THIRDS of those who had ages assessed were found to be adults.* https://www.thesun.co.uk/news/2005846/more-than-two-thirds-of-so-called-child-refugees-who-had-their-ages-assessed-were-found-to-actually-be-adults-official-figures-show/

Trump, D. J. (2019). *President Donald J. Trump has made it a priority to combat the heinous crime of human trafficking.*
UK Government. (2020). *UK Government modern slavery statement.*
United States Congress. (2006). *Trafficking victims Protection Reauthorization Act of 2005.*
UNODC. (2012). *Trade of innocents: Film captures reality of child trafficking for sexual exploitation.*
U.S Department of State. (2018). *Trafficking in Persons Report 2018. Office to Monitor and Combat Trafficking in Persons.*
U.S Department of State. (2022). *Trafficking in Persons Report 2022. Office to Monitor and Combat Trafficking in Persons.*
van Doore, K. E. (2016). Paper orphans: Exploring child trafficking for the purpose of orphanages. *The International Journal of Children's Rights, 24*(2), 378–407.
van Doore. (2021). *Orphanage Trafficking in International Law.* Cambridge University Press.
Vinkovi, M. (2010). The "unbroken marriage"–trafficking and child labour in Europe. *Journal of Money Laundering Control, 13*(2), 87–102.
Yea, S. (2017). Editorial: The politics of evidence, data and research in anti-trafficking work. *Anti-Trafficking Review, 8,* 1–13.
Young men and violence in Sierra Leone and Liberia. The Cultures and Practices of Violence Duke University Press.

2

Protecting Children: Childhood, Rights, and the Trafficked Child

2.1 Introduction

This book critiques the journey of child trafficking in international law from the start of the twentieth century to the present day. It therefore pre-dates the creation and adoption of children's rights within the international legal framework through the much-celebrated legally binding United Nations Convention on the Rights of the Child 1989 (hereafter, the CRC) However, the predecessor to the UN the League of Nations expressed an interest in both children and anti-trafficking in the early twentieth century.

The purpose of this chapter is to introduce the concepts of childhood, children's rights, and their relationship with international law. This introduction serves as the foundation for the subsequent analysis of the commercial sexual exploitation and the development of the "trafficked child". Understanding the broader context of children's rights and contestations of their universality is part of the puzzle required to understand the law and policy reforms adopted in relation to child trafficking. The subsequent chapters seek to analyse the international legal architecture and policies implemented to address the issue of child trafficking.

The Convention on the Rights of the Child (and the Optional Protocols thereto) remains the pivotal international instrument that has been implemented under the United Nations system regarding the protection and endorsement of children's rights. However, the legacy of the colonial contours of the new world order are often excluded within the context of children's rights.

2.2 Childhood, Children's Rights, and International Law

The International law on children's rights, in important ways, usurps state authority over the ideology of childhood, establishing complicated and exacting standards that all states should adopt (Linde, 2016). To address the international law of child trafficking and the rights of children under the international legal framework, it is important to firstly consider what we mean by 'children', 'childhood', and 'children's rights'. At first these concepts seem straightforward, however, upon closer inspection they are contestable notions (Akhtar & Nyamutata, 2020, 1).

2.2.1 Childhood

So long as we believe we are all party to an implicit covenant to care about children, and not to use them for our own private ends, especially not to use them for ends that conflict with the dominant vision of childhood as a state of innocence, dependency and Otherness. (O'Connell Davidson, 2005, 22)

Children and adolescents are often viewed with a level of sentimentality, often concocting a great sense of nostalgia when reflecting upon the period of "childhood". Children and childhood are often seen as special periods of time, ones that warrant protection due to the vulnerability of children and the evils of the world that we live within. However, despite the noble or moral notion to protect this highly romanticised period of childhood, this is not the case for a multiplicity of children globally. This text seeks to consider how the parameters of childhood and children are drawn and how different levels of protection, sympathy, and care are afforded to those who conform to pre-existing ideals of child victims of trafficking and related exploitation. The starting point here is a series of questions, such as when does childhood cease or begin? How does the state perceive childhood? How does the legal system define childhood? These questions appear to be simple but have complex answers in law (Bajpai, 2018, 299).

The concept of childhood is an interdisciplinary one, drawing upon historical, psychological, sociological, and social policy perspectives, therefore becoming a 'truly multidisciplinary activity' (Buck, 2014, 1). Speculation about children and their study is not recent (Menon and Saraswathi, 2018, 2) with systematic efforts to understand and care for children dating back at least 2500 years in the Indian Tradition for instance (Madan et al.,2018; Seshadri, 2018; Singhi & Saini, 2018). Another example, is found through Locke's assertion in 1764 that children are 'not born in [a] full state of equality though they are born into it'. The child as a category, therefore, was the only subject from whom freedom could be ethically kept or withheld from (Duane & Meiners, 2021, 60). As one commentator observed 'for much of history children have not been of particular interest to academics or policy makers' (Kelly, 2005, 375). With Rousseau and Montessori popularising what has become to known as 'romantic developmental ideas about children that viewed their essence as naturally innocent, pure and good, untainted by culture, resonances of which can be found in the writings of the Indian poet, novelist, song writer and educator Rabindranath Tagore', (Menon & Saraswathi, 2018, 2). Despite this long history of interest in understanding children and childhoods, the academic study of children is relatively recent (Buck, 2014, 5; Menon & Saraswathi, 2018, 3). The focus upon childhood has been favoured by the academic community, research initiatives since the 1990s (that are more highly linked to policy, and specific projects such as child trafficking) tended to primarily concern themselves with child protection (Ennew, 2008).

Through his work, Ariès and Baldick (1962) examined the iconography in art and literature over several centuries to identify an emerging 'discovery of childhood' and maintained that in medieval times, the idea of childhood did not exist. The works of Ariès 'sparked off a whole series of strictly historical debates: on whether the medieval period did in fact have an awareness of childhood, on the key periods in the 'discovery of childhood', on the nature of parent–child relations...' (Heywood, 2001, 5). However, 'ideas of childhood in the past exist in plenitude; it is not so easy to find out about the lives of children' (Cunningham, 2005, 2). The works of Ashish Nandy analysed the relationship of colonialism to ideologies of childhood and adulthood. Through drawing parallels between the characterisation of childhoods and of the colonised, Nandy illustrated how both (childhoods and the colonised) were both represented as culturally and politically immature and inferior (Nandy, 1987). As Veerman (1992) commented, ideas concerning the rights of children are dependent upon the prevailing image of childhood, and when that image changes, the ideas about the rights of the child also change.[1] Notions of the child and childhood have been heavily influenced by Western discourses and a romanticised ideal of childhood (Howard, 2017). In the Democratic Republic of Congo (DRC) for example, children's rights and NGO narratives have combined with a neoliberal agenda have acted as a filter for new values upon the concepts of a 'proper childhood' and 'responsible parenthood'. This has led to a clash of sorts, between these ideals and the economic and cultural context of Congolese society, which favours the importance of the family collective, and reciprocity and interdependencies within family relationships (André & Godin, 2014). The unintended consequences of this clash have meant that instead of protecting children, these representations of a proper childhood and responsible parenthood advocated by these NGOs have ruptured pathways of survival for the young and in some cases, have led to migration of older children to other artisanal mining sites away from home (Twum-Danso Imoh, 2014, 9). This clash coincides with the empirical research of Howard in Nigeria and Benin, where the rescue operations of NGOs in the region to resulted in the removal of children from working conditions that they had chosen due to a continued buy into 'rescue ideologies' (Howard, 2016, 2017).

---

[1] P.E. Veerman, 'To what extent did the image of childhood change?' In P.E. Veerman, *The rights of the child and the changing image of childhood* (Dordrecht/Boston/London: Martinus Nijhoff Publishers, 1992), 3–12, 10.

Since childhood is a socially constructed category, its boundaries vary historically and within and between societies (Ariès & Baldick, 1962; Pilcher, 1995). Liberal understandings of childhood frame children as lacking the capacity to make contracts, therefore child prostitution, child labour, child marriage in addition to migration for any of these purposes is deemed 'forced' (O'Connell Davidson, 2005). As Peleg asserts, childhood has been framed in 'coherent and homogeneous terms and therefore the universal child was a standardized child' (Peleg, 2019, 12). Within this construct children are residential, fixed, and inherently local (Ansell, 2009; Huijsmans, 2011; White et al., 2011). These perceptions of childhood are important as they influence contemporary law and policy upon children, in addition to inadvertently being tied to aid which is often used as a toll to enact reform. The relations of power that continue to underlie the apparent division between a singular, normative, childhood versus 'multiple childhoods' through the 'project of liberal tolerance that underlies the latter has inadvertently set up a 'separate but equal' comparative register for understanding the lives of children in the Global South (Balagopalan, 2018). Often, both representation of and responses geared towards children the 'poor child', especially the poor child of non-Western contexts (Hopkins & Sriprakash, 2015). This globalised model of childhood that emerged after the Second World War was important to the development of the international system, serving to consolidate power and legitimise international institutions and order (Linde, 2016).

The perception that children should not migrate is entrenched through their classification as inherently vulnerable. The definition of children is intrinsically linked with the development of the powerful protectionist discourse that continues to surround children today (Ost, 2009). Indeed, the problem with policies that are adopted in relation to children is that by their very definition policies involve generalisations (Menon & Saraswathi, 2018, 8). The fact of "children on the move" conflicts with the central notion of Western constructs of children that they are fixed within a protective family environment is illuminating in understanding contemporary responses to children within the anti-trafficking frameworks implemented. The notions of 'innocence' and 'purity' have featured prominently in Western post-enlightenment discourse on childhood, whilst notions of prostitution have centred on ideas of corruption, pollution, and impurity (Ennew, 1986). Additionally, the protectionist discourse identified by Ost in relation to the sexual exploitation of children has influenced both the historical and contemporary responses to child trafficking, exploitation and slavery which in turn serves as fuel to feed the anti-trafficking machine.

The new social concept of childhood as a period of life devoted to education and growth and not to work appeared as a formal definition in 1919, under Article 2 of the International Labour Organization Convention No. 5—Minimum Age (Industry). This social position of children manifested itself within the framework of the new international legislation concerning children. The principle of special protection of the child is enshrined in the Declaration of the Rights of the Child 1959 and this shift to the child being considered as a subject rather than an object of rights and duties is where our attention shall turn to.

2.2.2 Human Rights, Children's Rights, and International Law

The history of human rights, and the subsequent emergence of children's rights protected within the unique instrument adopted to prescribe and protect them, namely the UN Convention on the Rights of the Child, 1989 form an important context to the discussion of child trafficking and the anti-trafficking machine. One of the primary contentions of my research is the neglect of the histories of child trafficking and the legal and policy responses to this perceived threat. The role of children's rights and the broader discourse surrounding the protection of children is not unique to the contemporary legal under the United Nations but can be traced back to the activities of its predecessor, the League of Nations (hereafter, the League). The League aspired in the protection of and provision of welfare services for children, creating a Committee for the

Protection of Children in 1919[2] and the Declaration on the Rights of the Child (Buck, 2014). With the New York Times suggesting that inclusion of the international movement of child welfare within the League allowed a claim to universality: 'the children of the world will be under the protection of the League of Nations'.[3] The idea of protecting children is not per se a new or novel idea. What is new is the idea of universal consensus—that societies or nations states are not to be left to determine the best interests of children by themselves, but that they need to come together to articulate basic children's rights' (Saraswathi & Menon, 2018, 398). At a most basic level the term 'children's rights' refer to a range of civil, political, social, economic, and cultural rights that pertain to children and childhood (Stalford & Hollingsworth, 2017, 17). Children's rights can only be understood in the context of the wider human rights framework (Buck, 2014, 18) That framework emerged with the creation of the United Nations (hereafter, the UN) after the Second World War (1939–1945).

The figure of the child 'symbolizes the state of subjection that we are all born to, and destined to grow out of, and in that space between vulnerability and consent, freedom is a boon that only qualified adults can grow out of' (Duane & Meiners, 2021, 60). Essentially, children were a category that freedom could be withheld from, with the denial of rights to women and enslaved populations (for example) often justified through comparing them to children (Brewer, 2012). Over the course of the twentieth century, the legal and social status of the child evolved considerably. The role of the League with regard to children is significant, pre-dating the development of the current international

---

[2] The Secretariat of the League was authorised to create a Child Welfare Committee composed of two dozen members, half of them delegates representing countries and half of them representing voluntary associations. That committee constituted one of the main forerunners of the Economic and Social Commission of the United Nations (ECOSOC). See further Marshall, 'The construction of children as an object of international relations: The Declaration of Children's Rights and the Child Welfare Committee of League of Nations, 1900–1924', *The International Journal of Children's Rights*, 7(2) (1999), 103–148.

[3] Quoted by Gordon L. Berry to T.J. Johnson, 2 April 1924, ALON, 1919–1927, R680, 12/35597/34652. As the Belgian congress of 1921 did not invite countries previously at war with Belgium, the inclusion in the League made for a collaboration between former enemies, in the spirit promoted by the SCIU. PVCE, SCIU, 38th session, 24 March 1921, AUIPE. (Quoted in Marshall, 1999, 120).

human rights law regime. In 1919, the signatories of the Treaty of Versailles and founding members of the League of Nations pledged to protect the young and to 'endeavour to secure and maintain fair and humane conditions of labour for men, women and children'.[4] It should be commented here that the international concern for the plight of children in armed conflict was one of the main motivating factors underlying the adoption of the Declaration of the Rights of the Child in 1924. (Akhtar & Nyamutata, 2020, With Marshall, 1999, 106) identifying the disastrous impact that the war in the Balkans had upon children, which correlates with the perception that it took the suffering of "white European populations" to kick start concerns of human rights. At this point, the meaning of such commitment was vague, it referred at least to the conventions of child labour recently adopted by the International Labour Office.[5] In 1919 a Committee for the Protection of Children was set up by the League. Eglantyne Jebb (1876–1928) founder of British Save the Children Fund and Save the Children International Union in Geneva, was an early influential campaigner for children and succeeded in getting the League to act (Akhtar & Nyamutata, 2020, 21). According to the Honorary President of the International Union for Child Welfare, Andree Morrier, the final text of the Geneva Declaration was ready in May 1923 when the PM was Baldwin.[6] In September 1924, the General Assembly of the League of Nations, at the request of the British delegation headed by Labour Prime Minister Ramsay Macdonald, adopted unanimously a Declaration of Children's Rights[7] (Marshall, 1999, 103) (Fig. 2.1).

Although the Declaration of 1924 was merely a non-binding resolution of the League of Nations, it carried significant moral force. The Declaration of the Rights of the Child was a 'brief five-point document which had first been promulgated by the non-governmental Save the

---

[4] Covenant of the League, Article 23. The Treaty of Versailles also mentioned the protection of the Young in its preamble (Quoted in Veerman, *The rights of the child*, 156). Ghébali, 'Aux origines de l'ECOSOC', 473.

[5] See further Marshall (1999).

[6] See further, The Declaration of the Rights of the Child (https://international-review.icrc.org/sites/default/files/S0020860400006987a.pdf). Accessed September 2022.

[7] Geneva Declaration of the Rights of the Child, adopted 26 September 1924, League of Nations OJ Spec. Supp. 21, at 43 (1924).

> Declaration of Geneva
>
> By the Present Declaration of the Rights of the Child, commonly known as the "Declaration of Geneva", men and women of all nations, recognising that all Mankind owes to the Child the best that it has to give, declare and accept as their duty that, beyond and above all considerations of race, nationality or creed:
>
> i. THE CHILD must be given the means requisite for its normal development, both materially and spiritually.
> ii. THE CHILD that is hungry must be fed; the child that is sick must be nursed; the child that is backward must be helped; the delinquent child must be reclaimed; and the orphan and the waif must be sheltered and succoured.
> iii. THE CHILD must be the first to receive relief in times of distress.
> iv. THE CHILD must be put in a position to earn a livelihood and must be protected against every form of exploitation.
> v. THE CHILD must be brought up in the conscience that its talents must be devoted to the service of his fellow-men.

Fig. 2.1 The Declaration of the Rights of the Child, drafted by the Save the Children Fund International in 1922–1923 and adopted by the Assembly of the League of Nations in 1924 (*Source* Save the Children Fund, London, Weardale Press, 1931)

Children International Union led by the British campaigner, Eglantyne Jebb' (Buck & Nicholson, 2010, 47). The Declaration of Geneva that emerged in 1924, put forward an early version of an international vision for children's welfare and protection (Saraswathi & Menon, 2018, 398).

The 5 principles contained with the Declaration were directed to 'creating the conditions necessary for children to be protected and to enable them to develop into citizens who will contribute to their communities' (Akhtar & Nyamutata, 2020, 21). The Declaration is brief, neglecting gender, race, and class but advocating that the principles contained within are applicable to all nations. However, as has been demonstrated by the application of differing standards of law (such as the differing ages of consent as adopted by Italy) by the colonial powers for European and indigenous populations conflicts with the ambition of the Declaration and its applicability. A delegate of Australia (Mrs. Allan) praised the League for mirroring worldwide interest for child protection.[8] However, despite praise such as this, the League remained a "colonial club" with membership increasing to 48 in total by 1920 and 62 by 1935, respectively. In spite of the increases in membership the League was dominated by the imperial powers such as the British and French, with other imperialist empires extending their reach around the globe during this period of time such as Germany. The protection and advancement of the welfare and rights of children was not general, with racialised othering evidenced through analysis of the League of Nations' archives.[9] The Declaration ultimately reflects a paternal view of children, which did not shift until the adoption of the Convention on the Rights of the Child (CRC) some 65 years later. Moreover, the Declaration makes 'no suggestion here about welcoming or encouraging children's participation in decision-making or other aspects of children's self-determination' (Akhtar & Nyamutata, 2020, 21). The Declaration was reaffirmed by the League in 1934, but the intention was not to create a binding treaty but 'merely to create guiding principles for those working in international child welfare' (Akhtar & Nyamutata, 2020, 21). This Declaration was in fact the first of its kind, the first human rights declaration adopted by any inter-governmental organisation which preceded the Universal Declaration of Human Rights (UDHR) by 24 years. The Declaration was swiftly and universally accepted, with the domination of Britain upon various agencies of the League ensuring its progress (Marshall, 1999, 128). Under the auspices of the United Nations, a new text of the Declaration of the Rights of the Child was adopted in 1959. Like its predecessor, this document had no international legal binding force but its unanimous adoption by the General Assembly (GA) enhanced its authority. The language used within the text of the Declaration of 1959 reflects the conception of a child as more than merely passive recipient of international humanitarian aid, but rather as an active participant in the enjoyment of human rights and freedoms.

---

[8] Société des Nations, A.IV, 'Quatrième Rapport de la Commission de Contrôle à la Quatrième Commission', 4, in ALON, 1919 1927, R680, 12/38884/34652; 'International. L'Office international de protection de l'enfance et la Société des Nations', BUISE, 5, 20 (30 October 1924), 467.

[9] See further Chapter 3.

The 'devastating impact of the Second World War and founding of the United Nations in its aftermath have been the most recent modern inspiration behind the human rights movement in the twentieth century'.[10] It is frequently identified that the atrocities of the Second World War brought into being the International Human Rights Bill.[11] As illustrated by Mutua it took the suffering of whites to force the powers that be into action and that by comparison slavery and colonialism left the world largely indifferent.[12] Human rights remains a contested field, with fierce critiques identifying the irretrievably entrenched colonial logic within them. Consider here for example the post-colonial[13] critique that the human rights logic has all too often led to the annihilation of the 'Other' (Bhabha, 1994). Whilst, the narrative of human rights claims inclusivity, as identified by Marx and feminists such as de Gouges human rights were always an exclusionary concept (Dembour, 2018, 57). The 'civilising mission' was at the heart of colonialism's justification and remains so in deployment of new imperial forms, such as through the anti-trafficking machine and children's rights framework. This in turn links with the aims of this book to illustrate the problematic nature of the popular perception of the "trafficked child". A powerful image that perpetuates racial inequalities and holds up the ideal child victim, as weak, vulnerable, passive, more often than not white who requires rescuing by the benevolent charitable organisation, civil society, or the ideal state.

The next international statement of human rights emerged in wake of the Second World War under the auspices of the newly established United Nations. The Universal Declaration of Human Rights of 1948 (hereafter, UDHR) was the result of activity of the UN Commission on Human Rights (hereafter, the UNCHR) conducted under the

---

[10] Buck (2014, 18).

[11] Some would be ready to thank, albeit not without irony Hitler and Stalin for this gift, see further Sieghart, The lawful rights of mankind: an introduction to the international legal code of human rights (OUP, 1985), 35.

[12] Mutua, *Human rights: a political and cultural critique* (University of Pennsylvania Press, 2002), 16.

[13] The term 'post-colonial' has been used in a variety of ways and summarised in a formulation borrowed from Sidaway (2000, 24) is a commitment to 'critique, expose, deconstruct, counter and (in some claims) to transcend, the cultural and broader ideological legacies and presences of imperialism'.

chairmanship of Eleanor Roosevelt. The Declaration is not binding in international law, with the view that the document would be short, inspirational, and accessible, allowing for more detailed and binding treaty provisions to be implemented (Buck, 2014, 19). Article 1 of the UDHR stated that 'all human beings are born free and equal in dignity and rights. They are endowed with reason and conscience and should act towards one another in the spirit of brotherhood'. As illustrated by de Gouges, the exclusionary masculine language is obvious.

Despite its formal non-binding status, the UDHR has become the accepted universal standard of international human rights. It has almost certainly become part of what is termed 'international customary law' (Akhtar & Nyamutata, 2020, 21). Furthermore, the UDHR has inspired similar human rights instruments to be produced at the regional level. For example, the European Convention on Human Rights (Rome, 1950), the American Convention on Human Rights (the 'Pact of San Jose', Costa Rica, 1969), and the African Charter on Human and Peoples' Rights (the 'Banjul Charter', Nairobi, 1981). As envisioned, eighteen years later the (binding) treaty provisions appeared in the form of the International Covenant on Civil and Political Rights (ICCPR) and the International Covenant on Economic, Social and Cultural Rights of 1966 (ICESCR).[14] Combined, the UDHR, ICCPR and ICESCR encapsulate the International Bill of Human Rights. Arguably, there was no need to create a separate treaty on children's rights as the International Bill of Human Rights sought to protect everyone.

The field of children's rights is not an uncontested space, with critiques of the Western dominance emerging. The perpetuating roles of race, colonialism and patriarchy continue to influence children's rights law and policy, both historically and today in a way that almost mirrors their entrenched positions of power within the anti-trafficking and anti-slavery movements both historically and today. The historical development of

---

[14] ICCPR Opened for Signature on 16th December 1966, entered into force 23rd March 1976, Signatories: 74, State Parties 173, https://treaties.un.org/pages/ViewDetails.aspx?src=TREATY&mtdsg_no=IV-4&chapter=4&clang=_en. Accessed September 2020.

ICESCR opened for signature on 16th December 1966, entered into force January 3rd 1976, Signatories 71; State Parties 171, https://treaties.un.org/pages/ViewDetails.aspx?src=IND&mtdsg_no=IV-3&chapter=4&clang=_en#1. Accessed September 2020.

human rights briefly alluded to in the preceding discussion and the emergence of the UN 'Treaty bodies' that now deal with particular categories of human rights issues, including the Committee on the Rights of the Child supervision and monitoring of the Convention on the Rights of the Child (1989), have raised the issue of how far children's rights should be differentiated from the general international human rights instruments (Akhtar & Nyamutata, 2020, 20). The issue with the latter is that they have tended to focus on the rights of parents, and there may also be obligations on parents and institutions towards children, but these are likely to be unenforceable by children. Therefore, the recognition of children's rights may lead to an assumption that children have different rights from adults, with different justifications, rather than accommodating children as an integral part of the same human rights protection regime. As asserted by Van Beuren, children were invisible within the United Nations prior to the CRC. Whilst Alderson commented that children tended to be missing from the literature on human rights (Alderson, 2012, 1). It would seem preferable to regard children as part of the human family with everyone equally entitled to rights[15] (Akhtar & Nyamutata, 2020, 20). Any special or additional formulations of human rights would need to be premised on children's particular vulnerability or inexperience (Sawyer, 2006, 13). This strengthens the position that any instrument that purports to provide for children must be child-centred and independent of adult bias (Akhtar & Nyamutata, 2020, 20). This view that children ought to be given specific rights gained traction during the early twentieth century, culminating in a fully fledged code of children's rights in the United Nations Convention on the Rights of the Child (1989).

---

[15] 'The inherent dignity and…the equal and inalienable rights of all members of the human family'.

2.2.3 The United Nations Convention on the Rights of the Child 1989[16]

The UN Convention on the Rights of the Child adopted in 1989, 'was the culmination of over 100 years of international discourse on children's rights' (Twum-Danso Imoh, 2018, 1) and the successor to two (non-binding) Declarations, namely the 1924 Declaration on the Rights of the Child and the 1959 Declaration of the Rights of the Child.[17] The international 'consensus around the basic principle that children have rights worthy of protection has never been more comprehensive and vivid than it is today', evidenced by the fact that they are embedded within the 'lexicon of international human rights' with near-global voluntary adherence (Stalford & Hollingsworth, 2017, 18). Human rights treaties are the embodiment of hope and the UN Convention on the Rights of the Child 1989 (hereafter, CRC) as the primary international human rights treaty, is no exception (Van Beuren, 2018, 326). Within the context of international law, prior to the adoption of the CRC, children were generally invisible within the United Nations or were passive objects of concern for international law (Van Beuren, 2018, 327). The CRC for the first time in international law viewed children as rights-holders instead of 'objects of adult charity' (Veerman, 1992, 184). Indeed, as stated by Fottrell (2000, 1) the 'Convention elevated the child to the status of an independent rights holder'.

A common view now exists that the CRC has not only imposed a universal notion of what it is to be a child; it has prescribed and embedded what the substance and scope of children's rights should be (Faulkner & Nyamutata, 2020, 70). For instance, Detrick, in her detailed and authoritative annotation of each of the substantive articles of the CRC, notes that:

---

[16] Convention on the Rights of the Child | OHCHR (https://www.ohchr.org/en/instruments-mechanisms/instruments/convention-rights-child). Accessed October 2022.

[17] Proclaimed by the General Assembly, resolution 1386 (XIV), A/RES/14/1386 (20 November 1959).

> *While the Convention on the Rights of the Child may not be the last – or complete – word on children's rights, it is the first universal instrument of a legally binding nature to comprehensively address those rights. As such, it forms a universal benchmark on the rights of the child – a benchmark against which all future claims for evolution will and must be answered.* (Dettrick, 1999, 721)

Whilst, for Archard, the CRC is a 'codification of children's rights', defining a '…recognizable canon of thought about the rights of children' (108–109). It is plausible to argue that the CRC is the principal driving force behind a global children's rights culture, dominating international children's policy' (Holzscheiter, 2010, 87). This assertion about the CRC, 'as a largely uncontested and legally valid norm has contributed to making the UNCRC a dominant and compelling instrument for advancing human rights for children' (Quennerstedt et al., 2018, 39).

The impact of the CRC has been observed (Engle, 2010, 794; Richter & Dawes, 2008; Sloth-Neilsen, 2008; Tobin, 2005; Verhellen, 2000) and 'its global reach is unparalleled and today it is now the prevailing general framework for most international action on children's rights' (Myers, 2001, 39). The CRC has indeed had a major impact on the perception of childhood, children, and children's rights. It has been a major catalyst in changing the social and political status of children and for achieving significant advances in law, policy, and practice across the world. The Convention led numerous governments to introduce child centric legislation into their national legal systems. Such as Bolivia (Code of Children and Adolescent 1999), Brazil (Brazilian Child and Adolescent Act 1990), the Dominican Republic (Code for the Protection of Children and Adolescents 2004), Guatemala (The Law for the Fundamental Protection of Childhood and Adolescence), India (Juvenile Justice Care and Protection of Children Act 2000), Indonesia (Law on Child Protection 2004), Jamaica (The Child Care and Protection Act 2003), Mauritius (Children Act 2003), Maldives (The Law on the Protection of the Rights of Children 1991), Thailand (Child Protection Act 2004), and Peru (Children's and Adolescents' Code 2000). Furthermore, it has seeped into jurisprudence on children even in countries which have not incorporated the treaty into domestic law (Faulkner & Nyamutata, 2020, 70). For instance, the UK judiciary has liberally deferred to the CRC, in particular the "best interests" principle.[18] Drawing on Article 12, CRC on taking into account the opinions of the child, the President of the UK Supreme Court has asserted that 'courts increasingly consider it appropriate to take account of a child's views'.[19] Furthermore, whilst the USA is not party to the Convention, the American courts have also referenced the Convention.[20]

The CRC has been celebrated for its universal acceptance, with the 30th anniversary of the Convention in 2019 marked by a series of celebratory events.[21] Due to this "universal acceptance" the CRC is often viewed as a clear success, however critiques of the CRC are evident. With the potential for the CRC to perpetuate colonial tendencies if accepted uncritically as a global and definitive blueprint for children's rights (Faulkner & Nyamutata, 2020). The CRC is the centrepiece of the international legal framework on children. Whilst it has been advocated that the 'concept of childhood ... is still not truly universal' (Humbert, 2009, 16) and that the CRC 'reflects Euro-American views' (Buck, 2014, 241). Indeed, the:

Near global ratification of the UNCRC brought the lives of marginal children in India under intense scrutiny. This heightened visibility tended to read these children primarily as 'victims' and was backed up by empathetical studies that attested to their harsh realities and attendant urgency to take action. (Balagopalan, 2018)

Since the adoption of the CRC, the meanings attributed to children's rights within global academic and political arenas are largely based upon

---

[18] See, e.g., UK cases; Z. H. (Tanzania) v. Secretary of State for the Home Department [2011] UKSC 4, [2011] 2 AC 166; R. (on the application of Williamson and others) v. Secretary of State for Education and Employment and others [2005] UKHL 15; R. (A) v. Leeds Magistrates' Court [2004] EWHC 554 (Admin) [51]; R. (Kenny) v. Leeds Magistrates' Court [2003] EWHC 2963 (Admin) [42].

[19] Re M. (Abduction: Zimbabwe) [2007] UKHL 46, 55.

[20] See, e.g., Roper v. Simmons, 543 U.S. 551 (2005); Graham v. Florida, 130 S.Ct. 2011 (2010).

[21] https://www.ohchr.org/EN/HRBodies/CRC/Pages/CRC30.aspx. #CRC30. Accessed September 2020.

the text of the Convention (Quennerstedt et al., 2018). Prior to its adoption, the focus of UN bodies had been predominantly on younger children due to the lack of a globally agreed definition of childhood.[22] Questions of who a child is have for many been answered through Article 1, UNCRC, which explicitly stipulates that:

A child means every human being below the age of 18 years unless under the law applicable to the child, majority is attained earlier.[23]

Article 1 provided a globally accepted definition of childhood, which stipulates that childhood ends at the age of 18, or the age of majority within a particular state as determined by national law. The CRC filled the vacuum in terms of an international agreement upon a globally agreed definition of childhood, specifically stating that childhood ends at the age of 18, or the age of majority within a particular state as determined by national law.[24] Therefore, Article 1 affords states with relative flexibility, and the CRC Committee has sought to raise the standards considering this. Afterall, age limits 'are a formal reflection of society's judgment about the evolution of children's capacities and responsibilities' (Bajpai, 2017, 2). The African Union for example has explicitly enshrined a higher standard through the African Children's Charter, within which childhood is extended to 18 without any reference to the age of majority.[25] The CRC offers children a set of rights that are distinct from those accorded to adults (Ansell, 2014, 234). The very existence of the CRC both assumes and reinforces a distinction between children and adults, which for some commentators is problematic (Aitken, 2001; Burman, 1996; White, 2002). It is definition that causes disquiet amongst commentators (Abede & Tefera, 2018; Cheney, 2018; Okyere et al., 2021). The CRC filled a void,

---

[22] The CRC Committee in recent years has focused upon the rights of older children, which culminated in the adoption of a General Comment on the implementation of the rights of the child during adolescence. See further, CRC Committee, General Comment No. 20, CRC/C/GC/20 (6 December 2016).

[23] Article 1, Convention on the Rights of the Child 1989.

[24] Article 1, Convention on the Rights of the Child.

[25] Article 2, Definition of the Child, http://www.achpr.org/instruments/child/. Accessed August 2018.

providing an international agreement upon the definition of childhood. The fact remains that a distinction is drawn between children and adults under international law, replicated through regional and domestic legislation globally. Under the anti-trafficking legal architecture implemented, that distinction remains through the omission of the means element contained within the Trafficking Protocol. Moreover, the importance of local understandings of childhood are often neglected within the anti-trafficking machine as highlighted through the call for a 'social age category within existing child rights and human trafficking laws in Ghana' for example (Koomson & Abdulai, 2021).

Although prima facie an international standard of childhood has been accepted, in practice drawing a clear-cut distinction between "children" and "youth" or "adolescents" is difficult. For example, the UN asserts that a child falls between the age range of 0 and 17, whilst a youth is anyone between the ages of 15 and 24.[26] Differences in operational or practical understandings of children are even more problematic within the context of "children on the move". The idea that children are, fixed, inherently local and within the protective family environment conflicts to an extent with the picture offered by the United Refugee Agency (hereafter, UNHCR) and its Refugee Data Finder. The UNHCR[27] data from 2020 indicates that of the 82.4 million forcibly displaced people approximately 35 million or 42% are children below the age of eighteen.[28]

Since the adoption of the CRC in 1989, it has been supplemented by three optional protocols, namely the:

- Optional Protocol to the Convention on the Rights of the Child on the Sale of Children, Child Prostitution and Child Pornography (OPSC);
- The Optional Protocol to the Convention on the Rights of the Child on the Involvement of Children in Armed Conflict (OPAC); and finally

---

[26] See further, http://www.un.org/esa/socdev/documents/youth/fact-sheets/youth-definition.pdf. Accessed August 2018.
[27] UNHCR—The UN Refugee Agency (https://www.unhcr.org/). Accessed 20 July 2022.
[28] See further, https://www.unhcr.org/refugee-statistics/. Accessed August 2021.

- The Optional Protocol to the Convention on the Rights of the Child on a Communications Procedure (OPIC).

The first two were adopted in 2000, with the third in 2014, respectively. It should be highlighted that an Optional Protocol is not an amendment to the text of a UN Convention, it is simply an addition to the main Convention on any topic relevant in the original treaty. Therefore, such Protocols are 'optional' as States may not wish to have the burden of additional duties to those in the main Convention that they have already ratified (Akhtar & Nyamutata, 2020, 106). An in-depth analysis of the Optional Protocols, chiefly the OPSC will feature in Chapter 4, however it is important to note that the frustrations of Argentina with the slow drafting and negotiating period of the OPSC was highlighted through the states proactive role in the drafting process of the Palermo Protocol, driving the focus upon 'trafficking in minors'.

The protection of children 'as championed by the CRC in theory guarantees children everywhere regardless of race or gender; basic rights and protection against exploitation and abuse' (Omoike, 2014, 123). However, from which society those judgements emerge, and what impact it has had upon children globally, is a crucial point within the discourse of children's rights and more specifically relating to "children on the move", child labour, and exploitation.

The Four 'General Principles' of the Convention on the Rights of the Child

The CRC reflected a shift from the paternalistic perception of children to the advocation of them as autonomous rights bearers. One of the best known and most cited features of the CRC is 'a concept that is, in fact, entirely extra-Conventional. This is the proposition that four of its articles are not just rights in themselves but enjoy a special cross-cutting status in the implementation of the whole CRC' (Lundy & Byrne, 2017, 52). The UN Committee on the Rights of the Child at an early stage in the Convention's life, identified the 'general principles' (Articles 2, 3, 6, and 12) These four 'general principles' underpin the CRC and the concept of 'general principles' has a long history in human rights

> Article 2: all children should have equal enjoyment of their rights;
>
> Article 3 (1): the best interests of the child should be a primary consideration[1],
>
> Article 6: children have a right to life, survival, and development and
>
> Article 12: all children have a right to express their views and to participate in decisions that affect them in accordance with their age and capacity.

Fig. 2.2 The general principles of the Convention on the Rights of the Child

discourse (O'Boyle & Lafferty, 2006). However the notion that a particular Treaty could have its own bespoke principles was at the time they were adopted entirely novel (Lundy & Byrne, 2017, 52) (Fig. 2.2).

The general principles are all of relevance when it comes to the trafficking of children, from non-discrimination prescribed in Article 2 to the right to life, survival, and development of Article 6. Articles 3 and 12 of the CRC are two of the four general principles that are relevant within the context of agency. The issue of agency is something of a red herring in the legal responses to child trafficking, as the legal and policy responses highlight the continued silencing and culture of disbelief that impacts upon children and adolescents.[29] This observation forms one of the focal points within the book and will be elaborated upon throughout the text. The Committee on the Rights of the Child asserts that:

> *There is no tension between Articles 3 and 12, only a complementary role of the two general principles; one establishes the objective of achieving the best interests of the child and the other provides the methodology for reaching the goal of hearing either the child or children. In fact, there can be no correct application of article 3 if the components of article 12 are not respected.*[30]

---

[29] This point is illustrated neatly by the ECPAT UK and Hynes report from October 2022, which focused upon the positive outcomes for children who had been trafficked into the UK and adopted a participatory methodological approach to the research. See further—Creating stable futures: human trafficking, participation and outcomes for children | ECPAT UK (https://www.ecpat.org.uk/creating-stable-futures-human-trafficking-participation-and-outcomes-for-children). Accessed October 2022.

[30] UN Committee on the Rights of the Child (CRC), General comment no. 12 (2009): the right of the child to be heard (2009), http://www.refworld.org/docid/4ae562c52.html. Accessed March 2018.

This quote embodies a significant shift away from the League's position within the 1924 Declaration and its firm stance in not actively welcoming or encouraging children's participation in decision-making or other aspects of the child's self-determination (Akhtar & Nyamutata, 2020, 21). The Committee articulates that actively involving children in decisions about issues that are central to their own lives is the most effective way of determining what is in their best interests (Stalford & Byrne, 2018, 523). Although difficulties in determining what precisely is in the best interests of children remains, especially when values differ and conflict, the tension between protection and participation largely falls away (Bourdillon & Musvosvi, 2014, 119). The best interests principal acts as a guide for interventions that are targeted at protecting children, however empirical research with child domestic workers in Ghana and Nigeria for example has illustrated that the principle does not consider children's own perceptions of best interests (Omoike, 2014, 123). The CRC transformed children from being merely victims who were incapable to be active participants in their own destinies to active rights-holders. It has been identified that involving children in decisions about their own lives, and that it is conducted in a balanced and sensitive way the children's rights principles (Article 3 and 12 CRC) should be able to accommodate both agency and children's vulnerabilities simultaneously.[31] The UN CRC Committee recommends that children's experiences 'should be considered in decision-making, policymaking and preparation of laws and/or measures as well as their evaluation'.[32] In spite of provisions for the voices of children to be heard in matters that concern them, there is no provision that recognises that child workers views might be different (Omoike, 2014, 123). This fact is noteworthy as it replicates the way in which the CRC was drafted, it is a document that enshrines the rights of children to participate and the importance of the voice of the child. Yet, no children or adolescents were consulted or

---

[31] ibid. See further K.-F. Kaltenborn, 'Children's and young people's experiences in various residential arrangements: a longitudinal study to evaluate criteria for custody and residence decision making', *British Journal of Social Work*, 31 (2001), 81 which highlight a strong correlation between positive long-term outcomes for children's welfare and adherence to children's wishes.

[32] UN CRC Committee, General comment no. 12 (2009), UN Doc CRC/C/GC/12 (27/07/2009) para. 12.

involved in the drafting process of the Convention itself. How might the world's children respond to a document drafted on their behalf but with the other excluded and silenced them?

A relatively recent EU study on High-risk Groups for Trafficking in Human Beings advocated to 'strengthen the voice of the child (Article 12 CRC) within all services and support systems for children, and particularly those who fall within the high-risk groups for trafficking' including through training professionals and funding for testing of child protection systems.[33] There have been calls for stronger direct involvement of (former) trafficked children in research, which remains an exception in the field of trafficking (Dimitrova et al., 2016; Dottridge, 2002; Sax, 2018, 255). This involvement would need to be mindful that any participation of children having undergone traumatic experiences of trafficking and exploitation must be based upon clear ethical guidelines and child safeguarding standards.[34]

This moves from children as objects of paternalistic protection links to the renewed sociological emphasis placed upon the child's competence, active agency, autonomy and 'voice', which in turn fits neatly around the legal-orientated perspective of children's rights (Buck, 2014, 14). The move towards a constructivist model of the child, where the child has a more active and self-determining role is enshrined in the CRC. Moreover, the central ethos of the instrument concerns the agency of the child, and the standard adopted in the famous and much cited case from the UK of 'Gillick'[35] in 1986 which appears to emulate the evolving nature of the CRC. The 'central tension' of the CRC can be identified as the conflict between the best interest principle (Article 3) and the child's right to be heard (Article 12).[36] Striking the balance between the elements of protection and empowerment within the Convention is difficult (Buck, 2014, 30); which principle should prevail and who should

---

[33] A. Cancedda, B. De Micheli, D. Dimitrova, and B. Slot, Study on high-risk groups for trafficking in human beings (2015), 85.

[34] See further UNICEF, Reference Guide on protecting the rights of child victims of trafficking in Europe (2006).

[35] Gillick v West Norfolk and Wisbech Area Health Authority [1986] AC 112.

[36] See further David Archard, 'Children's rights' in Thomas Cushman (ed) Handbook of human rights (Abingdon: Routledge), 324–332.

determine it? In recent years there has been a focus upon the rights of older children, which culminated in the adoption of a General Comment on the implementation of the rights of the child during adolescence.[37] The Committee observed 'that the potential of adolescents is widely compromised because States parties do not recognize or invest in the measures needed for them to enjoy their rights'.

The focus upon the interrelated issues of autonomy, maturity, and intelligence is not isolated to public international law. Within the context of the child objection defence under the Hague Convention on the Civil Aspects of International Child Abduction[38] (hereafter, the Hague Convention) expressly refers to the "age and degree of maturity".[39] Adult decision-makers focus upon issues of the autonomy of the child, their maturity, and intelligence (Scullion, 2018). The difficulty is striking the balance between protecting children from harm and recognising their autonomy and respecting their wishes. This balancing act runs at the heart of the earlier statement from the UN Committee on the Rights of the Child, within which they explicitly stated that no tension exists between Articles 3 and 12 of the CRC. The dominant discourse that has developed considering child trafficking, conflicts directly with the assertion that no tension exists between Articles 3 and 12. The agency of all children under the Trafficking Protocol is removed through the omission of the means element by Article 3.

Granting the child, the status of an independent rights holder conflicts with the legal, social, and political construction of "child trafficking".

---

[37] UN Committee on the Rights of the Child (CRC), General Comment No. 20 (2016) on the implementation of the rights of the child during adolescence, 6 December 2016, CRC/C/GC/20, available at, General comment no. 20 (2016) on the implementation of the rights of the child during adolescence (https://digitallibrary.un.org/record/855544). Accessed July 2022.

[38] Convention of 25 October 1980 on Civil Aspects of International Child Abduction, entry into force: 1-XII-1983 with 101 contracting Parties to the Convention at the time of writing in August 2021. See further, https://www.hcch.net/en/instruments/conventions/full-text/?cid=24. Accessed August 2021.

[39] Article 13 (b) Hague Convention on the Civil Aspects of International Child Abduction. The Revised Brussels II Regulation of 2003 also explicitly references to the age or degree of maturity of children within the context of hearing children.

The dominant discourses that pervade trafficking emphasise and highlight the inherent vulnerability of the child, paralleled by the understanding that trafficking is generally dominated by vulnerable women and girls destined for a life of misery within the commercial sexual exploitation industry. The central ethos of the CRC was to promote the agency of children; however, the international legal framework of human trafficking can remove the agency of the child(Quénivet, 2017, 433). The issue of child soldiers provides a useful insight into the concept of agency, with some commentators articulating that denying the agency of children is not paternalistic as within the context of child soldiers it is an approach that would be suitable for adult offenders.[40] Moreover, the idea of creating an accountability mechanism exclusively within the parameters of private international law, that would extend both the current laws on agency in addition to vicarious liability has been raised within the context of child soldiers (Shah-Davis & Quénivet, 2010, 229).

The Agency of the Child

A critical source of vulnerability of children lies in their lack of full agency—in fact and under law (Gallagher, 2012, 284). The International Covenant on Civil and Political Rights (hereafter, the ICCPR) provides an example of the explicit recognition of this fact through Article 24 which states that the right of the child such measures of protection *as are required by his status as a minor*, on the part of his family, society, and the State.[41] Immaturity 'is the inability to use one's own understanding without direction from another' (Kant, 2009, 2) Moreover, as highlighted by Bajpai (2017, 2) age limits are merely a 'formal reflection of society's judgement about the evolution of children's capacities and responsibilities'. This case is most explicitly elaborated upon

---

[40] See further Noëlle Quénivet, 'Does and should international law prohibit the prosecution of children for war crimes?' *European Journal of International Law*, 28 (2017), 433 Within the context of reintegrating child soldiers into a community is often in the child's best interests to return to the community, moving on to observe that denying the child's agency is not a paternalistic approach, but within the context of child soldiers an approach which would be suitable for adult offenders in this specific context. See further Shilan Shah-Davis and Noëlle Quénivet (ed), *International law and armed conflict: challenges in the 21st century.*

[41] ICCPR, http://www.ohchr.org/en/professionalinterest/pages/ccpr.aspx. Accessed April 2018.

by 'classical liberal theorists in relation to children, who were excluded from the terms of the social contract on grounds that, since they were not qualified for the exercise of freedom and needed to be protected from their own irrational actions, as well as from others' (Archard, 1993; O'Connell Davidson, 2005). The notion of active agency has been increasingly recognised and a key controversy that has arisen both within child law and policy is the extent to which the child can be properly regarded as having a right to autonomy (Buck, 2014, 24). Autonomy is resonant of individual choice, liberty, and self-sufficiency and arguably holds a 'sacred status' within contemporary law[42] (Herring, 2010, 267). Moreover, it is fundamental to growth, development, and personal well-being.[43]

The starting point for a consideration of the agency of the child is the decision of a case from England and Wales, *Gillick v West Norfolk and Wisbech Area Health Authority*[44] (hereafter referred to as *Gillick*) As I was educated within the jurisdiction of England and Wales my point of reference is the decision in the case of Gillick—'in which it was held that a child, on being able to demonstrate sufficient competence to pass a functional capacity test, should be entitled to make his or her own decisions – have been neutralised subsequently by being made subject to overriding best interests principles grounded in the status of that person as a child' (Sandland, 2018, 125). The Gillick case specifically looked at whether doctors should give contraceptive treatment or advice to those under the age of sixteen without the consent of their parents.[45] The Gillick competence test provides that children under the age of sixteen that are judged to have 'sufficient understanding and intelligence' to enable them to understand fully the consequences and nature of the suggested treatment; then they should be able to make the decision to receive that treatment rather than their parents (Bucataru, 2016, 17). The Gillick competence test is based upon the maturity, intelligence, and

---

[42] See further Aoife Daly, *Children, autonomy and the courts: beyond the right to be heard* (Brill Nijhoff, 2017).
[43] Edward Deci and Richard M. Ryan, *Intrinsic motivation and self-determination in human behaviour* (First, Spinger US, 1985).
[44] [1986] AC 112.
[45] Gillick v West Norfolk and Wisbech Area Health Authority [1986] AC 112.

understanding of the individual child and has been adopted internationally as the standard by which children can be determined competent to consent to their own medical treatment[46] (Bucataru, 2016). However, the test does not exist without criticism, with deficiencies raised with the concept as a whole. A suggestion that a move towards provisions of the Mental Capacity Act 2005[47] could be applied to minors, potentially in conjunction with a newly developed common law test for child incapacity has been asserted (Scullion, 2018, 422).[48]

You may be wondering what relevance this has to the issue of child trafficking and what does this mean? The issue of agency is of vital importance when seeking to understand and critique the creation of the fear and moral revulsion of the phenomena. This perception of children hooks into the notion that 'those who were seen to be *actually* immature were unqualified for the exercise of freedom, and so needed to be protected for the exercise of freedom, and so needed to be protected both from others and themselves' (O'Connell Davidson, 2015, 83). The feel-good factor of rescue is appealing in a way that it avoids addressing structural issues and recognising the harms caused by anti-child trafficking initiatives upon those they purport to protect.

General Comments to the Convention on the Rights of the Child

The international law relating to child trafficking and more broadly to 'children on the move' is located within a variety of sources, with some key developments emerging through General Comments to the Convention on the Rights of the Child. A General Comment is quasi legal document published by the UN Committee on the Rights of the Child which was established under the Convention on the Rights of the Child. A GC is a treaty body's interpretation of human rights provisions,

---

[46] Anna-Maria Bucataru, 'Using the convention on the rights of the child to project the rights of transgender children and adolescents: the context of education and transition' *Queen Mary Human Rights Law Review*, 3 (2016), 17, 59.
[47] https://www.legislation.gov.uk/ukpga/2005/9/contents. Accessed July 2022.
[48] Dianne Scullion, 'The medical treatment of children' in Ruth Lamont (ed), *Family law* (First, 2018), 422.

thematic issues, or its methods of work. Moreover, general comments seek to clarify the reporting duties of States parties with respect to certain provisions and suggest approaches to implementing treaty provisions.[49] The purpose of this section is not to consider each of the 25[50] general comments that have been adopted but to acknowledge those of specific importance in relation to 'children on the move' and 'child trafficking'. Notably, a General Comment from 2006 sought to:

> *draw attention to the particularly vulnerable situation of unaccompanied and separated children; to outline the multifaceted challenges faced by States and other actors in ensuring that such children are able to access and enjoy their rights; and, to provide guidance on the protection, care and proper treatment of unaccompanied and separated children based on the entire legal framework provided by the Convention on the Rights of the Child (the "Convention"), with particular reference to the principles of non-discrimination, the best interests of the child and the right of the child to express his or her views freely.*[51]

The General comment explicitly references the role of non-discrimination as parallel with the best interests of the child and their right to participation to voice their own views. The GC does not explicitly refer to trafficking or child trafficking, but nevertheless relates to the categories of children who are often perceived as vulnerable to trafficking, namely "children on the move" and it is to this category of children our focus shall now turn.

---

[49] OHCHR | General Comments (https://www.ohchr.org/en/treaty-bodies/general-comments). Accessed October 2022.

[50] At the time of writing in October 2022 25 General Comments had been adopted with a 26th 'Children's rights and the environment with a special focus on climate change' in draft. See further, OHCHR | General Comments (https://www.ohchr.org/en/treaty-bodies/crc/general-comments). Accessed October 2022.

[51] CRC/GC/2005/6 page 5 accessed via Treaty Bodies Download (https://tbinternet.ohchr.org/_layouts/15/treatybodyexternal/Download.aspx?symbolno=CRC%2fGC%2f2005%2f6&Lang=en). Accessed October 2022.

2.3 International Law and "Children on the Move"[52]

The phrase "children on the move" is used by the United Nations High Commissioner for Refugees (hereafter, the UNHCR) to identify children of concern (asylum-seeking, refugee and stateless children) who move across international borders in search of protection and solutions, whether accompanied or alone.[53] In 2010 in Barcelona, Spain an International Conference on "Children on the Move" was convened as a 'first step in the process of re-examining policy and programmatic responses to the protection and support of children on the move'.[54] A series of reports and documents were produced for the conference and after its conclusion. One such report highlights how the 'exclusive focus on the crime of child trafficking has obscured the reality of why and how many children are moving across the world'.[55] The Report subsequently moves to illustrate that assumptions that 'adults who accompany or help children move are feeding the criminal trade in child trafficking, which is increasing alongside global migration'. The issue with assumptions is that they ignore the fact that 'millions of children currently on the

---

[52] This monograph uses the term "children on the move" to refer to children within and outside of international migration frameworks, whether they have been trafficked, smuggled, or are asylum-seeking or refugees. The phrase "children on the move" is used by the UNHCR to identify children of concern (asylum-seeking, refugee, and stateless children) who move across international borders in search of protection and solutions, whether accompanied or alone. See further Children on the Move: Background Paper, 'High commissioner's dialogue on protection challenges', *International Journal of Refugee Law*, 29(2) (1 June 2017), 356–381 In other contexts, such as the Inter-Agency Group on Children on the Move, this term has a broader meaning. See, for example, http://www.gmfc.org/en/action-within-the-movement/gmc-actions/actions-by-imperatives/other-campaigns-a-actions/current-actions/90-international-conference-on-children-on-the-move.

[53] See further Children on the Move: Background Paper, 'High commissioner's dialogue on protection challenges', *International Journal of Refugee Law*, 29(2) (1 June 2017), 356–338.

[54] International Conference on "Children on the Move" (https://www.ilo.org/ipec/Events/WCMS_145302/lang--en/index.htm).

[55] Leaving Home: Voices of Children on the Move, Global Movement for Children (2010), 3, https://resourcecentre.savethechildren.net/document/leaving-home-voices-children-move/. Accessed September 2022.

move across the world are travelling with their families or relatives'.[56] The dialogues relating to "children on the move" and child trafficking or modern slavery clash with the overwhelming focus of international law and policy upon the latter. The idea that children are fixed and inherently local is something that shapes and influences the adoptions of law and policy in this context. The problematic narrative of 'saving children' can hinder the adoption of laws and policies that enable and facilitate safe migration rather than inadvertently stripping children and adolescents of their agency and voices in the development of such frameworks.

For some, migration is a defining feature of the twenty-first century (Bakewell, 2008) with the world experiencing unprecedented levels of migration (Kapur, 2012). According to UNICEF, between 2005 and 2015 the number of child refugees more than doubled from 4 to 9 million, with 300,000 unaccompanied or separated children who moved across borders in 80 countries in 2015 and 2016, with 28% of trafficking victims were identified as children by the UNODC Trafficking in Persons Report 2014.[57] Although data is available, there is an evidentiary gap as migration data is rarely disaggregated by age.[58] Moreover, children may not be counted at all even if they migrate through legal channels (Huijismans, 2011) and this issue of data collection of adolescents was raised in a General Comment of the UN Committee in 2016. How has the international legal and policy framework responded to the supposed contemporary challenge of migration? Or perhaps better identified as a shift from south–south migration to south–north migration. Brittle and Desmet's (2020) review of children's rights research in the context of migration, for example illustrates a dearth in published research from Africa, Asia, and Latin America in spite of extensive internal and cross-national migration occurring in the regions. Some of

---

[56] Leaving Home: Voices of Children on the Move, Global Movement for Children (2010), 11, https://resourcecentre.savethechildren.net/document/leaving-home-voices-children-move/. Accessed September 2022.
[57] UNICEF Data brief: children on the move key facts and figures (2018), https://data.unicef.org/wp-content/uploads/2018/02/Data-brief-children-on-the-move-key-facts-and-figures-1.pdf. Accessed August 2018.
[58] See further, Data brief: children on the move key facts and figures (2018), https://data.unicef.org/wp-content/uploads/2018/02/Data-brief-children-on-the-move-key-facts-and-figures-1.pdf. Accessed August 2018.

the research conducted in the geographical region of Asia illustrates that 'Children are also migration actors' and subsequently call for reflections upon whose perspectives, concerns, and interests need to be considered in research, policy making, and advocacy in the region (Asis & Feranil, 2020). With Stalford and Lundy (2020) commenting that the 'global refugee crisis has acted as a honey pot for Western researchers, leading to a proliferation of work on unaccompanied children in particular'. Although this work may highlight States' failure to comply with their humanitarian obligations, much of this work signals an uncomfortable reversion to colonialist narratives, including the civilising function of Western (notably European) legal, policy, and humanitarian intervention and the intractable vulnerability and helplessness of child refugees.[59] The adult centric approach often documents the 'suffering and breaches of child rights' at the expense of collecting child inclusive data that may show children's resilience in such circumstances (Lundy, 2019, 597). Furthermore, the ethical approval processes complemented the need for any child to be protected from any potential harms of participating in research with the right of children to be heard (Goddard & Mudaly, 2009) and growing acceptance of methodologies and methods that enable children to participate in research on their own terms (Horgan, 2017).

The next avenue for exploration is the international legal framework currently in existence. How does it operate, and which instrument or instruments address children on the move? There is no single piece of legislation that systematically addresses the issue of children on the move in the world today (Bhabha and Dottridge, 2016). However, the CRC is a comprehensive compilation of legal standards for the protection of children, defining children as being below the age of 18 years, and the most widely ratified international human rights treaty today. As such it is often the first port of call when undertaking an analysis of the instruments adopted. The pre-history of the CRC involves a vision of the kind of 'childhood' that children everywhere should be able to enjoy

---

[59] L. Lundy and H. Stalford, 'The field of children's rights: taking stock, travelling forward', *The International Journal of Children's Rights*, 28(1) (2020), 1–13, Available From: Brill, https://doi.org/10.1163/15718182-02801010. Accessed 28 July 2022.

(Hart, 2006), a position that neglects the imposition of the Western romanticised image of childhood upon the world.

Internationally, there are a range of legal instruments, Conventions, Protocols, and Guiding Principles that serve to 'identify, define and disaggregate distinct populations of people who have been forcibly displaced' (Hynes, 2021, 7). This framework includes the 1951 Convention relating to the Status of Refugees[60] (hereafter the Refugee Convention, 1951), the associated 1967 Protocol relating to the Status of Refugees (hereafter, the Refugee Protocol 1967),[61] the International Convention on the Protection of the Rights of All Migrants and Members of Their Families, 1990,[62] and the Guiding Principles on Internal Displacement, 1998.[63] In addition to the two Protocols attached to the UN Convention on Transnational Organised Crime; The Trafficking Protocol 2000 and the Protocol against the Smuggling of Migrants by Land, Sea and Air 2000[64] (hereafter, the Smuggling Protocol, 2000).[65] This framework is supplemented by the instruments

---

[60] Signed Geneva 28 July 1951, entered into force 22 April 1954, in accordance with Article 43. With 149 State Parties to either (the 1951 or 1967 Protocol) or both, they define the term 'refugee' and outline the rights of refugees, as well as the legal obligations of States to protect them. The core principle is non-refoulement, which asserts that a refugee should not be returned to a country where they face serious threats to their life or freedom, moreover it is now considered a rule of customary international law.

[61] The Protocol required just 6 ratifications and entered into force on 4 October 1967. Instead of an international conference under the auspices of the United Nations, the issues were addressed at a colloquium of some thirteen legal experts which met in Bellagio, Italy, from 21 to 28 April 1965. The Colloquium did not favour a complete revision of the 1951 Convention but opted instead for a Protocol by way of which States parties would agree to apply the relevant provisions of the Convention, but without necessarily becoming party to that treaty. See further Goodwin Gill, https://legal.un.org/avl/ha/prsr/prsr.html. Accessed August 2021.

The 1967 Protocol removed the Refugee Convention's temporal and geographical restrictions so that the Convention applied universally.

[62] A multilateral treaty governing the protection of migrant workers and families. Signed on 18 December 1990, it entered into force on 1 July 2003 after the threshold of 20 ratifying States was reached in March 2003.

[63] See also the 2006 Protocol on the Protection and Assistance to Internally Displaced Persons (adopted by the Member States of the International Conference on the Great Lakes) (known as the 2006 Great Lakes IDP Protocol) 2009 African Convention on Protection and Assistance for Internally Displaced Persons in Africa (known as the 2009 Kampala Convention).

[64] Supplementing the United Nations Convention Against Transnational Organized Crime. Adopted 15 November 2000, Entered into force 28 January 2004.

[65] See also the 1954 Convention relating to the Status of Stateless Persons (known as the 1954 Stateless Convention) and the 1961 Convention on the Reduction of Statelessness.

that together form the International Bill of Rights,[66] Convention on the Prevention and Punishment of the Crime of Genocide, 1948,[67] the Convention on the Elimination of All Forms of Discrimination against Women (hereafter, CEDAW 1979)[68]; the Convention against Torture and Other Cruel, Inhuman or Degrading Treatment or Punishment 1984[69] and arguably the most important in relation to children the CRC, 1989.

There has been an increasing mismatch between legal and normative frameworks that define the existing protection regime and contemporary forms of migration (Zetter, 2015). Historically, international law has struggled with women and children migrating across international borders, a phenomenon that continues to plague the international legal responses to migration. For example, within the context of human trafficking, there has been a conscious move to stop those classified as vulnerable from migrating, serving to dissuade women and girls from moving to protect them from harm (Kapur, 2012, 30). Women and children "on the move" are frequently identified as deserving victims in need of rescue and rehabilitation, but only if they fall within the preconceived parameters of the ideal victim. The ideal victim encapsulates the "trafficked victim" or "sex slaves", images that rely upon the weakness, vulnerability, and naivety of both women and children (Sanghera, 2012). The impact of the "ideal victim" (Christie, 1986) is of importance within the context of international migration as it is used as a way of drawing a clear distinction between those to be classified as deserving of assistance and support and those (i.e., migrants) who are not.

---

[66] Declaration of Human Rights 1948; International Covenant on Civil and Political Rights 1966; and the International Covenant on Economic, Social and Cultural Rights 1966.

[67] Approved and proposed for signature and ratification or accession by General Assembly resolution 260 A (III) of 9 December 1948, entry into force 12 January 1951, in accordance with Article XIII.

[68] Adopted in 1979 by the UN General Assembly, is often described as an international bill of rights for women. Consisting of a preamble and 30 articles, it defines what constitutes discrimination against women and sets up an agenda for national action to end such discrimination. Aside from the CRC it is the only human rights treaty that explicitly references trafficking.

[69] Adopted and opened for signature, ratification, and accession by General Assembly resolution 39/46 of 10 December 1984 entry into force 26 June 1987, in accordance with Article 27 (1).

The legal frameworks for "children on the move" fall into three principal approaches—regulatory, criminalising, and protective (Bhabha, 2016). The regulatory approach (as adopted in most domestic and regional immigration law) relates to legislation that assumes 'children are dependents of the family unit, without autonomous agency' (Bhabha, 2016, 6). Such a staunch refusal to accept the rationality of youth labour migratory decisions can be attributed in large part to the strength and structure of the ideology of Western Childhood (Howard, 2017, 39). The criminalising approach applies to both 'smuggled' and 'trafficked' children, focusing on 'penalizing and preventing exploitative child migration' in a punitive fashion, dating back to legislation on the "White Slave Trade" (Bhabha, 2016, 7; Faulkner, 2019). Moreover, for children who are trafficked, the Palermo Protocol does not require states to treat victims of trafficking with the same long-term protection as for refugees (Bhabha, 2016). It is also argued that the child trafficking lens 'dominates current policy responses to the exploitation of children on the move', leading to some unintended effects, including 'removal' and 'rescue' from exploitation without substantive engagement with drivers or root causes of vulnerability in the first instance (Bhabha, 2016, 9). Finally, the protective approach relates to the CRC and other international laws and guidelines that provide a core set of universally applicable human rights for the protection of children (Hynes, 2021, 154).

2.3.1 The Global Compacts (2018)

The Global Compact for Safe, Orderly and Regular Migration[70] (hereafter, GCM) and the Global Compact on Refugees (hereafter, GCR) set forth objectives, commitments, and actions, informed by the principle of promoting the best interests of the child and child protection, which specifically address the needs of children. Both agreements specifically mention child migrants and child refugees and serve as benchmarks in discussing how migration affects children and what policies and

---

[70] (A/RES/73/195). Accessed via N1845199.pdf (https://documents-dds-ny.un.org/doc/UNDOC/GEN/N18/451/99/PDF/N1845199.pdf?OpenElement). October 2022.

programmes are required to respond to both their needs and aspirations.[71] Although, neither is a legally binding document they are a significant development at the international level. The purpose of this section is not to undertake an in-depth analysis of the Global Compacts, but to consider their role in addressing "children on the move" and how they operate in tandem to the anti-trafficking machine.

The first Global Compact to be discussed is the GCM which 'promotes existing international legal obligations in relation to the rights of the child and upholds the principle of the best interests of the child at all times, as a primary consideration in all situations concerning children in the context of international migration, including unaccompanied and separated children' (GCM, 2018, 15). There are a series of objectives contained within the GCM, of which seventeen (out of a total of twenty-three) specifically mention necessary actions directed at children in different stages of migration, including before departure, whilst they are migrating or in transit, upon arrival in their destination, and return and repatriation. In relation to trafficking 1 of the 23 Objectives for safe, orderly and regular migration[72] identified within the GCM explicitly states the objective to 'Prevent, combat and eradicate trafficking in

---

[71] M. M. B. Asis and A. Feranil, 'Not for adults only: toward a child lens in migration policies in Asia', *Journal on Migration and Human Security*, 8(1) (2020), 68–82, https://doi.org/10.1177/2331502420907375.

[72] Namely—(1) Collect and utilise accurate and disaggregated data as a basis for evidence - based policies. (2) Minimise the adverse drivers and structural factors that compel people to leave their country of origin. (3) Provide accurate and timely information at all stages of migration. (4) Ensure that all migrants have proof of legal identity and adequate documentation. (5) Enhance availability and flexibility of pathways for regular migration. (6) Facilitate fair and ethical recruitment and safeguard conditions that ensure decent work. (7) Address and reduce vulnerabilities in migration. (8) Save lives and establish coordinated international efforts on missing migrants. (9) Strengthen the transnational response to smuggling of migrants. (10) Prevent, combat, and eradicate trafficking in persons in the context of international migration (11) Manage borders in an integrated, secure, and coordinated manner. (12) Strengthen certainty and predictability in migration procedures for appropriate screening, assessment, and referral. (13) Use migration detention only as a measure of last resort and work towards alternatives. (14) Enhance consular protection, assistance, and cooperation throughout the migration cycle. (15) Provide access to basic services for migrants. (16) Empower migrants and societies to realise full inclusion and social cohesion. (17) Eliminate all forms of discrimination and promote evidence-based public discourse to shape perceptions of migration. (18) Invest in skills development and facilitate mutual recognition of skills, qualifications, and competences. (19) Create conditions for migrants and diasporas to fully contribute to sustainable development in all countries. (20) Promote faster, safer, and cheaper transfer of remittances and foster financial

persons in the context of international migration'.[73] Within Objective 10, a series of 10 points are identified as sub-categories, of interest is Objective 10 (e):

'Apply measures that address the particular vulnerabilities of women, men, girls and boys, regardless of their migration status, who have become or are at risk of becoming victims of trafficking in persons and other forms of exploitation, by facilitating access to justice and safe reporting without fear of detention, deportation or penalty, focusing on prevention, identification, appropriate protection and assistance, and addressing specific forms of abuse and exploitation'. The current Special Rapporteur on Trafficking in Persons, Siobhán Mullally stated in May 2022 that the:

> *Global Compact is rooted in the UN Convention on the Rights of the Child and a commitment to child rights. Risks of exploitation, including trafficking in persons, are most acute for those children in vulnerable situations, including unaccompanied and separated children, children living in situations of protracted irregularity, LGBT adolescents and youth, and children with disabilities. Too many children continue to face the risks of immigration detention.*[74]

The GCM (nor GCR) is not a legally binding document but sets out an alternative framework that attempts to guide and influence states in relation to their immigration policies. On the other hand, the GCR notes that children comprise more than half of the world's refugees (GCR, 2018, 76–77) and highlights that 'children, adolescents and youth' are a specific population in need of support (Asis & Feranil, 2020). However, without the political will or resources to enable such grand and noble

---

inclusion of migrants. (21) Cooperate in facilitating safe and dignified return and readmission, as well as sustainable reintegration. (22) Establish mechanisms for the portability of social security entitlements and earned benefits. (23) Strengthen international cooperation and global partnerships for safe, orderly, and regular migration.

[73] Page 6 GCM.

[74] UN Special Rapporteur on Trafficking in Persons, especially women and children, Siobhán Mullally Statement delivered at International Migration Review Forum (Round Table 2), New York, United Nations May 17, 2022.

desires to save, empower, and address structural factors such as inequalities and poverty of the classified 'vulnerable populations' then what is the point of such compacts?

2.3.2 The Clash: Fears of Migration and the Anti-Trafficking Machine

International law has struggled to adapt to the reality of "children on the move". The current international legal order is not isolated in its struggle to classify and categorise children within migration frameworks. The predecessor to the United Nations, the League of Nations (1919–1946) grappled with the challenges of "children on the move", through creating unequal levels of protection through the creation of an international legal framework that sought to protect children. How do children fit into this puzzle? With regard to children, migrants and displaced children are classified as either a victim or a threat (White et al., 2011) and the various international instruments that have been adopted of varying age and origin provide a complex architecture of overlapping definitions of "people on the move".[75] The preoccupation with whether or not the movement was organised by an adult, or whether it was actively chosen by the child or whether it led to harmful outcomes is frequently discussed under the rubric of "child trafficking". Similarly moral anxieties about and the policy interest in adult-controlled child mobility do not necessarily reflect a concern with the wishes or interests of the child in question. Linking back to the point that the omission of the means element in the Trafficking Protocol's definition removes the agency and capacity of the child to consent or wish to move, directly conflicting with

[75] Such as the UN Trafficking Protocol, International Convention relating to status of refugees 1951, 1967 Refugee Optional Protocol, 1990 Migrant Workers Convention, 2000 Migrant Smuggling Protocol, 1949 ILO Migration for Employment Convention (No. 97) 1975 ILO Migrant Workers Convention (No. 143) 2011 ILO Domestic Workers Convention (No. 189) Convention relating to the Status of Stateless Persons 1954 Convention on the Reduction of Statelessness (https://treaties.un.org/Pages/ViewDetails.aspx?src=TREATY&mtdsg_no=V-4&chapter=5&clang=_en) 1961, Art 14 (1) UDHR and the New York Declaration, 2016. For further information please refer to https://treaties.un.org/Pages/Treaties.aspx?id=7&subid=A&clang=_en Chapter VII; https://treaties.un.org/Pages/Treaties.aspx?id=5&subid=A&clang=_en Chapter V. Accessed August 2018.

the best interests and voice of the child principles advocated through the CRC.

> *Ruth* was 14 when she left Eritrea to journey to the UK, travelling via foot, lorry, boat and train. Her story was documented by the BBC in 2016, with her name changed to protect her identity in addition to creating cartoon depicting her journey and experience.*[76]

When Ruth began her journey 'across international borders, through different national structures and a range of legal or socially constructed categorisations and labels given to people which rarely capture the complexities and nuances of the experience during migration' (Crawley & Skleparis, 2018; Hynes, 2021; Richmond, 1994; van Hear, 2012; Zetter, 2007). This disjuncture between the conceptual and policy categories and the lived experiences of those on the move is evidenced (Crawley & Skleparis, 2018, 48; Howard, 2017; Sanchez, 2016; Stock, 2019). The role of agency in relation to children and adolescents is important, as identified by Martinis and O'Connell Davidson (2022) that with the 'exception of young children, people on the move are conscious agents, not passive objects, all journeys proceed based upon choices'.

Ruth's journey is her unique story, but she is not alone with countless children exercising their right of mobility due to a variety of reasons, fleeing conflict, poor opportunities in terms of education or employment, seeking a better life and making the journey as a family unit, as individuals, with a relative or a friend. Each story is different and does not necessarily fit into the simplistic narrative of 'migration' presented. The conceptual divisions between refugees, economic migrants, trafficked and smuggled persons, forced and voluntary labourers, child and adult migrants, and the idea of "modern slavery", 'deflect attention from the structures that limit the choices open to people on the move' (Martinis & O'Connell Davidson, 2022, 1). The impact upon children who find themselves caught between the rescue endorsed narrative that is

---

[76] https://www.bbc.co.uk/newsround/36714334. 'Ruth's story: One child's refugee's journey from Eritrea to England'. Accessed June 2021.

central to the anti-trafficking machine and the realities of irregular migration upon children. As many critical migration scholars have observed the journeys and experiences of people on the move do not neatly fall on one side or the other of the voluntary/forced and legal/illegal binaries or slot into easily administrative categories (Cresswell, 2006; Collyer, 2007; Innes, 2015; Martinis and O'Connell Davidson, 2022; Schapendonk et al., 2021; Stock, 2019). The implications of this fact for children are often detrimental, as highlighted through some of the jurisprudence of the European Court of Human Rights in the 2021 V.C.L.N case.

Why do we appear to have a categorical fetishism of organising children? Consider a jigsaw puzzle as a tool to understand the legal and policy responses and dominant discourse of "children on the move". A jigsaw puzzle includes a variety of irregularly shaped pieces that when correctly assembled forms an image or photograph or map for example. Each piece has defined parameters, which cannot be compromised, and each individual piece has its place. Consider then the 'ideal victim of child trafficking' as a piece of this puzzle, what happens when a child does not fit into that piece? Should they be discarded or allowed to slip between the cracks of the wider picture? Then reflect upon your perceptions of childhood, if a child does not confirm to that ideal—then where is their place in this puzzle?

The prevailing construction of childhood from the Global North as a period of innocence and dependence has led to the belief that the independent mobility of those deemed to be children is imagined to be fraught with danger. That danger is perceived, regardless of whether the child's movement is linked to earning opportunities, pleasure, or even safety. It chimes with the age-old perception that those who are vulnerable, such as women and children should not move. The significance of labels as a mechanism to draw distinctions between deserving and undeserving victims has been limited. Whilst feminist debates of human trafficking have become polarised by the concept of victimhood (Doezema, 2010; Limoncelli, 2010) alternative critiques of contemporary migration have arisen, with the notion of 'undesired categories of people' (Segrave et al., 2018, 2) and 'categorical fetishism' (Crawley & Skleparis, 2018) emerging. Within the context of children, the issue of forced migration through the form of trafficking or "modern-day slavery" (Bales, 2007; Kara, 2009) conflicts with the central ethos of the CRC, the agency of the child. Questions still arise around the provenance and representation of the CRC. In particular, the Convention is deemed to enshrine Western notions of childhood upon which its rights were constructed. However, the legacy of the colonial contours of the new world order are often excluded within the context of children's rights. It has been suggested that the new imperialism brandished under the guise of "children's rights" serves as an effective tool to "beat" the Global South, deflecting from the continued Western dominance within the field of children's rights (Faulkner & Nyamutata, 2020). The impact of this agenda, under the cloak of 'children's rights' has maintained the system of Western dominance and adherence, and the subsequent acceptance of Western standards and ideals. The links between the rhetoric of modern slavery and immigration policies remains an obscure and uncontested aspect of international law, this chapter seeks to deconstruct the hierarchy of status afforded by the contemporary international legal framework, advocating a child centric, child rights approach as endorsed by the CRC to children on the move.

In addition to the general principles, the CRC provides articles that deal specifically with refugees (Article 22) and trafficked children (Article 35) but not upon child migrants. This could be attributed to the belief that those who are vulnerable should not migrate, a perception that can be traced back to the era of the League of Nations through a Report of the 3rd Session from April 1924 which identified the need '… to protect women and child migrants against the dangers of becoming stranded after having commenced their journey and thereby falling easy prey to traffickers…'.[77] The quote is illuminating of contemporary understandings of migration, with states asserting their position as the protector and the traffickers as the private criminal actors who steal time, labour, and are the architects of violence and exploitation.[78] This classification of the heroic and ideal state conflicts with the legacies of colonialism upon

---

[77] Report of Work of the Third Session 11.04.1924 C.184. M.73.1924IV at 5.
[78] See further Jovana Arsenijević et al., 'A crisis of protection and safe passage: violence experienced by migrants/refugees travelling along the Western Balkan corridor to Northern Europe',

the contemporary world. Moreover, children who migrate today whether through legal or illegal routes fall outside of the Western constructed ideal of the child and childhood. Mohanty and Werbner (1988) identified the classification of children as passive victims in need of rescue with the extensive works of Enloe interrogating othering in relation to women and children. The durability of the entanglement or lumping together of women and children in public imaginations remains deeply problematic.

The overwhelming focus of legal responses to irregular or illegal migration has been to adopt more stringent anti-trafficking initiatives and more recently these efforts have been coupled with anti-slavery initiatives (O'Connell Davidson, 2015). Together they create a powerful discourse, one that advances the stereotypical three key actors of human trafficking: the victim, villain, and rescuer (O'Brien, 2021). The analysis of O'Brien, illuminates how race, ethnicity, gender, and global positioning work together to construct this simplistic story of the ideal victim, as a passive young woman, the villain as foreign, and the heroes as Western.[79] This construction of human trafficking serves as an undercurrent to the way that the hierarchy of status that has been created through the development of international law. The legal framework affords various levels of protection, the rights that are available, in addition to differing opportunities and the support systems that are in place. These factors depend upon the status or label afforded to the person in question, and that is why the system of dividing and classifying people within the context of migration is problematic, because of the consequences for the individual. With the undercurrents of race, patriarchy, and nationalism bubbling under the surface creating a toxic cocktail of conflicting ideas of migration.

The blurred categorisations afforded through the international instruments conflict with the aims of both policymakers and public discourse which seeks clear definitions. This is particularly true within the context

---

Conflict and Health, 11 (2017), 6 that identifies the overwhelming majority of violence perpetrated against minors was done so by state border officials rather than smugglers/traffickers in Serbia and Hungary.

[79] This is not a new analysis of trafficking with literature documenting the fears of white slavery, perpetrated by foreign traffickers at the turn of the twentieth century. See further, Allain (2017), Doezema (2010), Lammasniemi (2017).

of funding afforded to organisations that dedicate to end human trafficking or eradicate modern slavery, as without a clear definition how can you evidence the magnitude of the problem or collect data upon an issue that is not sufficiently defined? Migration regimes, like all other systems of ordering create hierarchal systems of rights (Crawley & Skleparsis, 2018) and the application of those hierarchal systems has led to the endorsement in a hierarchy of status created by contemporary legal responses to migration. What is the impact of this upon children? And more specifically upon those classed as victims of child trafficking, victims or modern slavery or undeserving others?

The international legal and policy responses have failed to adequately address the phenomenon of children on the move. The interplay between the various branches of international law, from refugee law, international human rights law, international criminal law, international child law, and law of armed conflict, amongst others to regional systems within the context of migration is complex. Policing national borders is a popular theme within the modern world, with some commentators have raising concerns for the safety and protection of migrants considering efforts to control them (Oberoi & Taylor-Nicholson, 2013). Coupled with increasing concern from both policymakers and the public about the evil or unknown 'other' who poses a threat to both the individual and the state. Arendt's critiques around the enforceability of human rights are relevant in this context. Moreover, as suggested by Bhabha (2009) migrant children—in what she calls 'Arendt's children'—are de facto stateless and do not have the same 'right to have rights' as other children. In other words, children might live in the cracks of an incomplete patchwork of nationally based legal provisions for children on the move (Hynes, 2021, XX).

The issue of "collateral damage" (GAATW, 2007) meaning the harming and endangering of the very people that the movement claims to save[80] or the supposed 'unintended harms' of anti-child trafficking need to be reviewed, as increasing research demonstrates harmful practices and how they can no longer be classed as 'unintended harms'.

---

[80] GAATW, *Collateral damage: the impact of anti-trafficking measures on human rights around the world* (Bangkok: GAATW, 2007), www.gaatw.org/Collateral%20Damage_Final/CollateralDamage_Frontpageswithcover.pdf.

The term "collateral damage" was coined through the GAATW 2007 report 'Collateral damage: The Impact of Anti-Trafficking Measures on Human Rights around the World' and the 'notion that efforts to combat trafficking in human beings caused collateral damage became common currency' (Dottridge, 2018, 342). The issue in respect of children and "collateral damage" is complicated, as you have.

> *idealistic policy-makers who imagine a perfect world in which children could remain in a parental home until adulthood (without engaging in economic activities) think they are asserting the principle that children's rights should not be violated when they support policies that make it riskier for children to migrate. In practice, some policies contradict the 'best interests' principle guaranteed by the UN Convention on the Rights of the Child.* (Dottridge, 2018, 352)

Initiatives with good intentions or well-intended to prevent or stop children from being exploited, prevent them from leaving home or intercepted whilst on the move were reported as problematic in the 1990s (Dottridge, 2018, 347). As identified by Howard, 'many anti-traffickers care deeply about what they do …'. A 'genuine' child saver, for example really *wants* to save children. In a similar vein just as a true believer in the Ideal State truly sees that state as a tool for protecting the vulnerable (Howard, 2017, 131). does not change the fact that the ultimate consequence of the aggregated individual decisions made by anti-traffickers is to ensure that we remain exactly where we are. And that where we are remains problematic for the very young people whose well-being (or lack thereof) represents the justification for most anti-traffickers being anti-traffickers in the first place (Howard, 2017, 131). Attempts to ensure that lessons are learnt, and that bad practice is discontinued has continued to be problematic in both West Africa and South Asia (Dottridge, 2018, 348). This interference or focus of Western States and Western-based organisations continues to cause issues. For example, 'Western-based organisations encountering shocking situations in West Africa for the first time have continued to suggest that the best way of protecting children would be to stop them moving, disregarding the substantial evidence of collateral damage caused to children by such initiatives' (Dottridge, 2021).

The collective concerns about the trafficking and exploitation of children have resulted in the creation of several movements, such as the 'long standing 'Not for Sale' organisation, and those aimed more generally at all victims of trafficking including 'Stop the Traffik' and the UN-backed 'Blue Heart Campaign' (Fussey & Rawlinson, 2017, 16). The partnerships between NGOs and law enforcement agencies in contemporary abolition has proven to be a lucrative field. The perception of Sharma that 'anti-trafficking is indeed a well-oiled machine' considering the activity of the Trump administration which authorised approximately $430 million to "fight sex and labor trafficking" since 2016 (Sharma, 2020). The lucrative nature of the anti-trafficking machine (Dottridge, 2014) can be illustrated through the example of the 'incredibly fast ascension of Invisible Children, the NGO behind the film Kony 2012' (Haynes, 2014, 29). In the year following the release of its video challenging celebrity "culture makers" to support the cause, exhorting viewers to secure the capture of Joseph Kony by purchasing posters and bracelets to "raise awareness" of the human rights abuses Kony had perpetrated, Invisible Children received a staggering $11,583,954 in private grants and contributions (Invisible Children, 2011). This collective action is interesting, as its 'indicative of the wider 'feel good' factor associated with new abolitionism, the sense of solidarity and collective identity for the 'we' who came together to fight this appalling anachronism' (O'Connell Davidson, 2015, 9). With Free the Slaves (2014) advocating that 'human trafficking is the modern-day slave trade—the process of enslaving a person'. Therefore, imagined this way trafficking becomes an assault on the core values of liberal democratic societies (Miller, 2006). As trafficking in persons and modern slavery took the 'high seat at the table of forced migrants, deserving sympathy and protection and intense moral opprobrium was directed towards those deemed to be traffickers or slavers (Martinis & O'Connell Davidson, 2022). This framing has been useful for both fundraising efforts of anti-trafficking and anti-slavery NGOS as well as politicians seeking to justify tighter border controls and more restrictive immigration policies' (Martinis and O'Connell Davidson, 2022).

2.4 Summary

This chapter has sought to serve as an in-depth introduction to the contestable notions of childhood and children's rights and their subsequent influence upon the law and policy responses aimed at eradicating the trafficking of children. The Convention and other UN childhood centric instruments have thus provided a 'language structure', as O'Byrne (2012) puts it, through which child rights claims can be made across the globe (Howard & Okyere, 2022). The new imperialism of the West brandished under the CRC adds to the clash between anti-trafficking, mobility, and rights. With the social construction of children as 'powerless objects all too easily translates into a stereotypical image of the victimized child, such that a child who does not conform to the stereotype (a child who is not pathetic, helpless, doe-eyed and innocent) cannot be imagined as a victim' (O'Connell Davidson, 2005, 59). This is of particular importance in the context of "children on the move", as often children and adolescents who develop strategies for fighting back or coping with conditions of deprivation are often viewed with great unease (Montgomery, 2001, 27).

Enforcing laws against trafficking or modern slavery is portrayed as upholding human rights, whilst many human rights of those concerned are systematically side-lined. Framing trafficking as a crime is beneficial for States—trafficking is subsequently understood as a deviancy to be cured or remedied by criminal law. Criminality (the advantage for states) is that states do not have to adjust state policies or tackle structural causes in a country or global economy. The role of right-wing politics, from the Conservatives in the UK, the Republicans in the USA (Australia also) in advancing concepts of evil traffickers as non-white criminals to be punished. With the systematic linkage with immigration by richer countries causing endless confusion and the issues of knowledge of trafficking, and more broadly mobility and the impact upon children needs to be considered under a lens of coloniality. The central ethos of the CRC revolves around the agency and participation of the child, which conflicts with the powerful narrative of the "trafficked child". This construction of innocence and purity or deserving and underserving victims' feeds into the conflicts of children's rights and the restrictive migration policies enacted by states globally.

References

Aitken, S. C. (2001). Global crises of childhood: Rights, justice and the unchildlike child. *Area (London 1969), 33*(2), 119–127.

Akhtar, R., & Nyamutata, C. (2020). *International child law*. Routledge.

Allain, J. (2017). White slave traffic in international law. *Journal of Trafficking and Human Exploitation. 1*(1), 1–40.

Alderson, P. (2012). Young children's human rights: A sociological analysis. *The International Journal of Children's Rights; CHIL, 20*(2), 177–198.

André, G., & Godin, M. (2014). Children's rights in the democratic republic of Congo and neoliberal reforms. In: A. Twum-Danso Imoh & N. Ansell (Eds.), *Children's lives in an era of children's rights the progress of the convention on the rights of the child in Africa*. Routledge.

Ansell, N. (2014). The convention on the rights of the child: Advancing social justice for African children? In: A. Twum-Danso Imoh & N. Ansell (Eds.), *Children's lives in an era of children's rights the progress of the convention on the rights of the child in Africa*. Routledge.

Ansell, N. (2009). Childhood and the politics of scale: Descaling children's geographies? *Progress in Human Geography, 33*(2), 190–209.

Archard, D. (1993). *Children: Rights and childhood* (3rd edn.). Routledge.

Ariès, P., & Baldick, R. (1962). *Centuries of childhood: A social history of family life*. Cape.

Asis, M. M. B., & Feranil, A. (2020). Not for adults only: Toward a child lens in migration policies in Asia. *Journal on Migration and Human Security, 8*(1), 68–82.

Bajpai, A. (2018). The Juvenile Justice (Care and Protection of Children) Act 2015: An analysis. *Indian Law Review (abingdon, England), 2*(2), 191–203.

Bajpai, A. (2017). *Child rights in India: Law, policy and practice*. Oxford India Paperbacks.

Bakewell, O. (2008). Research beyond the categories: The Importance of policy irrelevant research into forced migration. *Journal of Refugee Studies, 21*(4), 432–453.

Balagopalan, S. (2018). Colonial modernity and the 'child figure': Re-configuring the multiplicity in 'multiple childhoods. In: T. S. Saraswathi (Ed.), *Childhoods in India traditions, trends and transformations.*

Bales, K. (2007). What predicts human trafficking? *International Journal of Comparative and Applied Criminal Justice, 31*(2), 269–279.

Bhabha, H. K. (1994). *The location of culture*. Routledge.

Bhabha, J. (2016). *Children on the move: An urgent human rights and child protection priority*. Harvard FXB Center for Health and Human Rights.

Bhabha, J. (2009). Arendt's children: Do today's migrant children have a right to have rights? *Human Rights Quarterly, 31*(2), 410–451.

Bhahba, J., & Dottridge, M. (2016). *Recommended principles to guide actions concerning children on the move and other children affected by migration*.

Bourdillon, M., & Musvosvi, E. (2014). What can children's rights mean when children are struggling to survive? The case of Chiweshe, Zimbabwe. In: A. Twum-Danso Imoh & N. Ansell (Eds.), *Children's lives in an era of children's rights the progress of the convention on the rights of the child in Africa*. Routledge.

Brewer, H. (2012). *By birth or consent: Children, law, and the Anglo-American revolution in authority*. Omohundro Institute and University of North Carolina Press.

Brittle, R., & Desmet, E. (2020). Thirty years of research on children's rights in the context of migration. *The International Journal of Children's Rights, 28*(1), 36–65.

Bucataru, A. (2016). Using the convention on the rights of the child to project the rights of transgender children and adolescents: The context of education and transition. *Queen Mary Human Rights Law Review, 3*(59).

Buck, T. (2014). *International child law* (3rd edn.). Routledge.

Buck, T., & Nicholson, A. (2010). Constructing the international legal framework. In: G. Craig (Ed.), *Child slavery now*. Bristol University Press. http://www.jstor.org/stable/j.ctt9qgxmk.9

Burman, E. (1996). Local, global or globalized?: Child development and international child rights legislation. *Childhood (copenhagen, Denmark), 3*(1), 45–66.

Christie, N. (1986). The ideal victim. In: E. A. Fattah (Ed.), *From crime policy to victim policy*.

Collyer, M. (2007). In-between places: Trans-Saharan transit migrants in morocco and the fragmented journey to Europe. *Antipode, 39*(4), 668–690.

Crawley, H., & Skleparis, D. (2018). Refugees, migrants, neither, both: Categorical fetishism and the politics of bounding in Europe's 'migration crisis.' *Journal of Ethnic and Migration Studies, 44*(1), 48–64.

Cresswell, T. (2006). *On the move: Mobility in the modern western world*. Routledge.

Cunningham, H. (2005). *Children and childhood in western society since 1500*. Routledge.

Dembour, M. B. (2018). Critiques. In: D. Moeckli et al. (Ed.), *International human rights law*. Oxford University Press.
Detrick, S. (1999). *A commentary on the United Nations convention on the rights of the child*. Martinus Nijhoff Publishers.
Dimitrova, K., Ivanova, S., & Alexandrova, I. (2016). *Child trafficking among vulnerable Roma communities: Results of country studies in 7 EU member states*. Center for the Study of Democracy.
Doezema, J. (2010). *Sex slaves and discourse masters: The construction of trafficking*. Zed Book.
Dottridge, M. (2002). Trafficking in children in West and Central Africa. *Gender and Development, 10*(1), 38–42.
Dottridge, M. (2014). Editorial: How is the money to combat human trafficking spent? *Anti-Trafficking Review, 3*(3), 1.
Dottridge, M. (2017). Trafficked and exploited: The urgent need for coherence in international law. In: P. Kotiswaran (Ed.), *Revisiting the law and governance of trafficking, forced labour and modern slavery*. Cambridge University Press.
Dottridge, M. (2018). Collateral damage provoked by anti-trafficking measures. In: R. Piotrowicz et al. (Ed.), *Routledge handbook of human trafficking*. Routledge.
Dottridge, M. (2021). Between Theory and Reality: The challenge of distinguishing between trafficked children and independent child migrants. *Anti-Trafficking Review, 16*, 11–27.
Duane, A. M., & Meiners, E. R. (2021). Working analogues: Slavery now and then. In: Lebaron, G. et al. (Ed.), *Fighting Modern Slavery and Human Trafficking: History and Contemporary Policy*.
Engle, E. (2010). The convention on the rights of the child. *Quinnipiac Law Review, 29*, 793–819.
Ennew, J. (2008, September 19). *Conference on children's rights*. Swansea University.
Ennew, J. (1986). *The sexual exploitation of children*. Polity.
Faulkner, E. A. (2019). The development of child trafficking within International Law: A socio-legal and archival analysis. In: R. Deplano (Ed.), *Pluralising international legal scholarship: the promise and perils of non-doctrinal research methods*. Elgar.
Faulkner, E. A., & Nyamutata, C. (2020). The decolonisation of children's rights and the colonial contours of the convention on the rights of the child. *The International Journal of Children's Rights, 28*(1), 66–88.

Fottrell, D. (2000). *Revisiting children's rights: 10 years of the UN convention on the rights of the child*. Springer.

Fussey, P., & Rawlinson, P. (2017). *Child trafficking in the EU: Policing and protecting Europe's most vulnerable*. Routledge Studies in Crime and Society Routledge.

Gallagher, A. T. (2012). *The international law of human trafficking*. Cambridge University Press.

Global Alliance Against Traffic in Women. (2007). *The impact of anti-trafficking measures on human rights around the world*.

Global Movement for Children. (2010). *Leaving home: Voices of children on the move*. Accessible via https://resourcecentre.savethechildren.net/pdf/4914.pdf/

Goddard, C., & Mudaly, N. (2009). The ethics of involving children who have been abused in child abuse research. *The International Journal of Children's Rights; CHIL, 17*(2), 261–281.

Haynes, D. F. (2014). The celebritization of human trafficking. *The Annals of the American Academy of Political and Social Science, 653*(1), 25–45.

Heywood, C. (2001). *A history of childhood: Children and childhood in the West from medieval to modern times*. Polity Press.

High Commissioner's Dialogue on Protection Challenges. (June, 2017). Children on the Move: Background Paper, *International Journal of Refugee Law, 29*(2), 356–381. https://doi.org/10.1093/ijrl/eex016

Holzscheiter, A. (2010). *Children's rights in international politics: The transformative power of transnational discourse*. Palgrave Macmillan.

Hopkins, L., & Sriprakash, A. (2015). *The 'poor child'*. Education, poverty and international development series (1st Edn.).

Horgan, D. (2017). Child participatory research methods: Attempts to go 'deeper.' *Childhood, 24*(2), 245–259.

Howard, N. (2017). *Child trafficking, youth labour mobility and the politics of protection*.

Howard, N., & Okyere, S. (Eds.), (2022). *International child protection: Towards politics and participation*. Palgrave Studies on Children and Development. Palgrave.

Huijsmans, R. (2011). Child migration and questions of agency. *Development and Change, 42*(5), 1307–1321.

Humbert, F. (2009). *The challenge of child labour in international law*. 64. Cambridge University Press.

Hynes, P. (2021). *Introducing forced migration* (1st Edn.). Routledge.

Hynes. et al. (2022). *Creating stable futures: Human trafficking, participation and outcomes for children.* Accessible via https://www.ecpat.org.uk/creating-stable-futures-human-trafficking-participation-and-outcomes-for-children

Imoh, A. T. D., Bourdillon, M., & Meichsner, S. (Eds.). (2018). *Global childhoods beyond the north-south divide.* Palgrave Studies on Children and Development, Palgrave Macmillan Cham.

Innes, A. J. (2015). The never-ending journey? Exclusive jurisdictions and migrant mobility in Europe. *Journal of Contemporary European Studies, 23*(4), 500–513.

Kapur, R. (2012). Cross-border movements and the law: Renegotiating the boundaries of difference. In: K. Kempadoo et al. (Ed.), *Trafficking and prostitution reconsidered.* Routledge. https://www.taylorfrancis.com/books/9781315636269/chapters/10.4324/9781315636269-8

Kara, S. (2009). *Sex trafficking: Inside the business of modern slavery* (1st ed.). Columbia University Press.

Kelly, F. (2005). Conceptualising the child through an "Ethic of Care": Lessons for family law. *International Journal of Law in Context, 1*(4), 375–396.

Koomson, B., & Abdulai, D. (2021). Putting childhood in its place: Rethinking popular discourses on the conceptualisation of child trafficking in Ghana. *Anti-Trafficking Review, 16*, 28–46.

Lammasniemi, L. (2017). Anti-white slavery legislation and its legacies in England. *Anti-Trafficking Review, 9*, 64–76.

Limoncelli, S. A. (2010). *The politics of trafficking: The first international movement to combat the sexual exploitation of women.* Stanford University Press.

Linde, R. (2016). *The globalization of childhood: The international diffusion of norms and law against the child death penalty.* Oxford University Press.

Lundy, L. (2019). A lexicon for research on international children's rights in troubled times. *The International Journal of Children's Rights, 2019*(4), 595–601.

Lundy, L., & Byrne, B. (2017). The four general principles of the United Nations convention on the rights of the child: The potential value of the approach in other areas of human rights law. In: E. Brems et al. (Ed.), *Children's rights law in the global human rights landscape: Isolation, inspiration, integration?.*

Lundy, L., & Stalford, H. (2020). Editorial. *The International Journal of Children's Rights, 28*(2), 219–220.

Madan, A., Srinivasan, R., & Pandya, K. (2018). Parent-child relations: Changing contours and emerging trends. In: T. S. Saraswathi et al. (Ed.), *Childhoods in India: Traditions, trends and transformations*. Routledge.

Marshall. (1999). The construction of children as an object of international relations: The declaration of children's rights and the child welfare committee of league of nations. *International Journal of Children's Rights, 7*(2), 103–148.

Martins Junior, A., & O'Connell Davidson, J. (2021). Tacking towards freedom? Bringing journeys out of slavery into dialogue with contemporary migration. *Journal of Ethnic and Migration Studies, 48*(7), 1479–1495.

Martins, A., & O'Connell-Davidson, J. (2022). Crossing the binaries of mobility control: Agency force and freedom. *Social Sciences (basel), 11*(6), 243.

Miller, J. R. (2006). Slave trade: Combating human trafficking. *Harvard International Review, 27*(4), 70–73.

Mohanty, C. T., & Werbner, P. J. (1988). *Under western eyes: Feminist scholarship and colonial discourses*.

Montgomery, H. (2001). *Modern Babylon? Prostituting children in Thailand*. Berghahn Books.

Mutua, M. (2002). *Human rights: A political and cultural critique*. University of Pennsylvania Press. http://www.jstor.org/stable/j.ctt3fhtq0

Myers, W. E. (2001). The right rights? Child labor in a globalizing world. *The Annals of the American Academy of Political and Social Science, 575*(1), 38–55.

Nandy, A. (1987). *Traditions, tyranny and Utopias: Essays in politics of awareness*. Oxford University Press.

Nations, U. (1989). *Convention on rights of the child*.

Oberoi, P., & Taylor-Nicholson, E. (2013). The enemy at the gates: International borders migration and human rights. *Laws, 2*(3), 169–186.

O'Boyle, M., & Lafferty, M. (2006). Remedies in international human rights law. In: D. Shelton (Ed.), *The oxford handbook of international human rights law* (2nd Edn.). Oxford University Press.

O'Byrne, D. (2012). On the sociology of human rights: Theorising the language-structure of rights: The sociology of human rights. *Sociology (oxford), 46*(5), 829–843.

O'Connell Davidson. (2005). *Children in the global sex trade*. Polity Press.

O'Connell Davidson, J. (2015). *Modern slavery: The margins of freedom*. Palgrave Macmillan.

Okyere, S., Agyeman, N. K., & Saboro, E. (2021). 'Why was he videoing us?': The ethics and politics of audio-visual propaganda in child trafficking and human trafficking campaigns. *Anti-Trafficking Review, 16*, 47–68.

Omoike, E. (2014). In the best interests of the child: the case of child domestic workers in Ghana and Nigeria. In: Twum-Danso Imoh & N. Ansell (Eds.), *Children's lives in an era of children's rights the progress of the convention on the rights of the child in Africa*. Routledge.

Ost, S. (2009). *Child pornography and sexual grooming: Legal and societal responses*. Cambridge University Press.

Peleg, N. (2019). *The child's right to development*.

Pilcher, J. (1995). *Age and generation in modern Britain*. Oxford University Press.

Quenivet, N. (2017). Does and should international law prohibit the prosecution of children for war crimes? *European Journal of International Law, 28*(2), 433–455.

Quennerstedt, A., Robinson, C., & I'Anson, J. (2018). The UNCRC: The voice of global consensus on children's rights? *Nordic Journal of Human Rights, 36*(1), 38–54.

Richmond, A. (1994). *Global apartheid: Refugees, racism, and the new world order*. Oxford University Press.

Richter, L. M., & Dawes, A. R. L. (2008). Child abuse in South Africa: Rights and wrongs. *Child Abuse Review (Chichester, England: 1992), 17*(2), 79–93.

Sanchez, G. (2016). 'It's all in their brain': Constructing the figure of the trafficking victim on the US-Mexico border. *Anti-Trafficking Review, 7*, 97–114.

Sanghera, J. (2012). Unpacking the trafficking discourse. In: K. Kempadoo et al. (Ed.), Paradigm Publishers.

Saraswathi, T. S. et al. (Ed.). (2018). *Childhoods in India: Traditions, trends and transformations*. 1st Edn.

Sawyer, C. (2006). The child is not a person: Family law and other legal cultures. *Journal of Social Welfare and Family Law, 28*(1), 1–14.

Sax, H. (2018). Child trafficking—A call for rights-based integrated approaches. In: R. Piotrowicz et al. (Ed.), *Routledge handbook of human trafficking*. Routledge.

Schapendonk, J., Bolay, M., & Dahinden, J. (2021). The conceptual limits of the 'migration journey'. De-exceptionalising mobility in the context of West African trajectories. *Journal of Ethnic and Migration Studies, 47*(14), 3243–3259.

Scullion, D. (2018). The medical treatment of children. In: R. Lamont (Ed.), *Family law*. Oxford University Press.

Segrave, M., Milivojevic, S., & Pickering, S. (2018). *Sex trafficking and modern slavery: The absence of evidence* (2nd Edn.). Routledge.

Seshadri, S. R. (2018). Food and nutrition in childhood: Ensuring dietary adequacy, diversity and choice. In: T. S. Saraswathi et al. (Ed.), *Childhoods in India: Traditions, trends and transformations*. Routledge.

Sharma, N. (2020). Anti-trafficking is an inside job. Available from: https://www.opendemocracy.net/en/beyondtrafficking-and-slavery/anti-trafficking-inside-job/

Sidaway, J. D. (2000). Postcolonial geographies: An exploratory essay. *Progress in Human Geography, 24*(4), 591–612.

Sieghart, P. (1985). *The lawful rights of mankind: An introduction to the international legal code of human rights*. Oxford University Press.

Singhi, P., & Saini, A. G. (2018). The journey of paediatrics from Vedic to neoteric. In: T. S. Saraswathi et al. (Ed.), *Childhoods in India: Traditions, trends and transformations*. Routledge.

Sloth-Nielsen, J. (2008). *Children's rights in Africa: A legal perspective*. Routledge.

Stalford, H., & Hollingsworth, K. (2017). Judging children's rights: Tendencies, tensions, constraints and opportunities. In: Anonymous *rewriting children's rights judgments*. Hart Publishing Ltd. https://doi.org/10.5040/978 1782259282.ch-002

Stock, I. (2019). *Time, migration and forced immobility: Sub-Saharan African migrants in Morocco*. Bristol University Press.

Tobin, J. (2005). Increasingly seen and heard: The constitutional recognition of children's rights. *South African Journal on Human Rights, 21*(1), 86–126.

Twum-Danso Imoh, A. (2014). Realizing children's rights in Africa. In: A. Twum-Danso Imoh & N. Ansell (Eds.), *Children's lives in an era of children's rights the progress of the convention on the rights of the child in Africa*. Routledge.

Twum-Danso Imoh, A., Bourdillon, M., & Meichsner, S. (2018). *Global childhoods beyond the north-south divide*, Palgrave studies on children and development. Palgrave Macmillan Cham.

Van Beuren, G. (2018). Children's rights. In: D. Moeckli et al. (Ed.), *International human rights law*. Oxford University Press.

Van Hear, N. (2012). Forcing the issue: Migration crises and the uneasy dialogue between refugee research and policy. *Journal of Refugee Studies, 25*(1), 2–24.

Veerman, P. (1992). *The rights of the child and the changing image of childhood*. Martinus Nijhoff Publishers.

Verhellen, E. (2000). *Convention on the rights of the child: Background, motivation, strategies*. Garant Publishers.

White, S. C. (2002). Being, becoming and relationship: conceptual challenges of a child rights approach in development. *Journal of International Development, 14*(8), 1095–1104.

Zetter, R. (2015). *Protection in crisis: Forced migration and protection in a global era*. Migration Policy Institute.

Zetter, R. (2007). More labels, fewer refugees: Remaking the refugee label in an era of globalization. *Journal of Refugee Studies, 20*(2), 172–192.

3

The Emergence of Child Trafficking (1900–1946)

3.1 Introduction

The trafficking of children has received extensive attention from both academic and political fora in recent years. Numerous charities now exist that have joined forces to "combat modern slavery" yet there is little agreement amongst any of these key players as to what constitutes the trafficking of children and what falls outside the parameters of its reach. Despite the plethora of literature on 'human trafficking' in the modern era, upon further investigation, the limited engagement of contemporary research with the historical foundations of child trafficking is evident. Most of the existing scholarly literature on human trafficking—and child trafficking in particular—neglects to recognise the contemporary continuities between historical understandings of human trafficking, and the legal and policy responses to child trafficking adopted during the twentieth Century. There appears to be an assumption in many existing accounts that the historical context of human trafficking has been completed. In relation to the trafficking of children, this assumption is incorrect, and there is much we can learn from examining historical responses to child trafficking.

© The Author(s), under exclusive license to Springer Nature
Switzerland AG 2023
E. A. Faulkner, *The Trafficking of Children*, Transnational Crime,
Crime Control and Security, https://doi.org/10.1007/978-3-031-23566-5_3

This chapter will explain and critique the international legal architecture that was implemented to address child trafficking from the early twentieth century to the end of the Second World War, 1945. In addition to cataloguing the non-legislative actions of the League of Nations, through the activities of the Traffic in Women and Children Committee (hereafter, the LNTWC) as documented within the archival inquiry. Charting the historical evolution of child trafficking will demonstrate the influence of abolitionists upon the creation and adoption of international law. This chapter draws upon a range of primary and secondary sources primarily from the League of Nations archives, Geneva.[1] The materials include international voluntary association and League of Nations publications; country specific reports; notes from the organisations meeting and conferences, newsletters, minutes of meetings, and correspondences within and between voluntary organisations, the International Bureau, International Abolitionist Federation, and the League of Nations.[2]

The focal point of the archival research is upon the 'Summary of Annual Reports',[3] submitted to the LNTWC between 1922 and 1945. The 'Summary of Annual Reports' represent the most systematic and comprehensive review of trafficking conducted during the period and will not be examined in isolation., In addition to preceding the outbreak of the Second World War in 1939, the year 1938 marked a significant change in the composition of the questionnaires analysed with the question that specifically focused upon children being removed and the important that the Committee attached to receiving full information on new legislative or administrative measures implemented (Secretariat, 1939).

The aim of this analysis is to consider whether the rhetoric of the "other" continued from the Conventions of the early twentieth century, into the anti-trafficking responses globally and the impact upon children. The construction of third world women and children as passive victims of culture and tradition verges on decolonial feminism and is

---

[1] Library of the United Nations, Geneva, Switzerland visited between 2017 and 2018.
[2] Archives Consulted; The League of Nations Archives, Geneva, Switzerland; The National Archives, London, United Kingdom and The Women's Library Archive, London School of Economics (LSE), United Kingdom.
[3] Refer to Appendix ii—The Summary of Annual Reports.

increasingly used in this context (Mohanty & Werbner, 1988). Moreover, this chapter seeks to readdress the racial bias by examining the preoccupation with "trafficking for immoral purposes" and the impact that this preoccupation had upon children. Through deconstructing the fears of sexual slavery, this chapter seeks to highlight other forms of exploitation identified through the League of Nations archives, moreover, charting the application of ideas of childhood and exploitation within a diverse cultural melting pot of subjugated populations of the colonial era. Through broadening the constrained focus on white sex slaves, the chapter seeks to enrich our understanding of morals, race, and the exploitation of children in the nineteenth and early twentieth century.

3.2 Human Trafficking in the Twentieth Century—A Brief History

The history of human trafficking can be divided into three periods, firstly pre-League of Nations, secondly the League of Nations Era from 1919 to 1945 and finally the United Nations Era from 1945 to today (Allain, 2017, 1) The focus of this chapter transcends the first two periods, looking at the issue of child trafficking through the emergence of the international instruments to address "White Slave Traffic" during the early twentieth century.

Four different international instruments were passed between 1904 and 1933, were specifically developed to deal with the traffic of women and girls. Namely, the International Agreement for the Suppression of White Slave Traffic 1904, International Convention for the Suppression of the White Slave Traffic 1910, International Convention for the Suppression of Traffic in Women and Children 1921 and the International Convention for the Suppression of the Traffic in Women of Full Age 1933. The "White Slave Traffic" and the trafficking of women and young girls for the prostitution has been covered extensively by scholars (Allain, 2017; Doezema, 2010; Knepper, 2012; Laite, 2017; Lammasniemi, 2017; Limoncelli, 2010) but there has been little research that exclusively focuses upon children.[4] The interwar years of the twentieth century (1919–1939) are often overlooked within scholarly research of human trafficking. Considerable attention has been paid to the trafficking of women in the nineteenth century and twentieth century, however, child trafficking sits on the periphery.[5]

3.2.1 The International Instruments 1904–1933

The Conventions of 1904, 1910, 1921 and 1933 transcend the prima facie clear eras of the legal history of human trafficking. The 1933 Convention is only applicable to adult females only (provisions and title) however, Rao (2013, xiii) argued that it was applicable to minor girls and developed out of the context where minor girls were being trafficked with the use of false birth certificates to show that they were of full age. Pre-dating the League of Nations, the Agreement of 1904[6] and the 1910 Convention carved the way towards the development of an international legal framework that was primarily concerned with the trafficking of women and young girls for sexual exploitation. The 1904 Agreement and the 1910 International Convention were negotiated at the 1902 International Conference on the White Slave Traffic.[7] After establishing the constitutive elements of the crime of white slave traffic, the Legislative Committee sought to make the distinction of the offence itself, as between women and the girl child. Stipulating that 'the crime exists even with consent; as for a woman, the crime exists only where

---

[4] An exception to this is the work of Sunil Salankey Rao (2013, 2014).

[5] This is a more general issue within the field of children's rights scholarship as identified by leaders in the field such as Lundy that international children's rights scholarship is neglected/ignored.

[6] Signed by 13 States, namely Belguim, Denmark, France, Germany, Italy, Netherlands, Portugal, Russia, Spain, Sweden and Norway, Switzerland and the United Kingdom. According to the list provided by the Government of France at the time of the transfer to the Secretary General of the depositary functions in respect of the Agreement (https://treaties.un.org/Pages/ViewDetails.aspx?src=TREATY&mtdsg_no=VII-8&chapter=7&clang=_en) Accessed May 2021.

[7] The International Conference on the White Slave Traffic was held between the 15th and 25th July 1902 in Paris. As identified by Allain (2017) the conference was labelled as an 'international conference' but remained a European affair.

violence or threats have been visited upon her, or where she has been deceived'.

Within that 1902 conference, a disquiet over the term "White Slave Traffic" was expressed with a French jurist Renault considering the term to be 'very unsatisfactory'.[8] The issue of race was on occasion not an explicit concern but codified through what was implied through the arguments identified. One such example can be found through the assertion that "The victim procured in a northern country, conveyed across a central country, has been delivered up in a southern country".[9] The issue of race was not mentioned, but it is entrenched within the logic of the era and reveals the racial codes of the era. Within the quote, the issues of geography and movement stand out, as over the century's enforcement has embedded dominant relationships of extraction. The quote refers to the young white woman or girl, kidnapped, transported, and delivered to be sexually exploited by non-white men. None of this is explicitly referenced, but the implication of racism is embedded behind the language adopted.

The development of the pre-League of Nations legal regime upon the issue of the 'White Slave Traffic', according to Allain 'remains fundamental to understanding the evolution of what is today understood as human trafficking generally, and more specifically, trafficking related to sexual exploitation; and the dynamics which shapes its contemporary contours and the language use to define it' (Allain, 2017). The phrase 'White Slave Traffic' is problematic for its explicit racism, and will feature in this book in quotation marks to reflect the discomfort amongst scholars with the term. The phrase represents a unique view into a 'very different world of the early twentieth Century, one dominated by a Eurocentrism of overt racism, at the height of its colonial conquest' (Allain, 2017).

---

[8] Procès-Verbaux des Séances, Troisième Séance, Ministère des Affaires Étrangères, Conférence Internationale pour la Répression de la Traite des Blanches, Documents Diplomatiques, 1902, 112.

[9] Correspondence respecting the International Conference on the 'White Slave Traffic', held in Paris, July 1902, House of Commons Parliamentary Papers (United Kingdom), Miscellaneous No. 3 (1905), Cd. 2667, 9.

This section of the chapter will address the following questions: What was the significance of these instruments to the issue of child trafficking? Did the focus upon sexual slavery deflect from other forms of exploitation? What about the dynamics of gender, race, caste, class, and othering? Considering these reflections this chapter will now move to analyse the instruments implemented at the turn of the twentieth Century.

The International Agreement for the Suppression of the White Slave Traffic, 1904

The International Agreement for the Suppression of the White Slave Traffic[10] (hereafter, the Agreement of 1904) was formulated in Paris in 1902, signed in 1904 by 13 States.[11] Entering into force on the 18th July 1905 in accordance with article 8, the instrument was superseded by the Convention for the Suppression of the Traffic in Persons and of the Exploitation of the Prostitution of Others, concluded at Lake Success in 1950 and under the auspices of the newly formed United Nations. The Agreement of 1904 provided the first co-operative international effort directed at the suppression of the White Slave Traffic (Rao, 2013, 15). The Agreement, contained just 9 articles however they lay the foundations for the emergence of the anti-trafficking machine that emerged towards the end of the twentieth Century, culminating in the Trafficking Protocol 2000.[12]

Article 1 required each of the contracting governments to undertake the establishment of or 'name some authority charged with the coordination of all information relative to the procuring of women or girls for immoral purposes abroad'. The underlying sentiment links to the earlier quote from the 1902 Convention which did not explicitly refer to race but implied the kidnap of a white northern women or girls to be transported and sold for sexual exploitation in a southern or foreign

---

[10] Accessed via https://treaties.un.org/Pages/ViewDetails.aspx?src=TREATY&mtdsg_no=VII-8&chapter=7&clang=_en (May 2021).
[11] The States that signed the agreement were France, Germany, Britain, Italy, Russia, Sweden, Denmark, Belgium, Holland, Spain, Portugal, Norway and Switzerland.
[12] See Appendix I.

3 The Emergence of Child Trafficking (1900–1946)

land. The anti-immigration focus of the Agreement is clear, with Article 2 establishing that each of the Governments 'undertakes to have a watch kept, especially in railway stations, ports of embarkation, and *en route*, for persons in charge of women and girls destined for an immoral life'.[13] Conversely, the article identified persons in charge rather than explicitly focusing upon men.

One of the objectives of the Agreement of 1904 was to secure for women and underage girls effective protection against the White Slave Traffic.[14] Bristow (1977) through his examination of the international agreements highlighted that they were a compromise between States such as France who remained regulationist and States such as the Netherlands and Germany who had adopted abolitionist positions in response to domestic fears of white slavery. In this context, the provisions of the Agreement of 1904 applied only to female children of the 'white' race. The Agreement of 1904 did not apply to female children of races other than 'whites' nor to male children of any race (Obokata, 2006, 13). Highlighting the erasure of non-white populations, including girls and boys, Moreover, the 1904 agreement only addresses the fraudulent recruitment of women or girls for prostitution in another country, subsequently the tone for the subsequent (supplementary) international agreements.[15] Conversely, the 1904 Agreement did not equate 'white slavery' with 'prostitution' (Doezema, 2010, 110) however through Article 3 Governments were obligated to have 'declarations taken of women and girls of foreign nationality who are prostitutes'.[16] The provisions were largely administrative and were drafted to 'facilitate member States' implementation of their own programmes to detect trafficking and to repatriate and generally assist victims' (Rao, 2013). The Agreement, 'established central bureaus for the exchange of information on the traffic, set up aid in ports and railway stations for women and girls,

---

[13] Article 2 1904 Agreement.
[14] As identified by Rao (2013) the other objective was to secure for women of full age who had suffered abuse or compulsion effective protection against the criminal traffic known as the White Slave Traffic, international Agreement for the Suppression of the White Slave Traffic opened for signature 18th May 1904, 1 LNTS 83, preamble (entered into fore nineteenth July 1905).
[15] Article 1 of the 1904 Agreement.
[16] Article 3 of the 1904 Agreement.

and provided for the government repatriation of foreign women in prostitution and regulation of employment officed that linked emigrants to situations abroad' (Limoncelli, 2010, 9). Additionally, the 1904 Agreement emphasised the centralisation of information as a means of facilitating cross-border cooperation (Gallagher, 2012, 57). The significance of the 1904 agreement is that it set the tone for two subsequent and supplementary international agreements on trafficking, the International Convention for the Suppression of the White Slave Traffic, 1910 and the International Convention for the Suppression of the Traffic in Women and Children 1921 respectively (Allain, 2017; Doezema, 2010).

The International Convention for the Suppression of the White Slave Traffic, 1910

The 1910 Convention stipulated through Article 1 that 'whoever, in order to gratify the passions of another person, has procured, enticed, or led away, even with her consent, a woman or girl underage, for immoral purposes, shall be punished, notwithstanding that the various acts constituting the offence may have been committed in different countries.' Therefore, expanding the scope of the Convention to cover the 'recruitment process' or offence of a transnational nature. An interesting aspect of the Convention, is the stipulation that 'the Contracting Parties undertake to communicate to each other records of convictions in respect of offences covered by the present Convention where the various acts constituting such offences have been committed in different countries.'[17] Arguably this is an early indicator of the subsequent focus upon quantifying prosecutions as a marker for success in terms of eradicating the evil of 'white slavery' later to be subsumed by 'human trafficking' and 'modern slavery' as the scourge of the twenty-first Century.

The 1910 Convention through article 2 identified;

> *whoever, in order to gratify the passions of others, hired, abducted or enticed for immoral purposes, even with her consent, a woman or girl under twenty*

---

[17] Article 7 1910 Convention.

3 The Emergence of Child Trafficking (1900–1946)   113

years of age, or over that age in case of violence, threats, fraud or any compulsion.

Notably, for a 'woman or girl under twenty' consent was nullified and for women of the age of twenty-one, 'violence, threats, fraud or any compulsion' must have been used for the act to be considered as 'white slavery' (Doezema, 2010). This meant that the 1910 Convention explicitly made the prostitution of minors with or without their consent a punishable offence.[18]

The significance of the 1910 Convention is fourfold; firstly, it broadened the scope of the crime to include recruitment for prostitution within national boundaries. Secondly, it creates the means element of human trafficking subsequently adopted as one of the three elements of trafficking as identified through the twenty-first Century instrument, namely the Trafficking Protocol 2000 (Allain, 2017). Thirdly, the 1910 Convention identified that the prostitution of minors with or without consent was a punishable offence. Finally, and most significantly in relation to children, the 1910 Convention establishes the distinction between adults and children through the omission of the means element. This distinction between young victims ('in relation to whom the "means" by which they were procured were irrelevant') and adult victims (in relation to whom some evidence of compulsion as required) has survived through the omission of the means element in relation to children under the Trafficking Protocol of 2000 The legal framework for child trafficking was created almost a century prior to the adoption of the Trafficking Protocol, therefore the interwar period and the perceptions of children are of pivotal importance. The legacy of the White Slavery Conventions upon the subsequent development of the international legal framework adopted to address trafficking remains clear into the twenty-first century, through the adoption of Trafficking Protocol, 2000.

---

[18] International Agreement for the Suppression of the White Slave Traffic, signed at Paris, May 4th, 1910 (London: His Majesty's Stationary Office, 1912), WL 4/IBS/Box 128/LN.1.

A few States signed the first three instruments, including those appointed to participate in the League's Trafficking in Women and Children Committee such as Poland and Uruguay. As noted by Limoncelli (2010) 'all of the chief imperial powers—Great Britain, France, Spain, Belgium, the Netherlands, and Japan—were represented and indeed were the main actors in the movement both prior to and in the League of Nations'. Even though many governments signed the international instruments, the key distinction lies with the implementation of anti-trafficking measures, as the measures varied from country to country, primarily in their applications to colonial areas (Limoncelli, 2010, 11).

3.3 The League of Nations (1919–1945) and Human Trafficking

A general association of nations should be formed on the basis of covenants designed to create mutual guarantees of the political independence and territorial integrity of States, large and small equally.

Woodrow Wilson, 28th President of the US

Founded in the aftermath of the First World War, the League ostensibly sought, above all, the maintenance of peace following the horror of war. Yet, Article 23 of the Covenant of the League of Nations tasked the organisation with a diverse range of tasks 'that move beyond mediating inter-State relationships as they are traditionally conceived' (Legg, 2012, 652). The League also sought to address manifold issues of global importance or, as Legg identifies, 'technical' or socioeconomic' activities such as improving labour conditions, the treatment of "natives" and global health (Legg, 2012, 652). Moreover, the League targeted human security through regulating different forms of international mobility, including the fight against the traffic in women and children. The emerging discourses of the League in relation to trafficking and prostitution reflected an increasing preoccupation with managing and controlling the movement of women.

3 The Emergence of Child Trafficking (1900–1946)

Prior to the creation of the current international legal system, the League of Nations (1919–1946) was an integral feature of the international legal order in the early twentieth century. The League created a Committee for the Protection of Children in 1919 and adopted the Declaration on the Rights of the Child in 1924.[19] Although not legally binding, the Declaration exemplifies how children were constructed as a passive object of concern, rather than as an active subject capable of asserting their own rights against others. The paternalistic nature of the Declaration is clear and provides a stark contrast to the central ethos of the Convention on the Rights of the Child 1989 (hereafter, the CRC) that sought to recognise children as autonomous.

This chapter serves to address the often neglected interwar years of the twentieth century, therefore filling the vacuum in knowledge in relation to the traffic and exploitation of children during this period, through contributing to the scant body of work on the important period in between these epochs. As evidenced through their archives, the work of the League of Nations to investigate and combat the trafficking of women and children provides a rich context to enhance our understanding of morals, race, and the exploitation of children during the early twentieth century. The overwhelming focus of the international legal scholarly work has been upon the traffic of women and young girls but has not sought to focus solely on children. Thus, studies of children are an area of research that has been neglected. In particular, the trafficking and/or exploitation of boys has been largely neglected. The interwar years reflect a period often forgotten in relation to the development of anti-trafficking (Legg, 2012), with the shift from the 1933 Convention to the first Convention adopted in the new era of the United Nations in 1949.[20] Moreover, existing studies have been Eurocentric in focus, whilst this chapter examines reports from 123 States, territories, and colonies from every corner of the world.[21] Conversely, those studies that do examine child trafficking, are overshadowed by the overwhelming focus upon trafficking for prostitution. This focus is demonstrated by the

---

[19] The Geneva Declaration of the Rights of the Child was adopted 26th September 1924.
[20] Entered into force 1951.
[21] Limoncelli focuses upon 3 imperial powers, namely France, Italy and the Netherlands in the politics of anti-trafficking (2010).

League of Nation's specific focus upon the trafficking and exploitation of children for "immoral purposes".

3.3.1 The League of Nations: Anti-Trafficking

The League went on to administer all of the international accords, although not binding they did identify agreed-upon practices for States to follow (Limoncelli, 2010, 9). Through administering all of the international accords, anti-trafficking efforts constituted a major component of its social and humanitarian work.[22] The additional Convention of 1921, was developed under the auspices of the League of Nations, helping to 'further legitimize anti-trafficking efforts' (Limoncelli, 2010, 9) The role of the League in relation to the trafficking of women and children is interesting with scholars such as Legg attempting to reinsert the League into narratives of the shift from slavery to trafficking, whilst others, such as Doezema (2010) gloss over the interwar period in their accounts. Other scholars, such as Knepper (2013), Allain (2017), and Lamasniemi (2017) have focused upon the trafficking of women for prostitution and the development of "White Slave Traffic in International Law" respectively. The significance of trafficking and the League of Nations is not to be ignored lightly as efforts to address trafficking equated to a significant percentage of the League's budget by the 1930s (Legg, 2012). However, paradoxically, there has been very little scholarly attention on the practice of the trafficking of children in the era.

The 1921 Convention and 1933 Convention were concluded under the auspices of the League, which had itself mandated to supervise the execution of agreements with regard to the traffic of women and children.[23] The League's Traffic in Women and Children Committee (hereafter, the LNTWC), was a special working group was made up of nine delegates and five international voluntary associations, collecting reports

---

[22] League of Nations 1926. Social and Humanitarian Work, Geneva, Switzerland: League of Nations
[23] Covenant of the League of Nations, 225 CTW 195, June 28th 1919, entered into force January 10th, 1920, at ART XXIII. The same article called on Member States of the League to 'ensure fair and humane conditions of labour for men, women, and children, both in their own countries and in all countries to which their commercial and industrial relations extend'.

3 The Emergence of Child Trafficking (1900–1946)   117

on trafficking and prostitution from participating States, commissioned two research studies of the international traffic, drafted additional conventions in 1933 and 1937, and worked on all matters relating to the accords (Limoncelli, 2010, 9). With Article 23(c) of the Covenant establishing the League of Nations assigned to it general control over the execution of any agreements to be entered into with respect to trafficking.

> *Subject to and in accordance with the provisions of international conventions existing or hereinafter to be agreed upon, the Members of the League …(c) will entrust the League with the general supervision over the execution of agreements with regard to the traffic in women and children….*[24]

The Covenant's assignment was taken up in the first instance by the Brazilian Representative, M. Castao Da Cunha, who presented a report to the Council of the League of Nations (Council) as the Council sat in Rome, in May 1920 (Rao, 2013, 24). His recommendations were that the Council keep in touch with issues arising in relation to the White Slave Traffic by appointing a special attaché to the Secretary-General and that an international conference be called as soon as possible to deal with the subject.[25] Meanwhile, the delegate of Romania had observed in a note to the League of Nations that in most countries, whatever had been done in relation to the White Slave Traffic had been done upon the initiative of private individuals, rather than by governments.[26] In support of the Brazilian Representative's submissions, he stressed the importance of continued international cooperation.

> *It seems that during the war this criminal traffic decreased, in consequence of the many formalities which the countries at war required from travelers. Still*

---

[24] Article 23(c) of the Covenant of the League of Nations. The Covenant of the League of Nations came into force on 10 January 1920.

[25] Report by the Delegate of Roumania, *Note on International Measures to be Taken for the Suppression of Traffic in Women and Children*, LON Assembly, [3], LON Doc. [A.20/48/225(a).IV] (1920).

[26] Report by the Delegate of Roumania, *Note on International Measures to be taken for the Suppression of Traffic in Women and Children*, LON Assembly, [2], LON Doc. [A.20/48/225(a).IV] (1920).

we must mention the Eastern slave markets, where women and children were sold and which we know have taken place in Armenia and Asia Minor. The women and children come from different countries but mostly from the Near East. Now with the return of peace and relaxation of passport formalities it is to be feared that the traffic will take a new lease of life. International collaboration is the only means to fight against it.[27]

The Romanian delegate proposed various measures and they included a survey of States, the resolution to act, a questionnaire, a Convention, and finally a Conference. Acting in an unofficial and consultative capacity Abbott from the USA insisted the fight against the traffic in women could only proceed from a platform of social-scientific fact-finding. Furthermore, indicating that the official correspondence with governments was not enough because governments lacked the tools for proper social inquiry. Abbott urged a cross-border study to determine "whether there is an international traffic in women and girls for purposes of prostitution" and to establish "between what countries the traffic is being carried on, by what methods, and about the effectiveness of national measures undertaken to suppress the traffic".[28]

On June 30th, 1921, the League of Nations called a conference to assess compliance with pre-war treaties on the commercialised sex industry. Thirty-four nations sent delegates to Geneva, Switzerland making it the most enthusiastic response to date (Knepper, 2012, 784). The delegates agreed to a convention that included a resolution to replace references to "White slave trade" with "traffic in women" within international policy documents (Knepper, 2012, 784). The "White Slave Trade" as identified by Knepper had drawn on an analogy to the abolitionists and their successful movement for outlawing the importation of slaves from Africa, whilst the "Traffic in women" drew a parallel to the League's efforts concerning trafficking in opium and trafficking in armaments (Knepper & Azzopardi, 2011, 168–169).

---

[27] Report by the Delegate of Roumania, *Note on International Measures to be taken for the Suppression of Traffic in Women and Children*, LON Assembly, [3], LON Doc. [A.20/48/225(a). IV] (1920).
[28] League of Nations (1924), 3.

International Convention for the Suppression of Traffic in Women and Children 1921

The International Convention for the suppression of the traffic in women and children (hereafter, the 1921 Convention) was opened for signature from 30th September, 1921, to 31st March, 1922. The preamble to the Convention highlighted the anxiety of the participating States in relation to the trafficking of women and children. Explicitly stating that anxiety with the proclamation that;

> *being anxious to secure more completely the suppression of the Traffic in Women and Children described in the preambles to the Agreement of May 18, 1904, and to the Convention of May 4, 1910, under the name of "White Slave Traffic".*[29]

The 1921 Convention sought to intensify and reinforce the 1904 agreement and 1910 convention, after representatives of thirty-four nations met in Geneva to determine the extent of compliance with the two treaties (Knepper, 2013). The 1921 Convention marked a notable departure from the overtly racialised focus of previous attempts to address this issue of the trafficking of people namely, the 1904 and 1910 White Slave Traffic Conventions.[30] Through replacing the phrase 'White Slavery' with the more racially neutral 'traffic' in international law (Lammasniemi, 2017). This shift in language from the "White Slave Traffic" to the trafficking of women and children, prima facie presents a palpable shift from the racially motivated language of its predecessors (Allain, 2017; Attwood, 2013; Lammasniemi, 2017). Moreover, it was the first international instrument to directly address the trafficking of children by a special provision.[31] According to Roberts when the League adopted

---

[29] Preamble1921 convention, 10 (https://treaties.un.org/doc/Treaties/1921/09/19210930%2005-59%20AM/Ch_VII_3p.pdf) Accessed June 2021.
[30] The "White Slavery Conventions" namely the International Agreement for the Suppression of White Slave Traffic 1904, the International Convention for the Suppression of the White Slave Traffic 1910, the International Convention for the Suppression of Traffic in Women and Children 1921 and the International Convention for the Suppression of the Traffic in Women of Full Age 1933.
[31] League of Nations, *Monthly Summary of the League of Nations* (Vol. 1, 1921), 130.

the 1921 Convention 'the issue no longer had the power to stir up the populace or the authorities... The "white slave" myth remained a minor theme of popular melodrama, surfacing in many lurid films, for instance, but it had already done its worst in the hearts and minds of the people' (Roberts, 1992). Additionally, Roberts asserted that the League's concern with white slavery in 1921 was a result of migration routes used by prostitutes, including Jews escaping the pogroms of Eastern Europe.

Article 1 of the Convention called upon the High Contracting Parties to ensure that they were Parties to the Agreement of 1904 and the Convention of 1910 and to 'transmit, with the least possible delay, their ratifications of, or adhesions to, those instruments in the manner laid down therein'. 1921 did not create a new definition of trafficking, opting to adopt the definitions afforded within the Articles 1 and 2 of the 1920 Convention. Article 2 of the 1921 Convention did stipulate that Parties 'take all measures to discover and prosecute persons who are engaged in the traffic in children of both sexes'. This explicit recognition of trafficking as an offence perpetrated against children of 'both sexes' reflects a significant shift from the selectivity of 'white slavery'. Through Article 5, the 1921 Convention altered the age limit identified in the 1910 Convention from "twenty years of age" to "twenty-one completed years of age". In addition to identifying obligations upon parties to enact legislative or administrative measures to 'ensure the protection of women and children seeking employment in another country'.[32] Finally, highlighting the need to 'undertake in connection with immigration and emigration to adopt such administrative and legislative measures as are required to check the traffic in women and children'.[33] Providing insights into potential hubs for trafficking such as ports and railway stations, indeed advocating for the display of 'notices warning women and children of the danger of the traffic and indicating places where they can obtain accommodation and assistance'.[34]

---

[32] Article 6, 1921 Convention.
[33] Article 7, 1921 Convention.
[34] Article 7, 1921 Convention.

The 1921 Convention was extensively ratified (Webster & Herbert, 1933, 268) and legitimised anti-trafficking efforts under the auspices of the League of Nations (Limoncelli, 2010, 28). The following table identifies the date of adherence of States to the 1921 Convention, in addition to again highlighting members of the LNTWC (Table 3.1).

The Convention extended the protection to minors of either sex, raising the age of consent to twenty-one. However, Italy adopted a reservation for the age of consent specifically for indigenous women and children at sixteen. The issue of consent was identified by the Legislative Commission prior to the adoption of the 1910 Convention and sought to establish an 'essential distinction' between women and girls. The distinction around the issue of the age of consent as between girls who were minors (*fille mineur)* and those over the age of majority (*fille majeure*) (Allain, 2017, 8). However, this demarcation between the age of consent for white women and children and indigenous, serves not only to establish the boundaries of consent but also illustrates 'attempts to mark and maintain national and racial boundaries, as these boundaries constantly shifted in the context of empire' (Doezema, 2010, 70). The Convention provided for the extradition of traffickers and required State legislation or administrative measures to control employment agencies. A doctrinal analysis of the 1921 Convention fails to identify the impact that this shift in language had upon the trafficking and exploitation of children globally during the 1920s and 1930s.[35] This language of the 1921 Convention sought to signal a move away from the explicit and implicit racism afforded through the previous white slavery accords. The impact (if any) of this shift will be illustrated through the non-legislative actions of the League of Nations through the Summary of Annual Reports on the Trafficking of Women and Children', produced by the League of Nation's Secretariat as interrogated below.

---

[35] A doctrinal analysis is the traditional legal methodology and sometimes referred to as Black Letter. In essence the doctrinal analysis method focuses almost entirely on the law's own language of statutes and case law to make sense of the legal world.

Table 3.1 International convention for the suppression of traffic in women and children 1921

Country	1921	Date of adherence to the 1921 convention	League of Nations Traffic in Women and Children Committee (LNTWC)
Afghanistan	X	10/04/1935	
Albania	X	13/10/1924	
Austria	X	09/08/1922	
Belgium	X	15/06/1922	X
Brazil	x	18/08/1933	
British Empire Does not include the Island of Newfoundland, the British Colonies, and Protectorates, the Island of Nauru, or any territories administered under mandates by Great Britain	x	28/06/1922	X
Bulgaria	x	29/04/1925	
Chile	x	05/01/1929	
China	x	24/02/1926	
Colombia	x	08/11/2020	
Cuba	x	07/05/1923	
Czechoslavakia	x	29/09/1923	
Denmark This ratification does not include Greenland, the Convention, in view of the special circumstances, being of no interest for that possession	x	23/04/1931	X
Egypt	x	13/04/1932	
Estonia	x	28/02/1930	
Finland	x	16/08/1926	

3 The Emergence of Child Trafficking (1900–1946)   123

Country	1921	Date of adherence to the 1921 convention	League of Nations Traffic in Women and Children Committee (LNTWC)
France Does not include French Colonies, the countries in the French Protectorate or the territories under French Mandate	x	01/03/1926	x
Germany	x	08/07/1924	x
Greece	x	09/04/1923	
Hungary	x	25/04/1925	
Iran	x	28/03/1933	
Iraq	x	15/05/1925	
Italy	x	30/06/1924	x
Japan Does not include Chosen, Taiwan, the leased Territory of Kwantung, the Japanese portion of Saghalien Island and Japan's mandated territory in the South Seas	x	15/12/1925	x
Latvia	x	12/02/1924	
Lithuania	x	14/09/1931	
Luxembourg	x	31/12/1929	
Mexico	x	10/05/1932	
Monaco	x	18/07/1931	
Netherlands (including Netherlands Indies, Surinam and Curaçao)	x	19/09/1923	
Nicaragua	x	12/12/1935	
Norway	x	16/08/1922	

(continued)

Table 3.1 (continued)

Country	1921	Date of adherence to the 1921 convention	League of Nations Traffic in Women and Children Committee (LNTWC)
Poland	x	08/10/1924	X
Portugal	x	01/12/1923	
Romania	x	05/09/1923	X
Russia	x	18/12/1947	
Spain Does not include the Spanish Possessions in Africa or the territories of the Spanish Protectorate in Morocco	x	12/05/1924	X
Sweden	x	09/06/1925	
Switzerland	x	20/01/1926	
Thailand (Siam)	x	13/07/1922	
Turkey	x	15/04/1937	
United States		N/A	X
Uruguay	x	21/10/1924	X
Former Yugoslavia (former)	x	02/05/1929	

Note This table identifies the date of adherence of States to the 1921 Convention and is not exhaustive as it does not set out colonial areas or list countries that adhered after 1950 when the Convention of twenty-first March 1950 superseded, with all Parties thereto becoming Parties to the 1950 Convention in accordance with its article 28. For the text and status of all subsequent anti-trafficking Conventions, see further Chapt. 7 of Multilateral Treaties Deposited with the Secretary General (https://treaties.un.org/Pages/Treaties.aspx?id=7&subid=A&clang=_en) Accessed October 2020

3 The Emergence of Child Trafficking (1900–1946)

Non-Legislative Action of the League of Nations (1919–1939)

This chapter does not solely focus upon the legislative actions of the League but considers the broader context of non-legislative action. The context of the interwar period and the development of the League's position to both protect and provide for children after the Great War forms a significant context to anti-trafficking efforts. The institutions created under the League to address both trafficking and children were distinguishable from all other League Committees by the fact that 'certain private international organisations were permanently represented on them by assessors or advisory members' (Wertheimer, 1972, 127). What this means is that non-governmental organisations such as the British Red Cross were able to infiltrate and subsequently influence the activities of the committees.

3.3.2 The Advisory Committee on the Traffic in Women and Children

To monitor the 1921 Convention, the League Council created the Advisory Committee on the Traffic in Women and Children (hereafter, LNTWC). As one area of "technical work," this body functioned under the direction of Dame Rachel Crowdy, renowned for her efforts to organise volunteer corps of nurses during the First World War (Knepper, 2012, 785).

In 1923, the LNTWC heard that 'The White slave traffic assumed large proportions; young girls—and even young boys—swelled the personnel of the over-numerous houses of ill-fame'.[36] The focus on the "White slave traffic" by the international community demonstrates the narrow racial focus of sexual slavery. Consequently, much subsequent

---

[36] De Reding De Bibberegg, Delegate of the International Red Cross Committee and the International Red Cross Committee and the International 'Save the Children" Fund in Greece. League of Nations, Advisory Committee on the Traffic in Women and Children, Minutes if the Second Session, Geneva March 22nd–27th 1923 at 65.

academic analysis has similarly focused on white sexual slavery (Allain, 2017; Kempadoo, 2015; Laite, 2017; Lammasniemi, 2017; Limoncelli, 2010). The rhetoric of "white slavery" emphasised the loss of innocence of adolescent girls, creating the powerful image of "the innocent, young girl dragged off…to distant lands to satisfy the insatiable sexual cravings of wanton men' (McDOnald, 2004, 158). Such rhetoric demarked the non-white "other" as unworthy of protection and rescue. Despite the League's intervention, campaigners never really settled on a consistent definition of the problem.[37] (Knepper, 2012, 784) Purity reformers tended to understand trafficking as concerning women forced into prostitution, or child prostitution, but expanded their concern to issues such as obscene literature as part of the sexual immorality to be suppressed (Knepper, 2012, 784). Whilst feminist campaigners included arranged marriage, child marriage, voluntary migratory adult prostitution, and unsuitable adoptions of girls under the expansive umbrella term of trafficking. Moreover, they were regarded as victims of traffic women in any situation in which they were subject to unwanted sexual advances from men (Limoncelli, 2010, 14–15).

Committee members welcomed the introduction of scientific evidence as a counterweight to distortions in the press and entertainment (Knepper, 2016, 785). "Extravagant and baseless stories" had circulated in the public, and although experienced workers knew better, these stories "misled others and had mischievous results" (League of Nations, 1924, 3). As a result of sensational and dramatic accounts, claims about trafficking on a wide scale by systematic methods "may be perceived with caution and even credulity" (League of Nations, 1924, 4).[38] This focus upon quantification is something that has been replicated in the twenty-first Century, through the emergence of a series of global benchmarks,

---

[37] Even now, the definition remains contested terrain. Measures of human trafficking are impossible to separate from conceptual and practical problems in identifying a "victim of human trafficking" (Tyldum & Brunovksis, 2005, 21).

[38] For its part, the Bureau of Social Hygiene supported the study of traffic in women proposed by the Advisory Committee "because the subject is one in which we have long been interested and because we believe that this proposed step is essential to any solution of the problem".

such as the Global Slavery Index (GSI) and Global Estimates of Modern Slavery (GEMS).[39]

3.3.3 The Summary of Annual Reports: 1922–1945

This section of the chapter incorporates primary and secondary sources located within the League of Nations Archives, Geneva. The archival research undertaken for this chapter focuses predominately on the 'Summary of Annual Reports on the Trafficking of Women and Children', produced by the League of Nation's Secretariat.[40] The Annual Reports were completed for a period of twenty-three years, from 1922 to 1945 and were based on responses to questionnaires completed by States and territories from around the world. Thus, these reports represent one of the most systematic studies of trafficking globally. The reports were distributed to the Council and members of the League, specifically the Committee tasked with addressing 'Traffic in Women and Children'.

A series of questionnaires submitted annually, regarding the traffic of women and children formed the basis of these Annual Reports. The questionnaires contain the responses of Governments of numerous States, Colonies, Possessions, Protectorates, and Mandated Territories on matters concerning the trafficking of people in their respective territories. The question of who was responding on behalf of the Global South is not clarified within the documents. Given that States were doubtlessly aware that their responses would be recorded; the British, French, and Dutch (and their respective Colonial Empires) would have been mindful of the need to remain able to 'bask in their newly found status as freedom makers'. The interlinked discourses of empire and white slavery were brought to the fore through campaigns to tackle white slavery, through the focus upon the international traffic in white slaves and the

---

[39] See further Broome and Quirk, (2015), Anne T. Gallagher and Rebecca Surtees (2015), and Merry (2016).

[40] The reports were prepared by the Secretariat. The Secretariat, along with the General Assembly (met once annually) and Council (including 4 permanent members, Britain, France, Italy and Japan) were the main organs of the League. The Secretariat's primary function was to prepare the agenda and publish reports of meetings. Through carrying out the day-to day work of the League, under the direction of the Secretary General Sir Eric Drummond (1919–1933).

subsequent impact upon anti-trafficking efforts during the era of the League.

A Question of Children

The question of children moved numerical position during the 16-year period between 1922 and 1938 before its removal by the redrafting of the questionnaires in 1938. Nevertheless, a total of 406 written responses to the question have been analysed for the purposes of this chapter. The question asked;

> *In addition to any information in reply to previous questions, please State whether any other measures have been taken to protect children from exploitation for immoral purposes, especially whether any system of adopting, pawning or bartering of children exists.*

The question does not explicitly mention "traffic" or "trafficking" but chooses to emphasise the exploitation of children for "immoral purposes" and the subsequent need to protect them. The explicit focus upon the need to protect children provides an insight into the concerns of the international community. Namely, that the exploitation of children was acceptable, unless those children were to be exploited for reasons of immorality. The key questions that arise are—What happened? Where? How many children? Did any patterns emerge? Leading onto the final issue of whether there are lessons to be learnt from the past? The following table identifies explicit references to the traffic or trafficking within the respondent's response, with only 18 respondents explicitly referencing the issue of the sixteen-year period analysed (Table 3.2).

Of the 406 responses analysed during the timeframe, trafficking was referenced explicitly upon 18 separate occasions between 1923 and 1936. However, of those references only the responses from Bombay, Cochin–China, and the Straits Settlements—Singapore specifically Stated that an incident/s of trafficking had occurred. If trafficking had not occurred, then what were the explicit references?

An illustrative example is the response of the Netherlands East Indies in 1929 which stated that there were '163 young immigrants (104 men

3 The Emergence of Child Trafficking (1900–1946)

Table 3.2 Explicit references to Trafficking: 1922–1938

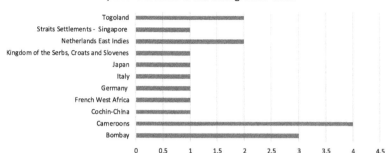

Explicit references to Trafficking: 1923–1936

and 32 women) placed under the supervision of the Batavia Government Department for the suppression of the traffic of women and children' further clarifying that the total number of 'young immigrants from both sexes under supervision is 563'.[41] The response referenced traffic through the department of the Batavia government but did not provide further information on the 'young immigrants' identified. The response failed to identify why so many young women and men had been placed under supervision and for what purpose other than to restrict mobility? This idea of keeping undesirables out, whilst imposing racist immigration controls and placing faith in the State as the rescuer is not new or isolated to the early twentieth century.

The narratives of white slavery had attempted to establish both gender and class boundaries, in addition to those of nation, colony and 'race' (Doezema, 2010, 70). Those interconnected issues play out within the archival story of anti-trafficking and the colonial era of restrictive mobility and racist ideologies. The response recorded from French West Africa in 1929 provides one of the most interesting insights, flagging up the interrelated issues of race, racism, and othering.

> *Question of half-castes has always been the subject of special care on the part of local Governments. In various colonies of French West Africa administration has set up orphanages for half-castes, where these children are cared for and*

---

[41] Summary of Annual Reports 1929C.164.M.59 1931 IV CTFE 498.

> *brought up until they are of age ... shown in previous reports that adoption did not exist in the native fetish worshipping community at present organised. Pawning of children assimilated to trafficking punished under same heading (whether accused is offender or accomplice) by Decree April 26th 1923*[42]

The response of French West Africa from the same year highlights the distinctions drawn between those of 'European status' and natives through the application of the relevant legislative mechanisms. The 'question of half-castes has always been the subject of special care' implicates the requirement for this sub-category of persons to be demarcated from both the white and non-white populations, belonging to neither but requiring special attention, nevertheless. The use of orphanages for the care of half-castes was not isolated to French West Africa, with imperial powers often forcibly removing half-caste and native children to charitable missions or homes to be reared in the correct manner i.e., white and Christian. The response illustrates the language used to demarcate difference and superiority of Europeans through references to "native", "fetish worshipping" and "half castes". The use of the terms was not isolated to the 1929 response, with references to 'half-castes', 'half breeds' and 'fetish worshipping tribes' documented in both 1923 and 1925, respectively. The legislative shift from the explicit racism of the 1904 Agreement and 1910 Convention using "white slavery" to the racially neutral traffic in women and children of the 1921 Convention, appears to of had a limited impact upon the perceptions of whiteness and classifications of others identified through the practice of reporting within French West Africa.

The other recorded responses identified what action the State had taken in relation to trafficking. In Cameroons, the response in 1923 was that 'very careful supervision is exercised in order to prevent abuses and the possibility of natives under the cloak of adoption engaging in the traffic' (Secretariat, League of Nations, 1923). Germany indicated that

---

[42] The penalties included between 1 month and 2 years imprisonment, with fines set between 2- and 500 francs. See further Summary of Annual Reports 1929C.164.M.59 1931 IV CTFE 498.

in 1924 'an important measure for the prevention of the traffic in children, the possibility is now being considered of forbidding newspapers to insert advertisements, under cypher, concerning offers of adoption.

Child Trafficking Identified

The responses analysed show five occasions within which the trafficking of children was explicitly identified. Three such instances recorded within Bombay (British Empire) in 1929, 1931, and 1932 respectively, with one instance in Cochin–China (French Empire) in 1927 and the final incident in the Straits Settlements—Singapore (British Empire) in 1933/34.

The response from Bombay (British Empire) is articulated in the same manner, explicitly identifying the 'very useful work' of the Children's Aid Society in 'protecting children from exploitation for immoral purposes'. The responses were generated through the 'Children's Home', but further details are omitted, in terms of the location, size if the home and under which organisation such as government or charity the home was governed. In 1929, 678 children were admitted to the Children's Home, with no further details about the children such as gender, age, or caste. The only additional detail provided was the justification for their placement within the Home such as 15 children who were victims of kidnapping and rape, 7 who were removed from brothels, with 5 children classed as victims of immoral traffic, 2 as victims of sodomy and 3 who were in "moral danger." The entry does not clarify if the identified cases of sodomy and moral danger, were subsets of the children trafficked for immoral purposes or distinct additional cases The information afforded in both 1931 and 1932 followed a similar rubric, identifying 717 and 798 children admitted to Children's Home in each year. In 1931, 2 children were of 'immoral traffic' and 7 rescued from moral danger. Whilst in 1932, 5 children were victims of immoral traffic and 7 were rescued from moral danger. No elaboration as to what constituted immoral traffic or moral danger were afforded.

The recorded response from Cochin–China (French Empire) is arguably the most interesting case of trafficking identified during the archival research. The entry identifies the 'traffic in aliens' and 'traffic in Ammamite boys' and girls' carried out upon a large scale due to the poverty of certain districts of Annam, with boys sold as domestic servants and girls placed into brothels. The entry provides further details, in terms of the difficulties in checking upon the illicit traffic as children are removed with parental consent and landed upon remote sections of the coast. Notably, the entry identifies trafficking that is transnational in nature and implicates 'Chinese organisations' who operate in Cholon and Saigon to recruit native women, girls, and boys for clandestine shipping to China.

The final instance of trafficking recorded during this period was identified in the Straits Settlements—Singapore (British Empire) in 1933/34. The three victims were between the ages of 13 and 15, with two separate instances being recorded. In the first both girls were Teochiu, classified as *mui tsai*. *Mui tsai*, which means "little younger sister" in Cantonese, describes the process of transferring girls from poor homes to do domestic work in the houses of rich families, in exchange for financial compensation to the girls' parents, plus board, lodging, and clothing for the girls (Rodriguez Garcia, 2012, 428). The girls complained that their master (a Hailam aged over 70) had indecently assaulted them on many occasions and had had intercourse with the elder of the two and that his wife was said to have abetted him. Subsequently, the master renounced all claim to their guardianship and made settlements of 500 and 750 dollars respectively in their favour. They were committed to the Po Leung Kuk, and later sent to school. However, in legal terms, *mui tsai* did not exist, so that in theory at least they were free to leave, unlike slaves, who belonged to their master or mistress (Rodriguez Garcia, 2012, 432). The term master was recorded within the reports and indicates the potential misclassification or misunderstanding of the *mui tsai* system.

The *mui tsai* system continued into the early decades of the twentieth century, but then something changed with the power of the humanitarian industry focusing upon the eradication of the *mui tsai* system. This activism manifested as 'protests by British parliamentarians and senior military men, European missionaries, journalists and Chinese Christian activists forced the British government to re-examine the subject. Political and social actors called for a ban on the sale and purchase of girls for domestic work or prostitution and likened the *mui tsai* custom to the worst forms of servitude' (Rodriguez Garcia, 2012, 433). The interrelated issues connected to the *mui tsai* system, namely slavery, traffic in children and child labour—together became the focus of the attention of the League's advisory committees and specialised bodies which had been set up with the express aim of making recommendations to the Assembly and Council on urgent international questions (Rodriguez Garcia, 2012, 434).

The second instance refers to a 14-year-old Cantonese girl was found in the custody of a 56-year-old Cantonese woman and was committed to the Po Leung Kuk on suspicion of being the victim of traffic. She later stated that her father had pawned her to the woman, who was about to sell her to a brothel-keeper to take to the Netherlands Indies. The woman in question absconded from bail before the hearing of the case. The two cases provide different pictures of exploitation and abuse perpetrated at that time, with the second scenario explicitly referencing trafficking whilst the former did not.

Exploitation

A considerable number of the responses analysed indicated that there was "nothing to report" in relation to the child focused question focused upon, however, what does this indicate? Is it to be understood that no exploitation of any children occurred? Notably exploitation was not defined, therefore leaving the interpretation, and understanding of exploitation to each of the respective respondents. Australia for example asserted that in 1925 'no trace of the exploitation of children in the Commonwealth for immoral purposes' existed within the colony. Although, this is a more substantial response than "nothing to report", what can be gauged from this perception considering our contemporary understanding of the role of the British Government in 'State sponsored exploitation of children'. This raises the issue of the British State-sponsored exportation of minors to colonies such as Australia and Canada. The ongoing Independent Inquiry into Child Sexual Abuse (hereafter, the IICSA inquiry) has heard evidence about exploitation and specifically sexual abuse experience by child migrants under the policy of the British Government. The point to highlight here is that the international law of the era and today distinguishes between State sponsored exploitation and exploitation perpetrated by organised criminal gangs or "evil human traffickers".

Another example can be found through Cyprus, which between 1924 and 1927 reported that a custom existed within the country where families received young orphans, poor girls, and sometimes the daughters of poor parents or relatives as servants.[43] The girls did not receive wages but lived with the family and were 'practically adopted'. This custom was identified on an annual basis within the responses, with additional information in certain years such as the responses from 1924 which identified that 'employers generally provide them with a dowry if they marry'.[44] The assertion was made that these girls were not 'exploited for immoral purposes'. The practice was therefore perceived as less harmful despite the exploitative element that was present. The general practice of labour without wages is prima facie classified as an acceptable or more agreeable exploitation of female children with enhanced levels of vulnerability. As the work did not encompass 'immoral exploitation' or sexual exploitation, it falls outside of the remit of the international communities' concern about children who were pawned, bartered, or adopted exclusively for immoral purposes. Exploitation (that is human exploitation) remains undefined in international law and despite its inclusion in the Palermo Protocol exploitation is not defined, it is enumerated (Allain, 2013, 2).

3.4 Empire, Race, and White Slavery

The undercurrent of race served as a prominent issue in the development of the international instruments and the subsequent international legal order that was established built upon the foundations of imperial

---

[43] See further Reports of 1924, 1925, 1926 and 1927.
[44] See further 1924 c.835.m.282 1925 IV.

expansion. Modern European imperialism[45] had dominated the globe by the early twentieth century, as by 1900 European States had portioned all of Africa, most of Asia and the part of the Pacific that had not been claimed by USA (Conklin & Fletcher, 1999, 4). Race and racism were the central organising frameworks that underpinned the spectacular success of slavery and colonialism. In the twentieth century, the political world order shifted from empires into national states, the political separation of 'natives' and 'migrants' became core to the cognitive scheme popularly used to define, explain, and order human mobility in the global north (Sharma, 2020). An aspect of the archival research sought to interrogate both what is and what is not said, and to consider how white supremacy over the "other" or "natives" became internalised within the logic of the common law and explicit in relation to the trafficking and exploitation of children. The continued prevalence of 'the other' can be further illustrated through the application of the 'White Slavery accord' of 1904 and 1910. The Dutch, for example, applied the accord equally throughout their empire, whilst the French did not apply the 1904, 1910, or 1921 Conventions to any colonies or protectorates nor mandated territories (Limoncelli, 2010). Further demarcations drawn by the imperial States can be seen through Italy who applied the 1921 Convention to its colonies but included a reservation lowering the age of consent for indigenous women and children to 16. Spain's adhesion to the 1921 Convention on 12th May, 1924, stipulated that 'This adhesion does not include the Spanish possessions in Africa nor the territories of the Spanish Protectorate in Morocco'. In short, they demonstrate the continued exceptionality of 'white' slavery, and the perpetuating implicit belief that non-white "other" as unworthy of protection and rescue. An additional link that should be noted is the utilisation of decolonial feminism in this context—the issue of white feminists speaking for all women whilst simultaneously portraying their non-white sisters as passive victims of culture and tradition (Davis, 1981).

---

[45] Imperialism is 'the process by which an expanding State dominated the territory, population, and resources of less powerful States or regions" and can take a colonial form involving "the imposition of direct military and administrative control, the influx of settlers from the imperialist country, and the systematic subordination of indigenous peoples' (Conklin & Fletcher, 1999, 1).

The 'intertwining of discourses of white slavery with concerns of empire can be seen in that part of the campaign against white slavery that focused on the international traffic in white slaves' (Doezema, 2010, 70) The rhetoric of "white slavery" emphasised the loss of innocence of adolescent girls, creating the powerful image of "the innocent, young girl dragged off… to distant lands to satisfy the insatiable sexual cravings of wanton men' (MacDonald, 2004, 158). Such rhetoric demarked the non-white "other" as unworthy of protection and rescue. Subsequently, that rhetoric needs contextualising within the era of colonial power. The role of the State in terms of advancing ideas of nationalism, the development of the nation State and drive towards restrictive borders feed into the construction of and response to "white slavery". Moreover, as identified by Sharma to 'better understand and historically situate the raging discourses on 'human trafficking' and 'modern-day slavery', we need to examine the period in which State regulations and restrictions on free human mobility were first enacted'. The perception of freedom and agency as white in dominant liberal thought interlink into the notions of innocence of the "white slave". Therefore, 'in this context, it is difficult to stress the restraining violence of slavery without suggesting that its victims were reduced to mere bodies, the passive objects of structural forces, and therefore, also hard to avoid reproducing the racist association between, blackness, dependency, and dishonour' (Brace & O'Connell Davidson, 2018, 23).

Through Europe's colonial ventures, freedom and unfreedom were distributed along racial lines and mobility emerged as a relational concept (Martins & O'Connell Davidson, 2022). The initial nineteenth-century organisation of border controls relied upon the 'discourse of 'rescue' and 'protection' of the very people whose mobility was coming under regulation' (Sharma, 2018, 123). Targeted human security through the regulation of different forms of international mobility, included the fight against the traffic in women and children (Legg, 2012). The potential to 'use anti-trafficking measures as a means of controlling migration, population, and sexual relations appealed to officials in democratic and authoritarian States alike' (Limoncelli, 2010, 11). The tropes of 'protection', 'freedom', and 'choice' were therefore central in the rationale to the ending of free human mobility across imperial State space (Sharma,

2018, 139). The increasing popular ideology of nationalism provided the rationale, with the imposition of State restraints on in-migration was done based on racist criteria of desirability' (Sharma, 2018, 129). Moreover, determining who was 'desirable' or 'undesirable' was integral to the process of nation-making' (Sharma, 2018, 140).

3.5 Summary

The focus of this archival research is upon the specific question that appeared in the questionnaires between 1921 and 1937 when a significant review of the questionnaire was undertaken. The Council (upon recommendation of the Committee) adopted on the 14th of May 1938 the new text of a questionnaire, which differs from the previous text on several points. It was identified that certain questions that 'produced few replies or replies of little value, and questions overlapping each other have been deleted or modified'.[46] The question which focused specifically upon children and has formed the focus of this archival investigation was consequently removed. The redrafting of the questionnaire reflected a shift in the approach to trafficking, with the repositioning of Question 7 to Question 1 illustrating the importance that the Committee attaches to receiving full information upon new legislative or administrative measures to tackle the traffic. This shift was also reflected in a move towards the monitoring of venereal diseases, immigration, and prosecutions.

In the context of human trafficking and the colonial enslavement of indigenous populations, the rhetoric of the earlier White Slave Conventions demarked the non-white "other" as unworthy of protection and rescue.[47] The 1921 Convention was meant to apply to all categories

---

[46] 101st session of the Council, May 14th, 1938.
[47] The International Bureau called the last international conference to consider the White Slave Traffic in 1913. A particular focus of attention was the suite of recommendations in relation to children which covered a range of matter—entertainment venues, exclusion of consent as a defence, places of refreshment, procuration of offence, carnal knowledge, research, employment agencies. nternational Conference on Traffic in Women and Children, *General Report on the Work of the Conference*, LON Council, [2], LON Doc. C.227.M.166.1921.IV (1921); Memorandum by the Secretary-General, *The Suppression of the White Slave Traffic in Women and*

of children, regardless of class, ethnicity, gender, nationality, race, and religion. What the responses demonstrate is that distinctions were identified between categories of children with some responses highlighting the racist language utilised in official documentation. The Dutch, French, and Italians were 'increasingly concerned with race in the interwar period, both at home and in colonies and rising anticolonial nationalism at that time exacerbated tensions about interracial sexual activity and miscegenation' (Limnocelli, 2010, 12).

References

Allain, J. (2013). *Slavery in international law: Of human exploitation and trafficking*. Martinus Nijhoff Publishers.

Allain, J. (2017). White slave traffic in international law. *Journal of Trafficking and Human Exploitation, 1*(1), 1–40.

Anonymous. (1902). *Procès-Verbaux des Séances, Troisième Séance, Ministère des Affaires Étrangères. In Conférence Internationale pour la Répression de la Traite des Blanches*. Documents Diplomatiques.

Attwood, R. (2013). *Vice beyond the pale: Representing "white slavery" in Britain, c.1880–1912*. University College London.

Brace, L. & O'Connell Davidson, J. (eds.) (2018). *Revisiting slavery and antislavery: Towards a critical analysis*. Palgrave Macmillan.

Bristow, E.J. (1977). *Vice and vigilance: Purity movements in Britain since 1700*. Gill and Macmillan.

Broome, A., & Quirk, J. (2015). The politics of numbers: The normative agendas of global benchmarking. *Review of International Studies, 41*(5), 813–818.

Conklin, A. L., & Fletcher, I. C. (1999). *European imperialism, 1830–1930: Climax and contradiction*. Cengage Learning.

Davis, A. Y. (1981). *Women, Race and Class*, Penguin Modern Classics.

De Reding De Bibberegg. (1923). *Delegate of the International Red Cross Committee and the International Red Cross Committee and the International*

Children, LON Assembly, LON Doc. [A].20/48/8. IV] (1920); Advisory Committee on Traffic in Women and Children, *Preparatory Documents, International Bureau for the Suppression of the Traffic in Women and Children*, LON Council, 1st sess., [17], LON Doc. C.365.M.216.1922.IV (1922).

'Save the Children" Fund in Greece. League of Nations, Advisory Committee on the Traffic in Women and Children, Minutes of the Second Session.

Delegate of Roumania. (1920). *Note on international measures to be taken for the suppression of traffic in women and children*.

Doezema, J. (2010). *Sex slaves and discourse masters: The construction of trafficking*. Zed Book.

Gallagher, A. T. (2012). *The international law of human trafficking*. Cambridge University Press.

Gallagher, A. T., & Surtees, R. (2015). Measuring the success of counter-trafficking interventions in the criminal justice sector: Who decides—and how? *Anti-Trafficking Review, 4*, 10.

Kempadoo, K. (2015). The modern-day white (wo)man's burden: Trends in anti-trafficking and anti-slavery campaigns. *Journal of Human Trafficking, 1*(1), 8–20.

Knepper, P. (2012). Measuring the threat of global crime: Insights from research by the league of nations into the traffic in women. *Criminology (Beverly Hills), 50*(3), 777–809.

Knepper, P. (2013). History matters: Canada's contribution to the first worldwide study of human trafficking. *Canadian Journal of Criminology and Criminal Justice, 55*(1), 33–54.

Knepper, P. (2014). International criminals: The league of nations, the traffic in women and the press. *Media History, 20*(4), 400–415.

Knepper, P. (2016). The investigation into the traffic in women by the league of nations: sociological jurisprudence as an international social project. *Law and history review; Law hist.rev.* 34 (1): 45–73.

Knepper, P., & Azzopardi, J. (2011). International crime in the interwar period: A view from the edge. *Crime, Law, and Social Change*, [Online] 56(4), 407–419.

Laite, J. (2017). Traffickers and pimps in the era of white slavery. *Past and Present, 237*(1), 237–269.

Lammasniemi, L. (2017). Anti-white slavery legislation and its legacies in England. *Anti-Trafficking Review, 9*, 64–76.

League of Nations Advisory Committee on the Traffic in Women and Children. (1924). *Report on the work of the third session. 7–11 April 1924 (Geneva: League of Nations, 1924)*.

League of Nations Report to the Council by the Advisory Committee on Traffic in Women and Children. *Advisory commission for the protection and welfare of children and young people. Report of the seventh session. United Nations Archives, Geneva*.

League of Nations, *Traffic in women and children resolutions adopted by the assembly, the Council and the Traffic in Women and Children Committee 1920–1929*. Vol. C.T.F.E. 359 (1).

League of Nations. (1920). *The suppression of white slave traffic—secretary-general—memorandum for presentation to the assembly, outlining the position as regards this question, and announcing the appointment of an officer within the secretariat, who will keep in touch with all matters relating to the traffic—document for the assembly: 8*, United Nations Archives, Geneva.

League of Nations. (1922). *Advisory committee on traffic in women and children (first session, June 28, 1922)—social section*. Preparatory documents submitted to the Committee.

League of Nations. (1926). *Annual reports on traffic in women and children (1926)—Italy*. United Nations Archives, Geneva.

League of Nations. (1937). *Monthly summary of the league of nations, February 1937*. In *Bandoeng conference on the traffic in women and children organisations and commissions of the league of nations*.

League of Nations. (1942). *Traffic in women and children—1941 reports on traffic in women and children (1st July 1940–30th June 1941)—Summary*. United Nations Archives, Geneva.

Legg, S. (2012). 'The life of individuals as well as of nations': International law and the league of nations' anti-trafficking governmentalities. *Leiden Journal of International Law, 25*(3), 647–664.

Limoncelli, S. A. (2010). *The politics of trafficking: The first international movement to combat the sexual exploitation of women*. Stanford University Press.

Martins, A., & O'Connell-Davidson, J. (2022). Crossing the binaries of mobility control: Agency, force and freedom. *Social Sciences (Basel), 11*(6), 243.

McDonald, W. F. (2004). Traffic counts, symbols & agendas: A critique of the campaign against trafficking of human beings. *International Review of Victimology, 11*(1), 143–176.

Merry, S. E. (2016). *The seductions of quantification: Measuring human rights, gender violence, and sex trafficking*. The University of Chicago Press.

Mohanty, C. T. & Werbner, P. J. (1988). *Under western eyes: Feminist scholarship and colonial discourses*.

Obokata, T. (2006). *Trafficking of human beings from a human rights perspective: Towards a holistic approach*. Martinus Nijhoff.

Rao, S. S. (2013). *Trafficking of children for sexual exploitation: Public international LAW 1864–1950*. Oxford University Press.

Rapporteurs, L.o.N. (1928). *Traffic in women and children I. Rapporteur's report adopted by the council on june 5th, 1928 h. Report to the Council of the Traffic in Women and Children Committee.*
Roberts, N. (1992). *Whores in history: Prostitution in western society*. Harper Collins.
Rodriguez Garcia, M. (2012). The league of nations and the moral recruitment of women. *International Review of Social History, 57*, 97–128.
Rodríguez García, M. (2015). Child slavery, sex trafficking or domestic work? The league of nations and its analysis of the Mui Tsai System. In: D. Hoerder et al. (ed.) *Towards a global history of domestic and caregiving workers* (1st edn).
Secretariat, L.o.N. (1921). *International conference on traffic in women and children—secretariat—general report on the work of the conference—council document.* Prepared by the Secretariat.
Secretariat, L.o.N. (1924). *Summary of annual reports for 1922 received from governments relating to the traffic in women and children.* Prepared by the Secretariat.
Secretariat, L.o.N. (1925a). *Traffic in women and children. Summary of Annual Reports for the year 1923.* Prepared by the Secretariat.
Secretariat, L.o.N. (1925b). *Traffic in women and children. Summary, prepared by the Secretariat, of Annual Reports for the Year 1923.*
Secretariat, L.o.N. (1925c). *Traffic in women and children. Summary, prepared by the Secretariat, of Annual Reports for the Year 1924.* Prepared by the Secretariat.
Secretariat, L.o.N. (1928). *Traffic in women and children. Summary of Annual Reports for 1926.* Prepared by the Secretariat.
Secretariat, L.o.N. (1930). *Traffic in women and children. Summary of Annual Reports for 1928.* Prepared by the Secretariat.
Secretariat, L.o.N. (1931). *Traffic in women and children. Summary of Annual Reports for 1929.* Prepared by the Secretariat.
Secretariat, L.o.N. (1932). *Traffic in women and children. Summary of Annual Reports for 1930.* Prepared by the Secretariat.
Secretariat, L.o.N. (1934). *Traffic in women and children committee. Summary of Annual Reports for 1932–33.* Prepared by the Secretariat.
Secretariat, L.o.N. (1935). *Traffic in women and children committee. Summary of annual reports for 1933–34.* prepared by the Secretariat.
Secretariat, L.o.N. (1936). *Traffic in women and children commitee. Summary of annual reports for 1934–35,* prepared by the Secretariat.

Secretariat, L.o.N. (1939). *Advisory committee on social questions. Summary of annual reports for 1937/38, prepared by the secretariat.* Traffic in Women and Children

Secretariat, L.o.N. (1941). *Advisory committee on social questions. Summary of annual reports for 1939/40 prepared by the secretariat.* Traffic in Women and Children.

Secretariat, L.o.N. (1942). *Advisory Committee on Social Questions. Summary of Annual Reports for 1940/41 prepared by the Secretariat.* Traffic in Women and Children

Secretariat, L.o.N. (1946). *Dvisory Committee on Social Questions. Summary of annual reports for 1944/45 prepared by the secretariat.* Traffic in Women and Children.

Sharma, N. (2018). Immigration restrictions and the politics of protection. In: Brace, L. & O'Connell Davidson, J. (eds.) *Revisiting slavery and anti-slavery: Towards a critical analysis.* Palgrave Macmillan.

Sharma, N. (2020). *Home rule.* National sovereignty and the separation of natives and migrants. Duke University Press. ISBN: 9781478000952.

Sharna, N. (2020). *Home rule.* Duke University Press.

Special Body of Experts on Traffic in Women and Children. (1922). *First enquiry on traffic in women and children—England.* United Nations Archives, Geneva.

Tyldum, G., & Brunovskis, A. (2005). Describing the unobserved: Methodological challenges in empirical studies on human trafficking. *International Migration, 43,* 1.

UK Parliament, *The international conference on the 'white slave traffic'.* House of Commons Parliamentary Papers.

Webster, C. K., & Herbert, S. (1933). *The league of nations in theory and practice.* Allen & Unwin.

Wertheimer, E. F. R. (1972). *The international secretaria: A great experiment in international administration.* Kraus Reprint Co.

4

Child Trafficking, Children's Rights, and Modern Slavery: International Law in the Twentieth and Twenty-First Centuries

4.1 Introduction

Child trafficking is not defined and regulated by one instrument alone. A complex set of international conventions seek to define and provide regulatory guidelines to signatory and ratifying states, as well as provide aspirational guidance for nation states on what trafficking is (Van Doore, 2016, 385). The international legal architecture that has been implemented during the era of the United Nations (1946–today) holds an integral position in the responses to child trafficking; however, the responses of the UN have not been limited to legislative mechanisms alone.[1] Arguably, the 'legal definition of trafficking in minors—and by extension, the approaches to victimised minors that follow from this legal categorisation—is oftentimes a black-and-white simplification of complex realities' (Oude Breuil & Gerasimov, 2021, 9). The issue of

---

[1] Such as Special Rapporteurs. ICAT, UNGIFT, UNODC Voluntary Trust Fund for Victims of Human Trafficking, Human Trafficking knowledge portal, Glo Act, the SDGs, UNICEF, IPEC, ILO, UN Human Rights Office, GEMS2017.

labels is important, with my preference for the phrase child trafficking and my disquiet with the phrase 'trafficking in minors'. Although the international legal landscape has evolved, the ideology of the young girl dragged off for sexual exploitation continues to hold prominence.

4.2 The Conflict of Definitions: Trafficking, Slavery, and Modern Slavery

Is child trafficking a form of modern slavery? Or is it a distinct crime committed against the state rather than a violation of the human rights of the victim? The relationship between prostitution, modern slavery, and human trafficking is much debated in the academic literature. By contrast, the discussion of children's involvement in prostitution as a form of modern slavery and human trafficking constitutes a silent consensus (Charnley & Nkhoma, 2020). Defining slavery has proven difficult in the contemporary world, with fierce debates over the parameters of what encompasses modern slavery.[2] The label slavery carries a political and emotional weight, however in legal terms, a special kind of pressure emerges—the prohibition of slavery is recognised as a rule of customary international law.[3] It is also regularly identified as a legal obligation *erga omnes*[4] and as part of *jus cogens*—a peremptory norm

---

[2] The author accepts modern slavery is a contestable term and prefers alternatives such as extreme exploitation but concedes to the use of the term without the punctuation to reflect my disquiet with the phrase modern slavery.

[3] See further Prosecutor V. Kunarac, Kovac and Vukovic, Case IT-96-23-T and IT-96-23/1-T, ICTY Trial Chamber, February 22, 2001 (Kunarac judgment), at para. 520. For an overview of this customary prohibition and its development, see M.C. Bassiouni, 'Enslavement as an international crime', *New York University Journal of International Law and Politics*, 23 (1991) 445.

[4] A legal obligation *erga omnes* is considered to be universal in character giving any State a legal interest in its protection and a capacity to bring suit against another State in the International Court of Justice. This legal right is vindicated irrespective of whether the State has suffered direct harm. The basis for this right was recognised by the International Court of Justice in Barcelona traction, Light and Power Company Limited (Belguim v Spain), [1970] ICJ Rep. 3 (Barcelona Traction) at paras. 33–34.

of international law.[5] With some advocating that the project of trying to find a definition of slavery "that might fit all [historical cases]" a "fruitless exercise in semantics" (Miers & Kopytoff, 1977, 7).

For most of human history, slavery has been a basis of society (Allain, 2013, 105). Legal systems throughout time have sought to govern and regulate slavery in multiple manifestations, from Ancient Greece and the Roman Empire to the contemporary moves to eradicate "modern slavery" in the UK and Australia. Different forms of slavery are known to be existed in prehistoric societies and 'have been present historically in most regions of the world' (Brace & O'Connell Davidson, 2018, 6). Therefore, it should perhaps be 'accepted that slavery has constituted the rule, not the exception in human history' (Allain, 2013, 10). Roman Law, for example, set out an elaborate regime that treats a slave as both a person and a thing (Allain, 2013, 18). However, where general Islamic law is concerned, Sharia recognises two legal means of enslavement, namely, the capture in the war of non-Muslims and slavery by birth (Schacht, 1975). For some commentators, Islamic law was often 'one of silence or quiet acquiescence' in relation to the 'cruel and sometimes life-threatening enslavement of women and children' (Freamon, 1998, 132). Different examples of child slavery can be drawn upon throughout history from Amistad's orphans (Lawrence, 2014) to the somewhat obscure 1848 Louisiana (USA) law that declared all children born in the penitentiary to African Americans serving life sentences would become property of the state. Upon turning ten, those children would be auctioned off and the proceeds diverted to the state treasurer as part of the "free school fund" (Derbes, 2013).

Over the course of the last two centuries, an 'international movement developed, which in law, abolished the slave trade, slavery and a number of lesser servitudes: forced labour, debt bondages, serfdom,

---

[5] The international law principle of jus cogens is a "peremptory norm of general international law" and is a "a norm accepted and recognized by the international community as a whole as a norm from which no derogation is permitted and which can be modified only by a subsequent norm of general international law having the same character" VCLT, at Art 53. See further on the status of the prohibition on slavery as an obligation *erga omnes* and as a *jus cogens* norm, Bassiouni, "Enslavement as an International Crime".

servile marriage, and child trafficking' (Allain, 2013, 105). The contestation over defining what has emerged as modern slavery has a complicated history, with attempts to define slavery and categorise its unique wrongs provoking scholarly clashes amongst classicists, philosophers, political theorists, anthropologists, sociologists, and legal academics (Allain, 2012; Chuang, 2014; Finley, 1964; Meillassoux, 1991; Miers & Kopytoff, 1977; Patterson, 1982; Rota, 2020). From Patterson's offer of a preliminary definition of slavery as the 'permanent violent domination of natally alienated and generally dishonored persons' to Bales' 'the total control of one person over another for the purpose of economic exploitation; to Honore's who are to be regarded as slaves in fact at the present day? … A slave is a person who, in fact though not in law, is subordinated to an unlimited extent to another person or groups or persons … and lacks access to state or other institutions that can remedy his or her inferior status'. With various definitions of slavery suggested by historians, sociologists, bodies of international governance, and legal scholars, it has proven difficult to find a sufficient definition, which is the observation 'to conclude that no definition is possible' (Rota, 2020). It has been asserted that the 'definitional conundrums surrounding the term 'slavery' have been, and remain, far from academic for anti-slavery activists' (Brace & O'Connell Davidson, 2018). With the definition of what qualifies as (or does not qualify) slavery appears as an increasingly important rhetorical device that serves in separating out which kinds of exploitation require political priority (Quirk, 2011, 2018). Therefore:

> *There is no definition of slavery that covers everything we scholars in the West want to call slavery while excluding those things we do not want to call slavery. This is because the notion of 'slavery' as a transhistorical, global reality spanning centuries and civilizations is a projection of Western scholarship…* (Brown, 2019, 18)

The perspective of Brown offers an interesting perspective upon the current situation over the often-conflicting definitions offered under the rubric of modern slavery. Policy measures implemented to address modern slavery 'are invariably presented with much thunder about the need to protect universal human rights and freedoms' (O'Connell Davidson, 2015, 3). Yet the legal architecture implemented conflicts with a human rights framing of the issues.

The term trafficking is used interchangeably with contemporary or modern slavery, exploitation, and labour by politicians, charities, media, scholars, and within society. Forced labour, slavery, and human trafficking are crimes that exist at the far end of what Jens Lerche identifies as the "spectrum" of labour exploitation (Lerche, 2007, 435). The terms are used interchangeably providing a broad appeal to humanitarian feeling (O'Connell Davidson, 2015, 6) and remain intrinsically linked, exploiting the emotive quality of slavery, and affording a level of exceptionality to the phenomena. The issues are to 'badness' what Apple Pie and Motherhood are to 'goodness' (Anderson, 2007). Moreover, contemporary slavery and human trafficking have emerged during the early twenty-first century as 'major sources of popular fascination and political preoccupation' (Bunting & Quirk, 2017). The construction of the global cause to fight the 'scourge of modern slavery' or the fight against human trafficking 'can be best understood as an unstable amalgamation of a wide range of diverse practices that go well beyond both legal definitions and historical experiences of slavery' (Bunting & Quirk, 2017, 6). The key question has 'gradually become which practices and institutions are sufficiently similar to legal slavery that they deserve to be legitimately classed as such' (Quirk, 2006, 566). Moreover, this new slavery discourse is caught up in 'classificatory conundrums' about where to draw the line between a slave and a non-slave, and about how to distinguish between literal and rhetorical claims of slavery (Quirk, 2006, 598). You may wonder what does this mean in relation to child trafficking?

To fully understand the re-emergence of child trafficking upon the international agenda as an issue of concern, it is integral to understand its position within the rhetoric of modern slavery. Running parallel with the obsession with the process of ranking harms, links our concern for children as a separate and exceptional group (O'Connell Davidson, 2005, 2). Whilst advocacy against modern slavery was once on the periphery, sidelined by the fascination of human trafficking for sexual exploitation, 'it has risen to the fore as the "catch-all" for a broad range of exploitative practices' (Chuang, 2014; O'Connell Davidson, 2015; Segrave et al., 2018). This is highlighted by the following statement from the UN Office of the High Commissioner for Human Rights.

> *The word "slavery" today covers a variety of human rights violations. In addition to traditional slavery and the slave trade, these abuses include the sale of children, child pornography, the exploitation of child labour, the sexual mutilation of female children, the use of children in armed conflicts, debt bondage, the traffic in persons and in the sale of human organs, the exploitation of prostitution, and certain practices under apartheid and colonial régimes.*[6]

The inclusion of abuses such as the sale of children, child prostitution, child pornography, and the sexual mutilation of children (amongst others) highlights the elasticity of the term of 'slavery' and the lack of definitional clarity within the international law of some of the issues identified such as child labour complicates their inclusion under the rubric of modern slavery. At an analytical level what constitutes slavery is problematic in that it is difficult to determine. Whilst at a 'political level, the main problem has been a tendency to invoke slavery as a rhetorical device in order to prioritize many different causes, such as rape as slavery, or economic injustice as slavery' (Quirk, 2021, 253). With the UK adopting this position recently in relation to "county lines" being classified as a form of modern slavery.

The interchangeable usage of the terms slavery and human trafficking through and within the "anti-trafficking machine" is legally inaccurate. As identified by Chuang in 2014;

> *Each of modern-day slavery's purported component practices—slavery, trafficking and forced labour—is separately defined under international law, subject to separate legal frameworks and overseen by separate international institutions. Conflating trafficking and forced labour with the far more narrowly defined (and extreme) practice of 'slavery'—however rhetorically*

---

[6] OHCHR, Fact Sheet No. 14 Contemporary Forms of Slavery OHCHR | Fact Sheet No. 14: Contemporary Forms of Slavery (Archive) (https://www.ohchr.org/en/publications/fact-sheets/fact-sheet-no-14-contemporary-forms-slavery-archive) Accessed October 2022.

effective—is not only legally inaccurate, but it also risks undermining effective application of the relevant legal regimes'. Legal definitions matter when it comes to providing a common basis for governments worldwide to collect and share data, facilitate extradition of criminal suspects, and to pursue policy coordination with other governments. They also matter when it comes to individuals directly affected by the legal regimes designed to identify perpetrators and provide redress to victims of slavery, trafficking and forced labor practices. (Chuang, 2014)

Furthermore, this 'rhetorical inflation reduces slavery to little more than a hollowed out place holder that covers virtually any form of exploitation or abuse' (Quirk, 2021, 254). As identified by Allain (2018, 3), in fact, and in law, the two respective regimes of slavery and human trafficking 'are distinct conceptually, but also have separate historical origins, and only come together with the negotiations of the Palermo Protocol'. By the continued conflation between slavery and trafficking for some commentators has been done to acknowledge other forms of exploitation that have been excluded or missed by the efforts of the international legal framework and international counter-trafficking policy regime (Allain, 2017, 61). Others have noted that the rise of modern slavery 'is a distraction: in the midst of hand-wringing over myriad forms of exploitation, attention is not being paid to the factors that contribute to and sustain such exploitation' (Segrave et al., 2018, 9). The focus of this chapter will now address the international legal framework implemented to addressed slavery and trafficking during the twentieth and twenty-first centuries, respectively, focusing upon the impact or implications of the approaches of law in relation to children.

4.3 The International Legal Framework of the Twentieth and Twenty-First Centuries: Slavery and Trafficking

The role which 'international law has played in the history of slavery is much more facilitator than inhibitor' (Allain, 2021, 1). Nevertheless, it is the focal point of this chapter that will examine the legal instruments adopted in the 'fight' against modern slavery and human trafficking. The instruments which form the core scaffolding of the legal architecture to address slavery and human trafficking[7] are the Slavery Convention of 1926 and the Supplementary Convention on the Abolition of Slavery, the Slave Trade, and Institutions and Practices similar to Slavery, 1956,[8] the International Labour Organization Forced Labour Convention 1930,[9] Universal Declaration of Human Rights, 1948, the Convention for the Suppression of the Traffic in Persons and of the Exploitation of the Prostitution of Others, 1949[10]; and finally the Optional Protocol to Prevent, Suppress, and Punish Trafficking in Persons, Especially Women, 2000.[11] Addressing issues from forced marriage to human trafficking, the instruments span fifty years, with the most recent (Palermo Protocol) adopted at the start of the twenty-first century. The other two international instruments concluded during this period to refer to trafficking were two of the core human rights treaties: The Convention on the Rights of the Child (CRC) which

---

[7] These instruments have further been supplemented by international and regional human rights treaties. Article 8 of the International Covenant on Civil and Political Rights 1966 (ICCPR) provides for the prohibition of slavery, servitude as well as forced labor, and similar provisions can be seen in the European Convention on Human Rights 1950, the American Convention on Human Rights 1969 and the African Charter of Human and Peoples' Rights 1980.

[8] Entered into force 30 April 1957, Signatories 35, Parties 124. https://treaties.un.org/pages/ViewDetailsIII.aspx?src=TREATY&mtdsg_no=XVIII-4&chapter=18&Temp=mtdsg3&clang=_en. Accessed November 2019.

[9] https://www.ilo.org/dyn/normlex/en/f?p=NORMLEXPUB:12100:0::NO::P12100_ILO_CODE:C029. Accessed 10 June 2021.

[10] Entered into forced 25 January 1950, Signatories 25, Parties 82. https://treaties.un.org/pages/ViewDetails.aspx?src=TREATY&mtdsg_no=VII-11-a&chapter=7&clang=_en. Accessed November 2019. See further Gallagher (2010), 'The abolitionist thrust of 1949 trafficking convention argued for a specific reference to prostitution' (Gallagher, 2010, 27).

[11] It is noteworthy that one of the three Optional Protocols to the Convention on the Rights of the Child 1989, the Optional Protocol on the Sale of Children (OPSC) holds significance within the context of children. The OPSC does specifically refer to trafficking and enshrines ideology of trafficking for "immoral purposes" as identified by the League of Nations as an issue of pressing concern. For an introduction to the international legal response to child sexual exploitation see further E.A. Faulkner, 'Chapter 8 Child sexual exploitation', Akthar and Nyamutata (ed.), *International child law* (Routledge, 2020); for a more specific focus upon the international legal instruments and history of child trafficking, see further E.A. Faulkner, 'The historical evolution of the international legal responses to the trafficking of children', *The Palgrave handbook of human trafficking* (2019a); E.A. Faulkner, 'The development of child trafficking within international law: A socio-legal and archival analysis', in Deplano et al., (eds.), *Pluralising international legal scholarship* (Elgar, 2019b), 104–126.

requires States Parties to take all appropriate measures to 'prevent the abduction of, the sale of or traffic in children for any purpose or in any form'[12] and the Convention on the Elimination of all forms of Discrimination against Women (hereafter, CEDAW) which requires all State Parties to take all appropriate measures to 'suppress all forms of traffic in women and exploitation of the prostitution of women'.[13] One omission from this list is the Slavery Convention of 1926,[14] which falls outside of the parameters of the United Nations era. However, due to its integral role in the contemporary definition of modern slavery, it will be included in this chapter's analysis of the international law governing trafficking and slavery.

By contrast to 'slavery and the Atlantic Slave Trade, human trafficking had its origins in seeking to address the "White Slave Traffic" in late nineteenth-century Europe' (Allain, 2018, 5). As identified in the previous chapter, the 'White Slave Traffic' focused upon the prostitution of white women and girls, prior to the emergence of the League of Nation's 1921 Convention. Moreover, human trafficking has 'embedded itself as a fundamental component of the contemporary international legal landscape' (Allain, 2018, 5). The fact remains that a distinction is drawn between children and adults under international law, replicated through regional and domestic legislation globally. The role of this distinction or the special classification of children as 'inherently vulnerable' plays an integral role in defining not only the parameters of what is tantamount to 'child slavery' or 'child trafficking' but who qualifies for the status of victim.

Most modern discussions of slavery and international law begin with the work of the League of Nations, which established a foundation upon which the most recent jurisprudence concerned with slavery was built (Quirk, 2012, 257). During the early twentieth century anti-slavery activists pressed for more expansive legal definitions and the political

---

[12] Article 35 CRC.
[13] Article 6 CEDAW.
[14] https://www.ohchr.org/EN/ProfessionalInterest/Pages/SlaveryConvention.aspx. Accessed 10 June 2021.

understanding of slavery (Brace & O'Connell Davidson, 2018). One example of this emerges from the Leagues' archives in Geneva, in a pamphlet entitled 'Slavery and the Obligations of the League', which identified slavery's 'barbaric cruelty, no less than its economic folly, should make a strong appeal to the civilized world civilized world ... with a plea for international enquiry and action ...'.[15] This growing awareness of the continued existence of slavery worldwide 'led to international action to combat it, facilitated by the growth of international organisations created after the First World War' (Craig et al., 2019, 8). The Question of Slavery (memorandum by the Secretary-General) involved the sending of letters to all members of the League in 1922 and a similar letter to non-member states asking them to 'supply the Council with any information on the existing situation as regards to the matter of slavery which they possessed and action they might see fit to communicate to it'. However, as persuasively demonstrated by Allain most international attention in this period was directed towards non-European governments most notably Liberia and Ethiopia rather than with European tutelage of 'backward peoples' (Allain, 2012, 256).

The League's Temporary Slavery Commission[16] (hereafter, TSC) was established in 1925 and tasked with examining slavery 'in all its forms'. One example of direct relevance to children was the condemnation by the TSC transfer of children for domestic service under the pretext of adoption as slave dealing.[17] The definition of the subsequent 1926 Slavery Convention emerges from the work of the TSC in operation between 1924 and 1926. As the work of the TSC is evident in the 'DNA of both the 1926 Convention and the 1956 Supplementary Convention'

---

[15] John H. Harris, Slavery and the Obligations of the League, The Anti-Slavery and Aborigines Protection Society, London, 1922 (27439—LoN document number).

[16] With members from France, Portugal, Belguim, Great Britain, Netherlands, Italy, Haiti and a representative of the International Labour Organization. Temporary Committee on Slavery, First Session of the Committee, report by M. Branting, 1924.

[17] Note the continuance of this practice in Cyprus as documented in archives research of previous chapter. See further Note the LoN (38385 document number) 'The Question of Slavery' 1924 SG Report Memorandum by the Secretary General A.25 1924 vi (Note—'freedom and protection of native labour' dealt with via an annexe, racialised distinction drawn (archives folder).

(Allain, 2013, 112). The TSC concluded that residual cases of slavery persisted, despite it having been abolished in law because the 'civilising influence of Colonial powers, however energetic and vigilant they may be cannot change completely in a few years habits ingrained by centuries'.[18]

4.3.1 The Slavery Convention 1926

Adopted under the auspices of the League of Nations, the Convention to Suppress the Slave Trade and Slavery 1926 (hereafter, the 1926 Slavery Convention) can be classed as the first modern international treaty for the protection of human rights (Nowak, 2005, 197). The drafting history and subsequent reception of the Slavery Convention have attracted considerable intellectual interest in recent years, following what Quirk (2012, 256) identified as a 'long period of relative neglect'. Whilst the fall of the Atlantic Slave Trade would coincide with the rise of the "White Slave Traffic", 'the international legal abolition of slavery itself is a more recent phenomena' (Allain, 2018, 4). At the time that the Slavery Convention was being developed, the most pressing issues upon the agenda were the ongoing slave systems in Africa, Asia, and the Middle East rather than 'New World' Slavery (Quirk, 2012, 256). During the drafting of the 1926 Convention, the process was heavily influenced by colonial politics, with various European officials working to circumscribe the scope of their international obligations in relation to legal slavery and its aftermath, forced labour, and related forms of human bondage.[19] The Convention also distinguishes forced labour, through Article 5 which stipulates that forced labour may only be exacted for public purposes and requiring state parties.[20] Although the Convention did not specifically mention child labour, certain forms of child labour in the form of domestic enslavement were meant to be included in the definition of the Convention (Humbert, 2009, 37).

---

[18] League of Nations (1925), *Temporary Slavery Commission Letter from the chairman of the commission to the president of the council and report of the commission.*

[19] Allain, The Slavery Convention 39–79, 101–124 (J. Allain, *The Slavery Convention: The Travaux Preparatoires of the 1926 League of Nations Convention and the 1956 United Nations Convention* [Martinus Nijhoff Publishers, 2008]).

[20] 'To prevent compulsory or forced labour from developing conditions analogous to slavery'.

> For the purpose of the present Convention, the following definitions are agreed upon:
>
> (1) Slavery is the status or condition of a person over whom any or all of the powers attaching to the right of ownership are exercised.
>
> (2) The slave trade includes all acts involved in the capture, acquisition or disposal of a person with intent to reduce him to slavery; all acts involved in the acquisition of a slave with a view to selling or exchanging him; all acts of disposal by sale or exchange of a slave acquired with a view to being sold or exchanged, and, in general, every act of trade or transport in slaves.

Fig. 4.1 Article 1 of the 1926 Slavery Convention

The 1926 Slavery Convention was signed at Geneva on 25 September 1926, entering into force in 1927 in accordance with article 12 (Fig. 4.1).

The League of Nations introduced the Slavery Convention in 1926, calling upon all states to criminalise enslavement and to put an end to slavery progressively and as soon as possible (Allain, 2018, 4). However, it is notable that the way in which the 1926 definition was 'operationalized by European authorities concerned with various slave systems which continued under colonial jurisdiction' (Quirk, 2012, 226).

The definition of slavery has caused controversy since its adoption with visible differences in opinion emerging about which practices should and should not be classified as slavery and therefore designated for elimination[21] (Humbert, 2009, 26). The 1953 Report of the Secretary-General indicates that the drafters of the 1926 Convention had in mind the concept of the authority of the master over the slave, comparable to that of *dominca potestas* in Roman Law.[22]

---

[21] See further the UN Sub-Commission on the promotion and Protection of Human Rights, Contemporary Forms of Slavery, Updated Review of the Implementation and Follow-up to the Convention on Slavery, working paper prepared by D. Weissbrodt and Anti-Slavery International, fifty-second session, 26 May 2000, E/CN.4.Sub.2/2000/3, para. 6.

[22] See Report of the Secretary-General on Slavery, the Slave Trade, and Other Forms of Servitude, E/2357 (1953) para. 36 fn 1 quoted in N. Lassen, 'Slavery and slavery like practices: United Nations standards and implementation', *Nordic Journal of International Law*, 57 (1988), 197–227, 205.

The 1926 Slavery Convention offered a definition of slavery as 'the status of a person over whom all or any of the rights attaching to the power of ownership are exercised'.[23] This phrase in the 1926 Slavery Convention definition is typically interpreted broadly (Allain & Hickey, 2012, 930) and the 2012 Bellagio-Harvard Guidelines on the Legal Parameters of Slavery.[24] On an alternate view "power" has been argued should be taken in its narrow sense (Penner, 2012). However, this broad interpretation 'may include claim rights, liberties, powers in the narrow sense and immunities and thus includes all or most of the 11 incidents of ownership identified by Honoré' (Rota, 2020). In this context, 'status' refers to a legally recognised 'state applicable in contexts in which slavery is legal, while "condition" refers to a state applicable in contexts in which slavery is illegal, so that a person who is treated as property will still count as a slave even if not recognised as property in law'[25] (Rota, 2020, 15). The definition afforded in the 1926 Slavery Convention, 'is accepted as the contemporary definition, having been considered in negotiations for both the 1956 Supplementary Convention and the 1998 Statute of the International Criminal Court and found to be satisfactory as being an accurate reflection of the term'[26] (Allain, 2013, 4).

The 1926 Slavery Convention definition was, in other words, a definition that fitted with what had till then, been understood as "chattel slavery but also required states to bring about the complete abolition of slavery in 'all its forms'" (Brace & O'Connell Davidson, 2018). The concept of 'slavery in all its forms' has been of particular interest to Quirk, who commented that it 'acquires legal and analytical currency through its incorporation within 1926 but can also be found in other international instruments such as the 1948 Universal Declaration of Human Rights'. Moreover, in recent times 'slavery in all its forms' tended

---

[23] Article 1 (1).

[24] https://glc.yale.edu/sites/default/files/pdf/the_bellagio-_harvard_guidelines_on_the_legal_parameters_of_slavery.pdf. Accessed 20 August 2021.

[25] This interpretation of 'statuses and 'condition' provided by the High Court of Australia in the Queen v Tang case (2008); see further Jean Allain, 'The Legal Definition of Slavery into the Twenty-First Century', in the Legal Understanding of Slavery, 199–219, 217.

[26] See further the 2008 Tang case before the High Court of Australia, which makes clear 'the definition is an applicable contemporary standard applying in situations of both de jure slavery, but more importantly in cases of de facto slavery' (Allain, 2013, 4).

to be viewed much the same as 'contemporary forms of slavery' and was prominently associated with the United Nations Working Group (1975–2006)[27] and the Special Rapporteur on Contemporary Forms of Slavery (2008–present).[28] This move away from chattel slavery reflects the understanding that 'one does not legally have to own a person as in the day of chattel slavery to be deemed to have enslaved a person' (Allain, 2013, 4). The 1926 definition, dictates that the 'simple ability to control a person so as to be able to treat them as a slave will fall foul of the standard of the 1926 Convention' (Allain, 2013, 4). The complexities of the concept of ownership can arguably be best understood in relation to illegal drugs as 'one cannot "own" a kilo of heroin in most jurisdictions; thus to dispute to its ownership cannot be vindicated in law' (Allain, 2013, 4).

The definition provided through the 1926 and 1956 Slavery Conventions deliberately drafted to be narrow in scope to avoid "spiralling interpretations" (Allain & Hickey, 2012). However, an alternative perspective accepts the fact that all these forms were never defined is frustrating and highlights that subsequently the burden fell upon signatories to the Convention to determine the scope of their new obligations (Quirk, 2012, 258). These "spiralling interpretations" illustrate how the drafters of the Slavery Conventions did not intend the definition of slavery to encompass every human rights violation that arose (Allain & Hickey, 2012). This fact is of crucial importance, particularly considering the increasing power of the anti-abolitionist movement which encapsulates the fears of stretching the parameters of slavery under the rubric of modern slavery. This narrowness of the Convention has been noted, with the Convention calling upon states to eradicate slavery 'in all its forms' but failing to 'list or explicate the different forms that slavery could take, nor did it clearly elucidate the difference (if any) between slavery and forced labour' (Brace & O'Connell Davidson, 2018, 18). In 1949 the Economic and Social Council (ECOSOC) appointed an Ad

---

[27] The Working Group on Contemporary Forms of Slavery no longer exists, and its successor is the mandate on contemporary forms of slavery, its causes and consequences, established in 2007 by Human Rights Council Resolution 6/14.

[28] The current SR is Professor Tomoya Obokata, appointed in 2020, see further, https://www.ohchr.org/EN/Issues/Slavery/SRSlavery/Pages/TomoyaObokata.aspx. Accessed August 2021.

Hoc Committee of Experts on Slavery, which identified that the definition did not cover the full range of practices related to slavery and that there were other equally repugnant forms of servitude that needed to be prohibited.[29] It is however advocated by Allain that the 1926 definition is the 'authoritative definition of slavery; as such, a reading which is consistent with the lived experiences of contemporary slaves allows us to escape from the definitional quagmire, by setting out a firm understanding of what constitutes slavery in a contemporary situation where the legal status no longer exists but the de facto situation persists' (Allain, 2013, 109). On the other hand, Quirk holds that the "language and drafting history of the Convention clearly envisages multiple forms of slavery, yet all of these forms can only be credibly classified as such in cases that satisfy the operative threshold of 'powers attaching to the right of ownership'" (Quirk, 2012, 259).

The case of pivotal importance in relation to children and the application of the 1926 definition is found through the case Siliadin v. France (2005) heard before the European Court of Human Rights. As a regional court, the European Court of Human Rights has heard several cases relating to trafficking, slavery, and forced labour. The two cases that are focused upon within this book have been selected for different reasons. The first case is Siliadan v. France (2005) which involved a teenage girl held in an exploitative situation of domestic servitude, notably the case was not pursued upon the basis of human trafficking. The second case V.C.L and A.N. v. United Kingdom (2021) involves two Vietnamese adolescents who were trafficked into the UK for exploitation by working as gardeners in cannabis factories. The Siliadan case offers an insight into the misinterpretation of the 1926 Slavery Convention, whilst the V.C.L and A.N case highlights the failures of the authorities to recognise and subsequently protect and empower victims of trafficking. The latter will be discussed in more detail later, but the case concerned two Vietnamese men who, whilst still adolescents, were charged with— and subsequently pleaded guilty to—drug-related offences after they were discovered working as gardeners in cannabis factories in the UK.

---

[29] UN Sub-Commission on the Promotion and Protection of Human Rights, Contemporary Forms of Slavery, E/CN.4/Sub.2/2000/3, para. 13.

Following their convictions, they were recognised as victims of trafficking by the designated Competent Authority responsible for making decisions on whether a person has been trafficked for the purpose of exploitation: this Authority identifies potential victims of modern slavery and ensures they receive the appropriate support. The applicants complained, mainly, of a failure on the part of the authorities to protect them in the aftermath of their trafficking, that the authorities had failed to conduct an adequate investigation into their trafficking and the fairness of the trial.[30] The focus of this section will turn to the interpretation of the 1926 definition of slavery.

Siliadan v. France (2006) 43 EHRR 16 (ECHR, 26 July 2005)

The European Court of Human Rights (hereafter, the ECtHR) considered the interpretation of the 1926 definition of slavery in the case of Siliadin v. France in 2005.[31] The applicant, a Togolese national having arrived in France in 1994 with the intention to study, was made to work instead as a domestic servant in a private household in Paris, France. She had been brought to France by her uncle. With the consent of her father, it had been agreed that she would work as a domestic servant until the cost of her air ticket was reimbursed, and her employer would also arrange for her continued education and regularise her immigration status. However, upon her arrival, her passport was taken away by her employer, and sometime after she was 'lent' to a couple with two small children to help with the housework, and thereafter 'kept' by them. The work required of her consisted of cleaning, cooking, washing, and childcare. The applicant was required to work 15-h days, seven days a week, and was rarely allowed to leave the house. On those occasions she was able to leave, this was only allowed to transport the owners' children, and exceptionally, to attend mass. She had no room of her own and slept on a

---

[30] European Court of Human Rights, Factsheet—Slavery, servitude and forced labour, January 2022 FS_Forced_labour_ENG (coe.int) (https://www.echr.coe.int/Documents/FS_Forced_labour_ENG.pdf) Accessed September 2022.

[31] Siliadin v France, App No. 73316/01 (ECtHR, 26 July 2005).

mattress on the floor in a room with the family's new-born baby. She did not receive any financial remuneration and did not attend school. A year after her arrival in France she managed to escape with help. However, she soon returned to the defendants out of a sense of obligation to her family. Almost four years after her arrival in France, a neighbour alerted the French Committee Against Modern Slavery, the applicant was rescued, and proceedings were brought against the couple under French criminal law for the charges of a breach of her right to human dignity, and for obtaining her services without payment (Nicholson, 2010).

The applicant complained about having been a domestic slave.[32] Moreover, the French criminal law did not afford her sufficient and effective protection against "servitude" or at least "forced and compulsory" labour. The ECtHR was called upon to consider whether the situation of domestic exploitation involving a child constituted slavery.[33] It is important to comment here that the case was not prosecuted based on human trafficking, but that the agreed facts would have supported such a charge (Gallagher, 2012, 187). The Court held (in a unanimous decision) that being deprived of personal autonomy, even in the most brutal way, is not in itself sufficient to constitute slavery. The Court held that the applicant had been held in "servitude" within the meaning of Article 4 of the European Convention on Human Rights and that she had also been subjected to forced labour.[34] In referring briefly to the possibility that the applicant was a slave within the meaning of Article 1 of the 1926 Slavery Convention, the Court held:

Although the applicant was, in the instant case, clearly deprived of her personal autonomy, the evidence does not suggest that she was held in slavery

---

[32] European Court of Human Rights, Factsheet—Slavery, servitude and forced labour, January 2022 FS_Forced_labour_ENG (coe.int) (https://www.echr.coe.int/Documents/FS_Forced_labour_ENG.pdf) Accessed September 2022.

[33] Although being heard almost 20 years ago, the case echoes the recent revelations that Sir Mo Farah had been trafficked to the UK for the purposes of domestic servitude.

[34] For an in-depth analysis of the case see further H. Cullen, 'Siliadin v. France: Positive obligations under Article 4 of the European Convention on human rights', *Human Rights Review*, 6 (2006), 585.

> *in the proper sense, in other words that Mr and Mrs B exercised a genuine right of legal ownership over her, thus reducing her to the status of an "object".*[35]

So, what does this mean? The ECtHR found that the applicant had not been enslaved because her employers, although exercising control over her, had not had "a genuine right of legal ownership over her reducing her to the status of an 'object'". The fact that slavery was illegal in France meant that despite the fact that 'the applicant was ... clearly deprived of her personal autonomy', her status did not correspond to 'the "classic" meaning of slavery was it was practiced for centuries' and embodied in the article.[36] This definition was interpreted narrowly by the ECtHR in the case so as to distinguish between slavery and servitude, and to construe the definition as relating to the concept of chattel slavery only (Nicholson, 2010).

The refusal of the ECtHR to apply Article 1 to the situation of a female adolescent who served for a period of four years as an unpaid domestic worker in France has been criticised. For example, the reasoning of the ECtHR on this point has been classes as a misinterpretation of the 1926 definition afforded to slavery, through reading that definition as linked to traditional chattel slavery and subsequently requiring a 'general right of legal ownership' (Gallagher, 2010, 187). The understanding of ECtHR in this case understood the 1926 definition of slavery as referring to *de jure* slavery. The case offers a potential for a schism between international criminal law and human rights law on this point of legal ownership. Distinct from the position of international criminal law, human rights law generally links the prohibition of slavery with both servitude and forced labour, subsequently creating an implied hierarchy of severity. The issue of hierarchies of harms is highlighted through the construction of the worst forms of child labour by the International Labour Organization. The idea that ranking some harms perpetrated against children as worse than others is problematic as it implies a notion that the severity of harm is less. As 'the existence

---

[35] Siliadin v France, at 33.
[36] As quoted in Allain Slavery Conventions at 4.

of this supposed "lesser" alternatives to slavery, in particular, servitude, provides a possibility, perhaps confirmed by *Siliadin v. France* for the threshold of slavery to be elevated beyond what has been recognized in judgments such as Kunarac' (Gallagher, 2010, 187).

The Court held, however, that the criminal law in force at the time had not protected her sufficiently, and that although the law had been changed subsequently, it had not been applicable to her situation. The Court concluded that the applicant had been held in servitude, in violation of Article 4 (prohibition of slavery, servitude, forced or compulsory labour) of the European Convention on Human Rights.[37] Additionally, through quoting Article 1 of the Supplementary Convention on the Abolition of Slavery 1956, the Court reminded the defendant State (France) that their duty was to take:

> … *all practicable and necessary legislative and other measures to bring about…the complete abolition or abandonment of [such] practices…*'[38] *The Court noted that '…the increasingly high standard being required in the area of the protection of human rights and fundamental liberties correspondingly and inevitably requires greater firmness in assessing breaches of fundamental values of democratic societies.*[39]

Therefore:

> *Children and other vulnerable individuals, in particular, are entitled to State protection, in the form of effective deterrence, against such serious breaches of personal integrity*[40] *… Article 4 enshrines one of the fundamental values of democratic societies…the member states' positive obligations under Article 4 of the Convention must be seen as requiring penalisation and effective prosecution of any act aimed at maintaining a person in such a situation.*[41]

---

[37] European Court of Human Rights, Factsheet—Slavery, servitude and forced labour, January 2022 FS_Forced_labour_ENG (coe.int) (https://www.echr.coe.int/Documents/FS_Forced_labour_ENG.pdf) Accessed September 2022.
[38] *Siliadin v. France*, 26 July 2005, 43 E.H.R.R. 16, 86.
[39] *Siliadin v. France*, 26 July 2005, 43 E.H.R.R. 16, 121.
[40] *Siliadin v. France*, 26 July 2005, 43 E.H.R.R. 16, 81.
[41] *Siliadin v. France*, 26 July 2005, 43 E.H.R.R. 16, 112.

4.3.2 The Supplementary Convention on the Abolition of Slavery, the Slave Trade, and Institutions and Practices Similar to Slavery 1956[42]

The Supplementary Convention on the Abolition of Slavery, the Slave Trade, and Institutions and Practices Similar to Slavery (hereafter, the 1956 Supplementary Convention) to the 1926 Slavery Convention was adopted by a Conference of Plenipotentiaries convened by Economic and Social Council resolution 608 (XXI) of 30 April 1956 and in Geneva on 7 September 1956.[43] The 1956 Supplementary Convention was adopted under the auspices of the United Nations, which drew inspiration from the UDHR that 'no one shall be held in slavery or servitude and that slavery and the slave trade shall be prohibited in all their forms'. The decision by the UN to adopt a new legal instrument that would inter alia address certain institutions and practices similar to slavery appears to support the narrow interpretation of the 1926 definition. What this means essentially is that if the 1926 legal definition had included related institutions and practices then there would have been no need to develop the Supplementary Convention, 1956. The Supplementary Convention is important for some commentators as it expanded the coverage of exploitation to include practices such as debt bondage and serfdom (Obokata, 2019, 529–552); however, the institutions and practices it recognised such as debt bondage, serfdom, and various practices around children and marriage all present their own problems of definition. As identified by Hathaway (2008), the Slavery Convention of 1956 did not "give more detail" to the prohibition of slavery that was set out within the 1926 Convention. With Rassam (2005, 829) indicating that the Supplementary Slavery Convention expanded the earlier definition of slavery to include institutions and practices similar to

---

[42] Supplementary Convention on the Abolition of Slavery, the Slave Trade, and Institutions and Practices Similar to Slavery | OHCHR (https://www.ohchr.org/en/instruments-mechanisms/instruments/supplementary-convention-abolition-slavery-slave-trade-and) Accessed July 2022.

[43] Entry into force: 30 April 1957, in accordance with article 13, https://www.ohchr.org/EN/ProfessionalInterest/Pages/SupplementaryConventionAbolitionOfSlavery.aspx. Accessed August 2021.

slavery, such as debt bondage, servile forms of marriage[44] serfdom, and the exploitation of child labour. A question that arises here as illustrated by Allain (2012) is 'what moved the parties negotiating the Supplementary Convention, 1956, to change tack and speak of "institutions and practices similar to slavery" rather than "servitudes"?'[45] The answer lies in the obligations which were being considered in the suppression of the four servile statuses at play: debt bondage, serfdom, servile marriage, and child exploitation.

Exploitation was not explicitly mentioned in the 1926 Slavery Convention. The social meanings of 'debt, forced labour, child labour, child marriage and cross-border marriages, uncover the space between not-slavery and freedom, and expose the risks of relying on broad dichotomies of choice and force' (Brace & O'Connell Davidson, 2018, 19). Through aligning 'slavery' with institutions and practices similar to slavery, it opened the possibilities to further expand the reach of the concept, with the 1956 Slavery Convention leading to a flurry of new conventions and declarations, many of them overlapping that add to the list of phenomena discussed under the rubric of contemporary slavery (Brace & O'Connell Davidson, 2018, 19). The types of child labour designated as exploitative by UNICEF and the ILO constitute a slavery-like practice which is prohibited by the Supplementary Convention.[46] Additionally, Obokata (2019) noted that human trafficking can be dealt

---

[44] Note that by seeking to address the issue of servile marriages, the Supplementary Convention calls on States Parties to prescribe, where appropriate, a minimum age of marriage, and to encourage both the registration of and the ability for the consent of both parties to be made freely in the presence of a civil or religious authority. Subsequently there was a Recommendation made by the Conference negotiating the Supplementary Convention, 1956, to the Economic and Social Council to consider the question of marriage as it relates to consent and setting a minimum age (E/CONF.24/23, p. 6).

[45] Slavery Convention (un.org) (https://legal.un.org/avl/ha/sc/sc.html) Accessed October 2022.

[46] According to ILO and UNICEF, there are eight main types of exploitative labour: hazardous working conditions, domestic service, street children, child labour in the informal economy, child slavery, trafficking and commercial sexual exploitation, children in armed conflicts, and illicit activities. See further, ILO, *A future without child labour, global report under the follow-up to the ILO declaration on fundamental principles and rights at work* (Geneva: International Labour Office, 2002), 22; ILO, *Targeting the intolerable: A new international convention to eliminate the worst forms of child labour,* leaflet (Geneva: International Labour Office, 1999); UNICEF, *The state of the world's children, report of the executive director* (Oxford University Press, 1997), 32; UNICEF, *End child exploitation, child labour today* (Florence: UNICEF, 2005).

with through the instruments relating to slavery and forced labour, such as the 1926 Slavery Convention and 1956 Supplementary Slavery Convention. What may be termed "child exploitation" emerged from considerations around fraudulent adoptions (Allain, 2012). However, the final provisions go beyond such adoptions, including the prospective exploitation of the child (Fig. 4.2):

> *Any institution or practice whereby a child or young person under the age of 18 years is delivered by either or both of his natural parents or by his guardian to another person, whether for reward or not, with a view to the exploitation of the child or young person or of his labour.*[47]

Article 1(d) of the Supplementary Convention refers to children and therefore will be the focus of the analysis. The article specifically focuses upon the child or adolescent as a possession to be protected rather than an autonomous being. This framing of children as possessions can be traced back in legal terms to the Roman legal system under *patria potestas*. What this meant was that the father had power over life and death—*patria potestas* principle, so the father could sell the child, for example. What we are talking about here was the fact that children were under the control of their parents, and this is how children are addressed under the Slavery Convention of 1956. Children historically were regarded as assets of property and therefore for some cheap labour, a resource to be capitalised upon, and subsequently exploited. Consider historical literature that illustrates this point such as Charles Dickens' Great Expectations where the child in question was an apprentice from the age of 6. When we think about the child, different times, different perspectives, and link that into how we think about how children were used or classed as a possession of the family. Although the Slavery Convention, considers the context where a child is under the care of a guardian, it is a traditional and reductive approach to children and adolescents. The focus upon financial gain or profit is interesting, as the language creates an explicit caveat that 'whether for reward or not' that a crime has still been committed if no financial gain has been made.

---

[47] The reference is to the 1956 Supplementary Slavery Convention section (d) which is included within the Fig. 4.2.

> **Section I. - Institutions and practices similar to slavery**
>
> **Article 1**
>
> Each of the States Parties to this Convention shall take all practicable and necessary legislative and other measures to bring about progressively and as soon as possible the complete abolition or abandonment of the following institutions and practices, where they still exist and whether or not they are covered by the definition of slavery contained in article 1 of the Slavery Convention signed at Geneva on 25 September 1926:
>
> (a) Debt bondage, that is to say, the status or condition arising from a pledge by a debtor of his personal services or of those of a person under his control as security for a debt, if the value of those services as reasonably assessed is not applied towards the liquidation of the debt or the length and nature of those services are not respectively limited and defined;
>
> (b) Serfdom, that is to say, the condition or status of a tenant who is by law, custom or agreement bound to live and labour on land belonging to another person and to render some determinate service to such other person, whether for reward or not, and is not free to change his status;
>
> (c) Any institution or practice whereby:
>
> (i) A woman, without the right to refuse, is promised or given in marriage on payment of a consideration in money or in kind to her parents, guardian, family or any other person or group; or
> (ii) The husband of a woman, his family, or his clan, has the right to transfer her to another person for value received or otherwise; or
> (iii) A woman on the death of her husband is liable to be inherited by another person;
>
> (d) Any institution or practice whereby a child or young person under the age of 18 years, is delivered by either or both of his natural parents or by his guardian to another person, whether for reward or not, with a view to the exploitation of the child or young person or of his labour.

Fig. 4.2 1956 Supplementary Slavery Convention

The language within Article 1, is masculine and could be dismissed as reflective of the time but it demonstrates the focus of the drafters and the exclusion of others from the spaces where the laws are created and in turn potential ways the law excludes sectors of society it purports to protect. A final point of note relates to the lifetime of the Working Group on Contemporary Forms of Slavery (1974–2006). The Working Group, developed an expansive understanding of contemporary forms of slavery beyond that of the legal parameters of slavery and practices similar to slavery as set out within the Slavery United 6 Convention, 1926, and Supplementary Convention, 1956.[48] Under its development

---

[48] See further Slavery Convention (un.org) (https://legal.un.org/avl/pdf/ha/sc/sc_e.pdf) Accessed October 2022.

of contemporary forms of slavery, the Working Group considered, inter alia, female genital mutilation, honour killings, and street children, and reported over various years on such diverse issues as child pornography, detained juveniles, early marriages, and incest.[49]

The provision contained within Article 1(d) was implemented with the practice of "sham adoptions" in mind according to the UN Sub-Commission on the Promotion and Protection of Human Rights in 2000.[50] The perception of "sham adoptions" was that they occurred when a family (generally in financial difficulty) gives or sells a child to a more affluent family, nominally to be adopted but in reality to work in the richer family's household without enjoying either the same status or the same treatment as ordinary children within the home they are adopted into.[51] The UN Sub-Commission also indicated that similar practices, where children were sent to households of relatives or others with the expectation that they will give special attention in regards to their education but in reality exploit them for labour.

A link here can be traced between the archival research, namely, through the identification of adoptive systems in Cyprus and the *Mui Tsai* system in the 1920s, where children were informally adopted to undertake domestic work within the home. It is interesting how legislative provisions were crafted with the aim of eradicating what was perceived as a harmful cultural practice of fake or sham adoptions for the purpose of exploitation, but not all scenarios were perceived as harmful. Consider the State-sponsored emigration of young white stock from the UK to the former colonies of Australia and Canada under the "Child Migrant Programme" (1920s–1970s), for example. The aim of the programme was twofold, firstly to relieve the pressure upon British orphanages and to boost the population of the colonies. The children

---

[49] See further E/CN.4/Sub.2. Accessed October 2022.

[50] UN Sub-Commission on the Promotion and Protection of Human Rights, Contemporary Forms of Slavery, Updated Review of the implementation of and Follow-up to the Conventions of Slavery, Addendum, fifty-second session, 26 May 2000, E/CN.4/Sub.2/2000/3/Add.1, para. 75.

[51] UN Sub-Commission on the Promotion and Protection of Human Rights, Contemporary Forms of Slavery, Updated Review of the implementation of and Follow-up to the Conventions of Slavery, Addendum, fifty-second session, 26 May 2000, E/CN.4/Sub.2/2000/3/Add.1, para. 75.

were between the ages of 3 and 14, coming from deprived backgrounds and often in some form of social or charitable care. The humanitarian industry again comes into play with charitable organisations such as Barnados, in addition to Anglican and Catholic Churches and local authorities helped to organise the emigration.[52] First-hand accounts of exploitation and abuse have recently emerged,[53] with a 2014 case in the USA Ellul v. Congregation of Christian Bros[54] emerging with the plaintiffs alleging violations of customary international law including slavery and involuntary servitude, child trafficking, forced child labour, and cruel, inhuman and degrading treatment or punishment in addition to common law claims of conversion, unjust enrichment, constructive trust, accounting, and breach of fiduciary or special duty.[55] Although the case was struck out upon procedural grounds (statute of limitations), it provides an insight into the global impact of state-sponsored migration aided by the humanitarian industry. The emerging stories of exploitation resulted in apologies from the former Prime Minister of the UK Gordon Brown in 2010[56] and former Australian Prime Minister Kevin Rudd in 2009.[57] Although not classified as sham adoptions, parallels exist in terms that the 130,000 children moved under the Child Migrant Programme were from.

---

[52] Britain's child migrant programme: why 130,000 children were shipped abroad | Child protection | The Guardian (https://www.theguardian.com/society/2017/feb/27/britains-child-migrant-programme-why-130000-children-were-shipped-abroad) Accessed July 2022.

[53] For example, successful claims for compensation on behalf of 215 former Fairbridge Farm (New South Wales, Australia) children, of whom 129 said they had been sexually abused, were made. The Australian royal commission on child abuse recently revealed 853 people had accused the Catholic order Christian Brothers, which also took in child migrants, of abuse.

[54] Ellul v. Congregation of Christian Bros., 2011 U.S. Dist. LEXIS 29887.

[55] Ellul v. Congregation of Christian Bros (unodc.org) (https://sherloc.unodc.org/cld/case-law-doc/traffickingpersonscrimetype/usa/2014/ellul_v._congregation_of_christian_bros.html?lng=en&tmpl=sherloc) Accessed July 2022.

[56] Britain's child migrant programme: Why 130,000 children were shipped abroad | Child protection | The Guardian (https://www.theguardian.com/society/2017/feb/27/britains-child-migrant-programme-why-130000-children-were-shipped-abroad) Accessed July 2022.

[57] Kevin Rudd says sorry to Britons forcibly shipped to Australia as children | Australia news | The Guardian (https://www.theguardian.com/world/2009/nov/16/kevin-rudd-apology-british-children) Accessed July 2022.

4.4 The United Nations (1945–Present Day)

The United Nations (hereafter, the UN) is an international organisation established on 24 October 1945 by 51 nations in response to the Second World War, with the aim to preserve peace through international cooperation and collective security (Akhtar & Nyamutata, 2020, 55). Currently made up of 195 Member States, the UN and its work are guided by the purposes and principles contained in its founding Charter.[58] Mutua echoes the review of Akthar and Nyamutata by asserting that the 'United Nations, formed after World War II by the dominant Western powers, aimed to create and maintain *global order* through peace, security, and cooperation among states'. Notably, Mutua goes on to identify that the global order that is created by the UN is dominated by the West and as such the critically important agenda of the UN has been the universalisation of European principle and norms, as the spreading of human rights which emerge out of Western liberalism and jurisprudence. The focus of this chapter will now turn to the legislative action of the UN since its inception that addresses slavery, trafficking, and the rights of children.

4.4.1 Universal Declaration of Human Rights (UDHR), 1948

Human rights are defined as certain fundamental rights to which every human being is entitled to, and are 'inherent in all human beings irrespective of colour, ancestry, sex, ethnic origin or social status' (Renzikowski, 2019, 13). As Kant articulated 'freedom is independence of the compulsory will of another; and in so far as it can coexist with the freedom of all according to a universal law, it is one sole original, inborn right belonging to every man in virtue of his humanity'.[59] The Universal Declaration of Human Rights (hereafter UDHR) is labelled as a 'milestone document in the history of human rights' and was adopted without a single dissenting vote (Shaw, 2021, 206). The UDHR was

---

[58] See further, https://www.un.org/en/about-us/un-charter. Accessed August 2021.
[59] Kant, I., *Metaphysik der Sitten* (first published in 1791) as referenced in Renzikowski (2019, 13).

collaboratively drafted by representatives with different legal and cultural backgrounds from all regions of the world. The focus in the aftermath of the Second World War 'story for international human rights law concerned the attempts made to create legal instruments protecting human rights. However, for some international law remains an instrument to pursue the interests of ancient colonial power (Galliie, 2008; Ramina, 2018). Of course, this meant securing agreement on what that concept actually covered' (Bates in Moeckli et al., 2018, 16). The preamble of the framing of the UN Charter in 1945 assertion that the peoples of the UN were:

> *Determined to save succeeding generations from the scourge of war, which twice in our lifetime has brought untold sorrow to mankind, and to reaffirm faith in fundamental human rights, in the dignity and worth of the human person, in the equal rights of men and women and of nations large and small.*

Utilising a post-colonial lens for analysis would infer that it took the suffering of white populations to spark international outrage and action which subsequently developed an exclusionary international human rights regime. Indeed, before the UN Commission on Human Rights began work, the politics of international human rights protection had become apparent, but by 1947, 'human rights' was rapidly becoming an ideological weapon in the war of words between East and West (Lauren, 1998, 228). For some commentators, the West was able to impose its philosophy of human rights upon the rest of the world due to its dominance of the United Nations at its inception (Ramina, 2018, 267). Moreover that immediately after the Second World War and after acquiring their political independence, the ex-colonies quickly realised that political independence was largely illusory without economic independence (Mutua, 2000). The lens of TWAIL to analyse the historical model of human rights illustrates its inability to respond to the needs of the Third World unless there is a radical rethinking and restructuring of the international order abandoning the efforts to 'universalise an essentially European corpus of human rights'.

In wake of the Second World War, it was recognised that 'no international human rights mechanisms has existed prior to and during the war which could have allowed interference between a state and its citizens in relation to even extreme human rights abuses' (Fenwick & Fenwick, 2018, 28). The European historical origins of human rights—the protection of emerging bourgeoisie against authoritarian monarchical regimes are enough to demonstrate their inadequacy to protect the Third World against violations of the same rights—by imperialist and neoclassicist practices (Ramina, 2018, 265).

The UDHR is generally agreed to be the foundation of international human rights law, adopted in 1948 it has 'inspired a rich body of legally binding international human rights treaties'.[60] International Human Rights Law reflects the 1956 Supplementary Conventions division between slavery and servitude or "slavery-like practices". The UDHR and ICCPR[61] both prohibit slavery and the slave trade and 'further stipulate that no person shall be held in *servitude*—a term that, although not defined by either instrument, is related normatively to the pre-human rights era concept of "servile status" (Gallagher, 2011, 182). Notably, the relationship between the two concepts of slavery and servitude is not settled.

The UDHR has not been free of critique with Lauterpacht dismissing it as being of 'controversial moral authority' (Lauterpacht, 1950, 279). Whilst Bachand identifies the three critiques of human rights that have emerged from TWAIL scholarship. Firstly, the relationship between universality and particularity—meaning that the current universal and official human rights corpus is based upon European philosophy, although the concept of human rights is not unique to European societies (Ibhawoh, 2007, 23). Secondly, human rights are to be perceived to civilise peoples mire in a savage and barbaric culture (i.e. the Third World) and a way to subsequently impose European standards often used as a toll for colonialist or imperialist practices and interventions (Bachand, 2010; Ramina, 2018, 264). Or as eloquently phrased by Mutua (2001) 'the "SVS metaphor"—savages, victims, saviours'. Thirdly,

---

[60] https://www.un.org/en/about-us/udhr/foundation-of-international-human-rights-law. Accessed June 2021.
[61] UDHR Art 4, ICCPR Arts 8(1) and 8(2) respectively.

the imposition of a form of political organisation and a form of states (Ramina, 2018, 265) with Mutua (1996) asserting that liberalism does not tackle the causes of real and economic equality, which is the main challenge in the Third World as opposed to a liberal state adopting a liberal democracy.

However, the UDHR is the starting point of the socio-legal history of slavery and human trafficking during the era of the United Nations. There was a consensus from the beginning that anti-slavery standards should be incorporated into the UDHR (Lassen, 1988, 103–119). The UDHR is not a treaty, but a declaration, which means that the principles of treaty interpretation are applicable *a maoire ad minus*[62] (Humbert, 2009, 46). With article 4 of the UDHR asserting that 'No one shall be held in slavery or servitude; slavery and the slave trade shall be prohibited in all their forms'.[63] This prohibition (albeit non-binding) gives the concept 'legal and analytical currency' (Quirk, 2012, 256) as the inclusion of slavery in all its forms arises from the 1926 Slavery Convention previously discussed.

---

[62] Note the main difference between a declaration and a treaty is that the latter is intended to create legal relations. This difference of course has to be borne in mind when applying the rules of the Vienna Convention on the Law of Treaties (VCLT), in particular, those regarding invalidity, termination, and suspension of treaties. There is however no reason why the rules of treaty interpretation should not be applied to other instruments in international law provided that the non-binding nature of such instruments is considered. This also applies a fortiori to documents of a non-diplomatic character.

[63] The Universal Declaration of Human Rights (UDHR) is a milestone document in the history of human rights. Drafted by representatives with different legal and cultural backgrounds from all regions of the world, the Declaration was proclaimed by the United Nations General Assembly in Paris on 10 December 1948 (General Assembly resolution 217 A) as a common standard of achievements for all peoples and all nations.

4.4.2 UN Convention for the Suppression of the Traffic in Persons and of the Exploitation of the Prostitution of Others, 1949[64]

In 1949, the various white slavery and trafficking agreements were consolidated into one instrument, namely, the Convention for the Suppression of the Traffic in Persons and of the Exploitation of the Prostitution of Other 1949. Prior to the adoption of the Trafficking Protocol in 2000, the instruments implemented had focused exclusively upon the trafficking of women and girls for sexual exploitation, from the four agreements adopted at the start of the twentieth Century and their focus upon sexual purity, race, and class to the UN Convention for the Suppression of the Traffic in Persons and of the Exploitation of the Prostitution of Others, 1949 (hereafter, The Trafficking Convention 1949).[65] The Trafficking Convention 1949 was approved by the General Assembly resolution 317 (IV) of 2 December 1949 and entered into force on 25 July 1951 in accordance with article 24. The preamble asserts that 'prostitution and the accompanying evil of the traffic in persons for the purpose of prostitution are incompatible with the dignity and worth of the human person and endanger the welfare of the individual, the family and the community'. The language used within the preamble shows a distinct lack of demarcation between prostitution and human trafficking. Declaring that both trafficking and prostitution are 'incompatible with the dignity and worth of the human being' and a danger to 'the welfare of the individual, the family and the community'.[66] This link between trafficking and sex work has been labelled as a 'convenient conflation' something that continues in contemporary imaginings of trafficking. The use of descriptive and emotive language is deliberate. The

---

[64] For an overview of the legislative history of the Convention, see UNESCO and the Coalition against Trafficking in Women, The Penn State Report: Report of the International Meeting of Experts on Sexual Exploitation, Violence and Prostitution, April 1999, Annex 1 (Penn State Report).

[65] https://www.ohchr.org/EN/ProfessionalInterest/Pages/TrafficInPersons.aspx. Accessed June 2021.

[66] 1949 Trafficking Convention, Preamble.

intention of the Trafficking Convention 1949 is to ensure that 'prostitution and the accompanying evil of the traffic in persons' are combatted to protect society. The preamble is reflective of the belief that social evils such as prostitution are a threat to society and rests upon assumptions that the family and community are wholesome, safe, and pure. The ideal of the family is particularly important with regard to children as the trafficking discourse today frequently relies upon the belief that children are kidnapped, tricked, or lured away from the protective family unit and sold into sexual slavery (Bhahba & Dottridge, 2016, 6; Dottridge 2021, 12).

The Trafficking Convention 1949 was limited to trafficking for prostitution, therefore entrenching the idea that the two are synonymous. This limitation ostensibly applied to both women and men and aimed to 'prohibit and control (undefined) practices of trafficking, procurement, and exploitation, whether internal or cross-border, and irrespective of the victim's age or consent' (Gallagher, 2018, 21). However, the Convention survived as the 'only specialist treaty on trafficking for more than half a century, and thereby as the primary source of reference and authority on this matter' (Gallagher, 2011, 62). The Convention is undoubtedly adopting an abolitionist approach to prostitution, linking the two issues together as social evils that must be combatted to protect the greater good and endorsing the rescue industry narrative. The Convention attracted and had retained a 'measure of political support from some States and sectors of civil society' (Gallagher, 2011, 61). Like its predecessors, the Convention afforded no definition of human trafficking and was primarily concerned with the movement of women and girls abroad for prostitution. The emphasis upon trafficking across borders is something that is a clear focus of the later Trafficking Protocol, this early stance that exploitation is worse if it is outside of the victim's native country is an idea that is not isolated to the 1949 Convention. The Convention was further limited in that it only attempted to deal with the process and result. The Convention did extend its scope beyond "movement", identifying prostitution and forced prostitution as matters for international regulation, therefore distinguishing between itself and the earlier legislative measures implemented earlier, with their deference to matters traditionally seen as within a State's domestic jurisdiction (Gallagher, 2011, 59).

Article 1 sought to punish the perpetrators and it specifically states through art 1 (i) that the consent of the victim is irrelevant.[67] This immediately infantilises and removes any agency or autonomy away from the 'victim'; therefore, enshrining the perspective that nobody can consensually work within the sex industry. It is not being advocated that children can consensually work with the industry and that practice cannot be condoned or justified but adult women and men can and do work consensually within the industry. The rescue industry has become a key part of the fight against human trafficking today and the various INGOs and NGOs that operate within that area endorse and advocate the idea that every person working within the sex industry requires saving.

Article 17 identifies the links of 'trafficking in persons of either sex for prostitution' and the issues of 'immigration and emigration'. The Article places an obligation on States Parties to check the trafficking of persons of either sex for prostitution, which is relatively significant as through acknowledging gender it widens its scope of application. Although the Convention adopts an abolitionist approach to prostitution (with art. 16 specifically identifying measures for the prevention of prostitution), it reflects a slight shift in the acceptance that prostitution does not only apply to women and girls. The purpose of the Convention is to prevent and criminalise the sex industry to protect society, little thought is given to what the perceived victims think, want, and need. Moreover, regarding children Article 17 specifically references children, requiring state parties to 'make such regulations as are necessary for the protection of immigrants or emigrants, and in particular women and children, both at the place of arrival and departure and whilst en route'. Additionally, Article 20 identifies the need to 'take necessary measures for the supervision of employment agencies in order to precent persons seeking employment, in particular women and children, from being exposed to the danger of prostitution'. The continued linkage between women and children has been explicitly identified by feminists as infantilising women

---

[67] Trafficking is seen by many as an inherently coercive environment, therefore it is incredibly difficult to determine true agency or consent see further Elliott.

but the ideology that those perceived as vulnerable should be protected and prevented from moving, through restrictions on their mobility and employment prospects maintains prominence today particularly in relation to children. This links to the activities of the League of Nations and the colonial legacies and restrictions of mobility discussed in the previous chapter.

The 1949 Convention has come under 'considerable and wide-ranging attack' (Gallagher, 2011, 61) despite retaining a level of support alluded to earlier. For example, human rights activists along with States that operate systems of legalised, licensed, or otherwise regulated prostitution have decried the instrument for not focusing sufficiently or solely on the more serious, coercive forms of sexual exploitation and forced prostitution.[68] For example, the 1949 Convention does not cover contemporary forms of sexual exploitation (Reanda, 1991) and provides no protection against the coerced or fraudulent movement of individuals of other sectors due to its constrained focus upon trafficking for prostitution (Knaus et al., 2000, 16). The position of the former UN Special Rapporteur on Violence against Women is reflective of this position:

> The 1949 Convention has proved ineffective in protecting the rights of trafficked women and combating trafficking. The Convention does not take a human rights approach. It does not regard women as independent actors endowed with rights and reason; rather, the Convention views them as vulnerable beings in need of protection from the "evils of prostitution". As such, the 1949 Convention does very little to protect women from and provide remedies for the human rights violations committed in the course of trafficking, thereby increasing women's marginalization and vulnerability to human rights violations.[69]

---

[68] See further UN Commission on Human Rights, 'Report of the Special Rapporteur, MS. Radhika Coomaraswamy, on violence against women, its causes and consequences, on trafficking in women, women's migration and violence against women', UN Doc. E/CN.4/2000/68, February 29, 2000 (Coomaraswamy, "Report", UN Doc. E/CN.4/2000/68) para. 22. N.V. Demleitner, 'Forced prostitution: Naming an international offence', *Fordham International Law Journal* 18 (1994) 163, at 174 "while the title of the., Convention speaks for the 'exploitation of prostitution', the text tends to refer solely to prostitution. This created a certain degree of ideological confusion, since the [1949] Convention's focus remained ambiguous as to whether all kinds of prostitution or only forced prostitution were at issue".
[69] Coomaraswamy, "Report" UN Doc E/CN.4/2000/68 at para. 22.

4.4.3 The UN Protocol to Prevent, Suppress, and Punish Trafficking in Persons, Especially Women and Children 2000

The UN Protocol to Prevent, Suppress, and Punish Trafficking in Persons, especially women and children (hereafter, the Palermo Protocol) which was adopted as a Protocol to the UN Convention against Transnational Organized Crime 2000, delivered the first legal definition of trafficking through Article 3. Negotiated within two years which was 'lightning speed on the UN clock' (Charnysh et al., 2015, 423), the Protocol entered into force in 2003 and has been exceptionally well ratified to date.[70]

The phrase "trafficking" has been used in several international instruments prior to the creation of the current international legal order.[71] It is notable that over the last 2 decades 'trafficking has been discussed predominately in the key of international law' (Kotiswaran, 2018, 9). Under international criminal law, itself a relatively new field emerging in the 1990s (Cryer et al., 2019, 3), individuals are held criminally responsible by a supranational court for crimes such as genocide and crimes against humanity and violations of *jus cogens* norms (Kotiswaran, 2018, 9). The Trafficking Protocol is better understood as an instance of transnational criminal law or the 'indirect suppression by international law through domestic penal law of criminal activities that have actual or potential trans-border effects' (Boister, 2003, 955). This framing of the 'problem of human trafficking as a transnational crime, best addressed through aggressive prosecution of traffickers'[72] at the time of adoption has shifted, with global anti-trafficking law and policy evolving significantly (Chuang, 2021, 179). The 'narrow characterisation

---

[70] https://treaties.un.org/Pages/ViewDetails.aspx?src=TREATY&mtdsg_no=XVIII-12-a&chapter=18&lang=en. Accessed 25 November 2020.
[71] Notably the "White Slavery Conventions" namely the International Agreement for the Suppression of White Slave Traffic 1904, International Convention for the Suppression of the White Slave Traffic 1910, International Convention for the Suppression of Traffic in Women and Children 1921, International Convention for the Suppression of the Traffic in Women of Full Age 1933, and the Convention for the Suppression of the Traffic in Persons and the Exploitation of the Prostitution of Others 1949.
[72] Protocol to Prevent, Suppress and Punish Trafficking in Persons, Arts 2, 4.

of trafficking and its monopolisation by the UN'S human rights system continued unchallenged until the last decade of the twentieth century' (Gallagher, 2018, 21). The 'catalyst for changes was the link established between trafficking and the newly identified international threats of migrant smuggling and transnational organised crime' (Gallagher, 2018, 21). This led to the development of a new legal instrument, outside of the human rights framework and within transnational criminal law. Compromised of two treaties, both adopted by the UN General Assembly in 2000, widely ratified, a parent instrument in the form of the United Nations Convention against Transnational Organized Crime (hereafter, UNCTOC) and a specialised treaty—the Protocol against trafficking in persons especially women and children. The relationship between the UNCTOC and its Protocols is set out within the Convention itself and four basic principles are identifiable. Firstly, as the Protocols were not intended to become stand-alone treaties as States must ratify the Convention before ratifying any of the Protocols[73] and a Party to the Convention is not bound by a Protocol unless it also becomes party to that Protocol.[74] Secondly, the Convention and its Protocols must be interpreted together, considering their stated purposes.[75] Thirdly, the provisions of the Convention must apply, *mutatis mutandis*, to the Protocols.[76] Essentially, this requirement means that in applying the Convention to the Protocols, modifications of interpretation or application should be made only when (and to the extent that) they are necessary.[77] Finally, the offences established by

---

[73] UNCTOC Article 37 (2). See, also the Legislative Guide, p. 253. The Legislative Guide points out this provision ensures that in a case arising under one of the Protocols to which the States concerned are parties, all of the general provisions of the Convention, for example relating to mutual legal assistance and the protection of victims will also be available and applicable.
[74] UNCTOC 2000, Article 37 (3).
[75] UNCTOC 2000, Article 37 (4); Trafficking Protocol 2000, Article 1 (1). See further the Legislative Guide—253–255.
[76] Trafficking Protocol 2000, Article 1 (2).
[77] Legislative Guide, p. 254. The Interpretative Note on Article 1 of the Trafficking Protocol states that 'this paragraph was adopted on the understanding that the words "*mutatis mutandis*" meant "with such modifications as circumstances require" or "with the necessary modifications". Provisions of the United Nations Convention Against Transnational Organized Crime that are applied to the Protocol under this article would consequently be modified or interpreted so as

the Protocols are to be regarded as offences established to the Convention. Consequently, the Convention's general provisions on issues such as victim protection, law enforcement cooperation, mutual legal assistance, and extradition, for example, are available and applicable to States in their implementation of the more specific and detailed provisions of the Protocols (Gallagher, 2018, 24).

The origins of the Trafficking Protocol can be traced back to Argentina's interest in the issue of trafficking in minors and to its 'dissatisfaction with the slow progress on negotiating an additional Protocol to the CRC to address child prostitution and child pornography'.[78] The informal preparatory meeting discussed the additional international legal instruments or protocols whose preparation the Ad Hoc Committee had been asked to consider. In that connection, the Governments of Austria and Italy submitted a working paper containing elements for an international legal instrument against illegal trafficking and transport of migrants. In relation to the proposed international legal instrument on the trafficking xxvi of women and children, the Chairman of the meeting called on interested delegations to submit a draft text in time for consideration by the Ad Hoc Committee at its first session XXV. According to the *Travaux Préparatoires*: United Nations Convention against Transnational Organized Crime specific proposals on additional topics to be included the 'trafficking of children' amongst other issues such as 'trafficking in illegal migrants', 'terrorism', and 'money laundering'.[79] Whilst the Government of Argentina played a pivotal role concerning the drafting of a new convention against 'trafficking in minors' with the political decision reached during the 7th session of the Commission that the additional instrument to be drafted should indeed address trafficking in women and children. The perspectives of different States involved in the drafting process of the Palermo Protocol can be seen through reading the submitted negotiated texts as catalogued in the *Travaux Préparatoires*. The USA, for example, in its draft submission identified the belief 'that women and children are particularly vulnerable to and

---

to have the same essential meaning or effect in the Protocol as in the Convention'—*Travaux Preparatoires* for the Organized Crime Convention and Protocols, p. 330.

[78] Travaux preparatoires; 320 Argentina (A/AC.254/8).

[79] *Travaux preparatoires* XX.

targeted by transnational criminal organizations engaged in trafficking in persons'.[80] As Argentina emphasised, the trafficking of women and children constitutes a universal concern and that.

> while there is a wide variety of international legal instruments containing provisions aimed at combating sexual exploitation of women and children, in particular the Convention on the Rights of the Child[81] and the Convention for the Suppression of the Traffic in Persons and of the Exploitation of the Prostitution of Others,[82] there is no such instrument whose specific objective is to deal with the problem of international trafficking in children for any purpose or of trafficking in both categories of person by criminal organizations.[83]

The focus upon child trafficking was spearheaded by the governments of Argentina and the United States, respectively, with a revised draft from both States emerging during the Second Session in March 1999.[84] Explicitly identifying the increasing activities of transnational criminal organisations, the profit from trafficking and that women and children 'are particularly vulnerable to and targeted by transnational criminal organizations'.[85] In addition to raising concerns that in the absence of such an instrument women and children would not be sufficiently protected.[86] It is notable that the proposal by Argentina was restricted to trafficking in women and children, contrasting with the United States position of recognising that women and children were both particularly vulnerable to trafficking, applied to trafficking in all persons.[87] Furthermore, according to the *Travaux Préparatoires* almost all countries expressed their preference for the Protocol to address all persons, rather than only women and children, ultimately agreeing that particular

---

[80] *Travaux preparatoires*; Negotiation Texts, First Session 19–29 January 1999 United States of America (A/AC.254/4/Add.3).
[81] United Nations, Treaty Series, vol. 1577, No. 27531.
[82] Ibid., vol. 96, No. 1342.
[83] *Travaux preparatoires*; 320 Argentina (A/AC.254/8).
[84] Argentina and United States of America (A/AC.254/4/Add.3/Rev.1).
[85] Part 2 Preamble 321 *Travaux preparatoires*.
[86] Ibid.
[87] Ibid.

attention should be paid to women and children.[88] Following the recommendation of the Ad Hoc Committee, the UN General Assembly (GA) modified the Committee's mandate to enable the scope of the Protocol to be expanded to cover trafficking in persons, especially women and children.[89]

Defining Human Trafficking

'In the late 1980s and early 1990s, divisions over (and positions on) a definition of trafficking began to emerge in the context of more specific debates relating to prostitution and the inadequacies of the current international legal framework to prevent the sexual exploitation of women' (Gallagher, 2010, 16). Subsequently, the Palermo Protocol was subject to 'fierce lobbying by transnational networks of feminist anti-trafficking NGOs', with the issues of consent highly contested (Doezema, 2010, 27). Furthermore, the complexities of sexist, racist, and the 'rescue industry' responses form part of the complicated web of anti-trafficking policies and reactions.

Although the Palermo Protocol contained an explicit definition of the meaning of "trafficking in persons", which appeared to 'consolidate existing international law concerning a range of forms of unacceptable exploitation' (Dottridge, 2017, 59). The significance of the definition of 'Trafficking in persons' through article 3 of the Palermo Protocol has been identified as a 'genuine breakthrough because it provided the necessary perquisite for the elaboration of a meaningful normative framework' (Gallagher, 2015, 2). A clear definition of human trafficking is crucial as the Palermo Protocol was intended to define a crime that can be both detected and prosecuted. Interestingly, since the adoption of the Palermo Protocol, the number of prosecutions internationally has fallen.

---

[88] *Travaux preparatoires* at 322.
[89] UN General Assembly Ad Hoc Committee on the Elaboration of a Convention against Transnational Organized Crime, Progress Report of the Ad Hoc Committee on the Elaboration of a Convention Against Transnational Organized Crime UN Doc. A/AC.254/30-E/CN.15/2000/4, 2000, para. 34.

The Protocol sets out a definition of trafficking that in essence 'renews obligations previously undertaken to suppress slavery and, most importantly … other types of exploitation domestically' (Allain, 2017, 60). Article 3 (a) of the Protocol reads;

> *"Trafficking in persons" shall mean the recruitment, transportation, transfer, harboring or receipt of persons, by means of the threat or use of fore or other forms of coercion, of abduction, of fraud, of deception, of the abuse of power or of a position of vulnerability or of the giving or receiving of payments or benefits to achieve the consent of a person having control over another person, for the purpose of exploitation. Exploitation shall include, at a minimum, the exploitation of the prostitution of others or other forms of sexual exploitation, forced labour or services, slavery or practices similar to slavery, servitude or the removal of organs;*

Article 3 (a) therefore establishes the three separate elements to the definition, (i) the action, (ii) the means, and (iii) the purpose or exploitation.[90]

The origins of the Palermo Protocol's definition can be traced back to the International Convention for the Suppression of the White Slave Traffic, 1910, which identified the terms 'abuse of authority', 'fraud', 'threats', and violence as the means elements (Allain, 2017, 31). Those changes coupled with the 'method' and 'purpose' of the Trafficking Protocol constitute the three elements of contemporary trafficking. The convergence of the two genealogies of the Atlantic Slave Trade and slavery and the White Slave Traffic and human trafficking 'only truly transpires in the year 2000 with the inclusion, as a type of exploitation, of slavery within the definition of trafficking in persons found in the Palermo Protocol' (Allain, 2018, 9).

As defined by the Palermo Protocol, trafficking does not refer to a single, unitary act leading to one specific outcome, but rather covers a

---

[90] For those familiar with the contemporary definition of human trafficking, the terms 'abuse of authority', 'fraud', 'threats' and 'violence' will stand out, as they have been maintained throughout the process from 1902 to the contemporary definition of the twenty-first Century (12) (PDF) *White Slave Traffic in International Law*. Available from: https://www.researchgate.net/publication/307937864_White_Slave_Traffic_in_International_Law. Accessed 5 May 5 2021.

process (recruitment, transportation, and control) that can be organised in a variety of ways and involve a range of different actions and outcomes (Anderson & O'Connell Davidson, 2003). The Palermo Protocol 'offers an expansive understanding of both the means of trafficking as well as the purpose for which one is trafficked, namely exploitation' (Kotiswaran, 2018, 11). The concepts of both coercion and exploitation are central to the Palermo Protocol, 'yet neither are defined and their meaning under international law is far from definitive even when clear' (Kotiswaran, 2018, 11).

A pivotal issue is the explicit requirement by the Palermo Protocol through Article 4 that 'those offences are transnational in nature and involve and organized criminal group'. The application of that definition is therefore constrained through the Protocol which specifically stipulates for trafficking to of occurred, the trafficked person must cross a national border and the perpetrators must be an organised criminal gang. The perception that organised crimes such as human trafficking are perpetuated by organised criminal groups is not a contemporary understanding. The links between organised criminal gangs and trafficking can be traced to different periods in the history of human trafficking, such as Chinese organisations at Cholon and Saigon recruiting 'native women, girls and boys for clandestine shipping to China' in 1927 (Faulkner, 2019). Moreover, the focus upon organised criminal gangs is not new, and particularly within the European Union (EU) legal and policy responses have been hindered by the overwhelming focus upon criminal actors and their actions that enable people to reach safety rather than upon the criminal regimes people are often fleeing (Squire & Pencowski, 2018). The Palermo Protocol is part of the arsenal of restrictive international instruments adopted to regulate illegal migration. What the legal framework and policymakers alike have failed to acknowledge is that certain forms of migration carry the highest risks of exploitation and abuse suggests that migrants are aware of the risks but still choose to proceed (O'Connell Davidson, 2015, 111). This is a key point, unfortunately, that agency is inadvertently stripped away from them through the adoption of the rescue narratives and the contemporary legal responses to migration such as the Palermo Protocol. Furthermore, the "ideal victim" has been constructed through the Palermo Protocol and enshrines the image as a weak, passive and inherently vulnerable victim as advocated by Durisin and Van der Maden 'she is the perfect victim—voiceless, vulnerable and easily manipulated' (2021, 149).

The Palermo Protocol: Defining Child Trafficking

As has been previously illustrated, international law recognises a distinction between children and adults; however, does this distinction require a separate definition for trafficking? In line with the Palermo Protocol, it is accepted that this is required, with this distinction recognised and the subsequent need for a different response (Gallagher, 2010, 323). After all, 'legal age standards have always been a shorthand for marking something else, most frequently thresholds of vulnerability or ability'[91] (Tambe, 2019).

The offence of child trafficking 'appears to have a clear definition in the UNTP and in laws based upon it' (Dottridge, 2021). The UN Trafficking Principles and Guidelines assert that.

> *The particular physical, psychological and psychosocial harm suffered by trafficked children and their increased vulnerability to exploitation require that they be dealt with separately from adult trafficked persons in terms of laws, policies, programmes and interventions. The best interests of the child must be a primary consideration in all actions concerning trafficked children, whether undertaken by public or private social welfare institutions, courts*

---

[91] In the 2000s and 2010s, there was a profusion of scholarship on how the legal ages of consent and marriage, in particular, mark vulnerability. See, for instance, Pamela Haag, *Consent: Sexual rights and the transformation of American liberalism* (Ithaca, NY, 1999); Holly Brewer, *By birth or consent: Children, law, and the Anglo-American revolution in authority*(Chapel Hill, NC, 2005); Vern L. Bullough, 'Age of Consent: A Historical Overview', in Helmut Graupner and Vern L. Bullough (eds.), *Adolescence, sexuality, and the criminal law: Multidisciplinary perspectives* (New York, 2004), 25–42; Matthew Waites, *The age of consent: Young people, sexuality and citizenship* (London, 2005); and Mrinalini Sinha, *Specters of mother India: The global restructuring of an empire* (Durham, NC, 2006).

of law, administrative authorities or legislative bodies. Child victims of trafficking should be provided with appropriate assistance and protection and full account should be taken of their special rights and needs.[92]

This quote identifies a threefold criterion, namely, the harm suffered, the 'best interests', and the 'special rights and needs of children' that need to be met. This perception of children illustrates the powerful protectionist discourse that dominates contemporary discussions about children. The vulnerability of children is an issue that repeatedly raises its head. A source of vulnerability for children emits from their lack of full agency, both and under law (Gallagher, 2010, 294). This fact is further aggravated by the absence of a parent or legal guardian, who can act in the child's best interests (Gallagher, 2010, 324). This links to the creation of a system of guardianship under the Modern Slavery Act (2015) in the UK, however. due to underfunding, language barriers amongst other issues the effectiveness has been undermined.[93] What is often not considered is whether the child can act for their own best interests, instead states such as the UK are developing responses to address the issue of agency through a trial of specialist independent advocates with the mandate to offer support to child victims of trafficking. Through the Modern Slavery Act (MSA) 2015, these advocates have now been afforded a statutory basis and the status they need to effectively support and represent the child. Although initiatives such as these fall in line with the consensus that children require extra levels of protection, it also serves to cement the vulnerability through unintentionally endorsing the child's lack of agency.

The trafficking of children is a crime distinct from the trafficking of adults since it is not necessary to establish the means used; with people under the age is eighteen, it is only necessary to establish the act and the purpose of trafficking the child. What does this mean in practice?

---

[92] UN Trafficking Principles and Guidelines. Guideline 8: Special measures for the protection and support of child victims of trafficking, Addendum to the report of the UN High Commissioner for Human Rights (E/2002/68/Add. 1) 10.
[93] See further Creating Stable Futures: Human trafficking, participation and outcomes for children | ECPAT UK (https://www.ecpat.org.uk/creating-stable-futures-human-trafficking-participation-and-outcomes-for-children).

This modification of the 'way the crime is defined, saying that there is no need for abusive means to be used, for example, when recruiting a child, for it to be considered a trafficking offence' (Dottridge, 2021, 13). This is not a new distinction, the links between the 1910 Convention and the Trafficking Protocol are not limited to the means of trafficking, but also hold relevance to child trafficking. The 1910 Convention established a distinction between adults and children through the omission of the means element. This distinction between young victims ('in relation to whom the "means" by which they were procured were irrelevant') and adult victims (in relation to whom some evidence of compulsion as required) has survived through the omission of the means element in relation to children under the Trafficking Protocol of 2000.

As far as children are concerned, the Palermo Protocol defines as a trafficking offence any situation in which a young person is recruited, transported, transferred, harboured, or received for the purpose of exploitation, whether the recruitment involves luring or abducting a child or the child is recruited voluntarily.[94] Moreover, if a 'child is recruited or moved with their agreement, the key distinction between a case of trafficking and one of recruitment into acceptable employment focuses on the nature of the young person's subsequent experience at work or while being exploited: whether the child is (or is intended to be) subjected to one of the forms of exploitation listed by the Protocol' (Dottridge, 2021, 14). A further issue is the lack of definitions afforded, with forced labour, for example, not clearly defined in relation to children. An additional complication concerns the age at which a child is recruited, for international standards stress the importance of each country specifying a minimum age for entry into employment (set at 14, 15, or 16 years). Although the ILO intimated in 2009 that recruiting children to work before the minimum age should be regarded as 'trafficking', this is not part of the UN Protocol's definition of child trafficking.[95] Further, public opinion and law enforcement agencies in many developing countries do not accord the same importance to respecting the minimum age

---

[94] Article 3.
[95] ILO, UNICEF and UN, GIFT, Training Manual to Fight Trafficking in Children for Labour, Sexual and Other Forms of Exploitation, Textbook 1: Understanding child trafficking (2009).

set by national law and international conventions, which international organisations are bound to use as their point of reference (Dottridge, 2021).

The strength and structure of the ideology of Western Childhood view children as what Qvortrup describes as 'human becomings', rather than beings, as somehow possessing less than the full personhood required to be legal–moral subjects able to offer meaningful consent (Qvortrup et al., 2009). This 'non-personhood is enshrined in the Palermo Protocol, which denies children the right to choose their exploitation and establishes that neither coercion nor consent matters in the legal definition of child trafficking, since trafficking equates to mobility and (the labour defined by the authorities as) exploitation' (Howard, 2017, 40). Crucially, however, the legal embodiment of this ideology necessarily contrasts with empirical 'reality' (Howard, 2017, 40). This issue goes beyond the gap between law and what happens in practice or reality. Serving to disrupt the rights of children under the justification of the moral crusade of anti-trafficking. The question of definitions in international law and the law of numerous jurisdictions as to what constitutes the crime of trafficking being committed against children are appropriate to distinguish between adolescent migrants in general and those victims of crime (at the hands of the trafficker) in particular (Dottridge, 2021, 13).

4.4.4 The Convention on the Rights of the Child (CRC) 1989

The focus of this chapter will now shift to critique the child-specific legislative framework of the United Nations, namely, the Convention on the Rights of the Child (hereafter CRC) and one of the CRC's three Optional Protocols, namely, the Optional Protocol on the Sale of Children, Child Prostitution, and Child Pornography (OPSC). The other two Optional protocols—the Optional Protocol on Children in Armed Conflict (OPAC) and the Optional Protocol on the Communications

Procedure (OPIC) are not covered by an in-depth analysis. It is noteworthy that the 2011 Optional Protocol (OPIC)[96] allows for an individual complaint and an inquiry procedure (in case of patterns of grave or systematic child rights violations) with significant potential application to child trafficking cases. The term 'child' spans what is invariably a condition of complete and absolute dependence on older carers through to what a state of partial or complete independence from such carers may be or indeed a state in which the person has acquired 'responsibility towards older or younger dependents' (O'Connell Davidson, 2005, 43). Childhood is frequently 'deployed as an already available, through a contextually qualified register, whose multiplicity serves to strengthen rather than vilify its obviousness' (Balagopalan, 2018, 23). This links in with ideas of childhood in migration research, with host communities and Greek officials, for example, perceiving childhood as a universal and linear process, strongly connected to chronological age (Gill et al., 2019). Differences between "childhoods" nationally and cross-nationally and divisions between children in terms of age, gender, class, race, 'cast', nationality, and disability, for example, are 'clearly relevant to any analysis of children's presence in the sex trade' and child trafficking, exploitation, and labour generally (O'Connell Davidson, 2005, 44).

Under the anti-trafficking legal architecture implemented, the distinction remains through the omission of the means element contained within the Trafficking Protocol, as previously discussed.

It was noted that.

while there is a wide variety of international legal instruments containing provisions aimed at combating sexual exploitation of women and children, in particular the Convention on the Rights of the Child and the Convention for the Suppression of the Traffic in Persons and of the Exploitation of the Prostitution of Others, there is no such instrument whose specific objective is to

---

[96] OPIC (at the time of writing) had 92 adopted decisions, 32 adopted views (decisions on the merits) and 1 concluded inquiry. Optional Protocol on a Communications Procedure—OPIC (childrightsconnect.org) (https://opic.childrightsconnect.org/) Accessed July 2022.

deal with the problem of international trafficking in children for any purpose or of trafficking in both categories of person by criminal organizations.[97]

This revealing quote highlights the perceived need for the adoption of the OPSC, however, the frustrations over the drafting process and slow progress were aired by Argentina during the negotiation of the Trafficking Protocol. The reference to the 1949 Convention is interesting, as the Convention explicitly references children on two occasions through articles 17 and 20 and remained the only comment upon the issue of trafficking for 50 years. Finally, the focus upon criminal organisations, fits in with the broader narrative of evil traffickers, and organised into ruthless foreign criminal gangs.

The CRC is in many ways distinctive amongst international treaties and unique in terms of international law generally (Akthar & Nyamutata, 2020, 86). The CRC was drafted over a lengthy period and mainly by the governments of Western Europe and North America and was subsequently 'firmly rooted in recent developments that have taken place with regards to children and their position in these societies' (Twum-Danso Imoh, 2014, 4). The Convention was swiftly embraced, with enthusiasm demonstrated by African governments with Ghana becoming the very first State to ratify the CRC in February 1990 (Twum-Danso Imoh, 2014, 4). Some suggest that ratification of CRC was considered part of the neoliberal package that developing countries had to accept to remain part of the international community (Adu-Gyamfi & Keating, 2013). It has also been claimed that States ratified the CRC under the impression that it would improve their international standing (Pupavac, 1997). Further, the approach of the CRC, it has been argued, was 'constructive and aid-orientated' and 'children's rights have become a legitimate road to access aid' (Reynolds et al., 2006, 298). Many African countries subsequently rushed to ratify the CRC, assuming that through ratification 'children's rights have become a legitimate road to access aid' (Ngokwey, 2004; Reynolds et al., 2006, 298). However, the universality claimed by the number of governments have ratified that the CRC is refuted by numerous commentators (Boyden, 1997; de Waal, 2002).

---

[97] Travaux preparatoires, p. 320.

Indeed, it is advocated that the 'respect for children's rights have grown since the adoption of the Convention … [It] inspired countless new policies and projects around the world' (Alderson & Morrow, 2004, 10). This was alluded to in earlier chapters which highlighted legislation adopted around the globe predominately to protect children. Whilst some countries made amendments to their constitutions, upon the continent of Africa, for example, children's acts have been introduced into the legislative framework of countries such as Uganda (1997), Ghana (1998), Kenya (2001), Nigeria (2003[98]), South Africa (2005), Tongo (2007), Tanzania (2009), Botswana (2009), and the Democratic Republic of Congo (2009).[99] However, the implementation in Sub-Saharan Africa is notably poor in comparison to countries in Western Europe and North America (Okyere, 2014, 98).

The CRC was produced after a lengthy drafting process that started in 1978, and this lengthy drafting process and the subsequent frustrations of Argentina played out in the development of the Trafficking Protocol. The significance of the CRC with regard to trafficking is that it is the only contemporary international human rights treaty to refer explicitly to trafficking apart from CEDAW.[100] The former Special Rapporteur on Trafficking indicates that the CRC is the main reference for the trafficking of children, with the OPSC holding particular relevance (Fig. 4.3).[101] Under Article 34 of the CRC;

Article 34 however fails to provide any clarification as to how a State is supposed to protect children from sexual exploitation. Focusing upon the vagueness of the provisions may seem pedantic since the intention

---

[98] Note—although the 2003 Nigerian Child Rights Act was passed at a federal level, it is only effective is state assemblies also enact it. As of February 2013, 10 of the country's 36 states had yet to pass the Act. See further Twum-Danso Imoh (2014, 14). Almost a decade later this has increased to 24/36 states—see further, Child Rights—National Human Rights Commission (nigeriarights.gov.ng) (https://www.nigeriarights.gov.ng/focus-areas/child-rights.html). Accessed September 2022.

[99] See further J. Sloth-Nielson, 'Domestication of children's rights in national legal systems in African context: Progress and prospects', in J. Sloth-Nielson (ed.), *Children's Rights in Africa: A legal perspective* (Farnham and Burlington, VT: Ashgate, 2008).

[100] Article 6—States Parties shall take all appropriate measures, including legislation, to suppress all forms of traffic in women and exploitation of prostitution of women.

[101] UN Human Rights, Office of the High Commissioner, International Standards, http://www.ohchr.org/EN/Issues/Trafficking/Pages/Standards.aspx. Accessed April 2018.

> States Parties undertake to protect the child from all forms of sexual exploitation and sexual abuse. For these purposes, States Parties shall in particular take all appropriate national, bilateral and multilateral measures to prevent:
>
> (a) The inducement or coercion of a child to engage in any unlawful sexual activity;
>
> (b) The exploitative use of children in prostitution or other unlawful sexual practices;
>
> (c) The exploitative use of children in pornographic performances and materials.

Fig. 4.3 Article 34 of the Convention of the Rights of the Child 1989

was to produce a Convention that was sufficiently broad enough to allow relative flexibility. However, consideration needs to be given as to whether the continual failure to provide specific definitions is proving detrimental to children. The main achievement of Article 34 is that it draws attention to sexual exploitation, an area which many states would often prefer to remain an underground issue (Humbert, 2009, 77). It has been noted that the qualification of sexual activities and sexual exploitation as 'unlawful', and subsequently to be prohibited under the CRC, is a major disadvantage. Furthermore, it could be argued, in light of the Suppression of Trafficking Convention 1949, that the prostitution of children under eighteen is per se unlawful. There is a compelling argument that with the consent of a child who is sexually emancipated, prostitution would be legal under the CRC (Humbert, 2009, 77).

Article 35 states that 'States Parties shall take all appropriate national, bilateral and multilateral measures to prevent the abduction of the sale of or traffic in children for any purpose or in any form'. Similarly, like CEDAW, which fails to define "all appropriate measures", Article 35 does not provide any illustration as to what it means or what obligations it specifically imposes upon States. The *Travaux Préparatoires* to the CRC reveals that besides national measures, bilateral and multilateral measures were considered necessary due to the international ramifications of the sale of, or traffic in, children (Detrick, 1999, 602).

Articles 34 and 35 are especially related, as the sale or traffic of children does occur for the purposes of sexual exploitation.[102] It is important

---

[102] As demonstrated by the findings of the UNODC Global Report on Trafficking in Persons 2012, 4.

to note that it was initially felt that the abduction of, sale of, or traffic in, children should be dealt with in a separate article of the CRC (Detrick, 1999, 598). It could be contested that this was reflective of a shift from the perception that trafficking and prostitution are synonymous. This perspective acknowledged the fact that the problem was and remains wider in scope than that of sexual exploitation (Detrick, 1999, 589). In contrast to the Suppression of Traffic Convention 1949, Article 35 does not link the prohibition of the sale of, and traffic of, children to prostitution; therefore, demonstrating a move away from the traditional understanding of trafficking.

Article 35 fails to explicitly state what 'for any purpose or in any form' means; it is intentionally vague. This vagueness of definition is unfortunately not a new issue; such debates surround numerous aspects of international human rights law. Consider then, how can States be held to account for their legal systems if the benchmark they are being measured against is not sufficiently defined? (Buck, 2014, 270). It is pivotal that States understand exactly what the international law requires of them if the international human rights legal system is to have any hope of influencing and attaching consequences to their actions (Gallagher, 2011, 8).

Pursuant to Article 35, states parties assume the obligation to prevent the abduction of, the sale and traffic of, children for any purpose or in any form, with the distinction between 'the abduction of children' and the 'illicit transfer and non-return of children abroad', which is dealt with earlier in the CRC.[103] Subsequently, as the CRC applies to all forms of trafficking, it thereby complements article 11 of the CRC which only applies to international abductions, following the UN's traditional mandate and focus upon the international sphere. A major importance of Article 35 is that it is the first international provision prohibiting the trafficking in children for the purposes of adoption (Humbert, 2009, 78). Trafficking for adoption is not an issue isolated to the contemporary world, with the League of Nations and Temporary Slavery Commission commenting on the cultural practice of adoption.

---

[103] Article 11, this article refers to parental abduction across international borders.

The relationship between Articles 34 and 35 has been mentioned earlier, but it is important to acknowledge that Article 35 is also especially related to Article 32 that deals with the economic exploitation of children. Articles 34 and 35 of the CRC clearly lay down the obligations of states parties to protect the child from all forms of sexual exploitation, sexual abuse, abduction, sale and trafficking. The major flaw of the CRC is its failure to define the terms "abduction", "sale" and "trafficking". Therefore, the exact scope and applicability of Article 35 is brought into question, despite its relatively clear incorporation of the obligations upon states parties. These obligations go beyond requiring the states party to punish offenders after the trafficking has occurred but also to prevent trafficking from occurring, therefore creating obligations with a horizontal effect (Humbert, 2009, 77).

The comprehensive framework provided by the CRC for the protection of the rights and dignity of children, as well as of their empowerment, should be considered in its entirety as a tool for understanding and responding to the trafficking and related exploitation of children (Gallagher, 2011, 65). One of the major strengths that have been attributed to the Convention is its ability to be used as a framework for understanding and measuring child trafficking and related commercial sexual exploitation of children in the broadest possible context.[104] The issue here is the consolidation of the perspective that commercial sexual exploitation is synonymous with trafficking. Article 35 aims at the prevention of the sale and traffic of children and constitutes the first broad and sufficiently binding framework for the potential effective control of international trafficking in children (Humbert, 2009, 78). However, this perceived "effective control" has failed to come into fruition over 20 years since adoption and over a decade after Humbert's analysis.

Article 11 promotes both bilateral and multilateral agreements to fight against the illicit transfer and non-return of children. Articles 32, 34, and 36 emphasise that children must be protected from every form of economic, sexual, or any other kind of exploitation. With Article 19

---

[104] According to a UNICEF sponsored report 'Children and prostitution: How can we measure the commercial sexual exploitation of children? A literature review and annotated bibliography" (UNICEF, 2nd Edition, 1996).

of the CRC linking exploitation to safeguards on the prevention and protection from violence against children, calling for a comprehensive child protection system.

Whilst Article 39 recognises the right of the child to physical and psychological recovery and social reintegration if they have been subjected to any forms of exploitation and abuse. Yet research which involves accounts and lived experiences of children highlights how deeply problematic being pulled out of their work when the intervening measures in Articles 24, 25, 26, 27, 28, and 32 of the CRC have not been put into place (Okyere, 2014, 101). The potential of such action may as identified by Okyere (2014, 101) push them into further distress rather than help them and was amply demonstrated in the often-cited care of the Harkin Bill[105] and Bangladeshi children working in garment factories (Rahman et al., 1999).

So where does the CRC leave us in terms of identifying child trafficking? Aside from the exploitation-focused provisions; the CRC contains a broad range of rights covering, civil, political, economic, social, and cultural rights of children, offering trafficked children access to adequate accommodation, health, including recovery from trauma, and education, as well as the protection of their personal integrity and liberty[106] (Sax, 2018, 257). However, the CRC fails to provide an authoritative definition of trafficking; leaving it open to interpretation, the danger being that trafficking is not understood in all its manifestations. And, the ambiguity does allow for broad definitions, which offer greater flexibility to the respective national frameworks in drawing up definitions of the acts to be penalised. The perception that trafficking and prostitution are synonymous has been detrimental to the understanding of trafficking, with the legacy of fears of "white slavery" influencing contemporary law and policy responses. The CRC has subsequently been

---

[105] Child Labour Deterrance Act (1993) USA. See further Mohammad Mafizur Rahman, et al. 'Child labor in Bangladesh: A critical appraisal of Harkin's Bill and the MOU-type schooling program', *Journal of Economic Issues*, 33, no. 4 (1999), 985–1003. JSTOR, http://www.jstor.org/stable/4227511. Accessed 21 October 2022.

[106] See further (in terms of general/structural measures of child rights implementation) UN CRC Committee, General Comment No. 5 (2003), UN-Doc CRC/GC/2003/5 (27/11/2003)—ranging from legal reform to co-ordination of all levels of government, adoption of national strategies, and developing a research agenda.

complemented by the Optional Protocol on the Sale of Children (hereafter, the OPSC) which set specific standards on criminalisation of these practices, investigation, mutual legal assistance, and international cooperation, as well as protection rights to assistance, safety, and privacy, and it is to the OPSC that our focus will shift to.

The Optional Protocol on the Sale of Children (OPSC)

Shortly after the drafting of the CRC, the issue of child sexual exploitation, particularly sex tourism, became of great concern. Subsequently, the United Nations appointed its first Special Rapporteur on the sale of children, child prostitution, and child pornography in 1990.[107] The former Special Rapporteur was concerned about whether the Convention on the Rights of the Child was sufficient to tackle child sexual exploitation, and by 1994, the UN Commission on Human Rights[108] had created a working group to examine the possibility of an Optional Protocol to the Convention on the Rights of the Child specifically related to the issue of (commercial) sexual exploitation.[109]

The Optional Protocol to the Convention on the Rights of the Child on the sale of children, child prostitution, and child pornography (hereafter, the OPSC) was adopted and opened for signature, ratification, and accession by the General Assembly resolution A/RES.54/263 of 25 May 2000, entering into force on 18 January 2002.[110] The preamble to the OPSC notes the grave concern at the 'significant and increasing international traffic of children for the purpose of the sale of children, child prostitution and child pornography'. Moving on to assert that the

---

[107] See further, https://www.ohchr.org/Documents/Issues/Children/SR/E-CN4-RES-1990-68.pdf. Accessed August 2021.

[108] The UN Commission on Human Rights (UNCHR) was replaced by the UN Human Rights Council (UNHRC) in 2006.

[109] UN Commission for Human Rights, need to adopt effective international measures for the prevention and eradication of the sale of children, child prostitution and child pornography, resolution 1994/90, 66th meeting (9 March 1994).

[110] State Parties 177, Signatory 8, and No. Action 12, https://indicators.ohchr.org/. Accessed June 2021.

'elimination of the sale of child, child prostitution and child pornography will be facilitated by adopting a holistic approach, addressing the contributing factors' such as the trafficking of children.

The OPSC[111] differs from the CRC in that it is more specific in terms of its definitions and its obligations on signatory States. The OPSC goes beyond the CRC in several important respects, in particular adopting an explicitly criminal justice approach and in detailing obligations accordingly (Gallagher, 2011, 67). Moreover, the OPSC has quickly established itself as the leading instrument specifically designed to tackle forms of child sexual exploitation.

Article 3 of the OPSC, marked a shift away from the focus of the Trafficking Protocol which specifically focused upon transnational organised crime and the violation of State sovereignty through crossing a national border, in addition to the explicit requirement of the involvement of 'organised criminal gangs'. Article 3 reads as follows (Fig. 4.4).

The listing of sexual exploitation first explicitly shows the continued view that trafficking and commercial sexual exploitation are synonymous. This perception is problematic in that it potentially hinders the successful identification of, and subsequent support provided to those the law purports to protect. Another interesting link between the 1910 Convention and the OPSC can be identified. The 1910 International Convention for the Suppression of White Slave Traffic imposed an obligation on the parties to punish anyone who recruited a young woman, below the age of majority, into prostitution, even with her consent. This resonates with the OPSC, broadly falling in line with the provisions of an instrument adopted almost a century after the former. Indicating that almost a century later, a change in language has occurred but not necessarily in relation to the ideology and moral panic surrounding child trafficking.

---

[111] OPSC had 121 signatories and 176 ratifications as of 8 October 2019.

Article 3

1. Each State Party shall ensure that, as a minimum, the following acts and activities are fully covered under its criminal or penal law, whether these offences are committed domestically or transnationally or on an individual or organized basis:

    (a) In the context of sale of children as defined in Article 2:

248

Volume 2171, A-27531

    (i) The offering, delivering or accepting, by whatever means, a child for the purpose of:

        a. Sexual exploitation of the child;

        b. Transfer of organs of the child for profit;

        c. Engagement of the child in forced labour;

    (ii) Improperly inducing consent, as an intermediary, for the adoption of a child in violation of applicable international legal instruments on adoption;

    (b) Offering, obtaining, procuring or providing a child for child prostitution, as defined in Article 2;

    (c) Producing, distributing, disseminating, importing, exporting, offering, selling or possessing for the above purposes child pornography as defined in Article 2.

2. Subject to the provisions of a State Party's national law, the same shall apply to an attempt to commit any of these acts and to complicity or participation in any of these acts.

3. Each State Party shall make these offences punishable by appropriate penalties that take into account their grave nature.

4. Subject to the provisions of its national law, each State Party shall take measures, where appropriate, to establish the liability of legal persons for offences established in paragraph I of the present Article. Subject to the legal principles of the State Party, this liability of legal persons may be criminal, civil or administrative.

5. States Parties shall take all appropriate legal and administrative measures to ensure that all persons involved in the adoption of a child act in conformity with applicable international legal instruments.

Fig. 4.4 Article 3 optional protocol on the sale of children, child prostitution, and child pornography

4.5 Summary

This chapter has sought to examine the international instruments that have been adopted over the course of the last century to address slavery and human trafficking. In addition to focusing upon the child-specific framework implemented under the auspices of the United Nations and a brief overview into some of the contemporary global action to address the phenomena. The slow process of creating and agreeing upon an Optional Protocol to the CRC created frustrations for the state of Argentina which took this to the negotiating table for the Palermo Protocol, an instrument that was drafted and adopted at an unprecedented pace. This amalgamation of anti-trafficking and anti-slavery law and policy has a powerful impact upon those frameworks are implemented in order to protect.

Although the explicit racism of the anti-trafficking instruments at the start of the twentieth century has been left behind, the legacy of race, colonialism, and patriarchy remains strong within the international legal framework adopted to address human trafficking and modern slavery. The unique appeal of the cause to fight modern slavery has seeped into the international arena, poisoning civil society with a moral crusade to end the 'trade in human misery' and free the slaves. Without addressing the structural factors and inequalities that plague contemporary society.

References

Adu-Gyamfi, J., & Keating, F. (2013). Convergence and Divergence between the UN convention on the rights of the children and the African Charter on the rights and welfare of the child. *Sacha Journal of Human Rights, 3*(1), 47–58.

Akhtar, R., & Nyamutata, C. (2020). *International child law*. Routledge.

Alderson, P., & Morrow, V. (2004). *Ethics, social research and consulting with children and young people*. Barnados.

Allain, J. (2008). *The Slavery Convention: The travaux preparatoires of the 1926 League of Nations convention and the 1956 United Nations convention*. Martinus Nijhoff Publishers.

Allain, J. (2012). *The legal understanding of slavery: From the historical to the contemporary*. Oxford University Press.

Allain, J. (2013). *Slavery in international law: Of human exploitation and trafficking*. Martinus Nijhoff Publishers.

Allain, J. (2017). White slave traffic in international law. *Journal of Trafficking and Human Exploitation, 1*(1), 1–40.
Allain, J. (2018). Genealogies of human trafficking and slavery. In R. Piotrowicz et al. (Ed.), *Routledge handbook of human trafficking*.
Allain, J. (2021). The histories of slavery and international law. In P. Ismard (Ed.), *Une histoire mondial de l'esclavage*. Editions de Seuil.
Allain, J., & Hickey, R. (2012). Property and the definition of slavery. *The International and Comparative Law Quarterly, 61*(4), 915–938.
Anderson, B. (2007). *Motherhood, apple pie and slavery: Reflections on trafficking debates*.
Anderson, B., & O'Connell Davidson, J. (2003). *Is trafficking in human beings demand driven?* IOM.
Anne, T. G. (2015). Two cheers for the trafficking protocol. *Anti-Trafficking Review, 4*, 14.
Bachand, R. (2010). Critical approaches and the third world: Towards a global and radical critique of international law. In *McGill University*.
Balagopalan, S. (2018). Colonial modernity and the 'child figure': Re-configuring the multiplicity in 'multiple childhoods. In T. S. Saraswathi (Ed.), *Childhoods in India traditions, trends and transformations*. Routledge.
Bassiouni, M. C. (1991). Enslavement as an international crime. *New York University Journal of International Law & Politics, 23*(2), 445.
Bhahba, J., & Dottridge, M. (2016). *Recommended principles to guide actions concerning children on the move and other children affected by migration*.
Boister, N. (2003). "Transnational Criminal Law"? *European Journal of International Law, 14*(5), 953–976.
Brace, L., & O'Connell Davidson, J. (Eds.). (2018). *Revisiting slavery and antislavery: Towards a critical analysis*. Palgrave Macmillan.
Brewer, H. (2005). *By birth or consent: Children, law, and the Anglo-American revolution in authority*. Chapel Hill, North Carolina; Published for the Omohundro Institute of Early American History and Culture, Williamsburg, Virginia by the University of North Carolina Press.
Brown, V. (2009). Social death and political life in the study of slavery. *The American Historical Review, 114*(5), 1231–1249.
Brown, J. A. C. (2019). *Slavery and islam*. Oneworld Academic.
Buck, T. (2014). *International child law* (3 ed.). Routledge.
Bunting, A., & Quirk, J. (Eds.). (2017). *Contemporary slavery: The rhetoric of global human rights campaigns*. Cornell University Press.

Charnley, H., & Nkhoma, P. (2020). Moving beyond contemporary discourses: Children, prostitution, modern slavery and human trafficking. *Critical and Radical Social Work, 2*(8), 205–221.

Charnysh, V., Lloyd, P., & Simmons, B. A. (2015). Frames and consensus formation in international relations: The case of trafficking in persons. *European Journal of International Relations, 21*(2), 323–351.

Chuang, J. (2021). Preventing human trafficking: The role of the IOM and the UN global compact on migration. In G. Lebaron, et al. (Eds.), *Fighting modern slavery and human trafficking: History and contemporary policy*. Cambridge University Press.

Chuang, J. A. (2014). Exploitation creep and the unmaking of human trafficking law. *The American Journal of International law, 108*(4), 609–649.

Chuang, J. (2015). The challenges and perils of reframing trafficking as 'modern-day slavery.' *Anti-Trafficking Review, 5*, 146.

Committee on the Rights of the Child. (2003). *General Comment No. 5 (2003) General measures of implementation of the Convention on the Rights of the Child*.

Craig, G., et al. (Eds.). (2019). *The modern slavery agenda: Policy, politics and practice in the UK*. Policy Press. https://www.bristoluniversitypress.co.uk

Cryer, R., Robinson, D., & Vasiliev, S. (2019). *An introduction to international criminal law and procedure* (4th ed.). Cambridge University Press.

Cullen, H. (2006). 'Siliadin v France': Positive obligations under article 4 of the European Convention on Human Rights. *Human Rights Law Review, 6*(3), 585–592.

de Waal, A. (2002). Realising child rights in Africa: Children, young people and leadership. In A. de Waal & N. Argenti (Eds.), *Young Africa: Realising the rights of children and youth*. Africa World Press.

Demleitner, N. V. (1994). Forced prostitution: Naming an international offense. *Fordham International Law Journal, 18*(1), 163.

Derbes, B. J. (2013). "Secret horrors": Enslaved women and children in the Louisiana state penitentiary, 1833–1862. *The Journal of African American History, 98*(2), 277–290.

Detrick, S. (1999). *A commentary on the United Nations Convention on the Rights of the Child*. Martinus Nijhoff Publishers.

Doezema, J. (2010). *Sex slaves and discourse masters: The construction of trafficking*. Zed Book.

Dottridge, M. (2017). Trafficked and exploited: The urgent need for coherence in international law. In P. Kotiswaran (Ed.), *Revisiting the law and governance of trafficking, forced labour and modern slavery*. Cambridge University Press.

Dottridge, M. (2021). Between theory and reality: The challenge of distinguishing between trafficked children and independent child migrants. *Anti-Trafficking Review, 16*, 11–27.

Durisin, E. M., & van der Meulen, E. (2021). The perfect victim: 'Young girls', domestic trafficking, and anti-prostitution politics in Canada. *Anti-Trafficking Review, 16*, 145–149.

European Court of Human Rights. (2022). *Factsheet—Slavery, servitude and forced labour.*

Faulkner, E. A. (2019). Historical evolution of the international legal responses to the trafficking of children—A critique. In J. Winterdyk & J. Jones (Eds.), *The Palgrave international handbook of human trafficking.* Palgrave.

Faulkner, E. A., & Nyamutata, C. (2020). The decolonisation of children's rights and the colonial contours of the convention on the rights of the child. *The International Journal of Children's Rights, 28*(1), 66–88.

Fenwick, H., & Fenwick, D. (2018). The case for a more ready resort to derogations from the ECHR in the current "war on terror". *European Human Rights Law Review, 4*, 303–310.

Finley, M. I. (1964). Between slavery and freedom. *Comparative Studies in Society and History, 6*(3), 233–249.

Freamon, B. K. (1998). Slavery, freedom, and the doctrine of consensus in Islamic jurisprudence. *Harvard Human Rights Journal, 11*, 1.

Gallagher, A. T. (2012). *The international law of human trafficking.* Cambridge University Press.

Gallagher, A. T. (2015). Two cheers for the trafficking protocol. *Anti-trafficking review, 4*, 14.

Galliie, M. (2008). Les theories tiers-mondistes du droit international (TWAIL). Un renouvellement? *Revue ktudes internationales, 39*(1), 17–38.

Gill, N., & Good, A. (2019). *Asylum determination in Europe ethnographic perspectives* (1st ed.). Springer International Publishing.

Gill, N. et al. (2019). *Asylum determination in Europe ethnographic perspectives* (1st ed.). In N. Gill & A. Good (Eds.). [Online]. Springer Nature.

Graupner, H., et al. (2006). *Adolescence, sexuality and the criminal law: Multidisciplinary perspectives* (Vol. 8). Routledge Journals, Taylor & Francis Group Ltd.

Haag, Pamela (2000). *Consent: Sexual rights and the transformation of American liberalism (Ithaca: Cornell University Press, 1999* (Vol. 87). Organization of American Historians.

Hathaway, J. C. (2008). The human rights quagmire of "human trafficking." *Virginia Journal of International Law, 49*(1), 1.

Howard, N. (2017). *Child trafficking, youth labour mobility and the politics of protection.*
Humbert, F. (2009). *The challenge of child labour in international law* (Vol. 64). Cambridge University Press.
Ibhawoh, B. (2007). Second world war propaganda, imperial idealism and anti-colonial nationalism in British West Africa. *Nordic Journal of African Studies, 16*(2), 221–243.
ILO, UNICEF, & UN. (2009). *Training manual to fight trafficking in children for labour, sexual and other forms of exploitation.*
Kotiswaran, P. (Ed.). (2018). *Revisiting the law and governance of trafficking, forced labor and modern slavery.* Cambridge University Press.
Knaus, K., Kartusch, A., & Reiter, G. (2000). *Combat of trafficking in women for the purpose of forced prostitution.*
Lassen, N. (1988). Slavery and slavery-like practices: United Nations standards and implementation. *Nordic Journal of International Law = Acta scandinavica juris gentium, 57*(2), 197–227.
Lauren, P. (1998). 'A very special moment in history', New Zealand's role in the evolution of international human rights. *New Zealand International Review, XXIII*(6), 2–9.
Lauterpacht, H. (1950). *International law and human rights.* Stevens.
Lawrence, B. (2014). *Amistad's orphans: An Atlantic story of children, slavery, and smuggling.* Yale University Press.
League of Nations. (1925). *Temporary slavery commission letter from the chairman of the commission to the president of the council and report of the commission.*
Lerche, J. (2007). Global alliance against forced labour? Unfree labour, neo-liberal globalization and the International Labour Organization. *Journal of Agrarian Change, 7*(4), 425–452.
Meillassoux, C. (1991). The anthropology of slavery: The womb of iron and gold. *Ufahamu, 19*(2–3), 3–21.
Miers, S., & Kopytoff, I. (1977). *Slavery in Africa historical and anthropological perspectives.* Wisconsin University Press.
Moeckli, D., Shah, S., & Sivakumaran, S. (2018). *International human rights law.* Oxford University Press.
Mutua, M. (2000). What is TWAIL? *American Society of International Law. Proceedings of the Annual Meeting. 94,* 31–38.
Mutua, M. (2001). Savages, victims, and saviors: The metaphor of human rights. *Harvard International Law Journal, 42*(1), 201.

Mutua, M. (2002). *Human rights: A political and cultural critique.* University of Pennsylvania Press. http://www.jstor.org/stable/j.ctt3fhtq0

Mutua, M. (2007). Standard setting in human rights: Critique and prognosis. *Human Rights Quarterly, 29*(3), 547–630.

Ngokwey, N. (2004). Children's rights in the Central Africa sub-region: Poverty, conflicts and HIV/AIDS as context. *The International Journal of Children's Rights, 12*(3), 183–216.

Nicholson, A. (2010). Reflections on Siliadin v. France: Slavery and legal definition. *The International Journal of Human Rights, 14*(5), 705–720.

Obokata, T. (2019). Human trafficking in Africa: Opportunities and challenges for the African Court of Justice and human rights. In K. Clarke et al. (Ed.), *The African court of justice and human and peoples' rights in context: Development and challenges.* Cambridge University Press.

O'Connell Davidson, J. (2005). *Children in the global sex trade.* Polity Press.

O'Connell Davidson, J. (2015). *Modern slavery: The margins of freedom.* Palgrave Macmillan.

OHCHR, U.N. (1991). *OHCHR, Fact Sheet No.14 contemporary forms of slavery.*

Okyere, S. (2014). Children's participation in prohibited work in Ghana and its implications for the Convention on the Rights of the Child. In A. Twum-Danso Imoh & N. Ansell (Eds.), *Children's lives in an era of children's rights: The progress of the Convention on the Rights of the Child in Africa.*

Oude Breuil, B., & Gerasimov, B. (2021). Editorial: Trafficking in minors: Confronting complex realities, structural inequalities, and agency. *Anti-Trafficking Review* (16), 1–9.

Patterson, O. (1982). *Slavery and social death: A comparative study.* Harvard University Press.

Piotrowicz, R. W., Rijken, C., & Uhl, B. H. (2018). Trafficking in transnational criminal law. In Anonymous (Ed.), *Routledge handbook of human trafficking* (1st ed.). Routledge.

Pupavac, V. (1997). Theories of conflict and children's rights. In *2nd Convention of the European association for the advancement of social sciences & nbsp.*

Quirk, J. (2006). The anti-slavery project: Linking the historical and contemporary. *Human Rights Quarterly, 28*(3), 565–598.

Quirk, J. (2007). Trafficked into slavery. *Journal of Human Rights, 6*(2), 181–207.

Quirk, J. (2009). New approaches to combating modern slavery. *Human Rights Quarterly, 31*(1), 257–267.

Quirk, J. (2011). *The anti-slavery project: From the slave trade to human trafficking.* University of Pennsylvania Press.

Quirk, J. (2012). Defining slavery in all its forms: Historical inquiry as contemporary instruction. In J. Allain (Ed.), *The legal understanding of slavery: From the historical to the contemporary.* Oxford University Press.

Quirk, J., & Rossi, B. (2022). Slavery and marriage in African societies. *Slavery & Abolition, 43*(2), 245–284.

Qvortrup, J., Corsaro, W., & Honig, M. (2009). *The Palgrave handbook of childhood studies* (1st ed.). Palgrave Macmillan UK.

Radhika Coomaraswamy. (2000). *Report of the Special Rapporteur, MS. Radhika Coomaraswamy, on violence against women, its causes and consequences, on trafficking in women, women's migration and violence against women.* UN Commission on Human Rights.

Rahman, M. M., Khanam, R., & Absar, N. U. (1999). Child labor in Bangladesh: A critical appraisal of Harkin's Bill and the MOU-Type Schooling Program. *Journal of Economic Issues, 33*(4), 985–1003.

Ramina, L. (2018). TWAIL—"Third World Approaches to International Law" and human rights: Some considerations. *Revista de Investigações Constitucionais, 5*(1), 261–272.

Rassam, A. Y. (2005). International law and contemporary forms of slavery: An economic and social rights-based approach. *Penn St. Int'l L. Rev., 23,* 809.

Reanda, L. (1991). Prostitution as a human rights question: Problems and prospects of United Nations Action. *Human Rights Quarterly, 13*(2), 202–228.

Renzikowski, J. (2019). *Kelsen versus Kant on the nature of law.* https://doi.org/10.1163/9789004390393_008

Reynolds, P., Nieuwenhuys, O., & Hanson, K. (2006). Refractions of children's rights in development practice: A view from anthropology—Introduction. *Childhood (Copenhagen, Denmark), 13*(3), 291–302.

Rota, M. (2020). On the definition of slavery. *Theoria (Lund, Sweden), 86*(5), 543–564.

Sax, H. (2018). Child trafficking—A call for rights-based integrated approaches. In R. Piotrowicz et al. (Eds.), *Routledge handbook of human trafficking.* Routledge.

Schacht, J. (1975). *An introduction to Islamic law.* Oxford: Clarendon Press.

Secretary General. (1924). *Question of slavery: Resolution adopted by the assembly at its meeting held on Monday, September 22nd, 1924.*

Segrave, M., Milivojevic, S., & Pickering, S. (2018). *Sex trafficking and modern slavery: The absence of evidence* (2nd ed.). Routledge.

Shaw, M. N. (2021). *International law*. Cambridge University Press.
Sinha, M., & Sturman, R. (2008). *Specters of mother India: The global restructuring of an empire* (vol. 20).
Sloth-Nielsen, J. (2008). *Children's rights in Africa: A legal perspective*. Routledge.
Tambe, A. (2019). *Tropical exceptions: Racial logics in twentieth century intergovernmental age of consent debates*. https://culturalstudies.ucsc.edu/2019/03/23/may-29-2019-ashwini-tambe-tropical-exceptions-racial-logics-in-twentieth-century-intergovernmental-age-of-consent-debates/
The Commission of Human Rights. (1990). *Sale of children*.
Twum-Danso Imoh, A. (2014). Realizing children's rights in Africa. In A. Twum-Danso Imoh & N. Ansell (Eds.), *Children's lives in an era of children's rights: The progress of the Convention on the Rights of the Child in Africa*. Routledge.
UN Commission on Human Rights (52nd sess.: 1996: Geneva). (1996). *Contemporary forms of slavery, updated review of the implementation and follow-up to the convention on slavery*. UN Commission on Human Rights.
UNICEF. (1996). *Children and prostitution: How can we measure the commercial sexual exploitation of children? A literature review and annotated bibliography*.
United Nations. *Travaux Préparatoires of the negotiations for the elaboration of the United Nations Convention against Organized Crime and the Protocols thereto*.
UNODC. *Background information ad hoc committee on the elaboration of a convention against transnational organized crime*. https://www.unodc.org/unodc/en/treaties/CTOC/background/adhoc-committee.html
van Doore, K. E. (2016). Paper orphans: Exploring child trafficking for the purpose of orphanages. *The International Journal of Children's Rights, 24*(2), 378–407.
Waites, M. (2005). *The age of consent: Young people, sexuality and citizenship*. Palgrave Macmillan.
Weissbrodt, D., & Anti-Slavery International. (2000). *Contemporary forms of slavery: Updated review of the implementation of and follow-up to the conventions on slavery*.

5

Child Trafficking: Contemporary Action in the Twenty-First Century

5.1 Introduction

The task of providing an extensive and authoritative overview of the contemporary action to eradicate modern slavery and human trafficking falls outside the parameters of this book. However, for illustrative purposes this chapter will aim to provide an overview of some of the contemporary action undertaken at the international level since the adoption of the Trafficking Protocol in 2000. The United Nations system prima facie is a large and responsible institution, with a degree of autonomy, however, the power and influence of the wealthy donor governments can be problematic (Dottridge & Howard, 2017). This section will consider some examples of contemporary action at the international level, starting with the Sustainable Development Goals of (hereafter, the SDGs) 2015 and finishing with an overview of some of the child trafficking cases that have been prosecuted within different jurisdictions around the world utilising data from the UNODC's Human

Trafficking Case Law Database.[1] The ILO and UNICEF, coupled with the mandates of the relevant Special Rapporteurs form a key component of this review of contemporary action. It should be commented that the various organisations of the UN such as the ILO and UNICEF can perhaps be better understood as competing companies as 'on everything that has to do with human trafficking, it's really been out and out naked, capitalist competition' (Dottridge, 2018).

5.1.1 The Contemporary Anti-Trafficking Crusaders

Contemporary antislavery and anti-trafficking crusaders—from Ivanka Trump to Boris Johnson—frequently invoke histories of slavery and the heroic efforts to combat it led by powerful white men like William Wilberforce and Abraham Lincoln (Kotiswaran, 2018; Lebaron & Pliley, 2021, 5; O'Connell Davidson, 2015). No doubt, these invocations aim to inspire and ignite antislavery efforts by positioning contemporary activism as part of a valiant multi-century struggle for freedom (Lebaron & Pliley, 2021, 5). However, these invocations have been flagged by historians such as Pliley (2021), Duane and Meiners (2021), Peck (2021) and Beutin (2017) about the 'misuse of history and how it can be distorted by contemporary antislavery efforts' (Lebaron & Pliley, 2021, 5). Moreover, the cross-partisan consensus appeal generated by the fight against forced labour, human trafficking, and modern slavery raises the issue of how to relate to such efforts is a complex and contradictory one for scholars and activists alike.

Fighting human trafficking and modern slavery over the last two decades has become a 'cause célébre,' (LeBaron & Pliley, 2021, 1). Similar to the increased visibility of poverty as an urgent global social problem in the final decades of the twentieth century 'as a result of democratization inspired and mobilized by iconic figures from Bill Gates to Bono' (O'Connell Davidson, 2015, 10). Poverty, ignorance, trickery,

---

[1] Case Law Database (https://sherloc.unodc.org/cld/en/v3/sherloc/cldb/index.html?lng=en). Accessed December 2022.

and 'the corruption of tradition' are frequently identified as the agency-denying dominant cause factors that drive trafficking (Howard, 2017). As 'poverty action is a key part of how millennials create a sense of self as a global citizen' (Roy, 2012). In a similar vein, the appeal of modern slavery allows for civil society and governments from both the left and right ends of the spectrum to champion the fight. With Kevin Bales (2013) asserting that 'a disease of our common being' that we can wipe out 'the way that we've wiped out smallpox'. Or in the eloquent words of O'Connell Davidson (2015, 11) 'freeing slaves is joyous, cheap and hugely personally rewarding—WE CAN ALL BE HEROES' in the words of Free the Slaves in 2013.

Moreover,

> *Multinational corporations host panels about fighting modern slavery at the World Economic Forum, UN Summits and rock music festivals. A motley civil society coalition of antislavery activists, students, churches and conservative anti-feminist organizations have banded together to eradicate slavery with an arsenal ranging from "slave raids" to awareness-raising campaigns. This coalition has spent billions of dollars on projects that promise to end slavery in our lifetime.* (LeBaron & Pliley, 2021, 1)

Policymakers and anti-trafficking campaigners who approach trafficking from a concern with immigration or crime control tend to argue that the term 'trafficked' should be extended to all migrants who end up in forced labour and slavery-like situations 'no matter how people arrive in these conditions' (Martins & O'Connell Davidson, 2022, 543). The current regime of national state control over human mobility is designed for the purposes of excluding "unwanted" people (Sharma, 2020). Indeed, borders are the 'product of histories of violent territorial expansion, settler colonialism, and slavery, histories that also produced racism' (Walia, 2021).

5.2 Global Sustainable Development Goals (SDGs)

The Sustainable Development Goals (hereafter, the SDGs) intrigue my intellectual curiosity. They have infiltrated many aspects of life. With a demonstrable 'strong interest in, and response to, the SDGs by governments, businesses and organisations in most countries'.[2] The SDG's are not going to disappear too soon, even if the targets to eradicate numerous social ills by 2030 pass by without coming to fruition. A prominent example can be found in the activities of universities globally. The position of universities in relation to knowledge production here is important, it interacts with the undercurrents of race, class, caste, nationality, gender, inequalities, poverty, and the legacies of colonialism in today's globalised world. The active response of universities globally to the SDG agenda is illustrated through the UN's Sustainable Development Solutions Network (SDSN) Northern Europe, which brings together more than 60 universities to 'identify and fill knowledge gaps, provide high-quality education for sustainable development, and provide advice and solutions for the transformation to a sustainable society'.[3] Keele University (UK) for example has posters around campus highlighting current activities such as 'The Beauty Bank' which collects spare unopened toiletries and beauty products for local food banks and refugee centres. In 2019, over 1000 items were collected and donated, providing a feel-good factor, and allowing the university to demonstrate its commitment to SDG 1 'No Poverty' and SDG 10 'Reduced Inequalities' respectively. You may wonder what relevance does this have to our discussion of contemporary action and child trafficking? It has everything to do with the appeal of acting "good", helping those in need or indeed

---

[2] Executive Summary, Australia, New Zealand Pacific Edition 'Getting Started with the SDGs in Universities: A Guide for Universities, Higher Education Institutions and the Academic Sector', University-SDG-Guide_web.pdf (https://ap-unsdsn.org/wp-content/uploads/University-SDG-Guide_web.pdf). Accessed October 2022.

[3] SDSN Northern Europe Connected and Committed to Sustainable Development (https://www.unsdsn-ne.org/). Accessed September 2022.

to be specific rescuing and saving children. But more importantly, it is to do with money. As identified the SDGs will be a major influencer on the strategies and actions of these stakeholders (governments, businesses and organisations) 'as well as on the development of finance flows—over the next 15 years'.[4] This fact coupled with the 'feel-good' factor or appeal to altruistic feeling is something that underlies the powerful appeal of contemporary efforts to eradicate child trafficking and modern slavery and is a key driver behind the anti-trafficking machine.

So, what are the Sustainable Development Goals? In 2015, the adoption of the 17 Sustainable Development Goals (SDGs) set a renewed development framework, the 2030 Agenda for Sustainable Development. Improving the capacity to deliver reliable data and statistics plays a significant role in this context. Each Goal includes indicators to measure improvements towards the agreed targets. However, such indicators can give an undue illusion of objectivity and reliability when they are neither neutral nor detached. The purpose of this section of the book is not to undertake an extensive review of the SDGs, but to consider and critique the ones of relevance to child trafficking and modern slavery, predominately SDG 8.7. Notably, trafficking appears in several goals, 'that puts them under the patronage of other institutions as well. So immediately there is enhanced competition, in this case between UN organisations' (Dottridge, 2018). I appreciate that other SDG's reference trafficking such as goal 5, which aims to eliminate all forms of violence against all women and girls in the public and private spheres, including trafficking and sexual and other types of exploitation, as well as to eliminate all harmful practices, such as child, early and forced marriage and female genital mutilation.[5] Another example can be found under Goal 16 which aims to end abuse, exploitation, trafficking, and all forms of violence against and torture of children. The SDG 16.2 can be linked to article

---

[4] Executive Summary, University-SDG-Guide_web.pdf (https://ap-unsdsn.org/wp-content/uploads/University-SDG-Guide_web.pdf). Accessed October 2022.

[5] The Special Rapporteur reports on combating and preventing the sale and sexual exploitation of children through the implementation of the Sustainable Development Goals from a child rights perspective to the General Assembly (A/73/174 and Corr.1) (17 July 2018).

37 of the Convention on the Rights of the Child, which also requires States parties to ensure that no child is subjected to torture or other cruel, inhuman, or degrading treatment or punishment. Whilst article 19 of the CRC contains a broader provision for the protection of children from mental and physical abuse. The SDG indicator 16.2 specifically calls upon Member States to end abuse, exploitation, trafficking, and all forms of violence and torture against children. Moreover, indicator 16.2.2 requires Member States to measure the number of victims of human trafficking per 100,000 population, by sex, age, and form of exploitation. To report on this indicator, Member States must gather trafficking data using defined methodologies to estimate the total number of trafficking victims.

The focus will now shift to consider SDG 8.7 which requires States to take measures to eradicate forced labour, end modern slavery and human trafficking and secure the prohibition and elimination of the worst forms of child labour, which includes the sale and/or the sexual abuse of a child through prostitution or for illicit activities.[6] This target invokes article 32 of the CRC, which prohibits any work that could impair the child's development, and article 35, which forbids the sale of children for any purpose or in any form. Through SDG 8.7 world leaders committed to.

> *take immediate and effective measures to eradicate forced labour, end modern slavery and human trafficking and secure prohibition and elimination of the worst forms of child labour, including recruitment and use of child soldiers, and by the end of 2025 end child labour in all its forms.*

The global community of 193 States set a target to end slavery by 2030. You may wonder what is the issue with such a noble cause? Well, 'once you have a target which is intrinsically unachievable, everything thereafter is building on sand' (Dottridge, 2018). The text of SDG 8.7 sets out an extensive list of commitments which highlights specific issues of concern such as forced labour, human trafficking, modern slavery. Each of those issues are crimes and umbrella terms existing at the far end of what Jens Lerche identifies as the "spectrum" of labour exploitation

---

[6] A/77/140 25.

(Lerche, 2007, 435). Goal 8 calls for immediate and effective measures to eradicate forced labour, end modern slavery and human trafficking and secure the prohibition and elimination of the worst forms of child labour, including recruitment and use of child soldiers, and by 2025 end child labour in all its forms. A further issue with goal 8.7 is that it throws a lot of jargon into the mix, in addition to the exclusion of survivors, whose 'voices are not yet at the heart of anti-slavery strategy' (Trodd et al., 2021, 203). However, 'no blueprint for achieving these objectives, nor any indicators set for SDG 8.7 except one around child labour' were identified (Trodd et al., 2021, 203). One of the actions taken in the step towards achieving SDG 8.7 has been the creation of Alliance 8.7, which is an 'inclusive global partnership committed to achieving target 8.7 of the 2030 Sustainable Development Goals'.[7] The focus of Alliance 8.7 is identified through their strategic objectives, namely accelerating action, conducting research and sharing knowledge and driving innovation, and leveraging resources.[8]

The inappropriateness of aiming to eradicate all child labour by 2025 conflicts with the central ethos of the CRC in relation to the agency of children, in addition to being unachievable. Moreover, 'successive targets and deadlines set by global leaders for meeting children's rights to adequate standards of living, education, healthcare, and other provisions have floundered in high-, middle-, and low-income countries alike' (Howard & Okyere, 2022). The aim to eradicate child labour does not correlate with what may be in the best interests of working children. This point has been highlighted clearly through the statistics published by the International Labour Organization. The focus upon child labour 'in all its forms' is problematic and illustrates the Western and romanticised ideals of childhood that shape and inform international law and policy. How such an arbitrary and unrealistic target to eradicate all child labour by 2025 was settled upon is unclear. What is clear is the simplistic idea that if you rescue or remove children from work, whether in agricultural or industrial locations and unequivocally improve their lives. What happens to those children or adolescents? If you simply remove

---

[7] ALLIANCE 8.7 (https://www.alliance87.org/the-alliance/). Accessed October 2022.
[8] Ibid.

all children and from all forms of 'child labour' what next? As illustrated by research conducted in Ghana, Dominican Republic, Bangladesh, and Myanmar,[9] if children are rescued from work but there are no schools or recourse for the lost income, whom is being helped by this noble rescue mission? The danger of the SDGs is that provide simplistic solutions to complex problems but as highlighted will play a significant role in the allocation of funding to tackle issues such as child labour, trafficking, and exploitation. This preoccupation with eradicating child labour is replicated through the focus of Alliance 8.7. SDG 8.7 targets specific harms perpetrated against children through the recruitment and use of child soldiers and the eradication of child labour by 2025, however, what this aim neglects to recognise is how child labour is perceived as a "harm" through a western lens (Faulkner & Nyamutata, 2020, 74). Targets to eradicate child labour serve as a catalyst for the creation of and perpetuation of "unintended harms" perpetrated against children; those whom the measures seek to protect. For example, the elimination of child labour from factories could lead to an increase in adult employment and wage rates, but might also negatively affect children's welfare if there are no adequate schools available and the children's only remaining option is to undertake more hazardous work in the 'informal sector' of the economy (Anker, 2000, 264). Empirical research illustrates a different perception of "child labour" from the children that are undertaking such labour. In Ghana, children's views show that poverty is the key driver behind their work in artisanal mining (Okyere, 2014, 92). For some commentators, the goals to eradicate modern slavery (8.7) and forced marriage (5.3) respectively 'cannot be achieved in isolation, but require a multi-SDG approach, one that accounts for simultaneous vulnerability factors' (Trodd et al., 2021, 211). And who better to undertake such a mission than actors from the Global North?

The SDGs can be observed as a mechanism that endorse imperial approaches to the rights of children, particularly with regards to child labour (Faulkner & Nyamutata, 2020, 74). Furthermore, the image of

---

[9] Clothes, Chocolate and Children—Department of Politics—University of Liverpool (https://www.liverpool.ac.uk/politics/research/research-projects/ccc/). Accessed October 2022.

child labour is too often portrayed as a phenomenon principally relevant to the developing countries (Akthar & Nyamutata, 2020, 275) whereas there is evidence of child labour in industrialised Europe, the USA, and other developed nations (Kilkelly, 2003; Selby, 2008). The ILO definitions are useful in understanding the nuances of children and work. However, there is no universally accepted definition of 'child labour'. Have we passed a tipping point where "unintended harms" can no longer be classed as such due to the wealth of research illustrating the harms of measures upon children?

5.3 The International Labour Organization (ILO)

The International Labour Organization (hereafter ILO) is a specialist agency of the United Nations charged with developing and enforcing labour standards. Founded in 1919, with the centenary of the organisation passing in 2019,[10] which saw the ILO actively encouraging researchers via their own Centennial Project to mine its archives 'to produce histories on a range of topics—for example, child labour—including big questions related to globalization, colonialism, the Cold War and development' (Boris & Rodriguez Garcia, 2021, 195). Both the League of Nations and the ILO indirectly addressed the issue of prostitution, with the latter considering prostitution a by-product of women emigrating without men in search of work (Boris, 2019, 17–52) and protection framed the ILO responses to commercial sex (Boris & Rodriguez Garcia, 2021, 197). Both the League of Nations and ILO would cite authority in their founding documents to address social evils. With Article 23C of the Covenant of the League of Nations entrusting the organisation with the monitoring international agreements on the trafficking of women and children,[11] whilst the ILO

---

[10] See further ILO 100 | The ILO Centenary (https://www.ilo.org/100/en/). Accessed December 2022.
[11] With the League of Nations establishing an Advisory Committee on the Traffic in Women and Children, which included a representative from the ILO see further Pliley (2010).

constitution charged it with protecting workers against disease and establishing labour standards (Boris & Rodriguez Garcia, 2021, 197).

From the 1930s, several more international Conventions which were often associated with the growing influence of the ILO which 'addressed differing aspects of slavery focusing on the position of children as well as adults' (Craig & Clay, 2017). The ILO Convention of 1930 (No. 29) defined forced or compulsory labour as 'all work or service which is exacted from any person under the menace of any penalty and which is exacted from any person under the menace of any penalty and for which the said person has not offered himself voluntarily'[12] The ILO viewed slavery as an integral part of the world of labour,[13] and 'its tripartite structure prescribed representation by governments, employers and workers, whilst the anti-traffic committee was made up of official delegates and representatives of private organizations dedicated to the fight against trafficking' (Rodriguez Garcia, 2012, 434).

In 1999 the ILO, passed the Convention on the Worst Forms of Child Labour[14] (hereafter, the WFCL Convention) At the time WFCL Convention appeared, the ILO estimated that 250 million children were at work, with some 80 million involved in what it refers to as 'the worst forms of labour' (NGO Group, 2001, 5). Article 2 of the WFCL Convention[15] defines a child as a person under the age of 18. This can be contrasted immediately with the CRC, which, whilst suggesting that the age of majority should be 18, allows that it can be lowered by domestic legislation.

The Preamble asserts that the

> *effective elimination of the worst forms of child labour requires immediate and comprehensive action, taking into account the importance of free basic*

---

[12] Article 2 (1).

[13] CTE/2nd Session/PV.17, Minutes of the Temporary Slavery Commission, second session, 22 July 1925, 6.

[14] International Labour Organization, Prohibition and Immediate Action for the Elimination of the Worst Forms of Child Labour Convention, ILO Convention No. 182 (17 June 1999). This Convention had 187 ratifications as of June 2021. https://www.ilo.org/dyn/normlex/en/f?p=1000:11300:0::NO:11300:P11300_INSTRUMENT_ID:312327. Accessed June 2021.

[15] See further Akthar and Nyamutata (2020) ICL for details on child labour within the international legal framework.

> For the purposes of this Convention, the term **the worst forms of child labour** comprises:
>
> (a) all forms of slavery or practices similar to slavery, such as the sale and trafficking of children, debt bondage and serfdom and forced or compulsory labour, including forced or compulsory recruitment of children for use in armed conflict;
>
> (b) the use, procuring or offering of a child for prostitution, for the production of pornography or for pornographic performances;
>
> (c) the use, procuring or offering of a child for illicit activities, in particular for the production and trafficking of drugs as defined in the relevant international treaties;
>
> (d) work which, by its nature or the circumstances in which it is carried out, is likely to harm the health, safety or morals of children.

Fig. 5.1 Article 3 worst forms child labour convention (C182)

education and the need to remove the children concerned from all such work and to provide for their rehabilitation and social integration while addressing the needs of their families.

The clear Western construction of childhood and perspective to children engaged in labour markets emerges, endorsing the focus upon the rescue of such children. Simplistic noble aims to 'save the children from the fields and place them into education' neglect and ignore local, cultural, and community understandings of children, childhood, and labour.[16]

The Instrument explicitly refers to trafficking in two distinct contexts within Article 3, the full text of which is contained within Fig. 5.1.

Article 7 of the WFCL Convention commits States parties, *inter alia*, to take measures to prevent a child's involvement in the worst forms of child labour and to aid those children who are working Accompanying the Convention is a recommendation that provides guidance to signatory States on how to implement the Convention. The Recommendation includes, for example, the suggestion that criminal offences should be invoked to tackle those who employ children in the worst forms of

---

[16] See further ATR 2021—CHILDHOOD IN ITS PLACE. Chocolate, clothes Stalford et al. project.

labour,[17] and Protocols on how information should be fed back to the ILO. An advantage of the Convention on the Worst Forms of Child Labour is that it brings together not just governments but also employers, NGOs, and trade unions. You may wonder why is this important? This global collaboration forms part of the broader global action upon eradicating harms perpetrated against children. Although the ILO intimated in 2009 that recruiting children to work before the minimum age should be regarded as 'trafficking', this is not part of the UN Protocol's definition of child trafficking[18] (Dottridge, 2021, 14).

5.3.1 International Programme on the Elimination of Child Labour (IPEC)

The ILO's International Programme on the Elimination of Child Labour (hereafter, the IPEC) was created in 1992 with the overall goal of the progressive elimination of child labour, which was to be achieved through strengthening the capacity of countries to deal with the problem and promoting a worldwide movement to combat child labour.[19] Whilst the goal of IPEC remains the prevention and elimination of all forms of child labour,[20] the priority targets for immediate action are the worst forms of child labour, which are defined in the ILO Convention on the worst forms of child labour, 1999 (No. 182).[21] The webpage of IPEC highlights that 'In line with Sustainable Development Target 8.7. IPEC+ focuses on the elimination of child labour in all its forms by 2025

---

[17] R190—Worst Forms of Child Labour Recommendation, 1999 (No. 190), Recommendation concerning the prohibition and immediate action for the elimination of the worst forms of child labour. Adoption: Geneva, 87th ILC session (17 June 1999), para. 12.

[18] See further ILO, UNICEF, and UN. GIFT, Training Manual to Fight Trafficking in Children for Labour, Sexual and Other Forms of Exploitation, Textbook 1: Understanding child trafficking, 2009). Moreover, public opinion and law enforcement agencies in many developing countries do not accord the same importance to respecting the minimum age set by national law and international conventions, which international organisations are bound to use as their point of reference.

[19] About the International Programme on the Elimination of Child Labour (IPEC) (https://www.ilo.org/ipec/programme/lang--en/index.htm). Accessed October 2022.

[20] Ibid.

[21] See further Fig. 5.1.

and the eradication of forced labour, modern slavery and human trafficking by 2030'.[22] At the time of writing it is unequivocally clear that neither of these targets will be met, which raises questions about why unachievable targets in relation to children are continually created. The increased ratification of both Conventions no.138 and 182 coupled with the 'intensification of child labour abolitionist efforts led by the ILO' (Howard & Okyere, 2022) respectively, the statistics of the ILO paint a different reality. For example, the number of children estimated by the ILO to be in conditions of illegal or hazardous work fell by only 3% between 2008 and 2012 and 1% between 2012 and 2016 (ILO, 2017, 11). Based on this rate of decline, by even the most optimistic assessment, at least 52 million children will still be found in hazardous work in 2025 (ILO, 2017, 11), when all such cases should have been 'eradicated', according to Target 8.7 of the Sustainable Development Goals (SDGs).

5.4 The Special Rapporteurs of the United Nations

This section will briefly consider the role of three Special Rapporteurs,[23] namely the Special Rapporteur on the sale and sexual exploitation of children, the Special Rapporteur on trafficking in persons, especially women and children and the Special Rapporteur on contemporary

---

[22] International Programme on the Elimination of Child Labour (IPEC) (https://www.ilo.org/ipec/lang--en/index.htm).

[23] Note the activities of the UN Special Representative of the Secretary-General on Violence Against Children (SRSG) (https://violenceagainstchildren.un.org/). Accessed October 2022 the SRSG is a global independent advocate in favour of the prevention and elimination of all forms of violence against children. The SRSG acts as a bridge builder and a catalyst of actions in all regions, and across sectors and settings where violence against children may occur, and the Special Representative of the Secretary-General for Children and Armed Conflict. The mandate of the Special Representative of the Secretary-General for Children and Armed Conflict was created by General Assembly resolution A/RES/51/77 (http://www.un.org/ga/search/view_doc.asp?symbol=A/RES/51/77%26Lang=EArea=UNDOC) following the publication, in 1996, of the report by Graça Machel on the impact of armed conflict on children (https://childrenandarmedconflict.un.org/mandate/the-machel-reports/).

forms of slavery, **including its causes and consequences**.[24] A Special Rapporteur is a title that are given to **independent experts** whose expertise is appointed by the Human Rights Council (formerly the U.N. Commission on Human Rights) with the mandate to monitor, advise and publicly report on human rights situations in specific countries (country mandates) and on human rights violations worldwide (thematic mandates). The thematic mandates cover a wide range of issues relating to civil, cultural, economic, political, and social rights, including the human rights of migrants, violence against women, the rights of internally displaced persons, freedom of religion, and arbitrary detention, amongst many others.[25] The most important issue is the mandate given to the expert as it is formulated in the resolutions of the Commission on Human Rights. These mandates could focus on reporting on violations, or on analysing a problem, or on assisting in the provision of technical assistance or on a combination of one or more of these features.[26] *The Special Rapporteurs are part of what is known as the Special Procedures*[27] *of the Human Rights Council. Special Procedures, the largest body of independent experts in the UN Human Rights system, is the general name of the Council's independent fact-finding and monitoring mechanisms that address either specific country situations or thematic issues in all parts of the world.*[28]

The Special Rapporteurs[29] have been particularly critical of the UK government's current shift in its approach to human trafficking and modern slavery. Issuing a joint statement in December 2022 asserting that the demonisation of victims of trafficking and modern slavery

---

[24] OHCHR I Special Rapporteur on contemporary forms of slavery (https://www.ohchr.org/en/special-procedures/sr-slavery). Accessed October 2022.

[25] Fact Sheet No. 27: Seventeen Frequently Asked Questions about United Nations Special Rapporteurs (Archive) (2001). Accessed October 2022.

[26] Ibid.

[27] OHCHR I Special Procedures of the Human Rights Council (https://www.ohchr.org/en/special-procedures-human-rights-council). Accessed October 2022.

[28] *Special Procedures' experts work on a voluntary basis; they are not UN staff and do not receive a salary for their work. They are independent from any government or organization and serve in their individual capacity.*

[29] Mr. Tomoya Obokata, Special Rapporteur on contemporary forms of slavery, including its causes and consequences; Ms. Siobhán Mullally, Special Rapporteur on trafficking in persons, especially women and children; Mr. Felipe González Morales, Special Rapporteur on the human rights of migrants.

'erodes public sympathy for measures to protect them and may lead to attacks on these groups by extremists', UN experts warned today, urging the UK to step up efforts to protect survivors.[30]

5.4.1 Special Rapporteur on the Sale and Sexual Exploitation of Children, Including Child Prostitution, Child Pornography, and Other Child Sexual Abuse Material

The UN Special Rapporteur SEC (formerly, the Special Rapporteur on the sale of children, child prostitution and child pornography) is mandated to analyse the root causes of sale and sexual exploitation of children, identify new patterns of the phenomena, exchange good practices to combat it, promote measures to prevent it, and make recommendations for the rehabilitation of child victims of sale and sexual exploitation. The mandate of the Special Rapporteur was created in 1990 and is the only mandate of the UN Special procedures system with an exclusive focus on children.[31] This is interesting given the explicit shift to create a separate legal framework of children's rights om the one hand but the failure to create an SR to exclusively focus on children as their mandate. This is perhaps due to the establishment of the Committee of the Rights of the Child but is worth commenting upon. The creation of the Special Rapporteur in this period reflects the fears and concerns of international policymakers with the commercial sexual exploitation of children and child sex tourism. Since its establishment, the mandate has been regularly renewed. In its resolution 7/13, the Human Rights Council mandated the Special Rapporteur, through visits and exchange of communications with Governments, to:

---

[30] UK: UN experts condemn attacks on credibility of slavery and trafficking victims | OHCHR (https://www.ohchr.org/en/press-releases/2022/12/uk-un-experts-condemn-attacks-credibility-slavery-and-trafficking-victims). Accessed December 2022.
[31] E-CN4-RES-1990-68.pdf (https://www.ohchr.org/sites/default/files/E-CN4-RES-1990-68.pdf). Accessed October 2022.

- Analyse the root causes of the sale of children, child prostitution, and child pornography
- Address all the contributing factors, including demand
- Identify new patterns of sale of children, child prostitution, and child pornography
- Identify, exchange, and promote best practices on measures to combat the sale and sexual exploitation of children
- Promote comprehensive strategies and measures to prevent the sale and sexual exploitation of children
- Make recommendations on the promotion and protection of human rights of children, actual or potential victims, as well as on the rehabilitation of child victims of sale and sexual exploitation
- Integrate a gender perspective throughout the work of the mandate.[32]

You will note that the issue of "child trafficking" is not explicitly mentioned. However, within a series of recent reports to emerge from the SR the issue of child trafficking is explicitly identified. For example, within the 2022 Report[33] trafficking is mentioned on 28 occasions with references to modern slavery and a call to 'end modern slavery' also emerging within the document. The 2022 Report observes that 'Protracted conflicts and emerging new ones are pushing millions of children into human trafficking, sale and exploitation.'[34] In addition to referencing how 'orphanage trafficking is one form of trafficking and modern slavery to which children in institutional care may be exposed for exploitation and profit'. The office of the SR has been relatively proactive upon its focus of child trafficking and related sexual exploitation. This operational focus can be determined by the mandate that has been adopted but indicates that attitudes and perceptions that trafficking is synonymous with sexual exploitation remain.

In terms of operation, to discharge the mandate, the Special Rapporteur will visit several countries (Buck, 2014, 169) to have policy-level

---

[32] https://ap.ohchr.org/documents/E/HRC/resolutions/A_HRC_RES_7_13.pdf.   Accessed October 2022.
[33] A/77/140 Accessed via N2242099.pdf (https://documents-dds-ny.un.org/doc/UNDOC/GEN/N22/420/99/PDF/N2242099.pdf?OpenElement). Accessed October 2022.
[34] Ibid.

discussions and consider how the States parties are discharging their obligations under OPSC. The Special Rapporteur produces an annual report to the Human Rights Council (for example the former SRSC Boer-Buquicchio, 2019[35]) which in turn reports to the UN General Assembly. Buck, whilst observing the valuable work that the Special Rapporteur performs, notes that a difficulty is that the office is under-resourced (2014, 170). The mandate of the Special Rapporteur has been underfunded since its creation and has operated without a specific budget from the Human Rights Council.[36] This is even though the mandate passed by the Human Rights Council requests the Secretary-General of the United Nations and the High Commissioner for Human Rights to 'provide all the human, technical and financial assistance' needed by the Special Rapporteur.[37] The under-resourcing of the office means that the Special Rapporteur is limited in the amount of research that can be commissioned and visits conducted. Ideally it would be beneficial for there to be an 'Office of the Special Rapporteur' that would employ a (small) number of staff to also conduct visits, commission and interpret research. Instead, a single mandate holder is in place and, whilst her role is invaluable, it does mean that its use is somewhat limited. Another problem with the Special Rapporteur is the extent to which it can be said that countries cooperate with her office. Despite States being requested to cooperate with the Special Rapporteur it does not appear that this always occurs.[38]

---

[35] Report of the Special Rapporteur on the Sale of Children, Child Prostitution and Child Pornography (2019) A/HRC/40/51, Sale and Sexual Exploitation of Children in the Context of Sports, 30.
[36] United Nations Special Rapporteur on the Sale of Children, Child Prostitution and Child Pornography (2016) 25 Years Fighting the Sale and Sexual Exploitation of Children: addressing new challenges: V.
[37] Human Rights Council, Mandate of the Special Rapporteur on the sale of children, child prostitution and child pornography, Resolution 7/13, 40th meeting (27 March 2008), para. 5.
[38] See further Faulkner in Akhtar, Rajnaara/Nyamutata, Conrad, International Child Law, 2020.

5.4.2 Special Rapporteur on Trafficking in Persons, Especially Women and Children[39]

The next SR to consider is the Special Rapporteur on the Trafficking in persons, especially women and children. The emphasis of the office reflects the Palermo Protocol, through its linkage between 'women and children' as a vulnerable subclass requiring specific attention. At its sixtieth session, the UN Commission on Human Rights adopted decision 2004/110, by which it decided to appoint, for a three-year period, a Special Rapporteur on trafficking in persons, especially women and children, to focus on the human rights aspects of the victims of trafficking in persons. Perhaps this appointment emerged from reflection upon the criminal justice thrust of the Palermo Protocol and the neglect of victim focused measures created. In July 2020, the mandate of the Special Rapporteur was extended again for three years by Human Rights Council.[40] The Special Rapporteur on trafficking in persons is the only exclusively focused international human rights mechanism for combating human trafficking. In contrast to the child criminal focus of the legal apparatus, the mandate has a global reach, and engages widely with law and policy forums, and with civil society.

5.4.3 Special Rapporteur on Contemporary Forms of Slavery, Including Its Causes and Consequences[41]

In March 2020, the Human Rights Council appointed Professor Tomoya Obokata as the Special Rapporteur on contemporary forms of slavery, including its causes and consequences. Although it is perhaps pedantic to focus upon the language implemented, the title of the office does

---

[39] See further OHCHR | Special Rapporteur on trafficking in persons, especially women and childrenhttps://www.ohchr.org/en/special-procedures/sr-trafficking-in-persons.

[40] Resolution 44/4 A/HRC/RES/44/4 (https://documents-dds-ny.un.org/doc/UNDOC/GEN/G20/188/68/PDF/G2018868.pdf?OpenElement). Accessed October 2022.

[41] See further, OHCHR | Special Rapporteur on contemporary forms of slavery (https://www.ohchr.org/en/special-procedures/sr-slavery).

not demarcate 'women and children' as a distinct vulnerable category of concern, but the approach is reflective of a different approach. Arguably creating a level of flexibility to pursue, consider and incorporate structural factors and immigration policies and rhetoric into the frame. The role is relatively new, with the United Nations Human Rights Council establishing the mandate in 2007 through resolution 6/14.[42] This move was to replace the Working Group on Contemporary Forms of Slavery that had been established in 1974 in order to better address the issue of contemporary forms of slavery within the United Nations system.[43] This shift towards contemporary slavery is not isolated to operations at the international level, but is a shift that has been reflected through the increasingly used term "modern slavery".

5.5 Unicef

The United Nations Children's Fund was created by the General Assembly on 11 December 1946 to provide emergency food and healthcare for children in countries that had been devastated by the Second World War (Akthar & Nyamutata, 2020, 65). In 1953, UNICEF became a permanent part of the UN system, and its name was shortened (from the original 'United Nations International Children's Emergency Fund'), but it has continued to be known by the popular acronym based on the old name.

The role of UNICEF in relation to child trafficking is interesting and forms part of the global action to eradicate this amongst other harms perpetrated against children. For example, UNICEF has advocated that one of the major strengths of the CRC is its ability to be used as a framework for both measuring and understanding trafficking and the related commercial sexual exploitation of children in the broadest

---

[42] Human Rights Council (https://ap.ohchr.org/Documents/E/HRC/resolutions/A_HRC_RES_6_14.pdf). Accessed October 2022.

[43] OHCHR | Overview of the mandate (https://www.ohchr.org/en/special-procedures/sr-slavery/overview-mandate). Accessed October 2022.

context.[44] "Trafficking is a very real threat to millions of children around the world, especially to those who have been driven from their homes and communities without adequate protection," said UNICEF Executive Director Henrietta Fore. "These children urgently need governments to step up and put measures in place to keep them safe." UNICEF and Inter-Agency Coordination Group against Trafficking (hereafter, ICAT) believe the number of children who fall victim to trafficking is higher than current data suggests.[45] For example, a study published in 2007 by Benin's Ministry of Family and Children and UNICEF estimated that over 40,000 Beninese children were 'victims of trafficking' according to the new (2006) law and that each year almost 15,000 children were trafficked.[46]

5.6 The Anti-Trafficking Giant—Understanding the Role of the USA, (TIP)

The role of the USA (hereafter the USA) is significant for understanding the anti-trafficking machine, as it was the USA that had the greatest single impact upon the evolution of an international consensus on the definition of trafficking (Gallagher, 2012, 22). With Janie Chuang pointing to the response of the USA to human trafficking as one that embodies a "global sheriff" character. The TVPA is the 'centrepiece of a major US foreign policy initiative that involves global monitoring and support for anti-trafficking NGOs around the world' (Engle Merry, 2018, 274). With significant pressure to enforce anti-trafficking laws

---

[44] Children and Prostitution: How can we measure the Commercial Sexual Exploitation of Children? A literature review and annotated bibliography (UNICEF, 2nd edn., 1996).
[45] Press release (29 July 2018) Children account for nearly one-third of identified trafficking victims globally. https://www.unicef.org/press-releases/children-account-nearly-one-third-identified-trafficking-victims-globally. Accessed June 2021.
[46] Centre de Formation et de Recherche en matière de Population (CEFORP), Etude Nationale sur la Traite des Enfants. Rapport d'analyse, Ministère de la Famille et de l'Enfant et l'UNICEF, Cotonou, 2007.

> 'SEVERE FORMS OF TRAFFICKING IN PERSONS. —The term "severe forms of trafficking in persons" means—
>
> (A) sex trafficking in which a commercial sex act is induced by force, fraud, or coercion, or in which the person induced to perform such act has not attained 18 years of age; or
> (B) the recruitment, harboring, transportation, provision, or obtaining of a person for labor or services, through the use of force, fraud, or coercion for the purpose of subjection to involuntary servitude, peonage, debt bondage, or slavery'[1]

Fig. 5.2 TVPA definition of severe forms of human trafficking

emerging from the US, despite the apparent structural reasons for widespread lack of enforcement as identified by Bunting and Quirk (2017, 14).

So how does the Victims of Trafficking and Violence Protection Act (hereafter, the TVPA) classify and address human trafficking and why is it important? Firstly, the TVPA addresses human trafficking through a three-pronged approach of prevention, prosecution, and protection. The TVPA garnered bipartisan support and was passed on 28th October 2000 and included the creation of immigration relief for survivors of human trafficking.[47] Notably at the time of the drafting of the TVPA calls continued for restrictive immigration measures by members of Congress. Despite the 'increasingly restrictive immigration environment, lawmakers were able to create and entirely new immigration benefit for trafficking survivors—the T-visa' (Raza, 2023, 64). The TVPA definition of severe forms of human trafficking is contained within the following text box, Fig. 5.2.

The US State Department therefore views human trafficking as an umbrella term for a series of activities (Engle Merry, 2018, 274) in which 'one person obtains or holds another person in compelled service'. The TVPA describes "compelled service" using a variety of different terms

---

[47] See further E:\PUBLAW\PUBL386.106 (https://www.congress.gov/106/plaws/publ386/PLAW-106publ386.pdf). Accessed December 2022.

such as involuntary servitude, slavery, debt bondage, and forced labour (Office to Monitor and Combat Trafficking in Persons, 2010, 7–8).

According to the US Department of State, the TVPA 'provides the tools to combat trafficking in persons both worldwide and domestically'.[48] However, for some commentators the desire to protect women and children who look like us, i.e. white European women and children is explicitly clear (Raza, 2023). The stories drawn upon to illustrate the problem of human trafficking, drawing upon narratives of white Eastern European women with the work of Raza identifying that some 'lawmakers make clear the TVPA is a result of the impact European Sex Trafficking victims made on them' (Raza, 2023, 70). Consider the position advocated that the 'resemblance of women and girls trafficked to the wives and daughters of many policymakers may have been one factor in arousing attention to the trafficking issue'. This fear of white slavery has been explored earlier within this text, but it is worth pausing to reflect and consider the continued role of race within the context of anti-trafficking legislative responses. This continuation of an emphasis upon ideal victims, namely European women and children, those who are deserving victims, and of human rights protections. This reliance upon the differences between genuine human trafficking victims (European women and children) and 'fraudulent non-white immigrants, lawmakers perpetuated racial hierarchies which contribute to the projects of racialization' (Raza, 2023, 75). Patterns and continuities can be drawn between this context[49] surrounding the TVPA and the implementation of the Modern Slavery Act in the UK and the 'hostile environment' that dominates immigration policy.

---

[48] https://www.state.gov/international-and-domestic-law/. Accessed July 2020.
[49] Consider (as just one example) Title 42 [Title 42 | U.S. Customs and Border Protection (https://www.cbp.gov/document/foia-record/title-42)] which has enabled the US government to exert it's authority under Title 42 public health law to rapidly expel migrants, and in some cases suspend the right to seek asylum under US law and international law. The origins of Tile 42 come from the Trump administration, invoking title 42 shortly after the coronavirus outbreak. The purpose of title 42 was to prohibit border control agencies from holding migrants in "congregant settings" or holding stations where COVID19 could spread rapidly. In effect, title 42 gifted the government the power to rapidly expel any migrant, without giving them any opportunity to make a case for staying in the country legally, including to seek asylum.

Within the US trafficking was classed as a 'vehicle for the sexual exploitation of women and children',[50] with the trafficking of men and trafficking for the purposes of labour exploitation only acknowledged as less urgent aspects of the same phenomena. The focus upon sexual exploitation is explicit, as the TVPA separately identifies "sex trafficking" a term that has been picked up within popular culture and helped to strengthen social and cultural understandings of human trafficking and related exploitation. This is important, especially in relation to children as this entrenched perception of trafficking as "sex trafficking" invokes the ideology and rhetoric of fears of the 'White Slave Traffic'.[51] Domestically (in the US) the discourse upon human trafficking and the subsequent development of anti-trafficking laws are 'rooted in the United States' history of slavery, anti-miscegenation laws and racial difference' (Raza, 2023, 65).

The TVPA established the Office to Monitor and Combat Trafficking in Persons in the State Department and mandated annual reports on human trafficking and anti-trafficking efforts globally, the Trafficking in Persons (TIP) Reports were launched in 2001 and labelled as the:

U.S. Government's principal diplomatic tool to engage foreign governments on human trafficking, it is also the world's most comprehensive resource of governmental anti-trafficking efforts and reflects the U.S. Government's commitment to global leadership on this key human rights and law enforcement issue.[52]

The TIP reports were launched in 2001 and produced annually since by the US Department of State with the most recent report of 2021

---

[50] Gallagher (2012, 23).
[51] For the US context, see further the White-Slave Traffic Act of 1910 (often referred to as the Mann Act) which was a federal law that criminalised the transportation of "any woman or girl for the purpose of prostitution or debauchery, or for any other immoral purpose". See further Brian Donovan (2005) White Slave Crusades: Race, Gender and Anti-vice Activism, 1887–1917, University of Illinois Press; Jessica Pliley (2014) Policing Sexuality: The Mann Act and the Making of the FBI, Harvard University Press.
[52] https://www.state.gov/trafficking-in-persons-report/. Accessed August 2021.

highlighting the impact of the Covid19 epidemic upon the issue of trafficking.[53] The TIP Report, is according to some experts 'the most far reaching and comprehensive global review of human trafficking undertaken by a government' (Laczko & Gramegna, 2003, 179). The TIP report noted in 2014 and 2015 that children involved in ranching are 'vulnerable to trafficking', but without noting that they were part of entire families in debt bondage. Its 2016 edition contains no reference to this long-term pattern of near slavery (Dottridge, 2018). This point is of interest, as it indicates that trends emerge and disappear within the data collection. Another illustrative example is through the inclusion of orphanage trafficking in Nepal (van Doore, 2021), and that the TIP reports do include the employment of child soldiers[54] as a form of trafficking in persons, which no one else does.

Annually the report assesses the extent of human trafficking globally, the nature of trafficking, and the state and NGO efforts to deal with it in most of the countries in the world. The TIP creates a ranking system, based upon the efforts of states they are ranked into three tiers (Tiers 1–3 respectively) and a Tier Two Watch List. Falling into the bottom tier (Tier 3) results in being sanctioned by the USA, and those sanctions have included the 'withdrawal of humanitarian aid and non-trade related foreign assistance, exclusion of government employees from funding for cultural and educational exchange programmes, and the opposition of the USA to assistance from international financial institutions such as the IMF and World Bank' (Engle Merry, 2018, 279). Therefore, the TIP has influenced, or perhaps better classed as forced or pressurised numerous governments to take action in the form of the development of new anti-trafficking laws and to 'change their policies towards trafficking,

---

[53] See further TIP 2021. https://www.state.gov/reports/2021-trafficking-in-persons-report/. Accessed August 2021.

[54] Note the 'Child Soldiers Prevention Act List'—Which states that 'Sect. 402 of the Child Soldiers Prevention Act, as amended (CSPA) requires publication in the annual TIP Report of a list of foreign governments identified during the previous year as having governmental armed forces, police, or other security forces, or government-supported armed groups that recruit or use child soldiers, as defined in the CSPA.' Available via the Trafficking in Persons Report 2022.

whilst its substantial investment of resources supporting anti-trafficking NGOs has reshaped the domestic debates about the issue in many countries' (Engle Merry, 2018, 279). The influential nature of the TIP can be well demonstrated, allowing the US perception of trafficking and its concerns of sex trafficking to emerge as a dominant force in the anti-trafficking machine. This new form of imperialism under the guise of anti-trafficking is a prime example of the continued colonial legacy upon contemporary anti-trafficking. Critical accounts of the relationship between colonial legacies and the construction of knowledge upon human trafficking have been highlighted.

The TIP Reports have faced criticism from a range of academics, with Engle Merry identifying that it is a skewed and a politically driven tool of disputed effectiveness. Along with other global north ranking mechanisms that have emerged, the TIP seeks 'to measure human trafficking according to global North paradigms' (Kempadoo & Shih, 2022, 6). Moreover, Dottridge commented that the 'focus on national prevalence of human trafficking means that an entrenched pattern of exploitation is ignored' (Dottridge, 2018, 161). Additionally, the ability of the TIP to raise awareness of human trafficking and the power and capacity it has created to support anti-trafficking efforts globally are areas of growing concern (U.S. Government Accountability Office, 2006, 2007; Wooditch, 2011). The TIP however, remains:

> *the most authoritative report on the issue of human trafficking on a global scale ... its combined effect as an exercise of soft power and sheer extent of the coverage has the potential not only to shape this particular field in terms of policy development and priorities but, more importantly, to define the issue of human trafficking itself.*[55]

Of note, is that the phrase "modern slavery" is not a term used within the TIP reports. Moreover, the interconnection of the TIP report with the wider system of USA international development aid and the process through which the information contained in the Report is compiled

---

[55] Bouckli et al. (2023)—Faulkner. E.A. MSGC (BUP).

is problematic. The issue of knowledge production is not isolated to the realm of anti-trafficking, but the power and prominence of anti-trafficking projects that are supported (financially) by the USA and the extent to which type of knowledge produced by the report appears to legitimise and promote specific kinds of interventions corresponding to that type of knowledge.

This section has not been a definitive guide to the role of the USA in contemporary anti-trafficking but hoped to draw attention to the importance of that metaphorical role of "global sheriff". Indeed, the expansion of the global sheriff metaphor to understand how white supremacy, racism, and coloniality fortify the USA and global North empire (Kempadoo & Shih, 2022, 6) is essential to understand the anti-trafficking machine.

5.7   The International Criminal Court (ICC)

The International Criminal Court (hereafter, the ICC) 'investigates and where warranted tries individuals charged with the gravest crimes of concern to the international community: genocide, war crimes, crimes against humanity and the crime of aggression'.[56] The ICC, resides in the Hague, Netherlands, and includes over 900 employees from approximately 100 States and operates 6 official languages, English, French, Arabic, Chinese, Russian and Spanish.[57] The preamble of the Rome Statute proclaims that 'during this century millions of children, women, and men have been unimaginable atrocities that deeply shock the conscience of humanity.'[58] This shock might only of occurred due to the suffering of white European populations in wake of the first and second world wars.

---

[56] About the Court | International Criminal Court (https://www.icc-cpi.int/about/the-court). Accessed September 2022.

[57] Ibid.

[58] Rome Statute of the International Criminal Court | OHCHR (https://www.ohchr.org/en/instruments-mechanisms/instruments/rome-statute-international-criminal-court). Accessed September 2022.

Human trafficking, or the approaches to the issue can be categorised and, in this context, the criminal law approach under the ICC. This approach is hegemonic, and 'views trafficking as an exceptional aberration to otherwise normal circuits of commerce and exchange in a globalised world, thus warranting the use of the heavy, corrective hand of the criminal law' (Kotiswaran, 2019, 376). Prior to the adoption of the UN Trafficking Protocol, a 'renewed focus on issues of exploitation by international lawmakers' (Dottridge, 2018, 61). This point is evidenced by the adoption of the Rome Statute of the International Criminal Court in July 1998 in addition to the three international instruments which specifically focused upon children—Convention on the Worst Forms of Child Labour (Convention no. 182), and the two Optional Protocols to the Convention on the Rights of the Child, the OPSC and OPAC. This apparent focus warrants a discussion as to omit the ICC and its role in advancing international criminal law relating to enslavement and trafficking would be an error. The focus of this text upon child trafficking and the international legal developments, needs to recognise the interlinked yet distinct fields of international law that is evoked, in this context international criminal law as opposed to international human rights law. The prohibition of slavery in general international law is based within international human rights law and is therefore directed towards States. So, for example, the violation of that prohibition (of slavery) will invoke the international legal responsibility of the offending State. This contrasts with international criminal law, within which the process of *enslavement* is set out and defined within the context of war, carrying individual criminal responsibility. The meaning of enslavement is not necessarily the same as slavery. this distinction reflects fundamental differences between the international regimes of criminal law and human rights law, as the latter regimes has made clear the normative distinctions between various types and degrees of exploitation of enslavement.[59] A human rights approach to human trafficking seeks to mitigate the harshness of the criminal law regime by bolstering the human rights

---

[59] See further Jean Allain Mobilization of International Law to Address Trafficking and Slavery (2009) paper presented at the Joint Stanford-University of California Law and Colonialism Africa Symposium, March 19–21, 2009.

of victims of trafficking.[60] However, the 2000 UN Protocol to Prevent, Suppress and Punish Trafficking in Persons, Especially Women and Children (Trafficking Protocol)[61] itself arose from the alignment of geopolitical interests of developed countries to police borders in the wake of globalisation.

The Rome Statute of the ICC[62] focused upon war crimes and crimes against humanity and included provisions on enslavement, which is classed as a crime against humanity and 'enforced prostitution, forced pregnancy, enforced sterilisation, or any other form of sexual violence of comparable gravity'. Regarding consent, the Rome Statute moved the 'focus back onto the use of coercion, categorising "enforced prostitution" as a crime against humanity' (Dottridge, 2018, 66). In relation to the legal responses to slavery, it is important to note the differences between the international human rights legal framework implemented that addresses slavery and those under international criminal law. Article 7(1) (c) Rome Statute of the ICC identifies *enslavement* as a crime against humanity when committed as part of a widespread or systematic attack directed against any civilian population, with knowledge of the attack. The Rome Statutes definition of enslavement is identical to the one provided within the 1926 Slavery Convention, but with an addition labelled curious by Gallagher (2012, 184). Article 7(2) reads;

---

[60] As Gallagher notes, the UN Trafficking Principles and Guidelines issued by the UN High Commissioner for Human Rights in 2002 'provided a way forward that has supported the evolution of a cohesive "international law of human trafficking" which weaves together human rights and transnational criminal law': AT Gallagher, 'Two Cheers for the Trafficking Protocol' (2015) 4 Anti-Trafficking Review 21. In 2005, the Council of Europe adopted a Convention on Action against Trafficking in Human Beings whereby the criminal law thrust of anti-trafficking provisions was softened vis-a-vis the victims of trafficking who were often prosecuted for committing crimes when trafficked. Council of Europe, Council of Europe Convention on Action Against Trafficking in Human Beings (16 May 2005) CETS 197.

[61] Protocol to Prevent, Suppress and Punish Trafficking in Persons, Especially Women and Children, Supplementing the United Nations Convention Against Transnational Organized Crime (adopted 15 November 2000, entered into in force 25 December 2003) 2237 UNTS 319.

[62] Rome Statute of the International Criminal Court | OHCHR (https://www.ohchr.org/en/instruments-mechanisms/instruments/rome-statute-international-criminal-court). Accessed September 2022.

'Enslavement' means the exercise of any or all of the powers attaching to the right of ownership over a person and includes the exercise of such power in the course of trafficking in persons, in particular women and children.

What does this mean? Essentially, that the term enslavement could also refer to situations of human trafficking. Furthermore, the Rome Statute also elaborates upon the elements of the crime of enslavement, which is understood to be relevant to human trafficking. The Preparatory Commission for the International Criminal Court report of 2000 identified that the crime of enslavement is identified as including the exercise by the perpetrator of:

any or all of the powers attaching to the right of ownership over one or more persons, such as by purchasing, selling, lending or bartering such a person or persons, or by imposing on them a similar deprivation of liberty.[63]

So, what has the ICC done explicitly in relation to the trafficking of children? In a 2016 Report it stated that the 'Office recognises that most crimes under the Statute affect children in various ways, and that at times they are specifically targeted.' Moreover, the Office of the ICC indicated in 2020 that they 'have sought to systematically investigate and prosecute sexual and gender-based crimes and crimes against or affecting children'.[64] With a 2016 policy paper proclaiming that 'crimes directed specifically against children include: the war crimes of child recruitment and use, the forcible transfer of children as an act of genocide, and

---

[63] Preparatory Commission for the ICC, Report of the Preparatory Commission for the ICC, Abbendum, Part II Finalized Draft Text of the Elements of the Crime, UN Doc PCNICC/2000/1/Add.2 November 2nd, 2000 (ICC Elements of Crimes).

[64] Statement of ICC Prosecutor, Fatou Bensouda, on the occasion of this year's International Day for the Elimination of Violence against Women | International Criminal Court (https://www.icc-cpi.int/news/statement-icc-prosecutor-fatou-bensouda-occasion-years-international-day-elimination-violence). Accessed October 2022.

trafficking of children as a form of the crime against humanity of enslavement or sexual slavery'.[65] An explicit reference to children is included in Article 7(2)(c) of the Rome Statute, which defines enslavement as a crime against humanity under Article 7(1)(c) as: "the exercise of any or all of the powers attaching to the right of ownership over a person and includes the exercise of such power in the course of trafficking in persons, in particular women and children".[66] As recognised in the Elements, Article 7(1)(c) may also cover instances in which children are subjected to forced labour or reduced to a servile status.[67] The ICC is not alone in addressing children and trafficking/slavery with regional courts such as the ECHR and Inter-American Court of Human Rights providing rulings on cases in recent years.

5.8 The Inter-American Court of Human Rights (IACtHR): 'Hacienda Brasil Verde Workers V. Brazil' 2016

The Inter-American Court of Human Rights was established under the American Convention on Human Rights in 1969 (sitting in San

---

[65] ICC (2016) Policy on Children, Paragraph 19, p. 12.

[66] This definition is repeated in the Elements, which state, in Footnote 11 to this provision: "It is also understood that the conduct described in this element includes trafficking in persons, in particular women and children." This footnote cites the 1956 Anti-Slavery Convention. Article 1(d) of that treaty calls for the abolition, inter alia, of "[a]ny institution or practice whereby a child or young person under the age of 18 years, is delivered by either or both of his natural parents or by his guardian to another person, whether for reward or not, with a view to the exploitation of the child or young person or of his labour." Other treaties that may prove useful in the interpretation of this aspect of Article 7 of the Statute include the 2000 Protocol to Prevent, Suppress and Punish Trafficking in Persons, Especially Women and Children, supplementing the United Nations Convention against Transnational Organized Crime and the 2000 CRC-OPSC.

[67] One of the elements relating to Article 7(1)(c) under the Elements is: "The perpetrator exercised any or all of the powers attaching to the right of ownership over one or more persons, such as by purchasing selling, lending, or bartering such a person or persons, or by imposing on them a similar deprivation of liberty." Footnote 11 to this element clarifies in relevant part: "It is understood that such deprivation of liberty may, in some circumstances, include exacting forced labour or otherwise reducing a person to a servile status as defined in the Supplementary Convention on the Abolition of Slavery, the Slave Trade, and Institutions and Practices Similar to Slavery of 1956."

Jose, Costa Rica) but did not commence operations until 1979. The 'Hacienda case' is noteworthy as it is the first case heard by the court that dealt with slavery and had the potential to form important legal precedent within the region. That fact alone has not excused the decision of the Court from scrutiny, particularly relating to the structural racial discrimination and its complexity within Brazil and other countries in the region.[68]

The case concerned the slavery-like working conditions of workers, some of whom were children in a privately owned estate "Hacienda Brasil Verde" which was a cattle ranch located within the State of Para, Brazil. This case was about slave labour used by the "Hacienda" or farm from the 1980s until the early 2000s and the State of Brazil's repeated failure to stop the practice, punish those responsible and provide remedies for the victims. The Court found Brazil in violation of several articles of the Inter-American Convention on Human Rights,[69] whilst it declined to exercise jurisdiction over some violations because the facts occurred before Brazil's acceptance of the Court's jurisdiction. The Court unanimously held that Brazil had violated—Article 6(1) (Prohibition of Slavery, Slave-Trade, Traffic in Women and Involuntary Servitude), in relation to Articles 1(1) (Obligation of Non-Discrimination), 3 (Right to Juridical Personality), 5 (Right to Humane Treatment), 7 (Right to Personal Liberty), 11 (Right to Privacy), and 22 (Freedom of Movement and Residence) of the American Convention, to the detriment of the eighty-five workers rescued on March 15, 2000, as well as in relation to Article 19 (Rights of the Child) of the Inter-American Convention which stipulates:

> Every minor child has the right to measures of protection required by his condition as a minor on the part of his family, society, and the state.

---

[68] See further Hacienda Brasil Verde Workers v. Brazil: Slavery and Human Trafficking in the Inter-American Court of Human Rights | OHRH (https://ohrh.law.ox.ac.uk/hacienda-brasil-verde-workers-v-brazil-slavery-and-human-trafficking-in-the-inter-american-court-of-human-rights/). Accessed September 2022.

[69] Article 6(1) Prohibition of Slavery, Slave-Trade, Traffic in Women and Involuntary Servitude; Article 8(1) Right to a hearing Within Reasonable Time by a Competent and Independent Tribunal; Article 25 Right to Judicial Protection.

The Court found these violations to the detriment of Mr. Francisco da Silva (who was at the time a child when he worked and subsequently escaped from the Hacienda Brasil Verde).

5.9 The United Nations Office on Drugs and Crime: Human Trafficking Case Law Database

Although some data exist upon child trafficking, it does not provide the whole picture and as the focus of this book is upon legal frameworks and child trafficking it would be amiss to not incorporate some case law examples from around the world. In October 2011, the United Nations Office on Drugs and Crime launched the 'Human Trafficking Case Law Database' (hereafter, HTCLD) as a 'global public online tool to collect and disseminate information on human trafficking prosecutions and convictions from all over the world'.[70] The HTCLD, offers a search tool and when entering "child trafficking" in July 2022 generates 2125 cases. This section will not endeavour to analyse every result found as that unfortunately falls outside the remit of this book, but to gain a small insight into how different legal systems globally have responded to child trafficking cases five cases will be discussed in chronological order: namely from Malawi, Guatemala, Philippines, and Bosnia and Herzegovina. Each case has been selected as it captured my interest when reading through the recorded cases on the HTCLD but should not be taken as an authoritative example of human trafficking law in action in each state.

5.9.1 Labour Exploitation Case, Malawi, 2005

A 2005 case from Malawi simply identified in the HTCLD as 'Banda' (albeit with limited facts available) indicated that the accused trafficked

---

[70] See further Human Trafficking Case Law milestone (https://www.unodc.org/unodc/en/human-trafficking/Webstories2017/human-trafficking-case-law-milestone.html). Accessed July 2022.

ten children under the age of 14 for the purpose of labour exploitation.[71] There is very little further information available upon this case, with no additional information provided as to how or why the children under the age of 14 were trafficked, there age, gender, ethnicity, or class. Aside from a comment from the Malawi Law Commission on the effectiveness or ineffectiveness of the current legal regime nothing further is obtainable via the database. The Malawi Law Commission referred to this case in illustrating how the Employment Act (Malawi) was unable to adequately punish perpetrators of trafficking in persons even though the formulation of the provision was arguably broad enough to capture offences which verge on trafficking.[72]

5.9.2 Illegal Adoption Case, Guatemala, 2009

The case in Guatemala (Case No. 38-2009) is interesting due to whether it qualifies as child trafficking, with a one-month-old child taken for the purpose of illegal adoption. The case involved several women working in tandem through an organisation ostensibly for the protection of children in order to abduct children and funnel them into illegal adoptions. Notably, the appeals court made a point of awarding both material and moral damages to the appellant, the victim's mother, noting that it is "easy to appreciate that the consequences that this fact has left in her person and in her family are serious, difficult to repair and will force her to incur expenses for a considerable time to try to bring her life back to more or less normal…"[73] As a general comment, the *Travaux Préparatoires of the negotiations for the elaboration of the United Nations Convention against Organized Crime and the Protocols* thereto state that where illegal adoption amounts to a practice similar to slavery (as defined in Article 1, paragraph (d) of the Supplementary Convention on the Abolition of Slavery, the Slave Trade, and Institutions and Practices

---

[71] Republic v Masautoso Banda, Criminal Case No. 347 of 2005.
[72] Banda (https://sherloc.unodc.org/cld/case-law-doc/traffickingpersonscrimetype/mwi/banda.html?lng=en%26tmpl=sherloc). Accessed July 2022.
[73] Case No. 38-2009 (https://sherloc.unodc.org/cld/case-law-doc/traffickingpersonscrimetype/gtm/2009/case_no._38-2009.html?lng=en%26tmpl=sherloc). Accessed July 2022.

Similar to Slavery), it will also fall within the scope of the Trafficking in Persons Protocol.[74] This interpretative note suggests that the intention of the drafters was that illegal adoption without the purpose of exploitation of the child would not fall under the crime of trafficking in persons.

5.9.3 Sexual Exploitation Case, The Philippines, 2011

In 2011, in the Philippines[75] a case was heard within which the accused were charged with recruiting, transporting, and then maintaining, for the purpose of prostitution, pornography, or sexual exploitation eight females and one male—seven of whom were children aged between 14 and 17 at the time. The court heard testimonies from three of the adolescents and viewed their testimonies in full faith and credit. Moreover, the Court also found that even if the minors gave their consent, this does not absolve the criminal liability of the accused. Under the Trafficking Protocol, the omission of the means element in relation to children is key here and that logic is followed in this context by the Court. Subsequently, the Court held that the trafficking is deemed qualified because the trafficked persons were children, and it was committed against at least three persons.[76]

5.9.4 Begging and Labour Exploitation Case, Bosnia and Herzegovina, 2017

In 2017 in Bosnia and Herzegovina a case identifies six children between the ages of 8 and 14 who were trafficked to beg on the streets without adequate clothing or protection in extreme conditions,

---

[74] (p. 347).
[75] CRIM. CASE NO. CBU-86668, Regional Trial Court, 7th Judicial Region, Branch 6, Cebu City.
[76] CRIM. CASE NO. CBU-86668 (https://sherloc.unodc.org/cld/case-law-doc/traffickingpersonscrimetype/phl/2011/crim._case_no._cbu-86668.html?lng=en%26tmpl=sherloc). Accessed July 2022.

including temperatures below −15 °C.[77] The defendant (M.E.) directed the children to beg passers-by for money and set an expectation that they would each collect at least 10–20 BAM (equivalent to between 5 and 10 Euros) In addition to forced begging, M.E. also forced the children to work for a furniture company and collect raw materials such as iron from garbage sites. What is noteworthy in this case is that of the two initial defendants, one was alleged to be the mother of three of the victims involved in the case. The case initially involved two defendants, however after defendant S. A. (the mother of three of the victims) pleaded guilty to the charges, the judge separated the case against her, and given the gravity of the offence, the proceedings against her were continued before the Municipal Court Tuzla, which had subject matter jurisdiction.[78]

The focus here has been upon some specific case law examples from around the world to try and provide an insight into the range of approaches in different legal jurisdictions to the interrelated issues of child trafficking, exploitation, and perceptions of slavery. They have been selected for the fact that they presented something interesting to me whilst undertaking my research, rather than their significance in relation to the application of the law. What has not been considered is the role or work on regional court systems and how they have approached the phenomena. For example, the Inter-American Court of Human Rights (IACtHR) in the case Hacienda Brasil Verde Workers v. Brazil was the first ruling by the Court which specifically addressed slavery in the Americas.

5.10 Summary

This chapter intended to draw together contemporary action and the legal responses to child trafficking to illustrate how they operate in a complimentary, yet often conflicting fashion. The contemporary action is not limited to the organisations, instruments, and policies that are

---

[77] 030K016017 (2017) M. E. Case (https://sherloc.unodc.org/cld/case-law-doc/traffickingpersonscrimetype/bih/2017/030k016017_2017_m._e._case.html?lng=en%26tmpl=sherloc). Accessed July 2022.
[78] Ibid.

contained within this chapter, as a full analysis unfortunately falls beyond the scope of this book. However, the contemporary action to eradicate child trafficking is important. It serves as a complimentary cog in the theoretical framework of the anti-trafficking machine. This chapter has sought to illustrate the power of anti-trafficking initiatives, the global extent of such action as demonstrated by the various regional instruments that had been adopted and developed in wake of the UN Trafficking Protocol in 2000. The levels of action that fears of child trafficking and human trafficking have fostered globally, are driven and underwritten by the complex ideologies of rescue, colonialism, nationalism, and mobility.

References

Anonymous. (1997). *Resolution adopted by the general assembly [on the report of the Third Committee (A/51/615)]*.
Anonymous. *Alliance 8.7*. https://www.alliance87.org/
Anonymous. *Office to monitor and combat trafficking in persons*. https://www.state.gov/bureaus-offices/under-secretary-for-civilian-security-democracy-and-human-rights/office-to-monitor-and-combat-trafficking-in-persons/
Anonymous. *SDSN Northern Europe*. https://www.unsdsn-ne.org/
Akhtar, R., & Nyamutata, C. (2020). *International child law*. Routledge.
Allain, J. (2009). Mobilization of international law to address trafficking and slavery. In *The Joint Stanford-University of California Law and colonialism Africa symposium*, March 19–21, 2009.
Anker, R. (2000). The economics of child labour: A framework for measurement. *International Labour Review, 139*(3), 257–280.
Bales, K. (2013). *Shining the light on modern slavery*. https://www.huffingtonpost.co.uk/professor-kevin-bales/modern-slavery_b_4114123.html
Beutin, L. P. (2017). Black suffering for/from anti-trafficking advocacy. *Anti-Trafficking Review, 9*, 14–30.
Boris, E. (2019). *Making the woman worker: Precarious labor and the fight for global standards, 1919–2019*. Oxford University Press. https://library.biblioboard.com/viewer/773dafd9-faaf-4fc0-94e6-005b46f1275c
Boris, E., & Rodríguez García, M. (2021). (In)decent work: Sex and the ILO. *Journal of Women's History, 33*(4), 194–221.

Bouckli, A., Papanicoloaou, G., & Dimou, E. (2023). Constructing 'indigenous people' reproducing coloniality's epistemic violence: A content analysis of the U.S. trafficking in persons report. In E. A. Faulkner (Ed.), *Modern slavery in global context: Human rights, law and policy*. Bristol University Press.

Buck, T. (2014). *International child law* (3rd ed). Routledge.

Bunting, A., & Quirk, J. (eds.) (2017). *Contemporary slavery: The rhetoric of global human rights campaigns*. Cornell University Press.

Commission on Human Rights. (1990). *Sale of children 1990/68*.

Craig, G., & Clay, S. (2017). Who is vulnerable? Adult social care and modern slavery. *The Journal of Adult Protection, 19*(1), 21–32.

Donovan, B. (2005). *White slave crusades*. University of Illinois Press. https://doi.org/10.5406/j.ctt1xcmjv

Dottridge, M. (2018). Collateral damage provoked by anti-trafficking measures. In R. Piotrowicz et al. (Ed.), *Routledge handbook of human trafficking*. Routledge.

Dottridge, M. (2021). Between theory and reality: The challenge of distinguishing between trafficked children and independent child migrants. *Anti-Trafficking Review, 16*, 11–27.

Dottridge, M., & Howard, N. (2017). *How not to achieve a sustainable development goal*. https://www.opendemocracy.net/en/beyond-trafficking-and-slavery/how-not-to-achieve-sustainable-development-goal/

Duane, A. M., & Meiners, E. R. (2021). Working analogues: Slavery now and then. In G. Lebaron et al. (Ed.), *Fighting modern slavery and human trafficking: History and contemporary policy*. Cambridge University Press.

Engle Merry, S. (2018). Counting the uncountable: Constructing trafficking through measurement. In P. Kotiswaran (Ed.), *Revisiting the law and governance of trafficking, forced labour and modern slavery*. Cambridge University Press.

Faulkner, E. A., & Nyamutata, C. (2020). The decolonisation of children's rights and the colonial contours of the convention on the rights of the child. *The International Journal of Children's Rights, 28*(1), 66–88.

Gallagher, A. T. (2012). *The International Law of Human Trafficking*. Cambridge University Press.

Howard, N. (2017). *Child trafficking, youth labour mobility and the politics of protection*. Palgrave Macmillan.

Howard, N., & Okyere, S. (Eds.). (2022). *International child protection: Towards politics and participation*. Palgrave Studies on Children and Development. Palgrave.

Human Rights Council. (2007). *Human Rights Council Resolution 6/14. Special Rapporteur on contemporary forms of slavery.*

Human Rights Council. (2008). *Resolution 7/13. Mandate of the Special Rapporteur on the sale of children, child prostitution and child pornography.*

Human Rights Council. (2020). *Resolution adopted by the Human Rights Council on 16 July 2020 44/4. Trafficking in persons, especially women and children: strengthening human rights through enhanced protection, support and empowerment of victims of trafficking, especially women and children.*

ILO. (1999). *Worst forms of child labour recommendation, 1999 (No. 190)*. https://www.ilo.org/dyn/normlex/en/f?p=NORMLEXPUB:12100:0::NO::P12100_ILO_CODE:R190

ILO. (2008). *Commercial sexual exploitation of children and adolescents—The ILO's response.*

ILO. *About the International Programme on the Elimination of Child Labour (IPEC)*. https://www.ilo.org/ipec/programme/lang--en/index.htm

ILO, UNICEF, & UN GIFT. (2009). *Training manual to fight trafficking in children for labour, sexual and other forms of exploitation, textbook 1: Understanding child trafficking.*

International Criminal Court. (2016). *Policy on Children.*

International Criminal Court. (ICC). *About the Court (International Criminal Court)*. https://www.icc-cpi.int/about/the-court

Kempadoo, K., & Shih, E. (2022). *White supremacy, racism and the coloniality of anti-trafficking* (Vol. 1. 1st edn.). Routledge.

Kilkelly, U. (2003). Economic exploitation of children: A European perspective. *Saint Louis University Public Law Review, 22*(2), 321.

Kotiswaran, P. (Ed.). (2018). *Revisiting the law and governance of trafficking, forced labor and modern slavery*. Cambridge University Press.

Kotiswaran, P. (2019). Trafficking: A development approach. *Current Legal Problems, 72*(1), 375–416.

Laczko, F., & Gramegna, M. A. (2003). Developing better indicators of human trafficking. *The Brown Journal of World Affairs, 10*(1), 179–194.

LeBaron, G., et al. (Eds.). (2021). *Fighting modern slavery and human trafficking: History and contemporary policy*. Cambridge University Press.

Lerche, J. (2007). Global alliance against forced labour? Unfree labour, neoliberal globalization and the international labour organization. *Journal of Agrarian Change, 7*(4), 425–452.

Martins, A., & O'Connell-Davidson, J. (2022). Crossing the binaries of mobility control: Agency, force and freedom. *Social Sciences (basel), 11*(6), 243.

Ministère de la Famille et de l'Enfant, & UNICEF. (2007). *Centre de Formation et de Recherche en matière de Population (CEFORP), Etude Nationale sur la Traite des Enfants. Rapport d'analyse.* Contonou.

NGO Group. (2001). A future without child labour. Global report under the follow-up to the ILO Declaration on Fundamental Principles and Rights at Work. Report of the Director-General, 2002. Accessible via ILO Global Report on Child Labour cites "alarming" extent of its worst forms.

O'Connell Davidson, J. (2015). *Modern slavery: The margins of freedom.* Palgrave Macmillan.

Office to Monitor and Combat Trafficking in Persons. (2021). *Trafficking in persons report (TIP) 2021.*

Office to Monitor and Combat Trafficking in Persons. (2022). *Trafficking in persons report (TIP) 2022.*

Office to Monitor and Combat Trafficking in Persons. *International and Domestic Law Office to Monitor and Combat Trafficking in Persons.* https://www.state.gov/international-and-domestic-law/

OHCHR. (2001). *Fact sheet no. 27: Seventeen frequently asked questions about United Nations Special Rapporteurs (Archive).* https://www.ohchr.org/en/publications/fact-sheets/fact-sheet-no-27-seventeen-frequently-asked-questions-about-united-nations

Okyere, S. (2014). Children's participation in prohibited work in Ghana and its implications for the convention on the rights of the child. In A. Twum-Danso Imoh & N. Ansell (Eds.), *Children's lives in an era of children's rights the progress of the convention on the rights of the child in Africa.*

Peck, G. (2021). Counting modern slaves: Historicizing the emancipatory work of numbers. In G. Lebaron et al. (Ed.), *Fighting modern slavery and human trafficking: History and contemporary policy.*

Pliley, J. R. (2010). Claims to protection: The rise and fall of feminist abolitionism in the League of Nations' Committee on the traffic in women and children, 1919–1936. *Journal of Women's History, 22*(4), 90–113.

Pliley, J. R. (2014). *Policing sexuality: The Mann act and the making of the FB.* Harvard University Press.

Pliley, J. R. (2021). Ambivalent abolitionist legacies: The league of nations' investigations into sex trafficking: 1927–1934. In G. Lebaron et al. (ed.), *Fighting modern slavery and human trafficking: History and contemporary policy.*

Preparatory Commission for the ICC. (2000). *Report of the preparatory commission for the ICC, Abbendum, Part II finalized draft text of the elements of the crime.*

Raza, A. (2023). Exploring the role of race and racial difference in the legislative intent of the trafficking victims protection act. In K. Kempadoo & E. Shih (Eds.), *White supremacy, racism and the coloniality of anti-trafficking* (Vol. 1, 1st edn.). Routledge. https://doi.org/10.4324/9781003162124-6

Rodriguez Garcia, M. (2012). The league of nations and the moral recruitment of women. *International Review of Social History, 57*, 97–128.

Roy, A. (2012). *The #GlobalPOV Project: 'Who sees poverty?'*

Selby, J. (2008). Ending abusive and exploitative child labour through international law and practical action. *Australian International Law Journal, 15*, 165–180.

Sharma, N. (2020). *Home rule*. Duke University Press.

Special Rapporteur. (2016). *25 years of fighting the sale and sexual exploitation of children: Addressing new challenges.*

Special Rapporteur. (2018a). *A/HRC/40/51: Sale and sexual exploitation of children, including child prostitution, child pornography and other child sexual abuse material—Report of the Special Rapporteur.*

Special Rapporteur. (2018b). *Report of the Special Rapporteur on the sale and sexual exploitation of children, including child prostitution, child pornography and other child sexual abuse material.*

Sustainable Development Solutions Network. (2017). *Getting started with the SDGS in universities Australia, New Zealand & Pacific edition a guide for universities, higher education institutions, and the academic sector.*

Temporary Slavery Commission. (1925). *Minutes of the temporary slavery commission, second session.*

Trodd, Z., Nicholson, A., & Eglen, L. (2021). Integrated and indivisible: The sustainable development agenda of modern slavery survivor narratives. In G. Lebaron et al. (Ed.).

U.S. Government Accountability Office. (2006). *Human trafficking: Better data, strategy, and reporting needed to enhance U.S. anti-trafficking efforts abroad.*

U.S. Government Accountability Office. (2007). *Human trafficking: Monitoring and evaluation of international projects are limited, but experts suggest improvements.*

UNICEF. (2018). *Children account for nearly one-third of identified trafficking victims globally.* https://www.unicef.org/press-releases/children-account-nearly-one-third-identified-trafficking-victims-globally

UNODC. *UNODC's human trafficking case law database.* https://sherloc.unodc.org/cld/en/v3/sherloc/cldb/index.html?lng=en

van Doore. (2021). *Orphanage trafficking in international law.* Cambridge University Press.

Walia, H. (2021). *Border and rule global migration, capitalism, and the rise of racist nationalism.* Haymarket Books.

Wooditch, A. (2011). The efficacy of the trafficking in persons report: A review of the evidence. *Criminal Justice Policy Review, 22*(4), 471–493.

6

Child Trafficking in Europe: Nationalism, Vulnerability, and Protection

6.1 Introduction

The final substantive chapter will consider the geographical location of Europe and the legal frameworks adopted to address trafficking, focusing upon the UK's fight to tackle what it terms 'modern slavery'. As the UK is situated within the geographical region of Europe and despite the ongoing issue of Brexit and how the entangled national and regional legislative frameworks will be untangled regarding trafficking, mobility, and human rights is yet to be fully critiqued and understood. This chapter will examine the regional action of the geographical region of Europe, including the legal and policy adoptions under the auspices of the European Union and Council of Europe. The EU and CoE are not the only regional organisations to make the trafficking in persons including children a key matter of political concern, the Organization for Security and Co-operation in Europe (OCSE)[1] and the Council of the Baltic Sea States also required acknowledgement.[2] As the former (EU and CoE) are the only ones to of developed legally binding standards relevant to child trafficking, namely the EU Directive 2011/36/EU and the CoE Convention on Action against Trafficking in Human Beings 2005. The focus of the chapter will then move to consider the legal and policy responses of the UK prior to and since the adoption of the Modern Slavery Act, 2015.

Described as 'a special evil in the abuse and exploitation of the most innocent and vulnerable' (UN, 2003). The trafficking of children has received extensive attention in recent years, with research conducted upon the phenomena in a range of geographical regions (Craig, 2010; Durisin & Meulen, 2021; Fussey & Rawlinson, 2017; Howard, 2017; Hynes, 2010; Koomson & Abdulai, 2021; Krsmanovic, 2021; Okyere et al., 2021; Soltis & Diaz, 2021). Despite the assertion that 'little is known about its magnitude' (UNICEF, 2011) statistics still continue to dominate discussions of the phenomena, with the ILO's 2002 estimate that 1.2 million children globally are trafficked each year remaining front and centre. According to UNICEF 'within and cross borders in Europe, children are trafficked into a variety of exploitative situations, violating their human rights and threatening their survival and development' (UNICEF, 2007). The trafficking of children is perceived mainly in connection with sexual exploitation, but the reality is a myriad of complexities. Children in Europe are trafficked for exploitation through labour, domestic servitude, begging, criminal activities, and

---

[1] See further the OCSE Action Plan to Combat Trafficking in Human Beings (with the 2013 Addendum); 2005 Adenedum Addressing the Special Needs of Child Victims of Trafficking for Protection and Assistance; 2015 Commentary to the OCSE Action Plan to Combat Trafficking in Human Beings and its addendums. In 2003 the post of the OCSE Special Representative and Co-Ordinator for Combatting Trafficking in Human Beings was established. Office of the Special Representative and Co-ordinator for Combating Trafficking in Human Beings (CTHB) | OSCE (https://www.osce.org/cthb). Accessed July 2022; the 22nd Conference of the Alliance against Trafficking in Persons, organized by the OSCE Office of the Special Representative and Co-ordinator for Combating Trafficking in Human Beings, 4 April 2022, Vienna, Austria.

[2] See further the Task Force against Trafficking in Human Beings; and Expert Group on Children at Risk, Guidelines Promoting the Human Rights and the Best Interests of the Child in Transnational Child Protection Cases (2015).

other exploitative purposes (Fussey & Rawlinson, 2017; Oude Breuil, 2021). Additionally, child trafficking is reported by Member States of the European Union as one of the trends that is increasing most sharply in the EU. The statistical data for 2013–2014 shows that out of the 15,846 registered victims of trafficking in the EU, at least 2375 were children.[3] Obviously, various caveats accompany any statistics or efforts to quantify human misery, with methodological inconsistencies continuing to thrive. As highlighted, 'the figures are given significant weight in the construction of narratives around victimisation and exploitation often accompanied by corresponding expressions of opprobrium for the trafficker and pity for their victims' (Fussey & Rawlinson, 2017, 17). Regardless of the statistics available, human trafficking continues to be an issue of much anxiety within Europe.[4]

6.2 The Anti-Trafficking Legal Regime of Europe

> *International law recognizes that children because of their reliance on others for their security and well-being are vulnerable to trafficking and related exploitation. It, therefore, accord children special rights of care and protection.* (OHCR, 2014, 43)

According to the UN OHCHR the special vulnerabilities of children including unaccompanied and separated children are recognised, affording special rights of care and protection. The anti-trafficking legal

---

[3] Report from the Commission to the European Parliament and the Council: Report on the progress made in the fight against trafficking in human beings (2016) as required under Article 20 of Directive 2011/36/EU on preventing and combating trafficking in human beings and protecting its victims at 5.

[4] See further, EU proposes new rules to fight trafficking in human beings (https://home-aff airs.ec.europa.eu/news/eu-proposes-new-rules-fight-trafficking-human-beings-2022-12-18_en). Accessed 3 December 2023 EU Action such as 'A modern form of slavery' EU Anti-Trafficking Commissioner, 2010; the creation of the 'EU Anti Trafficking Day' an annual event on 18 October. The awareness campaign was established by the Council of Europe and aims to raise public awareness of the global problem of human trafficking, in addition to emphasising the right of all human trafficking victims to justice and compensation.

regime of Europe includes the legal mechanisms adopted under the remit of the European Union (hereafter the EU) and the Council of Europe (hereafter the CoE).[5] Both organisations have played a prominent role in the development of the anti-trafficking machine of the region, which is not isolated to the creation of a legal regime but includes non-legal action to eradicate child trafficking and human trafficking more broadly. It is integral to understand that major differences between the CoE and EU in terms of their respective legal systems and how they work. The EU legal system is not a typical international legal system, as its laws enjoy primacy, some of its instruments enjoy direct effect, in addition to a system of national and supranational judicial enforcement for example. There is a danger of miscommunication through the presentation of the organisations and their respective instruments alongside each other, as I do not wish to misrepresent them as of equal importance in national legal systems.[6] Instruments of the EU and CoE have different effects in domestic law, and this is not a uniform matter.

A common theme that can be traced through the definitional debates and the adopted debates of various organisations such as the UN and the

---

[5] The Council of Europe and European Union are two distinct organisations, with their own set goals and objectives. The EU is made up of three main EU Institutions (EUI) namely the European Parliament which represents EU citizens and is directly elected by them, the Council of the European Union, which is one of the EU's co-legislators and arguably its most powerful institution which represents the individual Member States and finally the European Commission which seeks to uphold the interests of the Union as a whole. See further, Glossary: European Union institutions (EUI)—Statistics Explained (https://ec.eur opa.eu/eurostat/statistics-explained/index.php?title=Glossary:European_Union_institutions_(EUI)#:~:text=The%20European%20Union%20institutions%2C%20sometimes%20abbreviated%20as%20EUI%2C,European%20Union%2C%20which%20represents%20the%20individual%20Member%20States%3B). Accessed July 2022.

The Council of Europe (CoE) Founded in 1949 by the Treaty of London and based in Strasbourg, France, the Council of Europe is the continent's leading human rights organisation. It has 47 Member States, 28 of which are members of the European Union. All Council of Europe Member States have signed up to the European Convention on Human Rights, a treaty designed to protect human rights, democracy, and the rule of law. The CoE is composed of The Committee of Ministers, which is the CoE's decision-making body, the Parliamentary Assembly of the Council of Europe (PACE), the Congress of Local and Regional Authorities, the Commissioner for Human Rights and the European Court of Human Rights (ECHR) which was established in 1959. It rules on individual or state applications alleging violations of the rights set out in the European Convention on Human Rights. See further, The Council of Europe and its various bodies—Europe in Strasbourg and Alsace (https://www.europeinstrasbourg.eu/en/institutions/council-europe.html). Accessed July 2022.

[6] This is not the case, although it may differ in some monist countries REFERENCES.

European Parliament (of the EU)[7] is the emphasis on cross-border trafficking. This demonstrates that the legal responses to human trafficking are primarily concerned with the statist control of borders (O'Connell Davidson, 2015; Sharma, 2018). The aspiration of preventing all unauthorised migration 'entails the indiscriminate criminalization of all those who assist in it, and in dominant discourse on trafficking as modern slavery, immorality and criminality is uniformly attributed to all those who assist with irregular travel' (O'Connell Davidson, 2015, 128). Moreover, this grand project is 'logical from the perspective of strengthening the state's right to control admission into its territory, but not is the primary concern lies with human rights' (O'Connell Davidson, 2015, 128). This links to the historical context of determining who is 'desirable' and 'undesirable' as an essential aspect of nation making (Sharma, 2018). The CoE's Convention, drafted after the Palermo Protocol, does appear to represent a minor shift away from this and can be viewed as a demonstratable departure from the focus upon borders and 'evil criminals'. The human rights orientation of the regional efforts is distinct from the international approach endorsed by the Palermo Protocol.

From a human rights perspective, the EU governments responses to trafficking and slavery are part of the problem, rather than the solution, and the 'direction of current policy risks not so much solving the problem of trafficking, but ending the right of asylum in Europe, one of the most fundamental of all human rights' (Morrison, 2000). The anti-trafficking responses of the region, culminating in "fortress Europe" veil the global political inequalities reflected in and intensified by border regimes (O'Connell Davidson, 2022). An illustrative example is that in 2020, the UNITED identified the deaths of more than 40,555 refugees and migrants that are attributable to the restrictive policies of the EU (UNITED, 2020). It has been noted that the existing European framework and its "existing biases" are problematic, as those biases cannot be 'detracted from the reality of the Dutch landscape of the trafficking of Roma children for criminal activities' (Oude Breuil, 2021, 93). This section will seek to critique the framework implemented and tease

---

[7] It is important to distinguish between the European Parliament of the EU and PACE, the CoE Parliamentary Assembly that has adopted numerous resolutions about trafficking in persons.

out the 'existing biases' and the role that they play. The Preamble to the CoE Convention on Action against Trafficking in Human Beings designates trafficking as a 'violation of human rights and an offence to the dignity and integrity of human beings'. In a similar vein, the EU Directive 2011 labels human trafficking as a 'serious crime' and 'gross violation of fundamental rights'.[8] With the instruments of both the EU and CoE concurring that human rights and the violation of them are of pivotal importance, the principle should also be upheld with regard to policymaking designed to assist states in ensuring compliance with basic human rights requirement, including that of freedom from slavery.[9] However, in practice 'we often find that whilst anti-trafficking (and anti-slavery) laws and policies are designed in compliance with Article 4 in principle, other policies and laws are commonly found to undermine their impact' (Skrivankova, 2018, 251). This section of the chapter will now turn to critique the adopted instruments as part of the regional anti-trafficking arsenal of both the CoE and EU in chronological order.

6.2.1 The Council of Europe

The CoE first began to work on human trafficking in the 1990s, when the issue was one of 'marginal relevance' to the activities of the international community.[10] The CoE adopted the 'first international instrument dealing comprehensively with these matters' (CETS 197, 12) in the form of the Recommendation No. R (91) on sexual exploitation, pornography and prostitution and trafficking children and young adults.[11] The Council's focus upon human trafficking and sexual exploitation

---

[8] Directive 2911/36/EU of the European Parliament and of the Council of 5 April 2011 on preventing and combatting trafficking in human beings and protecting victims, and replacing Council Framework Decision 2002/629/JHA, [2011] OJ L 101/1.

[9] As enshrined by the UDHR, Art 4 of the ECHR.

[10] Such as the establishment of a Group of Experts on trafficking in women identified key elements of action containing criminal justice response and measures to protect and support victims.

[11] CofE Recommendation No. R (91) on sexual exploitation, pornography and prostitution and trafficking in children and young adults. Also, the establishment of a Group of Experts on trafficking in women identified key elements of action containing criminal justice response and measures to protect and support victims.

is clear through the development and adoption of two instruments in 2000. The first instrument specifically related to trafficking for sexual exploitation,[12] whilst the second instrument outlined measures to protect children against sexual exploitation, including through trafficking.[13] The combined aim of these instruments was to develop a comprehensive strategy to tackle human trafficking effectively both within and beyond Europe (Gallagher, 2012, 111). They sought to achieve this objective by focusing efforts upon the eradication of definitional disparities, criminal justice measures, research, international cooperation, and aiding victims (Gallagher, 2012, 111). The CoE subsequently adopted the Convention on Action against Trafficking in Human Beings in 2005.[14] The CoE Convention is significantly different from the Trafficking Protocol 2000, as the latter has focused too much upon law enforcement and paying insufficient attention to the needs of trafficked persons (Piotrowicz et al., 2018, 41).

Council of Europe Convention on Action Against Trafficking in Human Beings 2005[15]

The Council of Europe Convention on Action against Trafficking in Human Beings (hereafter, the CoE Convention) applies to all forms

---

[12] Council of Europe, Committee of Ministers, Recommendation No. R (2000) 11 of the Committee of Ministers to Member States on action against trafficking in human beings for the purpose of sexual exploitation, adopted on 19 May 2000. https://wcd.coe.int/ViewDoc.jsp?id=355371. Accessed April 2018.

[13] Council of Europe, Committee of Ministers, Recommendation No. R (2001) 16 of the Committee of Ministers to Member States on the protection of children against sexual exploitation, adopted on 31 October 2001. https://wcd.coe.int/ViewDoc.jsp?id=234247. Accessed July 2015.

[14] The Council of Europe Convention on Action against Trafficking in Human Beings [CETS No. 197] was adopted by the Committee of Ministers on 3 May 2005 and opened for signature in Warsaw on 16 May 2005, on the occasion of the 3rd Summit of Heads of State and Government of the Council of Europe Member States. And entered into force on 01/02/2008—10 ratifications including 8-Member States. Currently 48 ratifications, Full list (https://www.coe.int/en/web/conventions/full-list?module=signatures-by-treaty&treatynum=197). Accessed October 2022.

[15] Council of Europe Convention on Action against Trafficking in Human Beings (CETS No. 197), Full list (https://www.coe.int/en/web/conventions/full-list?module=treaty-detail&treatynum=197). Accessed October 2022.

of human trafficking, whether national or transnational, or whether it is related or not to organised crime and whoever the victim regardless of gender or age and whatever form of exploitation.[16] The Preamble contained an explicit call for a "child rights approach" and that child-focused standards are mainstreamed across all implementation areas. The CoE Convention stands at the core of legally binding, comprehensive anti-trafficking standards (Sax, 2018, 256). The Convention follows a victim centred, human rights approach, covering all types of trafficking (national/international, non-organised crime related, and all forms of exploitation) and establishes an independent monitoring mechanism, Group of Experts on Action against Trafficking in Human Beings (GRETA).[17] Which is the only such mechanism to date in the anti-trafficking field.

The explanatory report to the Convention on Action against Trafficking in Human Beings (hereafter, the CoE Trafficking Convention) asserted that;

> *Trafficking in human beings is a major problem in Europe today. Annually, thousands of people, largely women and children, fall victim to trafficking for sexual exploitation or other purposes, whether in their own countries or abroad. All indicators point to an increase in victim numbers. Action to combat trafficking in human beings is receiving worldwide attention because trafficking threatens the human rights and the fundamental values of democratic societies.*[18]

This links to the extensive works of Enloe (2014) on 'women and children' as a single merged concept and the idea of innocence. The notion of children as eternal passive victims has been fiercely critiqued within the academic literature (Moharty, 1988; O'Connell Davidson, 2005). This continual linkage of women and children is demarked as 'the durable

---

[16] Summary, Full list (https://www.coe.int/en/web/conventions/full-list?module=treaty-detail&treatynum=197). Accessed October 2022.

[17] Home (https://www.coe.int/en/web/anti-human-trafficking). Accessed July 2022.

[18] Council of Europe Convention on Action against Trafficking in Human Beings, Explanatory Report CETS No. 197 at 1.

binding of the lives and fates of women and of children in public imaginaries' (Rosen & Twamley, 2018). The rhetoric of the CoE Trafficking Convention is clear; that human trafficking and the sexual exploitation of women and children are synonymous practices (Doezema, 2010; Kempadoo et al., 2012; Kotiswaran, 2018; O'Connell Davidson, 2014). One of the complaints of this book has been to contest the continual linkage between trafficking and commercial sexual exploitation and the heightened sense that the sexual exploitation of children is uniquely terrible (O'Connell Davidson, 2004, 2). The global panic around sex work and trafficking, has been fostered largely by the foreign policy of the USA and indirectly through the naming and shaming techniques of US anti-trafficking law, leading to the constant conflation of trafficking with trafficking for sex work and of trafficking for sex work with sex work (Kotiswaran, 2014).[19] The powerful image of a young girl tricked and sold into sexual slavery had captured imaginations for over a century. The idiom of the anti-trafficking machine and the thrust of abolitionist movements have been alluded to throughout this book. It is important to recognise that the abolitionist campaigns that fall under the anti-trafficking machine, are not united and harmonious nor are they a single unified movement.

The Palermo Protocol is a pivotal legal document that has had a considerable influence upon international, regional, and national legal provisions and regulations of the sex work that have been subsequently implemented. The scale of its influence can be seen in the CoE Trafficking Convention, which reflected the terminology and approach contained in the Palermo Protocol.[20] The definition of trafficking within with CoE Convention is taken directly from the Palermo Protocol, consisting in the case of children, of two elements only: the action and exploitative intention.[21] The timing of the CoE Trafficking Convention,

---

[19] See further Prabha Kotiswaran, 'Beyond Sexual Humanitarianism: A Postcolonial Approach to Anti-Trafficking Law' (2014) 4 UC Irvine Law Review 353.

[20] The total number of ratifications/accessions 48 ratifications in total With Belarus's ratification on 26/11/2013, and subsequent entry into force 1/03/2014 being the only non-member of the Council of Europe, http://conventions.coe.int/Treaty/Commun/ChercheSig.asp?NT=197&CM=&DF=&CL=ENG. Accessed October 2022.

[21] Article 4—Definitions For the purposes of this Convention: a "Trafficking in human beings" shall mean the recruitment, transportation, transfer, harbouring, or receipt of persons, by means

soon after the adoption of the first contemporary international treaty on trafficking, inevitably impacted upon its scope and purpose. In comparison to the drafting process of the Palermo Protocol, the development of the CoE Trafficking Convention was a relatively private affair, with significantly greater internal control (Gallagher, 2012, 113). However, the NGOs that were admitted to the CoE discussions had much more opportunity to make statements and to try and influence the provision. The Convention places an emphasis upon human rights and victim protection (even defining a victim) and applies to all forms of trafficking and to the trafficking of men, women, and children.

The definition of trafficking provided through Article 4 (a) mirrors exactly the corresponding provision of the Trafficking Protocol. For the purposes of this Convention Article 4:

> *"Trafficking in human beings" shall mean the recruitment, transportation, transfer, harbouring or receipt of persons, by means of the threat or use of force or other forms of coercion, of abduction, of fraud, of deception, of the abuse of power or of a position of vulnerability or of the giving or receiving of payments or benefits to achieve the consent of a person having control over another person, for the purpose of exploitation. Exploitation shall include, at a minimum, the exploitation of the prostitution of others or other forms of sexual exploitation, forced labour or services, slavery or practices similar to slavery, servitude or the removal of organs.*

What distinguishes the CoE Convention from the Palermo Protocol is that it defines a 'victim' of trafficking through Article 4 (e) stipulating

---

of the threat or use of force or other forms of coercion, of abduction, of fraud, of deception, of the abuse of power or of a position of vulnerability or of the giving or receiving of payments or benefits to achieve the consent of a person having control over another person, for the purpose of exploitation. Exploitation shall include, at a minimum, the exploitation of the prostitution of others or other forms of sexual exploitation, forced labour or services, slavery or practices similar to slavery, servitude, or the removal of organs; b The consent of a victim of "trafficking in human beings" to the intended exploitation set forth in subparagraph (a) of this article shall be irrelevant where any of the means set forth in subparagraph (a) have been used; c The recruitment, transportation, transfer, harbouring, or receipt of a child for the purpose of exploitation shall be considered "trafficking in human beings" even if this does not involve any of the means set forth in subparagraph (a) of this article; d "Child" shall mean any person under eighteen years of age; e "Victim" shall mean any natural person who is subject to trafficking in human beings as defined in this article.

that a victim 'shall mean any natural person who is subject to trafficking in human beings as defined in this article'. Additionally, it extends the scope of application through Article 2 asserting that 'all forms of trafficking in human beings whether national or transnational, whether or not connected with organised crime'.[22] This is a departure from the Palermo Protocol and demonstrates how the CoE has identified one of the main limitations of the Palermo Protocol in terms of the scope of its application. However, this is not the main distinguishing characteristic of the CoE Convention. The substantial emphasis placed upon protection and assistance, which confirms the rights of anyone deemed to of been trafficked to protection and assistance is. This is a stark contrast to the Palermo Protocol which suggested to states that they may wish to make protection and assistance available but without creating an obligation to do so. This departure *prima facie* appears to disrupt the contention that the main narratives have dominated instruments adopted since the Palermo Protocol. The CoE Trafficking Convention further distinguishes itself from the Palermo Protocol in recognising internal trafficking within its definition, thus eliminating the need for an international border to be crossed before the necessary elements of the crime are satisfied.[23] The CoE Trafficking Convention is built upon the foundations provided by the Palermo Protocol, whilst at the same time instilling a more explicit human rights-based approach to combat trafficking in persons. This raises the question of how the Convention aims to achieve these objectives. With regard to children, the CoE Trafficking Convention is again distinct from the Palermo Protocol, which failed to deliver recognition and protection of the rights of children. Considering this, the UN High Commissioner for Human Rights urged that the European Convention;

Acknowledge that the problem of child trafficking is a distinct one requiring special attention. The best interests of child victims must be considered

---

[22] Article 2—This Convention shall apply to all forms of trafficking in human beings, whether national or transnational, whether or not connected with organised crime.

[23] Article 2—This Convention shall apply to all forms of trafficking in human beings, whether national or transnational, whether or not connected with organised crime, http://www.coe.int/en/web/conventions/full-list/-/conventions/rms/090000168008371d. Accessed February 2017.

paramount at all times. Children should be provided with appropriate assistance and protection. Full account should be taken of their special vulnerabilities, rights and needs.[24]

The best interests of child trafficking victims are not always understood but often referred to of 'paramount importance'. Some academic studies for example have highlighted that in cases of exploitation within the family, structural causes should be addressed and that a criminal justice approach may not be in the best interests of the child (Hynes et al., 2022; Oude Breuil, 2021, 101; Warria et al., 2015, 326). Indeed 'applying the label of child trafficking victim may not (always) be in the children's best interest' (Oude Breuil, 2021, 103). For example, 'it may well be in the best interests of some children to leave home and start earning well before they turn 18' (Dottridge, 2021, 27). With the road towards ensuring the 'best interests of the child in cases of minors trafficked for exploitation in criminal activities is bumpy' (Oude Breuil, 2021, 87). The key point here emerges from the issue of childhood, with the Western 'romantic visions of childhood innocence, associated with Rousseau and Wordsworth, have sat alongside a variety of other depictions in the popular and governmental imagination' (Fussey & Rawlinson, 2017, 45).

When a comparison between the two instruments is drawn, the CoE Convention on trafficking offers an incredibly detailed framework for the protection of child victims of trafficking. This is significant because NGO requests to make protection of the rights of child victims a specific purpose of the Palermo Convention failed.[25] The CoE Convention reflects the belief that the child requires extra protection and care, with an entire range of provisions developed to complement the protection and assistance measures available to all victims. This endorses the perception of the child as weak, passive, and vulnerable and as requiring rescue by the heroic state from the clutches of the evil human traffickers. This perspective is not exclusive to children, consider the critique of Kempadoo (2015) that new representations of slavery in the Global

---

[24] N HCHR: Council of Europe Statement, 118.
[25] As highlighted by Gallagher, *The International Law of Human Trafficking*, 118, for example AI/ASI November 2004 Submission, at 5–6, 436.

South show 'colonized peoples as helplessly trapped by their repeating Sisyphean tasks, objects not subjects eternal victims who can only be liberated by white saviours' (O'Connell Davidson, 2015, 73).

The Convention refers explicitly to the notion of creating a protective environment for children. This is a concept that was being pushed for by UNICEF but was soon abandoned, creating a strange situation within which GRETA and the CoE must continue to refer to it, but UNICEF does not. Article 5 (5) for example mandates the creation of "protective environments" for children, linking anti-trafficking National Referral Mechanisms (NRM) to the concept of integrated child protection systems,[26] as promoted by UNICEF, the Council of Europe, the European Union, and Others.[27] It is commentable that the two systems have repeatedly failed to coincide, with the latest ODIHR NRM handbook of 2022[28] attempting to reconcile between the two, in comparison to the first version in 2004 within which children were largely ignored. The CoE Trafficking Convention contains an array of provisions specifically to address the needs of trafficked children. Article 5 addresses the prevention of trafficking in human beings, requiring that Parties take specific preventive measures regarding children. The provision refers to creating a "protective environment" for children to make them less vulnerable to trafficking and enable them to grow up without harm and to lead decent lives. This stance mirrors that advocated by the operational definition of the trafficking of children by IPEC.[29] This approach endorses the Western construction of childhood, failing to acknowledge

---

[26] See further the analysis contained in UNICEF/UNHCR/Save the Children/World Vision, A Better Way to Protect All Children: The Theory and Practice of Child Protection Systems (Conference Report, UNICEF, 2013).

[27] See further the initiative by the European Commission to establish quality criteria for such systems, as included in the Reflection paper "Coordination and Cooperation in Integrated Child Protection Systems", presented at the 9th European Forum on the Rights of the Child in June 2 2015.

[28] See further, ODIHR National Referral Mechanisms Handbook, 2nd Edition | OSCE (https://www.osce.org/odihr/510551). Accessed October 2022.

[29] The approaches of IPEC and the ILO have changed over time, with the operational definition asserting that 'trafficking in children is about taking children out of their protective environment and preying on their vulnerability for the purpose of exploitation'. See further, Trafficking in children (IPEC) (https://www.ilo.org/ipec/areas/Traffickingofchildren/lang--en/index.htm). Accessed October 2022.

how idyllic this construct is. For Fussey and Rawlinson (2017) what has been 'most influential if concentrating on legally relevant characterisations has been the Lockean picture of stages of childhood, in turn transposed through twentieth-century discourses (notably Piaget on the stages of moral reasoning)' Childhood innocence and vulnerability are constructions of the powerful protectionist discourse which currently prevails in the social and legal world (Ost, 2009, 4). These romantic visions 'somehow picture the innocent child, like the noble savage, as an almost asocial being, childhood is more typically depicted in terms of dependency on others, notably parents but also other socialising agencies such as education' (Fussey & Rawlinson, 2017, 45). A universal standard of what is the child does not exist; despite the assertion that the central importance of the CRC is that it provides a near-global normative legal standard, customised specifically to children (van de Glind, 2010, 100). In practice states are able to derogate from this legal standard, and many have enacted legislation or policies that are detrimental to the child, particularly in relation to borders, immigration with the undercurrent of racism, white superiority, and nationalism bubbling underneath.[30] Despite the widespread ratification of the CRC (1989) the concept of childhood, what constitutes as acceptable for a child and the distinction between children and adults and often male and female varies dramatically from state to state, with reasons given such as religious, cultural, structural, or economic for these classifications. The concept of the child is a constructed one, dominated by the Western liberal democracies that made it their mission in the aftermath of the Second World War to enshrine and develop human rights. Under international law the child is classed as anyone under the age of eighteen years, however each state can derogate from this standard.

In relation to assistance, services should therefore identify children, treat them as under-age in case of doubt, provide legal guardians if unaccompanied or otherwise warranted in the child's best interests (for example in the case of potential involvement of parents in the trafficking process) provide qualified shelters and staff, access to information

---

[30] See further immigration in the UK, USA, and Australia.

services and compensation, as well as a safe return only after best interests determination.[31] The CoE Trafficking Convention is reflective of the powerful protectionist discourse that dominates our understanding of children, particularly when it comes to protecting the child from harm. However, a recurrent implementation gap observed by GRETA is the lack of policies to address children in risk situations leaving institutions on their own—children who then "disappear".[32] The child is continually classified as a 'vulnerable class both within the social and legal world, a class that requires protection from physical and psychological threats (Ost, 2009, 6). The Palermo Protocol's conflicts with the central ethos of the CRC to classify the child as having agency and the ability to participate in decision-making does not sit comfortably with the CoE Convention. Regarding prosecution, the CoE Convention requires particular protection and safety for children as witnesses and victims during court proceedings. Furthermore, the application of the principle of non-punishment (Article 26) to children forced to commit petty crimes remains a critical case for State compliance.[33]

The decisive point of observation of the CoE Convention relates to the question of language and invocations of history. Although the preference for trafficking over modern slavery has been identified by Skrivankova (2018) invocations to 'historical' slavery do appear. An example can be found within the Explanatory Report (2005, CETS 197) which states that 'trafficking in human beings, with the entrapment of its victims, is the modern form of the old worldwide slave trade' (CETS 197, 1). This invocation is important, as the emotive power and legacy of the Trans-Atlantic Slave Trade are used as a tool to advocate fighting traffickers via more restrictive border controls and more punitive criminal measures. Furthermore, in 'speaking of transatlantic slavery, contemporary anti-slavery activities are always at pains to avow and condemn the

---

[31] Articles 10–16.
[32] CoE/GRETA, 5th General Report on GRETA's Activities (2016) 36–39.
[33] CoE/GRETA, 4th General Report on GRETA's Activities (2015) 33 and 54–55; Fourth further guidance on the application of this principle, also to children, see the OCSE Office of the Special Representative and Co-ordinator for Combating Trafficking in Human Beings, Policy, and Legislative Recommendations Towards the Effectove Implementation of the Non-punishment Provision with Regard to Victims of Trafficking (2013).

role of race and racism' (O'Connell Davidson, 2015). The current restrictive approaches of the geographical region of Europe, fails to mask to the undercurrent of race, racism, and nationalism that drive the feeling of need to close the borders and keep out the 'undesirables'.

6.2.2 The European Union[34]

The European Union (hereafter, the EU) has a 'range of instruments available to law enforcement agencies within the EU that provide police forces with both the tools and the powers to investigate organised crime, including modern slavery cases, both effectively and efficiently' (Skrivankova, 2018, 247). However, it is notable that the collaborative work may well be 'impaired by Brexit unless specific arrangements can be protected during and after the transition of the UK out of the EU' (Skrivankova, 2018, 247). The EU first became actively involved with the issue of human trafficking in the 1990s, which culminated in the release of the 1997 *Joint Action to combat trafficking in human beings and sexual exploitation of children*.[35] The title of the report supports the observation that the EU was primarily concerned with trafficking for the purposes of sexual exploitation, especially children. This interest has driven and shaped the EU's response to the phenomenon through consistently framing trafficking as inherently linked with sexual exploitation. This continued conflation is a pattern not isolated to the EU, which reflects the international and regional instruments implemented post-Palermo.

---

[34] The predecessor of the EU was created in the aftermath of the Second World War. The first steps were to foster economic cooperation: the idea being that countries that trade with one another become economically interdependent and so more likely to avoid conflict. The result was the European Economic Community (EEC), created in 1958, and initially increasing economic cooperation between six countries: Belgium, Germany, France, Italy, Luxembourg, and the Netherlands. The European Union is a unique economic and political union between 27 EU countries (https://europa.eu/european-union/about-eu/countries/member-countries_en) that together cover much of the continent. On 31 January 2020 the UK left the EU, https://europa.eu/european-union/about-eu/eu-in-brief_en#from-economic-to-political-union. Accessed August 2021.

[35] Joint Action of 24 February 1997 concerning action to combat trafficking in human beings and sexual exploitation of children (97/154/JHA), OJ L 063/2, 4 March 1997 (Joint Action on Trafficking).

The EU demonstrated its commitment to combatting the trafficking of human beings by identifying trafficking as one of its priorities for cooperation in combatting and preventing the crime.[36] Additionally, the EU Parliament resolution of the 19 May 2000 on the communication from the Commission called 'for further action in the fight against trafficking in women'. The EU Charter on Fundamental Rights provisions on slavery, forced labour, trafficking in human beings, and child labour[37] are significant due to the interpretative merit that they possess (Vinkovi, 2010, 91). This was true prior to the 2009 Lisbon Treaty, however the CFREU now has equal status with the TEU and TFEU. Whilst Article 5 (3) of the EU Charter of Fundamental Rights specifically provides that 'trafficking in human beings is prohibited'.

Since the entry into force of the Lisbon Treaty, the EU Charter has enjoyed equal status with the EU Treaties themselves (Article 6 (I) TEU). Therefore, the Directive is giving legal effect to the fundamental rights principles protected at the highest level of the EU legal order. Pre-dating the Trafficking Protocol (2000), the first EU soft law measure adopted was a *Joint Action on Trafficking in Human Beings*.[38] The Joint Action explicitly focused upon trafficking in human beings and the sexual exploitation of children. Singling out the sexual exploitation of children as an interwove yet distinct aspect of human trafficking. The Joint Action was subsequently replaced by the Framework Decision 2002,[39] and then the Directive 2011/36/EU, respectively.

---

[36] Treaty on European Union.
[37] Charter on Fundamental Rights of the European Union, 2007 Soft law instrument with primarily declaratory function, the charter has transformed from rhetoric ethos into articulated and powerful legal bulwark of common constitutional values of Member States to which the EU, ECJ, and national courts call on.
[38] Joint Action of 24/02/97 concerning action to combat trafficking in human beings and sexual exploitation of children.
[39] Also, developed a Joint Action on short-term residency permits for victims of.

EU Framework Decision on Combatting Trafficking 2002[40]

The EU Framework Decision[41] presupposes that the trafficking of human beings is widespread and that the trafficking of women and girls for sexual exploitation is the predominant form (Anderson, 2001, 184). The link between the Trafficking Protocol and the Framework Decision is strong. As the EU had already ratified the Protocol, the Framework Decision was expected to improve the implementation of the Palermo Protocol.[42] The Framework Decision retained the Trafficking Protocol's criminal justice focus, and in certain respects significantly expanded this focus through Articles 1–5, requiring the criminalisation and penalisation of a range of trafficking offences whether committed by natural or legal persons.[43]

Article 1 (3) stipulates that 'When the conduct referred to in paragraph 1 involves a child, it shall be a punishable trafficking offence even if none of the means set forth in paragraph 1 have been used'. Further stipulating that for the purposes of the Framework Decision, that a child referred to anyone under 18 years of age.[44] Through Articles 1–3, the Framework Decision defines several offences and penalties concerning trafficking in human beings for the purposes of labour or sexual exploitation. The clear focus of the Framework Decision was upon the criminalisation of human trafficking, demonstrating a clear preference for criminalisation over measures aiding victims. It can be contested that criminalisation is the preference as victim assistance measures can

---

[40] Directives and Framework Decisions do not enjoy direct applicability and therefore must be transported into domestic law. However, they may under certain conditions be capable of direct effect even if they are not so transposed. Article 10 (1) required all EU Member States to have transposed the provisions of the framework decision into domestic legislation by September 2004.

[41] Prior to the Treaty of Lisbon entering into force, a proposal for a replacement to the Framework Decision aimed at strengthening the provisions of its predecessor instrument was being formulated. Treaty of Lisbon abolished the decision-making system used to produce framework decisions.

[42] "EU urges Higher Priority on Trafficking in Women and Children" Europa Press Release, IP/01/325, 07/03/2001, http://europa.eu/rapid/press-release_IP-01-325_en.htm. Accessed April 2017.

[43] Articles 1–5 of the Framework Decision.

[44] Article 1 (4).

be expensive and challenging for the most developed states (Buck, 2014, 366). This stance is reflective of the Palermo Protocol and international policy responses to human trafficking at that particular moment in time.

The Framework Decision provided no acknowledgement of the need to protect the rights and interests of children, containing no provisions on the prevention of the trafficking of children or any provisions relating to the repatriation of the victim or remedies (Gallagher, 2012, 99). However, the preamble stated that 'Children are more vulnerable and are therefore at greater risk of falling victim to trafficking'. Despite this, only Article 7 addresses the protection of and assistance to victims, asserting that children who are victims of an offence referred to in Art. 1 should be considered as *"particularly vulnerable victims"*.[45] The phrase *"particularly vulnerable victims"* demonstrates the protectionist stance of the EU considering children, and links back to the preamble assertions of greater vulnerability. The Framework Decision further states that when the victim is a child, each Member State is under the obligation to take all possible measures to ensure the appropriate assistance is provided for his or her family.[46] There is no clarification as to whether family reunification options are to be classed as appropriate assistance in this context. This is interesting as it endorses the ideal construction of the child as part of a traditional family unit, this Western view, excludes the realities of children who move independently for work, for example in Benin, Vietnam, and the UK (Dottridge, 2021, 12). The meaning of 'appropriate assistance' was left unspecified, however as the Framework Decision is no longer in force this is now a moot point. The strongest criticisms that the Framework Decision received focused on what was left out and the missed opportunity to create a 'victim-centred' approach (Gallagher, 2012, 99).

The Decision can be classed as a retreat from the previous commitment of the EU outlined through the Joint Action of Trafficking which was repealed to be replaced by the Framework Decision 2002. The identification and subsequent acceptance of the weaknesses of the Framework Decision led to the Commission adopting and submitting to the

---

[45] Article 7 (2) Framework Decision 2002.
[46] Article 7 (3) Framework Decision 2002.

Council of the European Union two proposals; firstly, for a new framework decision on human trafficking,[47] and secondly, for a Framework Decision on combatting both the sexual abuse and exploitation of children.[48] The aims of both proposals were to strengthen the existing provisions of the predecessor instrument (Gallagher, 2012, 103). The timing of the proposals is significant as it implies that the two issues are intertwined and demonstrates the creation of linkages between the two and a 'powerful protectionist discourse' that seeks to protect children (Ost, 2009, 4). The Framework Decision emphasised the criminal aspects of human trafficking in line with the Palermo Protocol and was subsequently replaced by the 2011 Directive as the Treaty of Lisbon abolished the decision-making system used to produce framework decisions (Gallagher, 2012, 110).

Directive 2011/36/EU on Preventing and Combatting Trafficking in Human Beings and Protecting Its Victims

Adopted in the wake of the Lisbon Treaty, the legal basis of the Directive is broader than the earlier Framework Decision.[49] Consequently, it provides for a more human rights-based approach to the issue of human trafficking, however the limitations of a human rights-based approach to human trafficking has been illustrated by Malarek (2004) and Gallagher (2012). Cecilia Malmström (Commissioner for Home Affairs at the time) stated that the 'new ambitious rules adopted today will keep the EU at the forefront of the international fight against human trafficking by protecting victims and punishing the criminals behind this modern slavery'.[50] The creep of modern slavery into the

---

[47] Commission of the European Communities, Proposal for a Framework Decision on preventing and combatting trafficking in human beings and protecting victims.
[48] Commission of the European Communities, Proposal for a Framework Decision on combatting the sexual abuse, sexual exploitation of children, and child pornography.
[49] Directive 2011/36/EU of the European Parliament and of the Council of 5 April 2011 on preventing and combating trafficking in human beings and protecting its victims, and replacing Council Framework Decision 2002/629/JHA (OJ L 101, 1 15.4.2011).
[50] 21 March 2011, Human trafficking: Commission welcomes Council adoption of stronger EU rules Press Release IP/11/332, http://europa.eu/rapid/press-release_IP-11-332_en.htm. Accessed April 2018.

language adopted to address exploitation is indicated here. Furthermore, the Preamble articulates that;

> Children are more vulnerable than adults and therefore at greater risk of becoming victims of trafficking in human beings. In the application of this Directive, the child's best interests must be a primary consideration, in accordance with the Charter of Fundamental Rights of the European Union and the 1989 United Nations Convention on the Rights of the Child.[51]

This recognition of the extra vulnerability of children is compatible with the consensus of the perceived vulnerabilities of the child. Arguably, the explicit reference to 'the child's best interests' could provide a mechanism, within which children who demonstrate agency have the capacity to articulate their own views in compliance with the central ethos of the CRC. The general principles of the CRC including the right to non-discrimination and right to survival are potentially being adhered to or at least referenced relatively broadly.

The Directive defines trafficking in more detail than the Framework Decision, with additional forms of exploitation specifically included within its definition.[52] However, the reference to the Framework Decision in Article 11 (1) indicates that the rights in the Directive are intended to build upon the rights set out in the earlier legislative measure. Through adopting a more victim-centred, human rights approach the Directive highlights the need for the victim's perspective to be at the heart of any measures designed to tackle human trafficking. The Directive is also relatively innovative in not only adopting a victim-centred approach but also including a gender perspective. The current global economic configurations disproportionately affect women, particularly in the Global South. This, coupled with entrenched patriarchal values, has led some commentators to conclude that human trafficking

---

[51] Preamble to the Directive 2011/36/EU at paragraph 8, http://eur-lex.europa.eu/LexUriServ/LexUriServ.do?uri=OJ:L:2011:101:0001:0011:EN:PDF. Accessed June 2017.

[52] Article 1 (3) "Exploitation shall include, as a minimum, the exploitation of the prostitution of others or other forms of sexual exploitation, forced labour or services, including begging, slavery or practices similar to slavery, servitude, or the exploitation of criminal activities, or the removal of organs". A definition which is word for word of the definition provided through the Trafficking Protocol.

is best explained in terms of the socio-economic disadvantages faced by women (Winterdyk et al., 2012, 58).

The Directive has several Articles (13–16) that specifically address children and the preamble advocates that the 'child's best interests must be a primary consideration'.[53] The Directive also addresses age assessment, child-focused standards for protection and assistance, child participation, guardianship, and further provisions specifically upon unaccompanied children, child victim protection at court, and the prevention of child trafficking.[54] The use of the term 'best interests' in relation to children is a prominent theme within international child law. However, the obligations placed upon states are not specifically prescribed. The Preamble states that 'forced begging should be understood as a form of forced labour or services defined in the 1930 ILO Convention No. 29 concerning Forced or Compulsory Labour'; this was a significant development with regard to children. Article 2 (3) also explicitly refers to the trafficking in human beings for the purpose of removing organs, with the Preamble unequivocally providing that 'other behaviour such as illegal adoption or forced marriage[55] [is covered] in so far as they fulfil the constitutive elements of trafficking in human beings'.[56]

Article 1 sets out the objectives of the Directive, including to establish minimum rules for the definition of criminal offences, to create sanctions, and to introduce common provisions to strengthen preventative

---

[53] Preamble Directive 2011/36/EU on preventing and combatting trafficking in human beings and protecting its victims.

[54] See further Joint UN Commentary on the EU Directive—A Human Rights-Based Approach, issued in 2011 by UNODC, OHCHR, UNHCR, UNICEF, ILO, and UN Women.

[55] An interesting point has been made about forced marriage as a form of slavery, as forced motherhood is frequently a consequence of forced marriages and of life generally, and women should have the right to choose whether to terminate a pregnancy, here, in the UK for example women within Northern Ireland are not given that choice and are essentially being forced into motherhood by the Government. It should be noted that during the drafting of this monograph, the legal position of access to abortion in NI has since changed. Although not advocating that forced motherhood should be classified as a form of slavery, fi the parameters are going to be pushed to incorporate forced marriage then should a similar approach be adopted to forced motherhood? Media coverage of this issue has been minimal but this article is indicative of the issue, https://www.theguardian.com/world/2015/oct/31/abortion-ireland-northern-ireland-women-travel-england-amelia-gentleman. Accessed June 2017.

[56] Preamble Directive 2011/36/EU on preventing and combatting trafficking in human beings and protecting its victims, § 11.

measures as well as the protection of victims of trafficking. Arguably, by spelling out these dual objectives, the EU is giving greater cognisance to the rights of victims. There are, however, no provisions on residence status, as this was left to be dealt with only by the earlier Directive 2004/81/EC[57]—which makes such residence permits for third-country nationals dependent upon their willingness to cooperate with police, which in practice often creates obstacles for trafficked persons seeking assistance. This cooperation element was something that emerged within the discussions of the lived experiences of children and adolescents that had been trafficked into the UK and was highlighted within a 2022 report which adopted a participatory action model centering on the voices of those with lived experiences (Hynes et al., 2022). Furthermore, the 2004 Directive led to inconsistent application in relation to the trafficked children.

Article 8 provides that victims of trafficking shall not be prosecuted nor have penalties imposed upon them for their 'involvement in criminal activities which they have been compelled to commit as a direct consequence of being subjected to any of the acts referred to in Article 2'. Article 12 provides a significant development in that it expresses the access to the justice system for the purposes of claiming compensation, arguably moving further forward than the OPSC in terms of establishing a legal route to compensation (albeit not a clearly identified victim fund from the proceeds of their exploitation). Articles 13–16 of the Directive specifically relate to child victims of human trafficking; therefore demonstrating the distinction between adults and children under the law[58] (Fig. 6.1).

Article 13 recommends that child trafficking victims are provided with assistance, support, and protection, but the obligation upon states is not mandatory. Whereas, Article 14 (1) outlines the obligations of assistance and support to victims, including their physical and psychosocial recovery, whilst maintaining consideration of the child's views, needs, and concerns in addition to providing education as part of rehabilitation. Article 14 (2) is significant as it arguably served as inspiration

---

[57] Directive 2004/81/EC of 29 April 2004.
[58] Note—Framework Decision only dealt with children in Article 7.

> *(13) In combating trafficking in human beings, full use should be made of existing instruments on the seizure and confiscation of the proceeds of crime, such as the United Nations Convention against Transnational Organised Crime and the Protocols thereto, the 1990 Council of Europe Convention on Laundering, Search, Seizure and Confiscation of the Proceeds from Crime, Council Framework Decision 2001/500/JHA of 26 June 2001 on money laundering, the identification, tracing, freezing, seizing and confiscation of instrumentalities and the proceeds of crime (2), and Council Framework Decision 2005/212/JHA of 24 February 2005 on Confiscation of Crime-Related Proceeds, Instrumentalities and Property (3). The use of seized and confiscated instrumentalities and the proceeds from the offences referred to in this Directive to support victims' assistance and protection, including compensation of victims and Union trans-border law enforcement counter-trafficking activities, should be encouraged.*
>
> *(14) Victims of trafficking in human beings should, in accordance with the basic principles of the legal systems of the relevant Member States, be protected from prosecution or punishment for criminal activities such as the use of false documents, or offences under legislation on prostitution or immigration, that they have been compelled to commit as a direct consequence of being subject to trafficking. The aim of such protection is to safeguard the human rights of victims, to avoid further victimisation and to encourage them to act as witnesses in criminal proceedings against the perpetrators. This safeguard should not exclude prosecution or punishment for offences that a person has voluntarily committed or participated in.*
>
> *(15) To ensure the success of investigations and prosecutions of human trafficking offences, their initiation should not depend, in principle, on reporting or accusation by the victim. Where the nature of the act calls for it, prosecution should be allowed for a sufficient period of time after the victim has reached the age of majority. The length of the sufficient period of time for prosecution should be determined in accordance with respective national law. Law enforcement officials and prosecutors should be adequately trained, in particular with a view to enhancing international law enforcement and judicial cooperation. Those responsible for investigating and prosecuting such offences should also have access to the investigative tools used in organised crime or other serious crime cases. Such tools could include the interception of communications, covert surveillance including electronic surveillance, the monitoring of bank accounts and other financial investigations.*
>
> *(16) In order to ensure effective prosecution of international criminal groups whose centre of activity is in a Member State and which carry out trafficking in human beings in third countries, jurisdiction should be established over the offence of trafficking in human beings where the offender is a national of that Member State, and the offence is committed outside the territory of that Member State. Similarly, jurisdiction could also be established where the offender is an habitual resident of a Member State, the victim is a national or an habitual resident of a Member State, or the offence is committed for the benefit of a legal person established in the territory of a Member State, and the offence is committed outside the territory of that Member State.*

Fig. 6.1 Article 13–16 EU Directive 2011/36

for the Modern Slavery Act of the UK 2015. It outlines the appointment of a guardian or representative upon the identification of a child victim of human trafficking.[59] Article 15 details the protection to be

---

[59] The imp[ortance of guardianship was emphasised through the Creating Stable Futures: Human trafficking, participation and outcomes for children | ECPAT UK (https://www.ecpat.org.uk/creating-stable-futures-human-trafficking-participation-and-outcomes-for-children) (2022).

afforded to child victims during criminal investigations and proceedings, whilst Article 16 addresses the issue of unaccompanied children. The issue of unaccompanied children has been problematic, particularly with regard to the UK and Section 67 of the Immigration Act 2016 frequently referred to as the Dubs Amendment.[60] Although, not linked to the Directive 2011/36/EU it is illustrative of the complexities surrounding unaccompanied children, and the subsequent identification of them as victims of trafficking, refugees, or migrants.

The Directive 2011/36 resonates with the emphasis in the CoE Trafficking Convention that states should adopt a child-sensitive approach when dealing with child trafficking victims. It further seeks to reduce children's vulnerability to trafficking by creating a protective environment for them.[61] The Directive stipulates that when the age of the victim is uncertain and there are reasons to believe that the person in question is a child 'that person is presumed to be a child in order to receive immediate access to assistance, support and protection in accordance with [the articles of the Directive which relate specifically to assistance, support, and protection for child victims]'.[62] Article 14 deals with the assistance and support for child victims in general, whilst Article 15 specifically deals with the protection of child victims in the course of criminal investigations and proceedings. Although a compensation for a victim's provision has been introduced by the Directive, it appears to be less innovative than it may first appear and is less far-reaching than Article 15 of the Council of Europe Convention.[63] Finally, Article 18 (4) focuses upon discouraging demand, a rather vague concept which fails to accept that tackling demand will not bring about an end for exploitation,

---

[60] See further, Factsheet: Section 67 of the Immigration Act 2016 ('Dubs amendment')—GOV.UK (https://www.gov.uk/government/publications/policy-statement-section-67-of-the-immigration-act-2016/factsheet-section-67-of-the-immigration-act-2016). Accessed October 2022: C. McLaughlin (2018). '"They don't look like children": child asylum-seekers, the Dubs amendment and the politics of childhood,' *Journal of Ethnic and Migration Studies*, [Online] 44 (11), 1757–1773.

[61] Article 7.

[62] Article 13 (2).

[63] See further on the failure of the OPSC to establish a 'Victim Fund' from the proceeds of exploitation as identified in Akthar & Nymamutata International Child Law (2020).

inequality, or injustice. The inclusion of this discrete offence is anomalous and arguably, it fits more comfortably alongside the other criminal offences found in Articles 2[64] and 3 of the Directive.[65]

Non-Legislative Actions of the European Union and Council of Europe

Since the late 1980s, the Council of Europe (CoE) has invested considerable efforts in the fight against trafficking in human beings. These efforts culminated in the adoption, in May 2005, of the Convention on Action against Trafficking in Human Beings and the setting up of a mechanism to monitor compliance with the obligations contained in it. This monitoring mechanism is composed of the Group of Experts on Action against Trafficking in Human Beings (hereafter, GRETA), a multidisciplinary panel of 15 independent and impartial experts,[66] and the Committee of the Parties to the Convention.

On the other hand their EU Anti-Trafficking Coordinator (based within the European Commission), founded in 2011 and continuing to have a profound impact with the office utilising the position to influence the orientation of subsequent reports.[67] The EU Anti-Trafficking Coordinator (at the time of writing in 2022, Diane Schmitt) is responsible for improving coordination and coherence among EU institutions, EU agencies, Member States and international actors, and for developing

---

[64] Report from The Commission to The European Parliament and The Council Report on the progress made in the fight against trafficking in human beings (2016) {SWD (2016) 159 final}.

[65] The idea of National Special Rapporteurs and an Anti-Trafficking Commissioner at the EU level has led Cullen to suggest that this network of rapporteurs could be important in linking the EU's system with that of the CoE Convention, which establishes an expert committee to monitor implementation, as well as UN which has a Special Rapporteur on trafficking in persons especially women and children.

[66] They are elected by the Committee of the Parties for a term of office of four years, renewable once. See further, Resolution CM/Res(2013)28 on rules on the election procedure of the members of the Group of Experts on Action against Trafficking in Human Beings (GRETA) (https://wcd.coe.int/ViewDoc.jsp?id=2119269&Site=CM&BackColor Internet=C3C3C3&BackColorIntranet=EDB021&BackColorLogged=F5D383) (adopted by the Committee of Ministers of the Council of Europe on 24 October 2013).

[67] See further, EU Anti-Trafficking Coordinator (https://home-affairs.ec.europa.eu/policies/int ernal-security/organised-crime-and-human-trafficking/together-against-trafficking-human-beings/ eu-anti-trafficking-coordinator_en). Accessed October 2022.

existing, and new EU policies to address Trafficking in Human Beings. This includes monitoring the implementation of the EU Strategy on Combatting Trafficking in Human Beings (2021–2025).[68]

The European Commission Report[69] on the progress made in the fight against trafficking in human beings (2016) and the 2017 EU Guidelines on the Promotion and Protection of the Rights of the Child—Leave no Child Behind are two selected examples of non-legislative contemporary action in recent years. The 2016 report was written to identify the progress made in the 'fight against trafficking in human beings' as required under Article 20 of Directive 2011/36/EU on preventing and combating trafficking in human beings and protecting its victims. The Commission recommends that concerted and coordinated efforts are made to prevent and address child trafficking. Namely through reducing the vulnerability of at-risk children, through providing adequate support to child victims, and finally by ensuring that a child protection dimension is incorporated into all measures targeting children. This final recommendation was to be incorporated particularly through the fortification of integrated child protection systems and their cross-border cooperation. These observations in the 2016 European Commission report highlight how the focus of the EU is upon the trafficking of children for the purposes of sexual exploitation.[70] This encompasses a focus on the "stereotypical victim", as the EU is choosing to identify who is a 'deserving' victim. The Member States of the EU have adopted controversial policies and stances with the current refugee or 'migration crisis in the Mediterranean'. The 2016 report demonstrates the continued role of the state, framing themselves as the heroic rescuer, focusing upon evil criminals and their prosecution rather than addressing the role that states themselves have in causing and driving crises including the ongoing plight of refugees within Europe. On a policy level, child trafficking was

---

[68] See further, files_en (https://home-affairs.ec.europa.eu/system/files_en?file=2021-04/14042021_eu_strategy_on_combatting_trafficking_in_human_beings_2021-2025_com-2021-171-1_en.pdf). Accessed October 2022.

[69] From the Commission to the European Parliament and Council.

[70] With regard to child prostitution, the Child Sexual Abuse Directive also indirectly helps the fight against child trafficking by obliging Member States to ensure that the act of engaging in sexual activity with a child where recourse is made to prostitution is criminalised and subject to a minimum level of imprisonment penalties.

subsequently addressed in the EU Strategy towards the Eradication of Trafficking in Human Beings (2012–2016) with Action A.3 asking for the creation of child protection systems for trafficked children and model standards for guardianship, for instance. Most recently, in 2017, the EU Foreign Ministers adopted the revised EU Guidelines on the Promotion and Protection of the Rights of the Child—Leave no Child Behind.[71] The report explicitly references child trafficking in 3 different contexts all under sections addressing the Sustainable Development Goals.

6.3 The European Court of Human Rights

The European Court of Human Rights (hereafter, the ECtHR) was established on 21 January 1959, with a mandate to ensure that States which had signed up to the Convention for the Protection of Human Rights and Fundamental Freedoms, commonly known as the European Convention on Human Rights (hereafter the ECHR) adhered to their obligations.[72] The ECHR opened for signature in Rome on 4 November 1950 and came into force on 3 September 1953. It was the first instrument to give effect to certain rights stated in the UDHR and make them binding.[73] The ECHR is an international treaty under which the Member States of the Council of Europe promise to secure fundamental civil and political rights, not only to their own citizens but also to everyone within their jurisdiction. The ongoing issues with "fortress Europe" and the perceived threat of irregular/illegal migration and the electrified undercurrent of race, extraction, and exclusion create a toxic cocktail of conflict over the realities of this aspiration.

The role of the ECtHR is not to be ignored, with the case of V.C.L and A.N v the United Kingdom (2021) considered in detail in the subsequent chapter. The pivotal case in the context of slavery pre-dating the 2021 decision emerges in the decision of the case of Rantsev v. Cyprus

---

[71] See further, Guidelines on the Promotion and Protection of the Rights of the Child | EEAS Website (https://www.eeas.europa.eu/node/45976_en). Accessed July 2022.
[72] Article 19 European Convention on Human Rights.
[73] https://www.echr.coe.int/Pages/home.aspx?p=basictexts&c=. Accessed June 2021.

and Russia,[74] the applicant, a Russian national, brought a complaint against the Republic of Cyprus and Russia in the ECtHR in relation to the death of his 20-year-old daughter. The ECtHR found a violation of Article 4 of the European Convention (Prohibition of slavery and forced labour). It should be emphasised here that the case law of the ECtHR in Article 4 imposes broader positive obligations on the state that are not limited to individual conduct and criminalisation (Mantouvalou, 2018, 13). The Court clarified the positive obligations upon States to investigate allegations of trafficking and to implement measures to prevent and protect people from human trafficking. The Court unanimously found that trafficking fell within the scope of Art. 4. Notably, the trafficking in human beings is not specifically referred to in the European Convention and has only ever been considered by the Court on one prior occasion, in Siliadin v France Application 73316/01.[75]

In Rantsev the Court said:

the duty to penalise and prosecute trafficking is only one aspect of Member States' general undertaking to combat trafficking. The extent of the positive obligations arising under Article 4 must be considered within this broader context.[76]

The positive obligations of State authorities in relation to sex trafficking, include an obligation to criminalise, to prosecute and investigate, to take positive operational measures to protect individuals at risk to prevent this from materialising, and to put in place an appropriate legislative and administrative framework (Mantouvalou, 2018, 14). An implication of Rantsev was that a very restrictive visa regime was incompatible with the ECHR, because the conditions of that visa were linked to trafficking and exploitation.[77] As highlighted by Mantouvalou, the expectation that 'as part of the drive to combat modern slavery, amendments would be made

---

[74] See further, https://ec.europa.eu/anti-trafficking/legislation-and-case-law-case-law/rantsev-v-cyprus-and-russia-application-no-2596504_en. Accessed July 2021.

[75] See further, https://ec.europa.eu/anti-trafficking/node/4557. Accessed July 2021.

[76] Rantsev, para 285.

[77] Rantsev, para 293.

to particularly restrictive classes of visa, which place workers in a position of vulnerability to exploitation' (Mantouvalou, 2018, 14).

6.4 Case Study: The UK of Great Britain and Northern Ireland

The United Kingdom (hereafter, the UK) signed the Palermo Protocol in 2000 and ratified it in 2006. The legal context of the UK needs to be commented upon here, as there are 3 separate legal jurisdictions within it, namely England and Wales, Scotland, and Northern Ireland.[78] A critical issue that has emerged from the ongoing research and debates following the enactment of this legislation is the contradictions and tensions between the legislative frames within the 3 UK legal jurisdictions. The initial amendments to law within the respective jurisdictions of the UK were piecemeal, based on an assumption that trafficking was an immigration offence 'involving foreign nationals brought to the UK that occurred mainly to make money from commercial sex' (Dottridge, 2021, 22). However, this changed when the UK ratified the Council of Europe Convention on Action against Trafficking in Human Beings (2005) in December 2008. The CoE Trafficking Convention required state parties to take a broader approach and to protect the rights of trafficking victims.[79] Moreover, the issue of modern slavery has been identified as a compliance one, with new legislation implemented in the state of California in the USA through the Transparency in Supply Chains Act, 2010, the UK's Modern Slavery Act (MSA, 2015) and most recently Australia's Modern Slavery Act (2018).

---

[78] With different instruments implemented in each, namely the Human Trafficking and Exploitation Act (Scotland) 2015, https://www.legislation.gov.uk/asp/2015/12/contents. Accessed October 2022; Human Trafficking and Exploitation (Criminal Justice and Support for Victims) Act (Northern Ireland) 2015, https://www.legislation.gov.uk/nia/2015/2/contents. Accessed October 2022.

[79] Some actions included the establishment of the Human Trafficking Centre in 2007, later subsumed into an All-Parliamentary Group on Human Trafficking in 2015. With the UK Government announcing anti-slavery day to be celebrated annually on 18 October 2010.

6.4.1 The Rise of Modern Slavery in the UK

Modern slavery is a term that is commonly used in the UK to describe several situations including the trafficking in human beings and forced labour, including the trafficking of children. Moreover, in relation to children, the issue of 'county lines' has fallen under the rubric of 'modern slavery' as the expanse of term continues.[80] However, the term that is 'most commonly used internationally, and in Europe in particular, is 'trafficking in human beings' (Skrivankova, 2018, 243). What has led to the adoption and universal acceptance of modern slavery as a concept, enshrined into domestic law via the Modern Slavery Act (hereafter the MSA) in 2015[81]? What impact does this shift have in relation to children and their rights, or restrictions upon them? Does the UK move to eradicate 'modern slavery' reflective of the start of a global shift towards the rhetoric of modern slavery rather than human trafficking? For some commentators, the advocacy against modern slavery was one sidelined by the focus upon human trafficking, but it has risen to the fore as a 'catch-all' for a broad range of exploitative practices (Segrave et al., 2018, 9). The question that you may be turning over at this point and reflecting upon is why is language important? Consider the argument by Segrave et al. (2018) that this shift has 'serious implications – the essential one is that it is a distraction in the midst of hand-wringing over myriad forms of exploitation, attention is not being paid to the factors that contribute to and sustain such exploitation'.[82]

The UK Government (at the time a coalition government between the Conservative Party and the Liberal Democrats) outlined its strategic response to modern slavery in the Modern Slavery Strategy, published in November 2014.[83] Additionally, the Inter-Departmental Ministerial

---

[80] County lines is a form of criminal exploitation where urban gangs persuade, coerce, or force children and young people to store drugs and money and/or transport them to suburban areas, market towns, and coastal towns (Home Office, 2018).
[81] Royal assent received 26/03/2015. Entered into Force 29/10/2015.
[82] See further A. Kidd, E.A. Faulkner and L. Arocha, How UK asylum system creates perfect conditions for modern slavery and exploitation to thrive, *The Conversation*, 2019, https://theconversation.com/how-uk-asylum-system-creates-perfect-conditions-for-modern-slavery-and-exploitation-to-thrive-113778. Accessed August 2021.
[83] Home Office, Modern Slavery Strategy.

Group on Modern Slavery published its annual report in October 2013 which highlighted activity to fight modern slavery across the UK, as well as providing information on the nature and scale of the problem.[84] In 2015 the Modern Slavery Marketing Campaign Evaluation Report was published, stating that the total cost of the media campaign was £2.18 million.[85] The effectiveness of awareness-raising campaigns has been fiercely disputed, with Haynes asserting that the money should be prioritised for direct assistance.[86] The National Crime Agency (hereafter, the NCA) has designated modern slavery as a threat,[87] subsequently identifying the importance attached to tackling human trafficking and other forms of enslavement as serious organised crimes (Van Dyke, 2017, 131). The NCA has also launched the Modern Slavery Human Trafficking Unit (hereafter, the MSHTU) which identifies child-related crimes such as commercial sexual exploitation, forced begging, illegal drug cultivation, organised theft, and benefit frauds as a distinct category of exploitation linked to human trafficking.[88] These examples have been used to illustrate how proactive the UK has been with regard to human trafficking and modern slavery. The fight against these issues is one that has garnered support from a wide variety of actors, particularly within

---

[84] Home Office Policy Paper Human trafficking: Inter-departmental ministerial group report, 2013. https://www.gov.uk/government/publications/human-trafficking-inter-departmental-ministerial-group-report-2013.

[85] Modern slavery marketing campaign evaluation report, July 2015, 4, https://www.gov.uk/government/uploads/system/uploads/attachment_data/file/451964/150806_Modern_Slavery_Evaluation_for_publication_FINAL.pdf. Accessed June 2017 See further The current Home Secretary, Amber Rudd, pledged £11 million for groups fighting modern slavery. Home Office Announcement, 27/10/2016, https://www.gov.uk/government/news/home-secretary-pledges-11-million-for-groups-fighting-modern-slavery. Accessed April 2018.

[86] Dina Haynes, The wastefulness of human trafficking awareness campaigns, The wastefulness of human trafficking awareness campaigns | openDemocracy (https://www.opendemocracy.net/en/beyond-trafficking-and-slavery/wastefulness-of-human-trafficking-awareness-campaigns/). Accessed December 2022. See further E. Shih, 'The fantasy of spotting human trafficking: Training spectacles in racist surveillance', *Wagadu* 22 (2021), 105–137. E. Shih & J. Quirk, *Introduction: Do the hidden costs outweigh the practical benefits of human trafficking awareness campaigns?* Available from: https://www.opendemocracy.net/en/beyond-trafficking-and-slavery/introduction-do-hidden-costs-outweigh-practical-benefits-of-huma/.

[87] NCA, National Strategic Assessment of Serious and Organised Crime 2016, http://www.nationalcrimeagency.gov.uk/publications/731-national-strategic-assessment-of-serious-and-organised-crime-2016/file. Accessed July 2017.

[88] Modern Slavery Human Trafficking Unit (MSHTU), http://www.nationalcrimeagency.gov.uk/about-us/what-we-do/specialist-capabilities/uk-human-trafficking-centre. Accessed July 2017.

the UK.[89] The bipartisan appeal of the language of "modern slavery" can be identified through support from businesses, charitable organisations, religious leaders, and politicians. The commitment of the UK to the abolition of contemporary slavery is clear through the considerable amounts of funding that have recently been dedicated to the cause and the passing of the Modern Slavery Act in 2015.[90]

Speaking in 2013, Theresa May (then the Home Secretary) stated that 'The first step to eradicating the scourge of modern slavery is acknowledging and confronting its existence. The second is accepting it is the responsibility of us all to abolish it once and for all'.[91] Marketing herself as the William Wilberforce of the twenty-first century, and "firmly nailing her colours to the contemporary abolitionist mast"[92] May announced the intention to introduce a Modern Slavery Bill in August 2013.[93] The significance of this Act needs to be understood, as at first glance the Act appears noble in its aim to protect the vulnerable, rescue the weak, and prosecute the evil, what this deflects from is the lack of awareness that exploitation is a consequence of capitalism and stringent immigration policies implemented here within the UK. A key issue is that to unproblematically accept colonial slavery as the standard against which any claims to forced or compulsory labour are measured in the twenty-first century, as in the case of the European Convention on

---

[89] Organisations such as Anti-Slavery International founded in 1839, through AHRC projects based in the UK such as 'Antislavery Usable Past', www.usablepast.ac.uk. Accessed March 2017, to politicians such as Theresa May, Fiona Bruce and Frank Field.

[90] The current Home Secretary Amber Rudd pledged £11 million for groups fighting modern slavery. Home Office Announcement, 27/10/2016, https://www.gov.uk/government/news/home-secretary-pledges-11-million-for-groups-fighting-modern-slavery. Accessed March 2017.
More recently the government announced a fund of £40 million to tackle child sexual abuse and child trafficking, with £2.2million specifically for organisations working to protect children at risk of trafficking. Home Office Announcement, 16/02/17, https://www.gov.uk/government/news/government-delivers-40-million-to-tackle-child-sexual-abuse-and-child-trafficking. Accessed March 2017.

[91] Theresa May, *The Telegraph*, 24/11/2013, http://www.telegraph.co.uk/comment/10470717/Theresa-May-Slaves-may-work-in-your-nail-bar-too.html. Accessed March 2017.

[92] J. O'Connell Davidson, *Viewpoint: What's wrong with modern slavery? Why Theresa May in Wilberforce's clothing won't appeal to all*, 5/11/2013, http://discoversociety.org/2013/11/05/586/. Accessed March 2017.

[93] Paragraph 8, Background, Explanatory Notes, Modern Slavery Act 2015, http://www.legislation.gov.uk/ukpga/2015/30/notes/division/3. Accessed March 2017.

Human Rights or the Modern Slavery Act 2015 in England and Wales (Bhandar, 2018).

The UK has sought to strategically position itself as a world leader in terms of the fight against the scourge of modern slavery. The claim that the UK government that it is the 'world leader in addressing modern slavery is not only demonstrably false, or at best, very partial' (Skrivankova, 2018, 258). Furthermore, the 'UK government has often conveyed a feeling that its own national framework is adequate for addressing trafficking and modern slavery – a feeling not supported by the outcomes of governmental practice and that it does not need the additional impetus provided by international frameworks' (Craig, et al. 2019, 11). This view is arguably reflective of the blindness of "Little England" an all-powerful nation that needs no one, a level of superiority, righteousness, and privilege that strides ahead with the idea 'Briton rules the waves and Britons never ever will be slaves'. Despite this persona, the UK has now incorporated most of the UN, ILO, and European Conventions in addition to the EU regulations and Directives into domestic law and policy, however it 'often did so with hesitancy, and in some cases only partially' (Balch & Geddes, 2011). However, consider the point raised by Balch which questions whether 'promises to eradicate modern slavery, and to stamp out the criminals that Theresa May referred to as 'slave-drivers' (May 2017) empty and doomed to fail? Will they do nothing to reduce severe forms of exploitation?' (Balch, 2018, 75).

The question remains—what is modern slavery? As a term 'modern slavery' has become widespread in debates within the UK around the most severe forms of exploitation, not least because of the Modern Slavery Act adopted in 2015 which uses the term as un umbrella concept to cover those forms (Craig, et al. 2019, 3). Despite the adoption of the language of 'modern slavery', a unified understanding of what does and does not encompass 'modern slavery' is yet to be (if ever) agreed. The mission of Free the Slaves to end slavery is highlighted as one that 'presupposes that 'modern slavery' constitutes a uniquely intolerable moral wrong, and that it can be separated from other social and global ills for purposes of practical intervention and for the purposes of quantification, something particularly important to their project' (O'Connell Davidson, 2015, 8).

'Modern slavery worldwide takes many forms, some of them very modern phenomena, others historically familiar, and includes chattel slavery, forced labour, debt bondage, serfdom, forced marriage, the trafficking of adults and children, child soldiers, domestic servitude, the severe economic exploitation of children, organ harvesting; many of them exist in the UK or in other countries linked to it through the supply of goods and services' (Craig et al., 2019). The appropriateness of the language of slavery has been questioned by Dottridge, with Beutin rejecting the equation with the historical trans-Atlantic slave trade (2017), in addition to the crucifixion of the UK's approach to modern slavery, denouncing it as 'reactionary and undermining human rights' (O'Connell Davidson, 2015). The emphasis anti-slavery campaigns are often placed upon the victims, reduced to 'objects of trade'. They abound with visual imagery of women and girls as slabs of meat, or packed in jam jars or sardine tins, or with bodies barcoded ready for sale, or as inanimate objects such as puppets, or as decapitated heads of packaged as sex toys (Andrijasevic, 2007; Aradau, 2004; O'Connell Davidson, 2015, 18).

The UK has been proactive in its campaign to eradicate modern slavery and human trafficking as demonstrated through legal, policy, and social campaigns in response to the issue. Indeed, as identified by Craig et al. the emergence of concerns about the severe exploitation of people within global supply chains 'unexpectedly came to the fore during debates leading the MSA'. More recent manifestations in the UK 'include large-scale farming of cannabis plants by young Vietnamese boys imprisoned in domestic properties, and the use of children and adults by, predominately Eastern European criminal gangs to beg, pickpocket or shoplift' (Craig et al. 2019, 8). As articulated by Skrivankova the UK being part of a regional response is essential for the UK's anti-slavery policing capability.[94]

The EU Directive adopts and expands upon both the definitions and obligations contained within the Trafficking Protocol and the CoE Convention on Action against Trafficking. To ensure full compliance with the obligations contained within the EU Directive in England and

---

[94] 2018, 258.

Wales, Parliament made changes to the Sexual Offences Act 2003 and the Asylum and Immigration (Treatment of Claimants, etc.) Act 2004 through Sections 109 and 110 of the Protection of Freedoms Act 2012.[95] Additionally, in relation to slavery, servitude, and forced or compulsory labour, the UK has ratified the ILO Convention (No. 29) Concerning Forced or Compulsory Labour. In addition, the UK has added a prohibition of forced or compulsory labour to the existing prohibition of slavery and servitude contained within the 1926 Slavery Convention. Moreover, in 2000 the UK ratified the ILO Convention (No. 182) concerning the Prohibition and Immediate Action for the Elimination of the Worst Forms of Child Labour, which commits signatory states to take immediate action to both prohibit and eliminate the worst forms of child labour. Furthermore, the ECHR through Article 4 prohibits holding a person in slavery or servitude or requiring a person to perform forced or compulsory labour. However, as highlighted by O'Connell Davidson 'contemporary states efforts to combat trafficking go hand in glove with their wider actions against illegal migration' (2015, 130). The UK is a prime example of the interplay or clash between the priorities of the Modern Slavery Act 2015, the Nationality and Borders Bill[96] and the hostile environment.

6.4.2 The Modern Slavery Act 2015

The Modern Slavery Act 2015 (hereafter, the MSA) received Royal Assent on 26 March 2015, with the six-year anniversary of the Act recently passing. The Home Office claimed that the Modern Slavery Act was the 'first of its kind in Europe' enacted with the aim of specifically addressing slavery and trafficking in the twenty-first century.[97] Through consolidating existing legislation upon human trafficking and slavery, the

---

[95] Modern Slavery Act, Explanatory Notes, Background, paragraph 5, http://www.legislation.gov.uk/ukpga/2015/30/notes/division/3. Accessed July 2017.
[96] Passed second reading in July 2021 in the House of Commons.
[97] 26 March 2015, News Story, Historic law to end Modern Slavery passed, Home Office, https://www.gov.uk/government/news/historic-law-to-end-modern-slavery-passed. Accessed March 2017.

Act has been heralded as a 'historic milestone' by the former Home Secretary (and former Prime Minister of the UK) Theresa May stated that 'This landmark legislation sends the strongest possible signal to criminals that if you are involved in this vile trade you will be arrested, you will be prosecuted and you will be locked up. And it says to victims, you are not alone - we are here to help you'.[98]

The MSA and parallel legislation in Scotland[99] and Northern Ireland[100] have been both lauded and critiqued since their introduction and adoption. The MSA was heralded by the UK Home Office as a mechanism that will 'give law enforcement the tools to fight modern slavery, ensure perpetrators can receive suitably severe punishments for these appalling crimes and enhance support and protection for victims'.[101] Over two years since its enactment, in December 2017, the National Audit Office published a highly critical report on the UK response to modern slavery.[102] The Act had a number of aims, namely to consolidate and simplify the existing offences into a single Act,[103] introduce 'suitably severe punishment' which included life sentences, enable law enforcement to stop boats where slaves are suspected of being held or trafficked, introduce a defence for victims of slavery and trafficking and in relation to children make 'provision for independent child trafficking advocates' for example.[104] As children are the focus of this book, it would

---

[98] News Story. Historic law to end Modern Slavery passed. Home Office, Karen Bradley MP and the Rt Hon Theresa May MP, 26 March 2015, https://www.gov.uk/government/news/historic-law-to-end-modern-slavery-passed. Accessed June 2015.

[99] Human Trafficking and Exploitation Act (Scotland) 2015, https://www.legislation.gov.uk/asp/2015/12/contents. Accessed July 2021.

[100] Human Trafficking and Exploitation (Criminal Justice and Support for Victims) Act (Northern Ireland) 2015, https://www.legislation.gov.uk/nia/2015/2/contents. Accessed June 2021.

[101] Modern Slavery Act, Home Office, 10 June 2014, https://www.gov.uk/government/collections/modern-slavery-bill. Accessed July 2021.

[102] https://www.nao.org.uk/report/reducing-modern-slavery/. Accessed July 2021.

[103] The Act consolidates and seeks to clarify the offences of human trafficking for sexual (Sexual Offences Act 2003) and non-sexual (Asylum and Immigration Act 2004) exploitation into one substantive offence of human trafficking whilst providing the separate offence of slavery, servitude, and forced or compulsory labour (Coroners and Justice Act 2009) and an offence for preparatory offences (committed with a view to committing a trafficking offence).

[104] See further—Beddoe and Brotherton critiqued the British Modern Slavery Act of 2015 over potential obstacles in prosecuting cases where the movement of victim (s) is difficult to prove.

be an error to not comment upon the support available generally to victims of modern slavery or the provision of child advocates. Heralded as 'world-leading'[105] in terms of the fight against "modern slavery", since its implementation has seen the government of Australia follow suit adopting a Modern Slavery Act of its own in 2018.[106] The MSA of Australia explicitly states that the Act requires 'some entities to report on the risks of modern slavery in their operations and supply chains and actions to address those risks, and for related purposes'.[107] Malcolm Turnbull's government introduced Australia's Modern Slavery Act, but was also deemed by the UN Special Rapporteur on torture and other cruel, inhuman or degrading treatment or punishment to have 'violated the right of the asylum-seekers including children to be free from torture or cruel, inhuman or degrading treatment' through its failure to provide adequate detention conditions; end the detention of children; and stop the escalating violence and tension at its offshore processing centres (Martins Junior & O'Connell Davidson, 2021; McDonell, 2016).

Subsequently through the passage of the Modern Slavery Act in the UK in 2015, a statutory defence was set out in England and Wales through Section 45 which provides for a defence for victims who commit criminal offences because of their exploitation. Burland (2018) has commented that this section is frequently disregarded by criminal justice agencies within the UK. However, organisations such as ECPAT have

---

See C. Beddoe and V. Brotherton, *Class Acts? Examining modern slavery legislation across the UK*, Anti-Trafficking Monitoring Group, London, 2016, https://www.antislaverycommissioner.co.uk/media/1253/class-acts.pdf.

[105] https://www.telegraph.co.uk/news/2016/07/30/we-will-lead-the-way-in-defeating-modern-slavery/. Accessed July 2021.

[106] Modern Slavery Act 2018 No. 153, 2018, https://www.legislation.gov.au/Details/C2018A00153. Accessed July 2021.

[107] https://www.legislation.gov.au/Details/C2018A00153. Accessed July 2021 Note the Dutch gov—Child Labour Due Diligence Law. India Committee for the Netherlands, 'Child Labour Due Diligence Law for Companies Adopted by Dutch Parliament' (8 February 2017) at http://www.indianet.nl/170208e.html. France—Human Rights Due Vigilence Law European Coalition for Corporate Justice, 'French Corporate Duty of Vigilance Law' (February 2017) at https://businesshumanrights.org/sites/default/files/documents/French%20Corporate%20Duty%20of%20Vigilance%20Law%20FAQ.pdf. In the US, the Federal Acquisition Regulation prohibits selling a product sourced overseas through federal contracts, if it is mined, produced, or manufactured by forced child labour. Federal Acquisition Regulation, 48 CFR §101, at 22.15.

expressed concerns it is not appropriate for children or compliant with international legislation on child trafficking.[108] These concerns proved justified in the unfolding case of two Vietnamese nationals trafficked to the UK for the purposes of cannabis cultivation and their treatment by the system of the UK.[109] With a UNICEF briefing report in 2017 commenting that the clause is yet to be tested in court, but has been used in the investigation stage since entering into force. There is a statutory duty on local authorities under s.51 MSA to notify the Secretary of State through the National Referral Mechanism (NRM) where there are 'reasonable grounds' to believe that an individual may be a victim of modern slavery. Additionally, the perception of trafficking of children and commercial sexual exploitation and or abuse as synonymous continues to be an issue. One of the reasons why trafficking for the purposes of sexual exploitation is continually identified as the most common purpose for trafficking is that commercial sexual exploitation is arguably more visible and identifiable than other forms of exploitation.[110] It could however be due to a structural bias that exists within the dominant paradigms surrounding trafficking. In the UK and Europe, for example, attention is paid to 'child sex trafficking' which covers any minor in prostitution, endorsing the anti-prostitution rhetoric that often dominates trafficking debates. This accompanies the anti-immigration thrust of anti-trafficking policies and activities, consequently giving rise to a 'radicalised panic around the "sexual grooming" of white girls by immigrant men' (Kempadoo et al., 2012, xvi). The continued racialisation and sexualisation of trafficking is important with regard to children, as it invokes a 'moral panic' response.

In England and Wales, Independent Child Trafficking Guardians (ICTGs)[111] are an independent source of advice for trafficked children

---

[108] See further, https://www.ecpat.org.uk/News/landmark-victory-european-court-human-rights-child-trafficking. Accessed 23 June 2021.
[109] This case will be discussed in detail in the subsequent Chapter.
[110] UNODC Global Report on Trafficking in Persons 2012 did however identify that trafficking for the purposes of sexual exploitation accounted for 58% of all the trafficking cases detected globally however the report fails to identify exactly what percentage of the children identified as victims were trafficked for sexual exploitation.
[111] See further, Interim Guidance for Independent Child Trafficking Guardians (accessible version)—GOV.UK (www.gov.uk). Accessed 1 October 2022.

who can speak up on their behalf and act in their best interests. The Home Office is required by Section 48 of the Modern Slavery Act 2015 to provide ICTGs to all potentially trafficked children in England and Wales. Since May 2021, ICTGs were available in two-thirds of Local Authorities.

The National Referral Mechanism

In the UK, the number of referrals into the National Referral Mechanism (hereafter, NRM),[112] the UK's framework for identifying and supporting potential victims of modern slavery, offers an insight into patterns of trends of modern slavery and how the overall system designed to address it is functioning.[113] If the potential victim is under the age of eighteen, or may be under eighteen, an NRM referral must be made—children cannot be referred in using a Duty to Notify (DtN) referral. Child victims do not have to consent to be referred into the NRM and must first be safeguarded and then referred into the NRM process.[114] The operation of the NRM is not free from scrutiny and has recently become a focal point of the current conservative government as part of their anti-immigration campaign. To the point a joint statement from three of the UN Special Rapporteurs[115] has been issued, specifically focusing upon the activity of the UK in 2022. "We are alarmed by the rise in

---

[112] National referral mechanism guidance: adult (England and Wales)—GOV.UK (https://www.gov.uk/government/publications/human-trafficking-victims-referral-and-assessment-forms/guidance-on-the-national-referral-mechanism-for-potential-adult-victims-of-modern-slavery-england-and-wales).

[113] See further, Modern Slavery: National Referral Mechanism and Duty to Notify statistics UK, end of year summary, 2021—GOV.UK (https://www.gov.uk/government/statistics/modern-slavery-national-referral-mechanism-and-duty-to-notify-statistics-uk-end-of-year-summary-2021/modern-slavery-national-referral-mechanism-and-duty-to-notify-statistics-uk-end-of-year-summary-2021). Accessed 1 October 2022.

[114] See further, National referral mechanism guidance: adult (England and Wales)—GOV.UK (https://www.gov.uk/government/publications/human-trafficking-victims-referral-and-assessment-forms/guidance-on-the-national-referral-mechanism-for-potential-adult-victims-of-modern-slavery-england-and-wales). Accessed October 2022.

[115] Namely, *Mr. Tomoya Obokata, Special Rapporteur on contemporary forms of slavery, including its causes and consequences; Ms. Siobhán Mullally, Special Rapporteur on trafficking in persons, especially women and children; Mr. Felipe González Morales, Special Rapporteur on the human rights of migrants.*

unsubstantiated claims by public officials and Government departments regarding persons seeking protection under the Modern Slavery Act and the National Referral Mechanism in the past days and weeks". Government officials have voiced such claims in the media and on 13 December 2022, the current Prime Minister Rishi Sunak is reported to of delivered an oral statement to Parliament in which he said that "the threshold for someone to be considered a modern slave will be significantly raised".[116]

Rhetoric aside, the annual NRM statistics indicate a long-term trend of annual increases since 2009 when the system was founded, apart from 2020 when the number of referrals was flat due to pandemic-related disruptions. In 2021, 5468 children were referred as potential victims of modern slavery, an increase of 9% on the previous year (5028).

Graph 6.1 demonstrates the data available since the creation of the NRM in 2009, focusing upon the total number of referrals, the number of children (aged 17 or under) and an emerging category since 2019 where the age group of the referrals is not known or recorded. The category of 'age not known' subsequently increases over the next four years, but no further explanation can be determined. At the time of writing the data for 2022 is incomplete, with the first three quarters only available and has therefore not been included in the graph. What is noteworthy is that at the end of 2021, the number of referrals for children and the category of 'age not known' equates to half of the total number, with 43% for children and 7% for the 'not known' categories respectively (Graph 6.2).

6.4.3 Children: Slavery, Trafficking, and Exploitation

The need to demarcate children as an exceptional category has been alluded to throughout this book, and the focus upon the response of the UK and more specifically within the legal jurisdiction of England and Wales is an illustrative example. Not only in light of legal and policy developments in the twenty-first century but dating back to

---

[116] UK: UN experts condemn attacks on credibility of slavery and trafficking victims | OHCHR (https://www.ohchr.org/en/press-releases/2022/12/uk-un-experts-condemn-attacks-credibility-slavery-and-trafficking-victims). Accessed December 2022.

288   E. A. Faulkner

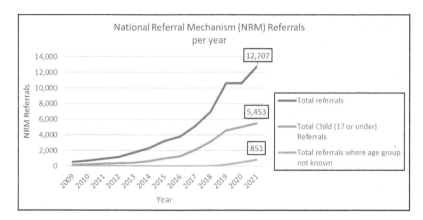

Graph 6.1 National Referral Mechanism (NRM) referrals (2009–2021) (*Source* Author. Data extracted from the quarterly statistics available via National Referral Mechanism statistics—GOV.UK [www.gov.uk]. Accessed February 2023)

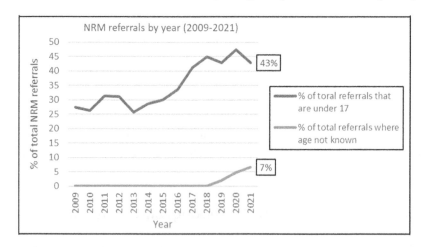

Graph 6.2 NRM annual referrals: Children and 'age not known' (2009–2021) (*Source* Author. Data extracted from the quarterly statistics available via National Referral Mechanism statistics—GOV.UK [www.gov.uk]. Accessed February 2023)

the early twentieth century and the peak of fears of "White Slavery" which was a perceived threat to the innocence, purity, and morality of young white girls. This notion of innocence remains powerful with contemporary responses, acutely identified by Duane and Meiners as 'the precious innocence of children that animates so much of the modern fundraising lexicon – and humanitarian actions that draw upon those funds'. The fascination of England with rescuing children is not new or isolated to the twenty-first century, as references to saving children from the 'clutches of the traffickers' can be found within the first report upon Traffic of Women and Children in England in 1925. In this case, the child in question was fourteen-year-old Fanny Zilbermann, of French origin. The point here is to illustrate the re-birth of child trafficking/slavery as a grave societal concern, and to pose the question—why are children a unique category? Indeed, consider that 'children haunt the legal and imaginative rhetoric defining and combatting modern-day slavery, as they facilitate a sentimental model of care that negates the rights of those who require caretaking' (Dunae & Meiners, 2021, 59). To translate, this means that children occupy the role of victims, who need rescue, and are a unique category as that need they are disqualified for freedom. This notion links back to Locke's Enlightenment freedom, which held at its heart as an opposition between adult and children, a binary that is separated by capacity for reason (Locke, 1764).

Child trafficking affects a wide group of young people (Cooper et al., 2017). In the UK potential child victims of modern slavery must be referred 'as soon as practicable to the NRM by a first responder and assessed by a competent authority (a trained decision maker) within the UK' (DfE, 2017, 5). The reality of child trafficking for some is 'much more complicated than the arbitrary categorisation established in the NRM' (Setter, 2018, 124). Additionally, the perception of trafficking of children and commercial sexual exploitation and or abuse as synonymous continues to be an issue. One of the reasons why trafficking for the purposes of sexual exploitation is continually identified as the most common purpose for trafficking is that commercial sexual exploitation is arguably more visible and identifiable than other forms of exploitation.[117] It could however be due to a structural bias that exists within the dominant paradigms surrounding trafficking. In the UK and Europe, for example, attention is paid to 'child sex trafficking' which covers any minor in prostitution, endorsing the anti-prostitution rhetoric that often dominates trafficking debates. This accompanies the anti-immigration thrust of anti-trafficking policies and activities, consequently giving rise to a 'radicalised panic around the "sexual grooming" of white girls by immigrant men' (Kempadoo et al., 2012, xvi). The continued racialisation and sexualisation of trafficking are important with regard to children, as it invokes a 'moral panic' response.

A different kind of trafficking emerges in the context of the UK. One that focuses on the threat of 'Asian sex gangs' as a new trafficking threat (Cockbain, 2018).[118] In the UK child sexual exploitation (hereafter, CSE) and human trafficking are both legally defines and are distinct yet overlapping terms. Differential treatment of minors who fall victim to sexual exploitation based on their nationality in the UK has been documented by Krsmanovic (2021). In addition to the work of Burland which documents the differing outcomes of referrals to the National Referral Mechanisms for EU citizens and non-EU citizens. This conflicts with the advocation by Kevin Bales that 'in the new slavery race means little'. If this were the case then why would the emerging research from within the UK indicate otherwise, and that the exceptionality of British victims reflects a wider shift to victims as insiders?

The travel aspect of the UK definition of trafficking may but does not need to be an element of CSE for example. The role of the media in the UK in 'constructing the sexual exploitation of British children as

---

[117] UNODC Global Report on Trafficking in Persons 2012 did however identify that trafficking for the purposes of sexual exploitation accounted for 58% of all the trafficking cases detected globally however the report fails to identify exactly what percentage of the children identified as victims were trafficked for sexual exploitation.

[118] See further, Jail for 'sexual predators' who led Asian gang that abused girls as young 12 | Daily Mail Online (https://www.dailymail.co.uk/news/article-1345084/Jail-sexual-predators-led-Asian-gang-abused-girls-young-12.html). Accessed July 2022; Revealed: conspiracy of silence on UK sex gangs | The Times (https://www.thetimes.co.uk/article/revealed-conspiracy-of-silence-on-uk-sex-gangs-gpg5vqsqz9h). Accessed July 2022.

a phenomenon to be approached differently than the sexual exploitation of trafficked minors who are non-British nationals' (Krsmanovic, 2021). This specific focus on Britons as potential victims is noteworthy, implicating that certain victims are legitimate and others not. With the abhorrence of slavery as a 'defining characteristic of the US', a nation committed, in (former) President Barack Obama's 2012 words 'to the enduring cause of freedom' and 'steadfast in [its] resolve to see that all men, women and children have the opportunity to realize this greatest of gifts'. This love of freedom was regarded 'as equally fundamental to Canadian, Australian, British and other Western European societies' (O'Connell Davidson, 2015, 11). As advocated by the former PM and Home Secretary at the time Theresa May, the idea of slaves in their own back garden was 'scarcely believable'. These fears of exploited Britons were noted by the British government in the summer of 2018, publicly expressing 'concerns that holiday makers heading to Majorca might end up trapped in modern slavery' (Faulkner, 2018). This focuses on Britons as victims marked a departure from the established convention of focusing upon 'outsiders' as both the victims and perpetrators, such as foreign nationals working in nail bars, car washes, and other foreign nationals forcing them to do so. The implied racism of a codified suspicion towards those with low local language ability, insinuates or hints how modern slavery is increasingly caught up in growing ideas of nationalism. Furthermore, this stereotypical media representation of CSE cases as trafficking 'reinforces the white slavery myth of foreign men coming to the UK to corrupt local (white girls) and force them into prostitution' (Krsmanovic, 2021, 84).

The League of Nations allowed distinctions to be drawn between those of White European status, and 'natives', 'fetish worshipping tribes', and the 'indigenous'. Those distinctions between us and them, remain but are not as explicit in the adoption of distinct laws for each (note Italy age of consent for natives lower than Italian nationals in colonies) but are implied through the racially informed, biased system of contemporary immigration and hypocrisy of anti-slavery initiatives.

6.4.4 "Categorical Fetishism" and Children in the UK

The issue of labels and language is important but 'should not mask the fact that what is at stake is the most appropriate care solution for each individual child' (Cantwell, 2017, 247). However, different labels or categories impose different standards of protection, care, and obligations upon the UK Government for example. With recommendations in 2022 calling upon the Home Office to ensure that the immigration and asylum system does not re-traumatise children, with an emphasis on those procedures that have the potential to increase the risk of exploitation (Hynes, 2022). In relation to children the UK Government has several obligations that arise, specifically when reviewing 'Looked after Children' (hereafter, LAC) and more specifically unaccompanied asylum-seeking children (hereafter, UASC). The classification of children as UASC is problematic as they are often unlawfully excluded from the duties and protections that are afforded (in theory) to all children in England and Wales. This subsequently places them at risk of significant harm.[119] Local authorities[120] have a duty to provide leaving care services and support to all young people who are leaving care including, asylum-seekers and refugees who fall under the umbrella term of "children on the move". This transition from 'looked after children' to adulthood is important, as highlighted by Kohli (2002) 'young asylum seekers approaching adulthood are, unlike their indigenous peers, at risk not just of social exclusion as they leave care but also of having citizenship denied to them'. Empirical research conducted highlights this issue, with participants identifying the multiple and persistent barriers to accessing documentation in addition to challenges in securing decisions relating to their immigration status. For example, only 2% of child trafficking victims between 2019 and 2020 with irregular migration status in the UK were granted the leave to remain, of which they are entitled to

---

[119] See further, Safeguarding children who may have been trafficked—GOV.UK (https://www.gov.uk/government/publications/safeguarding-children-who-may-have-been-trafficked-practice-guidance). Accessed October 2022.

[120] See further, Local government structure and elections—GOV.UK (https://www.gov.uk/guidance/local-government-structure-and-elections). Accessed October 2022.

under international law.[121] Indeed, as highlighted through the work of ECPAT, Hynes and Connolly from 2022 many of the young victims consulted about their views and experiences of trafficking indicated that the UK immigration procedures were often worse than their experiences of exploitation.[122]

The UK Government has specific obligations under domestic, regional, and international law to UASC. Under the UN Convention on the Rights of the Child for example, children are entitled to non-discrimination, protection, and care in addition to participation and decisions made considering their best interests. In domestic legal frameworks for example, under the Children Act 1989, for example Section 17 identifies 'all children in need', with Section 22 identifying 'those in need of care and being looked after by the local authority'. There is, importantly no requirement for a child to be 'ordinarily resident' to trigger these duties, the child's presence is sufficient (Hynes, 2022). Additionally, the views of the child are taken into account 'as would be appropriate given the age and understanding of the child'.[123] You may wonder why my focus has shifted slightly to consider the position of the care of UASC, well the following Statutory Guidance from 2017 explicitly links the two categories together through the 'Care of unaccompanied migrant children and child victims of modern slavery'.[124] The Guidance emphasises that 'Unaccompanied migrant children and child victims of modern slavery, including trafficking can be some of the most vulnerable children in the country' (Statutory Guidance, 2017, 3).

Graph 6.3 draws together the available data on those classified as 'UASC' and referrals of children (age 17 and under) to the NRM

---

[121] See further, New data obtained from the Home Office shows only 2% of child victims of trafficking are given Discretionary Leave to Remain in the UK | ECPAT UK (https://www.ecpat.org.uk/news/new-data-obtained-from-the-home-office-shows-only-2-of-child-victims-of-trafficking-are-given-discretionary-leave-to-remain-in-the-uk). Accessed October 2022.

[122] ECPAT and Hynes report.

[123] CA 1989, s.22 (5) (a) and (b).

[124] See further, Care of unaccompanied migrant children and child victims of modern slavery—GOV.UK (https://www.gov.uk/government/publications/care-of-unaccompanied-and-trafficked-children). Accessed 1 October 2022.

mechanism since 2009. The purpose of this is not to draw a comparison between the two categories, but to follow on from the Statutory Guidance in 2017 which explicitly links the two categories.

However, some observations can be drawn or hypothesized from the visualization of the data, such as the relatively sharp increase in child NRM referrals and that the two data sets marginally separated in 2020 with UASC at 5080 and NRM 5021, with the latter surpassing in 2021. It is time to pause and reflect to consider why this is the case?

The issue of immigration is important in contemporary society and the issue of the language adopted by the current Conservative Government illustrates how polarised the discussion of migration, belonging, citizenship, race, ethnicity, class, gender, and otherness remains. With the current Home Secretary referring to those crossing the English Channel in boats as an "invasion", with the current Prime Minister Rishi Sunak supporting the stance and language of Bravermann as it 'conveys the scale

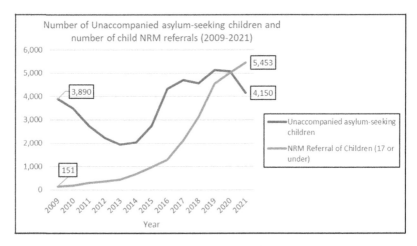

Graph 6.3 Unaccompanied asylum-seeking children and NRM Referrals (2009–2021) (*Source* Author. Data extracted from the quarterly statistics available via National Referral Mechanism statistics—GOV.UK [www.gov.uk]. Accessed February 2023 and Statistics: looked-after children—GOV.UK [www.gov.uk]. Accessed February 2023)

of the challenge' in Autumn 2022.[125] The historical context here is clear, as deciding who are 'desirable' and 'undesirable' is an essential aspect of nation making (Sharma, 2018).

The Immigration Act 2016 provided for the transfer of responsibility for the care of UASC children from Local Authorities where they arrive to the care of other LA with greater capacity, which used to be upon a voluntary basis until 2021. However, a decade of austerity has led to a chronic funding crisis within children's social care, with LA's being eligible for £143 (per child, per night) under the National Transfer Scheme (NTS).[126] Which sounds more than sufficient, right? However, Ofsted through a series of emails told the Department of Education (DfE) that the housing of children in hotels created "unacceptable safeguarding risks".[127] It has been commented that the practice of putting UASC into hotels 'risks establishing yet more unlawful unregistered children's homes'.[128] Notably, under the Care Standards Act 2000, it is unlawful for authorities to provide a child with care if their accommodation is not registered with Ofsted as a children's home.[129] This fact has not dissuaded the current Government away from the policy, with a total of 1251 children being placed into hotel accommodations between July 2021 and February 2022.[130]

---

[125] The High Court decision are the lawfulness of the Rwanda Policy illustrates the contentious nature of contemporary immigration debates within the jurisdiction. See further, Suella Braverman restates Rwanda deportation goal after court ruling | Immigration and asylum | The Guardian (https://www.theguardian.com/uk-news/2022/dec/19/asylum-seekers-rwanda-uk-plan-legal-high-court). Accessed December 2022.

[126] See further, National Transfer Scheme to become mandatory for all local authorities—GOV.UK (www.gov.uk).

[127] See further, Asylum children living in hotels 'unacceptable'—Ofsted—BBC News (https://www.bbc.co.uk/news/uk-england-kent-58957838). Accessed October 2022.

[128] Yvette Stanley, National Director of Ofsted, Safeguarding risks for 600 unaccompanied asylum-seeking children—BBC News (https://www.bbc.co.uk/news/uk-england-kent-59262516). Accessed October 2022.

[129] Care Standards Act 2000 (https://www.legislation.gov.uk/ukpga/2000/14/contents).

[130] Parliamentary Question by Mrs. Emma Lewell-Buck 18/02/2022 and answer by Minister Kevin Foster.

The Hypocrisy of Modern Slavery and the UK

It has been repeatedly demonstrated that measures to clamp down on irregular migration, often enacted in the name of combatting modern slavery and trafficking have had dire consequences for people entitled to protection under the international law of refugees as well as for others on the move. For example, as illustrated by Howard and Okyere (2022) the forced separation of child migrants from their parents or adult companions, alongside the confinement of children in torturous and inhumane immigration detention facilities or refugee camps, are routine aspects of border control in the USA, Europe, Australia, and many other places (O'Connell Davidson, 2016). As highlighted by the UN Task Force to End Deprivation of Liberty of Children, every day, in over 100 countries, migrant children are detained; whether alone or with their families. It is important to highlight that detaining migrant children is not in their best interest; it is a form of violence and a child rights violation. With dwindling opportunities for legally authorized international migration have prompted the expansion and diversification of markets for clandestine migration services (Alpes, 2011; Kempadoo et al., 2005).

The modern anti-slavery campaigns are often reflective of:

> *a neoliberal white chivalrous crusade across the world, born of a moral sense of goodness that shores up the power and subjectivity of the North, with the 'developing' Global South and East as the dumping grounds for helping imperatives involving rescue and charity.* (Kempadoo, 2015, 8)

This idea of morality is not new to contemporary abolition, with the historical campaigns of fears of the 'White Slave Traffic' manifesting in a similar web of morality, rescue, and racism. The anti-trafficking machine in the UK has manifested itself as a moral crusade to rescue those poor unfortunate souls from the clutches of the twenty-first-century slave masters. The 'trafficker is depicted as a hyper-exploitative, vampire capitalist who valorizes his workers without concern for their well-being' (Howard, 2018, 518). This views links to the popular and cultural societal perspectives and in turn 'creates grounds for further discrimination, and other underlying factors that push minority communities into further vulnerability to victimization and over-policing by law enforcement agencies' (Krsmanovic, 2021, 84). What is often neglected is the undercurrent of racism that is concealed by a smokescreen of morality, to do good whilst simultaneously encouraging the perpetuation of exploitation and hostile anti-immigrant policies. People who enter the UK illegally for example are characterised as either undesirable migrants or victims of 'modern slavery'. Our use of labels such as slave, trafficking victim, refugee, and migrant highlights our need to distinguish between those who deserve protection and those who do not. Echoing Kipling's sentiment in 'The White Man's Burden',[131] the anti-slavery machine effectively charges those from superior cultures with the "civilising mission" that Kipling mandated in the twentieth century. The continued use of slavery as a tool to invoke a powerful emotive response is the issue here, as such a conception promotes overly simplistic solutions—such as awareness-raising campaigns or that the removal of children from the fields into education will eradicate the issues (Balch et al., 2019; Okyere, 2014). The narrative produced by the anti-trafficking machine distorts our conceptions of labour, exploitation, and inequality by calling for us to "free the slaves" without recognising that this concept blames the perpetuation of slavery upon the 'toxicity of certain cultures', evoking Western imperialism, and endorsing Kipling's sentiment. Consider the point, that:

> *Slave Codes historically obliged all white citizens to police the movement of slaves, so increasingly in the UK, the entire community is being mustered to monitor unauthorized movement, with employers, universities and now private landlords all under a legal obligation to check the status of migrants and report those suspected of living in the country without authorization, or breaking the terms on which they have been permitted to enter.* (O'Connell Davidson, 2015)

The hypocritical position of the former Prime Minister of the UK Theresa May and her strong advocacy for anti-slavery campaigns on

---

[131] http://www.kiplingsociety.co.uk/poems_burden.htm. Accessed July 2021.

the one hand but on the other lead a 'government that in many ways', generates the conditions creating severe labour exploitation (Lewis et al., 2017). The campaign against modern slavery is highly hypocritical, as the 'moral stance of the contemporary abolitionist movement' hides a deeply and perhaps unconscious racist and imperialist bias. An example of this can be found through the numbers of those purported to be modern slaves by organisations such as the Walk Free foundation 'hide an implicit racist bias. The "best" states fighting modern slavery are all Euro-American, the worst African and Asian'. This is an incomplete and selective view, that praises UK legislation on the one hand whilst overlooking the 'lethal consequences of UK immigration policies or the effects of neo-liberalism on the non-West', a form of cultural imperialism, on the other. Therefore, the contemporary abolitionist movement is 'being wielded as a hypocritical weapon of morality … [which does not] acknowledge the West's role in perpetuating inequality, injustice and exploitation overseas' (Faulkner, 2017) of which much slavery, a legacy of colonialism and imperialism, is a part' (Craig et al. 2019, 20).

6.4.5 The UK and the European Court of Human Rights

An illustrative case was decided in 2021 by the European Court of Human Rights in relation to two Vietnamese victims of trafficking and the UK.[132] This case study focuses upon two Vietnamese nationals and their treatment by the UK, which ultimately led to a significant ruling from the European Court of Human Rights in February 2021. Prior to an analysis of the facts of the case and the wider context a brief introduction to the European Court of Human Rights is necessary.

---

[132] *V.C.L. and A.N. v. the United Kingdom* (applications nos. 77587/12 and 74603/12).

> Article 26 – Non-punishment provision Each Party shall, in accordance with the basic principles of its legal system, provide for the possibility of not imposing penalties on victims for their involvement in unlawful activities, to the extent that they have been compelled to do so.

Fig. 6.2 The Non-punishment provision of the Council of Europe Trafficking Convention 2005

The European Court of Human Rights

V.C.L. and A.N. v. The United Kingdom

The legal framework for the non-punishment of trafficking victims is set out in Council of Europe Convention on Action against Trafficking in Human Beings.[133] This instrument had been signed by the UK on 23/03/2007, ratified on 17/12/2008, and entered into force on 1/04/2009.[134] The CofE Convention is 'significant not only for its contribution to the rights of victims of THB and the fight against traffickers, but particularly for its independent monitoring mechanism, which aims to evaluate on a regular basis the parties' compliance with their obligations' (Piotrowicz et al., 2018, 41). The criminalisation of potential trafficked cannabis gardeners in the UK is 'highly inappropriate from a moral standpoint and, just as significantly, also contradicts the expectations of the 2005 Council of Europe Convention on Action against Trafficking in Human Beings and policy and legislation on the non-punishment of trafficked persons in the UK' (Burland, 2018, 167). Through the CoE Convention Article 26 states are expected to provide for the non-punishment of trafficked persons as highlighted in Fig. 6.2.

---

[133] Adopted by the Committee of Ministers of the Council of Europe on 3 May 2005 and entered into force on 1 February 2008. The Convention builds upon existing international instruments, but goes beyond the standards previously established, and strengthens protections afforded to victims. See further, https://www.coe.int/en/web/gender-matters/the-convention-on-action-against-trafficking. Accessed August 2021.

[134] Reservation—In accordance with Article 31, paragraph 2, of the Convention, the UK reserves the right not to apply Article 31, paragraph 1.d or 1.e, of the Convention. See further, https://www.coe.int/en/web/conventions/full-list/-/conventions/treaty/197?module=declarations-by-treaty&numSte=197&codeNature=2&codePays=UK. Accessed August 2021.

In the period following the adoption of the CoE Trafficking Convention, policy, and legislation in each of the jurisdictions within the UK has been adopted to prevent people from being punished for criminal acts committed as a direct consequence of their trafficking.[135] However, this has not been the reality.

Subsequently through the passage of the Modern Slavery Act in the UK in 2015, a statutory defence was set out in England and Wales through Section 45 which provides for a defence for victims who commit criminal offences because of their exploitation.[136] A report by UNICEF (2017, 8) commented that the statutory defence from punishment for trafficked persons in England and Wales had to date yet to be tested in court, but that it had been used at the investigation stage. However, organisations such as ECPAT have expressed concerns it is not appropriate for children or compliant with international legislation on child trafficking.[137] An ECPAT UK Report illustrated concerns about the extent to which judges sitting in criminal courts understand the non-punishment provision (Finch, 2017, 63). Additionally, UNICEF highlighted that 'Information obtained through interviews with defence lawyers and the police in England indicates some serious shortcomings in the implementation of the non-punishment principle … evidence also shows that there are some defence lawyers who remain unaware of the statutory defence' (UNICEF, 2017, 7). These concerns proved justified in the unfolding case of two Vietnamese nationals trafficked to the UK for the purposes of cannabis cultivation and their treatment by the system of the UK. A State that has tried to assert its dominance as the

---

[135] For example, policies on the non-punishment principle in Scotland published by the Crown Office Procurator Fiscal Service (COPFS 2010), in England and Wales it came from the Crown Prosecution Services (CPS 2011) and finally from the Public Prosecution Service in Northern Ireland (PPSNI 2013).

[136] In Northern Ireland, s. 22 of the Human Trafficking and Exploitation (Criminal Justice and Support for Victims) Act 2015, whilst the Human Trafficking and Exploitation (Scotland) Act 2015 did not include a non-punishment provision. Instead, it required that the Lord Advocate in Scotland provide guidance on the non-punishment of trafficked persons (HTSEA 2015 Section 8).

[137] See further, https://www.ecpat.org.uk/News/landmark-victory-european-court-human-rights-child-trafficking. Accessed 23 June 2021.

world leader in the fight against what former Prime Minister Theresa May labelled 'the scourge of forced labour, modern slavery and human trafficking'.[138] Ultimately, the 'introduction of legislation on the non-punishment of trafficked persons has not been a panacea in preventing them from being punished' (Burland, 2018, 180).

There is a long-standing recognition that people are trafficked into the UK for cannabis cultivation or gardening (Burland, 2018, 169; NCA, 2016, 33). Here is where the TIP reports come into fruition, as the first reference to human trafficking in the UK for cannabis cultivation emerged in 2007 which stated that 'Children, particularly from West Africa, are also trafficked to the U.K for force labor in cannabis factories' (USSD, TIP, 2007, 204) Interestingly and as highlighted by Burland (2018, 170) the issue of trafficking for cannabis cultivation in the UK had been discussed in every TIP report since 2009 (at the time of his 2018 publication). Moreover, it appears that the UK is 'unique in having a recognised long-term and sustained problem of trafficking for cannabis cultivation' (Burland, 2018, 170). With minimal references to the practice since the first TIP report emerged, and only identified within Ireland (2015 and 2016), Denmark (2014), and Albania (2017), respectively. It leads to the observation that this form of exploitation is relatively unique to the UK and that the following case to be focused upon provides an insight into the conflict between national and regional law in regard to child trafficking.

The case upon which this section will now focus upon begun in 2009 with the final decision being held in the ECtHR in early 2021. Therefore, the case straddles across a period after the entry into the CoE Trafficking Convention and the creation, adoption, and subsequent entry into force of the Modern Slavery Act (2015).

---

[138] https://www.gov.uk/government/speeches/pm-speech-to-unga-on-modern-slavery-behind-these-numbers-are-real-people.

Facts of the Case

The applications concerned the prosecution of the (then) minor applicants, both of whom were recognised as victims of trafficking by the designated Competent Authority, for criminal offences connected to their work as gardeners in cannabis factories in the UK.[139]

The case addresses the plight of two individuals, identified as the 'first applicant'[140] and 'second applicant'[141] within the official judgement of the ECtHR. The applicants were born in 1994 and 1992, respectively, residing in Middlesex and London. For clarity, the facts of the cases for each of the applicants will be dealt with separately, with an analysis of the applicant's Conviction and Sentencing following each applicant.

The First Applicant's Conviction and Sentencing

On 6 May 2009 the first applicant was discovered by police at an address in Cambridge during the execution of a drug warrant. The address was a four-bedroomed house which had been converted into a sophisticated cannabis factory containing 420 cannabis plants with a street value of more than GBP £130,000. The first applicant was found alone in the property, in possession of a mobile telephone, with credit, and GBP 100 in cash. Following his discovery, the first applicant was interviewed in the company by a legal representative and an appropriate adult. He claimed that he was fifteen years old (a fact which the Government now accepts to be correct), that he had been smuggled into the UK by his adoptive father, that upon arrival he had encountered two Vietnamese nationals who took him to the address in Cambridge, and that whilst he realised cannabis was being grown there, he had not known that it was illegal. He was charged with being concerned with the production of a controlled drug. Social services assessed the first applicant's age and concluded that

---

[139] Judgement p1.
[140] Applicant in application no. 77587/12 (hereinafter, "the first applicant").
[141] Applicant in application no. 74603/12 (hereinafter, "the second applicant").

he would turn eighteen in January 2010. A district judge in the Magistrate's Court[142] subsequently found in fact that he was at least seventeen years old. At a preliminary hearing before the Crown Court on 21 May 2009, the case was adjourned for a plea and case management hearing. A few days later Refugee and Migrant Justice, a legal advice and representation charity, informed the first applicant's then representative of concerns that he may have been the victim of human trafficking, and that the point had been noted by social services. They further indicated that social services might raise discontinuance with the Crown Prosecution Service[143] (hereafter, the CPS) but if not the matter ought to be taken up at court.

On 13 August 2009 the first applicant had a conference with counsel. There was no record of any exploration of the trafficking issue. The first applicant initially gave "not guilty" instructions and indicated that he was scared, but on receiving counsel's advice he confirmed that he intended to plead "guilty". On 20 August 2009, following the conference with counsel, the first applicant pleaded guilty to the production of a Class B drug.

On 4 September 2009, at a conference at which the first applicant was not assisted by an appropriate adult, different counsel advised him that he could apply for leave to vacate his guilty plea on the ground that he had been trafficked and subjected to forced labour. However, the first applicant instructed counsel that he was not in fear of the alleged traffickers. Nevertheless, sentencing was adjourned to await receipt of a report from social services on whether he was deemed to be the victim of trafficking. On 14 October 2009 the CPS reviewed their decision to prosecute and concluded that there was no credible evidence that the first applicant had been trafficked. The following day, however, the CPS received a letter from the UK Border Agency[144] (hereafter, UKBA) indicating that the circumstances of the first applicant's case had been

---

[142] It is worth noting that the courts system of the UK is complicated, having been the product of piecemeal evolution rather than designed from scratch.

[143] The CPS prosecutes criminal cases which have been investigated by the police and other investigative organisations in England and Wales. The CPS is independent and therefore makes decisions independently of the police and government.

[144] The UKBA closed in 2013 and was replaced by UK Visas and Immigration.

considered by one of the two Competent Authorities which concluded that there were reasonable grounds for believing that he had been trafficked. He was therefore granted a forty-five day "reflection period" and his case was adjourned on the basis that this was in his best interests. On 27 November 2009 UKBA sent a letter to the first applicant's representative. It noted that the trafficking-related criminal investigation was still ongoing but found that the first applicant's circumstances raised the following trafficking indicators: he had been found at a cannabis factory highlighting criminality involving adults; he was not enrolled in school; and he was not allowed to leave the property. It further stated that considering his "credible account"—which had remained consistent in the various meetings he had had with social services—it was considered that he had been trafficked to the UK. On 8 December 2009 the case was reviewed by the CPS lawyer, but the Chief Crown Prosecutor subsequently confirmed that it should be prosecuted. Although no official reasons were given for this decision, in a letter to a Member of Parliament on 10 December the then Director of Public Prosecutions explained that the prosecution had not been discontinued because the offences were extremely serious, there was no defence of duress and no unambiguous evidence of trafficking. At a hearing on 14 December 2009 the CPS argued that to be a victim of trafficking was not a defence; rather, the decision to prosecute was taken considering information they had and had to be kept under review. To apply to vacate would be pointless as duress was not a viable defence. The judge, however, indicated that an application to vacate was well-founded and set a timetable for listing in early 2010 if the application was to be made. In the cells afterwards the first applicant indicated that he wished to change his plea.

On 16 December 2009 defence counsel indicated to the first applicant's solicitors that social services were "outrageous" in advocating a change of plea. He reiterated his view that the fact that the first applicant was not frightened and was looking after the plants in return for help in finding his family made the issue irrelevant. At a hearing on 19 January 2010 the first applicant maintained his plea. It appears that this decision followed a meeting with his solicitors in which he was advised that the finding that he had been trafficked had not been definitively confirmed; that in any case the CPS were not required—and did not intend—to withdraw the prosecution; and that although the decision to prosecute could be challenged in the High Court, it was a lengthy process which had little prospect of success. In the Crown's submission, the evidence suggested that the first applicant was not a trafficked person. Counsel for the Crown went through the facts in detail, noting that he was found in an ordinary house with a mobile phone, credit, and money; in the trafficking assessment he had indicated that his family in Vietnam was not under threat; there were no debts owed to anyone in Vietnam; and he had not been abused prior to his arrest. They therefore found "no reason whatever" to revise their initial assessment that the first applicant should be prosecuted in the public interest. The first applicant was sentenced to twenty months of detention in a young offenders' institution.

The Second Applicant's Conviction and Sentencing

On 21 April 2009 police officers attended a residential premises in London following reports of a suspected burglary. They had been informed that a large body of men had been seen in the gardens to the rear of the premises, forcing their way in. When they got there, they discovered a very sophisticated cannabis factory. The second applicant, together with several other Vietnamese nationals, was found close to the premises, hiding from the marauders. They were all arrested. Upon his arrest, GBP 70 was found on the second applicant. With the assistance of an interpreter, he was interviewed at a police station. As he initially gave his year of birth as 1972, he was treated as an adult (it was later accepted that his actual year of birth was 1992). During the police interview he indicated that upon leaving Vietnam he had travelled to the UK via the Czech Republic. Soon after his arrival, he met some Vietnamese people, including a man ("H") who gave him accommodation, clothes, and food for a week. Whilst he was staying at the house, he was told that it was "best for him not to go out"; however, when asked if he was held there against his will, he said no. After a week, he was taken to the cannabis factory in a vehicle which was "covered up". According to the second applicant, the windows of the factory were bricked up, the only door was locked from the outside and he believed that the factory was guarded. His work included watering the plants and cooking. He slept, ate, and worked in the factory, and he was not paid for his work.

The second applicant claimed that in the beginning he did not know that the plants in the factory were illegal. However, he became suspicious and wished to leave as he was frightened. In or around this time H allowed him to leave the factory with some others for a few days, but when he told H, in the course of a telephone call, that he did not wish to return, H told him that he might be killed if he stopped working. He and the others were then picked up and returned to the factory. Following the interviews, the applicant was charged with being concerned with the production of a controlled drug of Class B, namely cannabis. At a hearing before the Magistrates' Court on 30 April 2009 the second applicant gave his year of birth as 1992. The case was thereafter approached on the basis that he was seventeen years old. The prosecution conducted a file review on 1 June 2009. They appear to have considered that the second applicant had been smuggled into the UK, since his parents had funded his journey to what was hoped would be a life with better prospects. The second applicant was granted legal aid. There is a note in the instructions to his counsel indicating that he had been "trafficked into the UK", although the source of that entry was not traced, and the applicant later accepted that he had not used that term.

Counsel saw the second applicant in a conference on 1 July 2009, taking instructions directly from him with the assistance of a translator. He told counsel that he had fled his home in Vietnam and come to the UK illegally via the Czech Republic. Upon arrival he contacted a cousin in London. Whilst looking for work, some Vietnamese people had introduced him to H, who provided him with accommodation, food, and money. He was then taken to work in the factory, which he initially thought was producing herbal medicine. He was mainly locked in the factory and was unable to go out. After approximately ten days he discovered that the plants were cannabis and asked to leave. He was threatened that if he left, he could or would be killed. Although on one occasion he went with some co-workers to the home of one of their relatives, H contacted them there and as a result of further threats they returned to the factory. As the second applicant accepted that he could have run away from the house of his co-worker's relative, counsel did not believe that a plea of duress would be likely to succeed. The second applicant pleaded guilty in July 2009.

Following his "guilty" plea, a member of the Youth Offending Team prepared a pre-sentence report.[145] The report indicated that the second applicant regretted his decision to accept the offer to work in the factory. He accepted that his motivation had been "financial gain", which was neither acceptable nor justifiable. He accepted responsibility for his decision to act and displayed a level of remorse. On 25 September 2009 the second applicant was sentenced to an eighteen-month detention and training order. He was given credit for his guilty plea, and the account was taken of his young age, the fact that he left Vietnam to make a better life for himself and his "excellent progress" in custody.

Commentary on the First and 'Second Applicants'

There are several issues which arise during the facts of the case section for both the first and second applicants in this case. Firstly, the language which states that the first applicant 'had been smuggled into the United Kingdom by his adoptive father'. Did the first applicant use the word smuggled or was this the language imposed upon him during the translation process? In relation to the second applicant, it appears that he was viewed as being smuggled into the UK as his parents had funded his journey in the hope of him being able to build a better life with improved prospects. It is interesting that a note appeared in his instructions to counsel that he had been trafficked into the UK, however the source of that information was not traced and the 'applicant later accepted that he had not used this term'. Where therefore did this link to trafficking emerge? Why was it discarded? What could have happened if this link had been accepted, or established?

Next, the determination of the first applicant's age, with both social services and the district judge of the Magistrates Court determining that the applicant was at least 17 years old. The 'second applicant' age determination is more problematic; in that he originally gave his date of birth

---

[145] Youth Offending Team (YOT) work with young people that get into trouble with the law, for further information see, https://www.gov.uk/youth-offending-team. Accessed August 2021.

as 1972 and was subsequently treated as an adult. His year of birth was some 20 years later in 1992, a staggering age difference and it evokes the question why was this not flagged as problematic? Research with "children on the move" has demonstrated that a variety of reasons exist as to why a child may lie about their age. They may be suspicious of authority, wish to remain with the unit they have made their journey with a lack of awareness of extra protections afforded to children and the belief that being viewed as an adult is a better option.

The facts indicate that the first applicant 'was not in fear of the alleged traffickers' however consider is fear a necessary piece of the puzzle in light of the omission of the means element of the Trafficking Protocol? In lay terms, this omission means that a child (identified as those under the age of 18 within the Palermo Protocol) does not need to prove that threats, fraud, or coercion have been used as they cannot consent to be trafficked. This idea of fear plays into the dominant perception of trafficking, that the ruthless traffickers dominate, abuse, and exploit their victims in a clear-cut manner. What if the power is more coercive or psychological than physical? Consider the second applicant who indicated that he was not held against his will but adhered to the advice that it was best not to go out. This interplay of psychological control ignored the preference for more obvious elements of control such as the use of physical violence or force. How can you be recognised as a victim if you do not fit into that piece of the puzzle which is the 'ideal victim of trafficking'? The issue of frontline workers being more proactive in recognising female victims of exploitation has been demonstrated through the research of Oude de Breil in the Netherlands who identified that girls were 'being more readily perceived as victims than boys, and interventions in the girls' cases geared towards protection, whereas boys were seen as 'little rascals' that should be punished' (Oude de Breuil, 2021). Both the first and second applicants were not viewed to fit the mould for a 'stereotypical victim of human trafficking'. The fact that the second applicant was identified as being motivated by "financial gain", rather than accepting the best of bad situation. Moreover, it was indicated that even if classed as a victim of trafficking this did not offer you a defence. Contrary to the non-punishment principle of the Palermo Protocol.

Although a trafficking assessment was completed for the first applicant, it was highlighted that his family in Vietnam were not under threat, no debts were owed, and he had not been abused prior to his arrest. These facts led to the conclusion that "no reason whatsoever" existed to revise the initial assessment which deemed that it was in the public interest to prosecute the first applicant. This simplistic focus upon threats, money, and physical abuse fits in with preconceived ideals of who is a trafficking victim, moreover a boy of Vietnamese nationality does not fit into the ideal of a young female white trafficking victim. The power of race, an undercurrent of nationality, ethnicity, class, and gender all strike a chord here and are presumed to be interrelated factors behind the treatment of the first and second applicants. It is of note that further appeals were also dismissed since prosecutorial discretion with the Court of Appeal finding that the CPS was not bound by the findings of anti-trafficking authorities.

The Appeals of the Applicants

Both applicants appealed against their conviction arguing inter alia that, as victims of trafficking, they should be entitled to protection, rather than prosecution. The Court of Appeal found that the non-punishment provision found in Article 26 of the Anti-trafficking Convention concerns the sentencing of victims and can neither affect the prosecutorial procedure nor extend the duress defence. It also found that there was no clear evidence of trafficking that should have made the CPS act differently and did not allow the appeals against the conviction. Doubts were also expressed regarding the reliability of the expert evidence provided by the applicants. However, the appeals against the sentences were allowed on account of their age and other factual considerations. The applicants sought permission to appeal to the Supreme Court, but their applications were refused. In 2013, the first applicant sought to review his criminal conviction following new medical evidence, but the Court of Appeal did not consider that the CPS was bound by the findings of anti-trafficking national authorities, and that the applicant's criminality had not been reduced to a point that prosecution should not have continued. Further appeals were dismissed.

The European Court of Human Rights Decision in V.C.L and A.N v. United Kingdom[146]

The ECtHR ruled in the case of V.C.L and A.N v United Kingdom on 16 February 2021. The Court started its assessment by reiterating that the positive obligation of states under Article 4 of the ECHR that requires prevention, victim protection, and investigation through an established legislative and administrative framework. Holding that violations of Article 4 ECHR and Article 6 (1) ECHR had occurred.

The ECtHR reiterated the procedural guarantees under Article 4, clarifying that the positive obligations of victim protection and investigation do not depend on a motion filed by a victim. Such obligations are triggered as soon as there are reasonable grounds to believe that there is credible suspicion of trafficking. Moreover, the ECtHR examined the Article 6 aspects of the case and found that the lack of proper investigation and assessment of the potential situation of trafficking deprived the applicants of valuable information regarding their status that could affect their prosecution, a deprivation that directly affected their right to defence.

6.5 Summary

This chapter sought to critique the issue of child trafficking within the geographical region of Europe, focusing upon the UK as a case study due to its position in the fight against modern slavery. Combined, the anti-trafficking legal regime of the EU and CoE and the UK's specific focus upon modern slavery form an integral part of the anti-trafficking machine. The undercurrent issues of race, racism, patriarchy, and white supremacy emerge through, in addition to the exceptionality of British

---

[146] European Court of Human Rights, V.C.L. and A.N. v. The United Kingdom, Applications nos. 77587/12 and 74603/12, 16 February 2021.

victims, a shift towards insiders as victims which echoes the ideology of the White Slave Traffic previously discussed.

This chapter has sought to grapple with some of the core themes within this book, focusing upon the role of the anti-trafficking machine in relation to children and the construction of the "trafficked child". The fascination with tales and visual representations of human misery, feed into the powerful rhetoric used to justify interventions which are potentially more harmful than beneficial to those they purport to protect.

The case of *V.C.N and A.N v UK* provides a unique insight into several issues surrounding child trafficking. In that the 'victims' in question were not the stereotypical or ideal victims that we as a society and in some frontline services come to expect. The ineffectiveness of the law to protect also deflects from the implicit racialisation of modern slavery, detracting and dehumanising potential victims as they do not fit as a piece of the intricate puzzle that is the clash between child trafficking, migration, and children's rights. The undercurrent of racism, nationalism, and patriarchy continue to bubble under the guise or smokescreen of "modern slavery" serving as a deflection from the myriad forms of exploitation that exist.

References

Alpes, M. J. (2011). *Bushfalling: How young Cameroonians dare to migrate.* Faculteit der Maatshappij en Gedragwetwnschappen.
Anderson, B. (2001). Why Madam has so many bathrobes?: Demand for migrant workers in the EU. *Tijdschrift Voor Economische En Sociale Geografie, 92*(1), 18–26.
Andrijasevic, R. (2007). Beautiful dead bodies: Gender, migration and representation in anti-trafficking campaigns. *Feminist Review, 86* (86), 24–44.
Antislavery usable past. www.usablepast.ac.uk
Aradau, C. (2004). The perverse politics of four-letter words: Risk and pity in the securitisation of human trafficking. *Millennium, 33*(2), 251–277.
Balch, A. (2018). Defeating 'modern slavery', reducing exploitation? The organisational and regulatory challenge. In G. Craig, et al. (Eds.), *The modern slavery agenda: Policy, politics and practice in the UK*. Policy Press.

Balch, A., & Geddes, A. (2011). Opportunity from Crisis? Organisational responses to human trafficking in the UK. *British Journal of Politics & International Relations, 13*(1), 26–41.

Balch, A., Stalford, H., Vaughn, L., & Johns, J. (2019). Focus on Labour Exploitation (FLEX) (Non-Governmental Organisation Partner) & Currie, S. (2019). *Clothes, chocolate and children: Realising the transparency dividend.*

Beutin, L. P. (2017). Black suffering for/from anti-trafficking advocacy. *Anti-Trafficking Review, 9*, 14–30.

Bhandar, B. (2018). *Colonial lives of property: Law, land, and racial regimes of ownership.* Duke University Press.

Breuil, B. O. (2021). 'Little rascals' or not-so-ideal victims: Dealing with minors trafficked for exploitation in criminal activities in the Netherlands. *Anti-Trafficking Review, 16*, 86–103.

Brotherton, V., & Beddoe, C. (2016). *Class Acts? Examining modern slavery legislation across the UK*. Anti-Trafficking Monitoring Group.

Buck, T. (2014). *International child law* (3rd ed.). Routledge.

Burland, P. (2018). Still punishing the wrong people: The criminalisation of potential trafficked cannabis gardeners. In G. Craig et al. (Ed.), *The modern slavery agenda: Policy, politics and practice in the UK.* Policy Press.

Cantwell, N. (2017). The human rights of children in the context of formal alternative care. In Vandenhole, W. et al. *Routledge international handbook of children's rights studies.* Routledge.

Cockbain, E. (2018). *Offender and victim networks in human trafficking.* Routledge.

CoE & GRETA. (2015). *4th general report on GRETA's activities.*

CoE & GRETA. (2016). *5th general report on GRETA's activities.*

Council of Europe (a). *Committee of Ministers, Recommendation No. R (2000) 11 of the Committee of Ministers to member states on action against trafficking in human beings for the purpose of sexual exploitation.*

Council of Europe (b). *Council of Europe convention on action against trafficking in human beings.*

Council of Europe (1991). *Council of Europe Committee of Ministers Recommendation No. R(91) 11 to member states concerning sexual exploitation, pornography and prostitution of, and trafficking in, children and young adults.*

Council of Europe, *Committee of Ministers, Recommendation No. R (2001) 16 of the Committee of Ministers to member states on the protection of children against sexual exploitation.* Accessed via https://www.coe.int/t/dg3/children/keylegaltexts/CMRec_en.asp

Council of the Baltic Sea States. (2015). *Guidelines promoting the human rights and the best interests of the child in transnational child protection cases*. Accessible via https://cbss.org/publications/guidelines-promoting-the-human-rights-and-best-interests-of-the-child-in-transnational-child-protection-cases/

Craig, G. (Ed.). (2010). *Child slavery now: A contemporary reader* (1st ed.). Polity Press.

Craig, G., et al. (Eds.). (2019). *The modern slavery agenda: Policy, politics and practice in the UK*. Policy Press.

Directorate-General for Migration and Home Affairs (European Commission) & European Commission. (2020). *Report from the Commission to the European Parliament and the Council: Third report on the progress made in the fight against trafficking in human beings (2020)*.

Doezema, J. (2010). *Sex slaves and discourse masters: The construction of trafficking*. Zed Book.

Dottridge, M. (2021). Between theory and reality: The challenge of distinguishing between trafficked children and independent child migrants. *Anti-Trafficking Review, 16*, 11–27.

Duane, A. M. & Meiners, E., R (2021). Working Analogues: Slavery Now and Then. In Lebaron, G. et al. (Ed.) Fighting Modern Slavery and Human Trafficking: History and Contemporary Policy.

Dugan, E. (2022). *Home Office reclassifies modern slavery as illegal immigration issue*. https://www.theguardian.com/world/2022/oct/13/home-office-reclassifies-modern-slavery-as-immigration-issue

Durisin, E. M., & van der Meulen, E. (2021). The perfect victim: 'Young girls', domestic trafficking, and anti-prostitution politics in Canada. *Anti-Trafficking Review, 16*, 145–149.

Dyke, R. V. (2017). Monitoring and evaluation of human trafficking partnerships in England and Wales. *Anti-Trafficking Review, 8*, 131–146.

Enloe, C. H. (2014). *Bananas, beaches and bases: Making feminist sense of international politics* (2nd ed.). University of California Press.

European Commission. (2011). *Human trafficking: Commission welcomes Council adoption of stronger EU rules Press Release IP/11/332*. http://europa.eu/rapid/press-release_IP-11-332_en.htm

Europe in Strasburg, *The Council of Europe and its various bodies*. https://www.europeinstrasbourg.eu/en/institutions/council-europe.html

European Union. (2017). *EU Guidelines on the Promotion and Protection of the Rights of the Child—Leave No Child Behind*.

European Parliament. (2001). *"EU urges higher priority on trafficking in women and children" Europa Press Release*. http://europa.eu/rapid/press-release_IP-01-325_en.htm

European Commission, *EU anti-trafficking coordinator (europa.eu)*. https://home-affairs.ec.europa.eu/policies/internal-security/organised-crime-and-human-trafficking/together-against-trafficking-human-beings/eu-anti-trafficking-coordinator_en

European Commission. (2014). *Report from the Commission to the European Parliament and the Council: Third report on the progress made in the fight against trafficking in human beings*.

European Commission. (2020). *EU law: Report from the Commission to the European Parliament and the Council: Third report on the progress made in the fight against trafficking in human beings (2020) as required under Article 20 of Directive 2011/36/EU on preventing and combating trafficking in human beings and protecting its victims*.

Eurostat, *Glossary: European Union institutions (EUI)*. https://ec.europa.eu/eurostat/statistics-explained/index.php?title=Glossary:European_Union_institutions_(EUI)#:~:text=The%20European%20Union%20institutions%2C%20sometimes%20abbreviated%20as%20EUI%2C,European%20Union%2C%20which%20represents%20the%20individual%20Member%20States%3B

Faulkner, E. (2018). *"Britons never will be slaves": The rise of nationalism and 'modern slavery'*. https://www.opendemocracy.net/en/beyond-trafficking-and-slavery/britons-never-will-be-slaves-rise-of-nationalism-and-modern-slavery/

Faulkner, E. A. (2017). *How the idea of 'modern slavery' is used as political click bait*. https://theconversation.com/how-the-idea-of-modern-slavery-is-used-as-political-click-bait-84877

Finch, N. (2017). *Lighting the way: Steps that lawyers, legal guardians and child trafficking advocates in the UK can take to better identify and protect children who may have been trafficked*.

Fussey, P., & Rawlinson, P. (2017). *Child trafficking in the EU: Policing and protecting Europe's most vulnerable*. Routledge Studies in Crime and Society Routledge.

Gallagher, A. T. (2012). *The international law of human trafficking*. Cambridge University Press.

Haynes, D. (2019). *The wastefulness of human trafficking awareness campaigns*. https://www.opendemocracy.net/en/beyond-trafficking-and-slavery/wastefulness-of-human-trafficking-awareness-campaigns/

Home Office. (2013). *Home Office Policy Paper Human trafficking: Interdepartmental ministerial group report.*
Home Office. (2014). *Home Office, Modern Slavery Strategy.* https://www.gov.uk/government/publications/modern-slavery-strategy
Home Office. (2015a). *Modern slavery marketing campaign evaluation report.*
Home Office. (2015b). *News Story, Historic law to end Modern Slavery passed.* 2015. https://www.gov.uk/government/news/historic-law-to-end-modern-slavery-passed
Home Office. (2016). *Home Secretary pledges £11 million for groups fighting modern slavery.* https://www.gov.uk/government/news/home-secretary-pledges-11-million-for-groups-fighting-modern-slavery
Home Office. (2017). *Government delivers £40 million to tackle child sexual abuse and child trafficking.* https://www.gov.uk/government/news/government-delivers-40-million-to-tackle-child-sexual-abuse-and-child-trafficking
Home Office & National Audit Office. (2017). *Value for money—Reducing modern slavery.*
Howard, N. (2017). *Child trafficking, youth labour mobility and the politics of protection.*
Howard, N. (2018). Abolitionist anti-politics? Capitalism, coercion and the modern anti-slavery movement. In L. Brace & J. O'Connell Davidson (Eds.), *Revisiting slavery and antislavery: Towards a critical analysis.* Springer International Publishing.
Howard, N., Okyere, S. (Eds). (2022). International Child Protection. *Palgrave Studies on Children and Development.* Palgrave Macmillan. https://doi.org/10.1007/978-3-030-78763-9_1
Human Rights Due Vigilence Law European Coalition for Corporate Justice. (2017). *French Corporate Duty of Vigilance Law.* https://businesshumanrights.org/sites/default/files/documents/French Corporate Duty of Vigilance
Hynes, P. (2010). Global points of 'vulnerability': Understanding processes of the trafficking of children and young people into, within and out of the UK. *The International Journal of Human Rights, 14*(6), 952–970.
Hynes et al. (2022). *Creating stable futures: Human trafficking, participation and outcomes for children creating stable futures: Human trafficking, participation and outcomes for children.*
ILO, UNICEF & UN. GIFT. (2009). *Training manual to fight trafficking in children for labour, sexual and other forms of exploitation, Textbook 1: Understanding child trafficking.*

India Committee of the Netherlands. (2017). *Child Labour Due Diligence Law for companies adopted by Dutch parliament.* http://www.indianet.nl/170208e.html
International Labour Organization. *Trafficking in children (IPEC).* https://www.ilo.org/ipec/areas/Traffickingofchildren/lang--en/index.htm
Kempadoo, K. (2015). The modern-day white (wo)man's burden: Trends in anti-trafficking and anti-slavery campaigns. *Journal of Human Trafficking, 1*(1), 8–20.
Kempadoo, K., et al. (Eds.). (2005). *Trafficking and prostitution reconsidered: New perspectives on migration, sex work, and human rights* (1st ed.). Paradigm Publishers.
Kempadoo, K., et al. (Eds.). (2012). *Trafficking and prostitution reconsidered: New perspectives on migration, sex work and human rights* (2nd ed.). Paradigm Publishers.
Kidd, A., Faulkner, E. A., & Arocha, L. (2019). *How UK asylum system creates perfect conditions for modern slavery and exploitation to thrive.* Conversation. https://theconversation.com/how-uk-asylum-system-creates-perfect-conditions-for-modern-slavery-and-exploitation-to-thrive-113778
Kotiswaran, P. (2014). Beyond sexual humanitarianism: A postcolonial approach to anti-trafficking law. *UC Irvine Law Review, 4*(1), 353.
Kotiswaran, P. (Ed.). (2018). *Revisiting the law and governance of trafficking, forced labor and modern slavery.* Cambridge University Press.
Koomson, B., & Abdulai, D. (2021). Putting Childhood in Its Place: Rethinking popular discourses on the conceptualisation of child trafficking in Ghana. *Anti–Trafficking Review, 16*, 28–46.
Krsmanovic, E. (2021). Child trafficking vs. child sexual exploitation: Critical reflection on the UK media reports. *Anti-Trafficking Review, 16*, 69–85.
Malarek, V. (2004). *The Natashas: Inside the new global sex trade.* Arcade Publishing.
Mantouvalou, V. (2018). The UK Modern Slavery Act 2015 three years on. *Modern Law Review, 81*(6), 1017–1045.
Martins Junior, A., & O'Connell Davidson, J. (2021). Tacking towards freedom? Bringing journeys out of slavery into dialogue with contemporary migration. *Journal of Ethnic and Migration Studies, 48*(7), 1479–1495.
May, Theresa (2016). *My government will lead the way in defeating modern slavery.* https://www.telegraph.co.uk/news/2016/07/30/we-will-lead-the-way-in-defeating-modern-slavery/

McDonell, E. (2016). *Australia set to ban asylum seekers from entering Australia: It is time to hold Australia accountable*. Available from: https://ohrh.law.ox. ac.uk/australia-set-to-ban-asylum-seekers-from-entering-australia-it-is-time-to-hold-australia-accountable/

Modern Slavery Act. (2015). (explanatory notes) Accessible via https://www.legislation.gov.uk/ukpga/2015/30/notes/contents

Morrison, J. (2000). The Policy Implications Arising from the Trafficking and Smuggling of Refugees into Europe. *Documentation of the European Conference "Children First and Foremost–Policies towards Separated Children in Europe"*. Save the Children. Stockholm.

National Crime Agency (NCA). *Modern Slavery Human Trafficking Unit (MSHTU)*. https://nationalcrimeagency.gov.uk/contact-us/6-modern-slavery-human-trafficking-unit

National Crime Agency. (2016). *National strategic assessment of serious and organised crime 2016*.

O'Connell, Davidson. (2005). *Children in the Global Sex Trade*. Polity Press.

O'Connell Davidson, J. (2011). Moving children? Child trafficking, child migration, and child rights. *Critical Social Policy, 31*(3), 454–477.

O'Connell Davidson, J. (2013). Troubling freedom: Migration, debt, and modern slavery. *Migration Studies, 1*(2): 176–195.

O'Connell Davidson, J. (2015). *Modern slavery: The margins of freedom*. Palgrave Macmillan.

OHCR Annual Report. (2014). Accessible via OHCHR Report 2014 | OHCHR.

Okyere, S. (2014). Children's participation in prohibited work in Ghana and its implications for the Convention on the Rights of the Child. In A. Twum-Danso Imoh & N. Ansell (Eds.), *Children's lives in an era of children's rights the progress of the convention on the rights of the child in Africa*. Routledge.

Okyere, S., Agyeman, N., & Saboro, E. (2021). 'Why was he videoing us?': The ethics and politics of audio-visual propaganda in child trafficking and human trafficking campaigns. *Anti-Trafficking Review, 16*, 47–68.

Organization for Security and Co-operation in Europe. (2003). *OSCE action plan on combating trafficking in human beings*.

Organization for Security and Co-operation in Europe. (2005). *Addendum to the OSCE action plan to combat trafficking in human beings: Addressing the special needs of child victims of trafficking for protection and assistance*.

Organization for Security and Co-operation in Europe. (2022). *National Referral Mechanisms—Joining efforts to protect the rights of trafficked persons: A practical handbook—Second edition*.

Organization for Security and Co-Operation in Europe (OCSE). *Office of the special representative and co-ordinator for combating trafficking in human beings (CTHB)*. https://www.osce.org/cthb

Ost, S. (2009). *Child pornography and sexual grooming: Legal and societal responses*. Cambridge University Press.

Piotrowicz, R., et al. (Eds.). (2018). *Routledge handbook of human trafficking*. Routledge.

Rosen, R., & Twamley, K. (2018). *Feminism and the politics of childhood: Friends or foes?* UCL Press.

Sax, H. (2018). Child trafficking—A call for rights-based integrated approaches. In R. Piotrowicz, et al. (Eds.), *Routledge handbook of human trafficking*. Routledge.

Segrave, M., Milivojevic, S., & Pickering, S. (2018). *Sex trafficking and modern slavery: The absence of evidence* (2nd ed.). Routledge.

Sharma, N. (2018). Immigration restrictions and the politics of protection. In L. Brace & J. O'Connell Davidson (Eds.), *Revisiting slavery and anti-slavery: Towards a critical analysis*. Palgrave Macmillan.

Shih, E. (2021). The fantasy of spotting human trafficking: Training spectacles in racist surveillance. *Wagadu: A Journal of Transnational Women's & Gender Studies, 22*, 105–137.

Shih, E., & Quirk, J. (2017). *Introduction: Do the hidden costs outweigh the practical benefits of human trafficking awareness campaigns?* https://www.opendemocracy.net/en/beyond-trafficking-and-slavery/introduction-do-hidden-costs-outweigh-practical-benefits-of-huma/

Skrivankova, K. (2018). The UK's approach to tackling modern slavery in the European context. In G. Craig, et al. (Eds.), *The modern slavery agenda: Policy, politics and practice in the UK*.

Soltis, K., & Taylor Diaz, M. (2021). Ganged up on: How the US immigration system penalises and fails to protect Central American minors who are trafficked for criminal activity by gangs. *Anti-Trafficking Review, 16*, 104–122.

The Times. (2011). Revealed: Conspiracy of silence on UK sex gangs. *The Times*.

UK Government. *Factsheet: Section 67 of the Immigration Act 2016 ('Dubs amendment')—GOV.UK*. https://www.gov.uk/government/publications/policy-statement-section-67-of-the-immigration-act-2016/factsheet-section-67-of-the-immigration-act-2016

UNHCR, UNODC, UNICEF, ILO & UN Women. (2012). *Joint UN Commentary on the EU Directive on human trafficking—A human rights-based approach.*
UNICEF. (2011). *The state of the world's children 2011.*
UNICEF. (2017). *Victim, not criminal: Trafficked children and the non-punishment principle in the UK.*
UNODC. (2012). *UNODC global report on trafficking in persons 2012.*
UNTIED. (2022). *The fatal policies of fortress Europe.* https://unitedagainstrefugeedeaths.eu/
US State Department. (2007). *Trafficking in persons report 2007.*
US State Department. (2014). *Trafficking in persons report 2014.*
US State Department. (2015). *Trafficking in persons report 2015.*
US State Department. (2016). *Trafficking in persons report 2016.*
US State Department. (2017). *Trafficking in persons report 2017.*
van de Glind, H. (2010). Child trafficking: A modern form of slavery. In G. Craig (Ed.), *Child slavery now.* Bristol University Press. http://www.jstor.org/stable/j.ctt9qgxmk.12
Vinkovi, M. (2010). The "unbroken marriage"—Trafficking and child labour in Europe. *Journal of Money Laundering Control, 13*(2), 87–102.
Warria, A., Nel, H., & Triegaardt, J. (2015). Challenges in identification of child victims of transnational trafficking. *Practice (birmingham, England), 27*(5), 315–333.
Winterdyk, J., et al. (Eds.). (2012). *Human trafficking: Exploring the international nature, concerns, and complexities.* CRC Press.

7

Conclusion: A Tale of Child Trafficking and the Shift to Modern Slavery

What was the point of the book? This book set out to chart the history over child trafficking and its relationship or imagination under international law, regional law (focusing upon Europe), and domestically in the UK over the course of two centuries. A grand aspiration, but the story is not over as the issue of child trafficking is in the process of a re-birth under the guise of modern slavery. The trafficking of children is extremely effective in cultivating strong responses, from society, individuals, politicians, celebrities, and religious leaders alike. The feel-good factor of being involved, taking up arms to save the worlds helpless children—not to say that this need isn't genuine but problematic. The simplistic solutions of saving children through interventions (whether legal, policy or rescue missions) cause harms to those they purport to protect. They silence children, exclude them and swaddle them in protective cloak of the romanticised vision of Western childhood. However, this protection is not available or gifted to all children. Just those who fall into the category of deserving or as Sharma identified in the colonial context of mobility who is 'desirable' or 'undesirable' as a central organising framework of nation making. Contemporary action to protect children through restricting their mobility and enforcing the Western construct of childhood upon the world's children creates an intricate web of conflicts. What is important and so frequently skipped over, neglected, and ignored is that fears of child trafficking are not new. Child trafficking is not a phenomenon that is exclusive to the twenty-first century—however we have collectively failed to recognise this or to learn from the mistakes of the past.

The contemporary parallels between the white slave traffic and contemporary human trafficking have been well documented (Allain, 2017; Doezema, 2010). From the inspiration that the 1910 Convention provided for the Trafficking Protocol in 2000, from the use of threats, fraud, coercion to the omission of the means element in regard to children it's power should not be neglected. This book aims to supplement that body of knowledge through an intricate analysis of child trafficking and anti-trafficking from the early twentieth century to today. Building upon the well documented fears of the 'White Slave Traffic' that emerged from the UK in the latter half of the nineteenth century, culminating in the 1904 Agreement and 1910 Convention White Slave Traffic respectively. The League moved to adopt its own Convention in 1921, explicitly removing the reference to white slavery and replacing it with women and children, creating a more racially neutral Convention (Lammasniemi, 2017). However, the legacy and power of the rhetoric of white slavery played a significant role in shaping perceptions of trafficking. Through an analysis of the summary of annual reports, the archival research sought to demonstrate how fears of the trafficking of children or exploitation of children for immoral purposes were unfounded and that the interwoven issues of racism, white supremacy, colonialism, and patriarchy had been covered in a smokescreen shielded by the moral cause to save women and children from sexual exploitation and the ruin associated with it. Moreover, that other exploitative practices were detected but as they were not of immoral nature, they were not deemed harmful.

Focusing upon the international legal framework crafted under the auspices of the United Nations, from human rights to migration and trafficking is the world not a better place? That depends upon your perspective, international law has long been documented as a tool of oppression and that the concerns of human rights only emerged in wake of the suffering of white populations in wake of the Second World War. The counter narrative of TWAIL illustrates that it was European colonialism (in the Fifteenth and Nineteenth Centuries) that formed the background for the emergence of international law as we know today. The purpose of international law is to both rationalise and regulate the subjugation of non-European lands and people (Anghie, 2005). With the much celebrated (due to its universal acceptance) convention on the rights of the child encompassing the Western construct and often romanticised ideals of children and childhood deflecting from its power as a tool of oppression or a stick to beat the global south with (Faulkner & Nyamutata, 2020). In a similar vein or parallel mechanism of oppression enters the Palermo Protocol in 2000. The protocol focused upon the statist control of borders and identified explicitly that for trafficking to of occurred a National border must have been breached and the perpetrators must be an organised criminal gang. This finds resonance in the 1927 League of Nation's anti-trafficking work which identified the trafficking of children in Cochin China by organised criminal gangs.

The neglect of the historical context of child trafficking is detrimental to the cause of anti-trafficking but also in terms of advancing policies and laws which integrate the empowerment and voices of those they purport to protect. The ideology and rhetoric of fears of White Slavery continue to shape and inform contemporary responses and perceptions to the phenomena. How do we break this cycle? A cycle which profits from the human misery of victims and is well harnessed and utilised as a moral beacon call to action by the multifaceted anti-trafficking machine. The fascination with tales and visual representations of human misery, feed into the powerful rhetoric used to justify interventions which are potentially more harmful than beneficial to those they purport to protect.

The aim was to address or begin to address some of the issues within the narrative of child trafficking and trafficking/modern slavery more generally. In social policy, development and humanitarian circles, few social problems elicit condemnation more quickly than those involving children. Why, perhaps you may wonder? If we consider the issues of trafficking, exploitation, or labour, are viewed quite rightly negatively but when you add the word "child" into the mix it manifests an additional level of horror and disgust. Anti-trafficking has always been an 'inside job' as eloquently articulated by Sharma.

> *This is true in at least two ways. First, we have an alliance between anti-trafficking organisations and state officials, who have worked together to embed the anti-trafficking framework into both international agreements and national and local laws. This alliance has actively dismissed the concerns of feminists, including sex workers, who have spoken up about the harms that tend to occur whenever anybody gets it in their head to 'save women and children'. It has also sidelined evidence that anti-trafficking measures tend to intensify the harms already being done by immigration and anti-sex work policies.* (Sharma, 2020, 17)

The willful dismissive attitude that doing harm by doing good is often the reality of anti-trafficking and anti-slavery initiatives that drive contemporary abolition. Protecting children has long been established as an effective tool for soliciting sympathy, money, and weapons (Enloe, 2014). To 'justify its importance, antitrafficking advocates appropriate the history of racial chattel slavery and its abolition to gain urgency, legitimacy, and moral outrage for their cause, but then minimise that same history to make trafficking today the most pressing social problem to address' (Beutin, 2017, 15). However, sceptics have 'raised alarm bells about the research and scholarship attached to the antislavery movement, which they see as relying on poor quality estimates and data that value awareness-raising potential over scholarly integrity—ultimately, many scholars see large swathes of anti-slavery research as an obstacle to develop accurate understandings of the problem and evidence-based policy to combat it' (LeBaron et al., 2021, 2). As Kempadoo (2015) has argued, anti-modern slavery and anti-trafficking campaigns have not led to a reduction or eradication of these phenomena, but rather to stronger ideologies against prostitutes, infantilising rescue missions to save 'innocent victims', greater police surveillance and programmes to apprehend pimps and traffickers, and greater controls on migration (Charnley & Nkhoma, 2020, 210).

Despite the considerable power of the anti-trafficking discourse in the global North, we find relatively low figures of trafficked victims and even lower conviction rates in contrast to the global South (Kotiswaran, 2017, 40). According to the Walk Free Foundation in 2016, of the 45.8 million slaves identified as victims of modern slavery globally with approximately 58% living in Bangladesh, China, India, Pakistan, and Uzbekistan, respectively. India for example has the highest absolute numbers of "modern slaves" in the world, at approximately 18.3 million (Walk Free Foundation, 2016). As highlighted through the work of Kotiswaran there is 'little surprise then, that mega-NGOs at the frontlines of the abolitionist movement like Walk Free, Free the Slaves and Freedom Fund are increasingly turning their attention to the global South, particularly in regions like South Asia to fund counter-trafficking initiatives'. Another example of this flurry of activity can be identified in Ghana. The NGO International Justice Mission (hereafter, IJM) has been working with the Anti-Human Trafficking Unit (AHTU) of the Ghana Police Service since 2015, and with other government agencies to conduct anti-child trafficking raids across the remote island communities on the Lake Volta in Ghana (Okyere et al., 2021, 48). However, not all anti-trafficking initiatives perpetuate harms, with the NGO Terr des Hoomes in Benin and the African Movement of Working Children and Youth working in Benin both providing starkly anti-abolitionist examples of good practice (Howard, 2017, 132).

The dominant narrative of child trafficking is simplistic and ethnocentric, with the issues of race, racism, nationalism, patriarchy, white supremacy, and legacy[1] of colonialism simmering under the surface, neglected, and ignored as 'fighting trafficking' is a noble and moral crusade. This creates a kaleidoscope as a lens for analysis of child trafficking and is illustrative of the power, dominance, and continued harms perpetuated under the operation of the anti-trafficking machine. As Boyden would identify these anti-trafficking efforts as 'misguided good intentions' (1997). The anti-trafficking machine as a theoretical framework is useful as it illustrates a number of issues, such as its failure to recognise differences between children and adolescents, resting upon assumptions that all children are weak, passive, eternal victims in need

---

[1] The author recognises that referencing the 'legacy' of colonialism implies that it is extinct. However, the continued impact of colonialism continues to influence and control law, policy, politics, and society globally.

of rescue. However, if a child cannot be recognised as fully autonomous, it follows that there is a need for some adult or state constraint on a child's autonomy, with most commentators now accepting the justification for at least some paternalistic intervention (Buck, 2014, 31). Critiques around choice, consent and agency are central within human trafficking debates and the conflicts within the theoretical framework anti-trafficking machine. Some commentators have termed this 'infantilised femininity' and concerns about women and children who move (Anderson, 2007, 2013; Gould, 2010; Palmary, 2010). Human trafficking is seen—perhaps justifiably by many commentators as an inherently coercive environment within which it is difficult to determine true agency or consent (Elliott, 2015) Although seldom studied through a 'forced migration lens, people who are trafficked as subject to degrees of force, coercion or coercive control, with debates about agency and consent ongoing in this field (Hynes, 2021, 79) particularly in relation to children. The questions of consent, choice, and agency are reiterated, as is the role of the State in the protection of victims of trafficking, but also in 'creating and producing vulnerability through legislation, policy and practice resting on border controls (Hynes, 2021, 87). The responses of the states of Benin[2] and the UK for example in their 'adoption of anti-trafficking law and policies have come to regard a broad swath of children who migrate to earn a living, without being coerced, as victims of trafficking' (Dottridge, 2021, 12). The conflation of issues around agency and representations of women and children as passive victims, is an issue which has been explored in relation to gender within the broader contexts of forced migration (Hynes, 2021, 87) including refugee and Internally Displaced People camps (Fiddian-Qasmiyeh, 2014). Moreover, conflict over the role of consent in trafficking has continued and flourished under the anti-trafficking machine, with debates about agency and consent ongoing within the field (Hynes, 2021, 79).[3]

---

[2] The references to 'Benin' within theis book are all to the Republic of Benin in West Africa and not to the city of Benin in neighbouring Nigeria. A place which according to Dottridge is a 'place of origin of substantial numbers of trafficked women as well as girls'.

[3] See further Bridget Anderson, *Motherhood, apple pie and slavery: reflections on trafficking debates* (2007); Kyunghee Kook Kook, K. (2018) '"I want to be trafficked so i can migrate!": cross-border movement of North Koreans into China through brokerage and smuggling networks',

7 Conclusion: A Tale of Child Trafficking and the Shift ...

It is striking that the global north politicians who most vocally denounce the evil of 'modern slavery' often at the same time pursue highly illiberal, often lethal, border control and immigration policies (Martins Junior & O'Connell Davidson, 2021, 2). For example, the UK has effectively positioned itself as a world leader against the 'trade in human misery' or modern slavery. This position has been refuted by numerous critics of the law and policies implemented with the confirmation that modern slavery is not about human rights but an issue of immigration and crime being confirmed through the updated ministerial portfolios in late 2022. A noble aim for some but when coupled with the explicit racism and othering of the undesirable number 1 (not Harry Potter in this case) but the wicked "cockroach" (Anderson) the migrant. The hypocrisy of little England is fascinating, as a shift has occurred in recent years from fears of slavery being perpetrated by foreigners to foreigners (outsiders) to British nationals (insiders) exploited by foreigners. The racialised coding behind this shift is clear and echoes the fears of the League and predating it back to the initial white slavery fears of the nineteenth century.

This focus upon the stereotypical 'trafficked child' is serving as a way of infantilising the child, branding them as victims in need of rescue and rehabilitation. The current panic surrounding the trafficking of children is influencing the development of policies that are often detrimental to "children on the move". The "trafficked child" is successfully damaging the way that we respond to the issues of child labour, migration, and exploitation. That image has been constructed within a (Ost, 2009) that dominates discussions around children, inadvertently stripping children of the autonomy contained within, for example, the CRC. Moreover, for 'anti-child traffickers, the young labour migrants moving for challenging work illegally across borders because they have no alternative literally embody the breakdown of the ideologies of Western Childhood, the Ideal State and Neoliberalism' (Howard, 2017, 131). The endorsement of a hierarchical framework of status serves to draw discrete and concrete boundaries between deserving and undeserving 'victims. The

---

The ANNALS of the American Academy of Political and Social Science, 676(1), 114–134, 10.1177/0002716217748591.

lack of access to safe migration routes is not acknowledged nor the impact of the sometimes-lethal immigration policies adopted by states such as the UK, Australia, and the USA.

The undercurrent of racism, nationalism, and patriarchy continue to bubble under the guise or smokescreen of "modern slavery" serving as a deflection from the myriad forms of exploitation that exist. The ineffectiveness of the law to protect also deflects from the implicit racialisation of modern slavery, detracting and dehumanising potential victims as they do not fit as a piece of the intricate puzzle that is the clash between child trafficking, migration, and children's rights and from preconceived ideals of the "trafficked child" or the pornographers of pain and human misery. Little has been learnt from lessons of the last. This book has sought to re-centralise the history of child trafficking and international law to address the ahistorical state of the research upon child trafficking and modern slavery.

The link between the Western dominance of children's rights and the creation of the anti-trafficking machine is problematic. Couple with the emergence of the TIP as an effective tool to persecute underperforming states, a hierarchical and imperial system is established and maintained. This hierarchical system enforces colonial power and the dominance of the Western world over the Global South. With limited and restricted options/recourse for dissent in wake of the moral crusade to rescue the world's children. The "anti-trafficking machine" has emerged as Hokusai's wave, reimagining of Kipling's 'White Man's Burden' and engulfing all who challenge its moral crusade. Sadly, not all children are born 'free and equal' with the perpetuation of child victim pornography and racist influence of populism infecting the Western world and in turn perpetuating systematic inequalities globally. Neglecting the past has been proven as harmful in several ways from the recurring use of bad practices in relation to children engaged in labour, migration, and those perceived as trafficking victims. Fears of child trafficking are not new; it is a re-emergence of the issue like a Phoenix from the ashes. The opportunity exists to learn from lessons of the past and the ongoing research that highlights the "collateral damage" or what can no longer be classed as unintended harms of laws and policies enacted under the anti-trafficking machine.

References

Allain, J. (2017). White slave traffic in international law. *Journal of Trafficking and Human Exploitation, 1*(1), 1–40.
Anderson, B. (2007). *Motherhood, apple pie and slavery: Reflections on trafficking debates.*
Anghie, A. (2005). *Imperialism, sovereignty and the making of international law* (Vol. 37). Cambridge University Press.
Beutin, L. P. (2017). Black Suffering for/from anti-trafficking advocacy. *Anti-Trafficking Review, 9*, 14–30.
Boyden, J. (1997). A comparative perspective on the globalisation of childhood. In: A. James & A. Prout (Eds.) *Constructing and reconstructing childhood: Contemporary issues in the sociological study of childhood* (2nd ed.). Falmer Press.
Buck, T. (2014). *International child law* (3rd ed.).
Charnley, H., & Nkhoma, P. (2020). Moving beyond contemporary discourses: Children, prostitution, modern slavery and human trafficking. *Critical and Radical Social Work, 2*(8), 205–221.
Doezema, J. (2010). *Sex slaves and discourse masters: The construction of trafficking.* Zed Book.
Dottridge, M. (2021). Between theory and reality: The challenge of distinguishing between trafficked children and independent child migrants. *Anti-Trafficking Review, 16*, 11–27.
Elliott, J. (2015). *The role of consent in human trafficking.* Routledge.
Enloe, C. H. (2014). *Bananas, beaches and bases: Making feminist sense of international politics* (2nd ed.). University of California Press.
Faulkner, E. A., & Nyamutata, C. (2020). The decolonisation of children's rights and the colonial contours of the convention on the rights of the child. *The International journal of children's rights, 28*(1), 66–88.
Fiddian-Qasmiyeh, E. (2014). *The ideal refugees: Gender, islam, and the sahrawi politics of survival.* Syracuse University Press.
Howard, N. (2017). *Child trafficking, youth labour mobility and the politics of protection.*

Hynes, P. (2021). *Introducing forced migration* (1st Edn.). Routledge.
Kempadoo, K. (2015). The modern-day white (wo)man's burden: Trends in anti-trafficking and anti-slavery campaigns. *Journal of Human Trafficking, 1*(1), 8–20.
Kook, K. (2018). I want to be trafficked so I can migrate!: Cross-border movement of North Koreans into China through brokerage and smuggling networks. *The Annals of the American Academy of Political and Social Science, 676*(1), 114–134.
Kotiswaran, P. (2017). *Revisiting the law and governance of trafficking, forced labor and modern slavery*. Cambridge University Press.
Lammasniemi, L. (2017). Anti-white slavery legislation and its legacies in England. *Anti-Trafficking Review, 9*, 64–76.
LeBaron, G. et al. (Ed.). (2021). *Fighting modern slavery and human trafficking: History and contemporary policy*. Slaveries since emancipation. Cambridge University Press.
Martins Junior, A., & O'Connell Davidson, J. (2021). Tacking towards freedom? Bringing journeys out of slavery into dialogue with contemporary migration. *Journal of Ethnic and Migration Studies, 48*(7), 1479–1495.
Okyere, S., Agyeman, N. K., & Saboro, E. (2021). 'Why was he videoing us?': The ethics and politics of audio-visual propaganda in child trafficking and human trafficking campaigns. *Anti-Trafficking Review, 16*, 47–68.
Palmary, I. (2010). Sex, choice and exploitation: Reflections on anti-trafficking discourse. In I. Palmary, E. Burman, K. Chantler & P. Kiguwa (Eds.), *Gender and migration: Feminist Perspectives*. Zed Press.
Sharma, N. (2020). *Anti-trafficking is an inside job*. https://www.opendemocracy.net/en/beyond-trafficking-and-slavery/anti-trafficking-inside-job/
Thea de Gruchy, Vearey, J., Marlise, R., & Quirk, J. (2015). Doing more harm than good: The politics of child trafficking prevention in South Africa. *Open Democracy (London)*.
Walk Free Foundation. (2016). Global Slavery Index, Accessible via Downloads|Global Slavery Index.

Appendix A: The White Slavery Agreement of 1904 and Convention of 1910

The International Agreement for the Suppression of the White Slave Traffic, 1904

His Majesty the King of the UK of Great Britain and Ireland and of the British Dominions beyond the Seas, Emperor of India; His Majesty the German Emperor, King of Prussia, in the name of the German Empire; His Majesty the King of the Belgians; His Majesty the King of Denmark; His Majesty the King of Spain; the President of the French Republic; His Majesty the King of Italy; Her Majesty the Queen of the Netherlands; His Majesty the King of Portugal and of the Algarves; His Majesty the Emperor of all the Russias; His Majesty the King of Sweden and Norway; and the Swiss Federal Council, being desirous of securing to women of full age who have suffered abuse or compulsion, as also to women and girls under age, effective protection against the criminal traffic known as the 'White Slave Traffic' have decided to conclude an Agreement with a view to concerting measures calculated to attain this object, and have appointed as their Plenipotentiaries, that is to say: [List of plenipotentiaries not reproduced here.]

Who, having exchanged their full powers, found in good and due form, have agreed upon the following provisions:

Article 1

Each of the Contracting Governments undertakes to establish or name some authority charged with the coordination of all information relative to the procuring of women or girls for immoral purposes abroad; this authority shall be empowered to correspond direct with the similar department established in each of the other Contracting States.

Article 2

Each of the Governments undertakes to have a watch kept, especially in railway stations, ports of embarkation, and en route, for persons in charge of women and girls destined for an immoral life. With this object instructions shall be given to the officials, and all other qualified persons, to obtain, within legal limits, all information likely to lead to the detection of criminal traffic. The arrival of persons who clearly appear to be the principals, accomplices in, or victims of, such traffic shall be notified, when it occurs, either to the authorities of the place of destination, or to the diplomatic or consular agents interested, or to any other competent authorities.

Article 3

The Governments undertake, when the case arises, and within legal limits, to have the declarations taken of women or girls of foreign nationality who are prostitutes, in order to establish their identity and civil status, and to discover who has caused them to leave their country. The information obtained shall be communicated to the authorities of the country of origin of the said women and girls, with a view to their eventual repatriation. The Governments undertake, within legal limits, and as far as can be done, to entrust temporarily, and with a view to their eventual repatriation, the victims of criminal traffic when destitute to public or private charitable institutions, or to private individuals offering the necessary security.

The Governments also undertake, within legal limits, and as far as possible, to send back to their country of origin those women and girls who desire it, or who may be claimed by persons exercising authority over them. Repatriation shall only take place after agreement as to identity and nationality, as well as place and date of arrival at the frontiers. Each of the Contracting Countries shall facilitate transit through its territory.

Correspondence relative to repatriation shall be direct as far as possible.

Article 4
Where the woman or girl to be repatriated cannot herself repay the cost of transfer, and has neither husband, relations, nor guardian to pay for her, the cost of repatriation shall be borne by the country where she is in residence as far as the nearest frontier or port of embarkation in the direction of the country of origin, and by the country of origin as regards the rest.

Article 5
The provisions of the foregoing Articles 3 and 4 shall not affect any private Conventions existing between the Contracting Governments.

Article 6
The Contracting Governments undertake, within legal limits, to exercise supervision, as far as possible, over the offices or agencies engaged in finding employment for women or girls abroad.

Article 7
Non-Signatory States can adhere to the present Agreement. For this purpose they shall notify their intention, through the diplomatic channel, to the French Government, who shall acquaint all the Contracting States.

Article 8
The present Agreement shall come into force six months after the exchange of ratifications. If one of the Contracting Parties denounces it, this denunciation shall only have effect as regards that party, and that only twelve months after the date of denunciation.

Article 9
The present Agreement shall be ratified, and the ratifications shall be exchanged, at Paris, with the least possible delay.

IN FAITH WHEREOF the respective plenipotentiaries have signed the present Agreement, and thereunto affixed their seals.

DONE at Paris, the 18 May 1904, in a single copy, which shall be deposited in the archives of the Ministry of Foreign Affairs of the French Republic, and of which one copy, certified correct, shall be sent to each Contracting Party.

International Convention for the Suppression of the White Slave Traffic, 1910

The Sovereigns, Heads of States, and Governments of the Powers hereinafter designated. Being equally desirous of taking the most effective steps for the suppression of the traffic known as the 'White Slave Traffic', have resolved to conclude a Convention with this object, and a draft thereof having been drawn up at a first Conference which met at Paris from 15 to 25 July 1902, they have appointed their plenipotentiaries, who met at a second Conference at Paris from 18 April to 4 May 1910 and agreed upon the following provisions:

Article 1
Whoever, in order to gratify the passions of another person, has procured, enticed, or led away, even with her consent, a woman or girl under age, for immoral purposes, shall be punished, notwithstanding that the various acts constituting the offence may have been committed in different countries.

Article 2
Whoever, in order to gratify the passions of another person, has, by fraud, or by means of violence, threats, abuse of authority, or any other method of compulsion, procured, enticed, or led away a woman or girl over age, for immoral purposes, shall also be punished, notwithstanding that the various acts constituting the offence may have been committed in different countries.

Article 3
The Contracting Parties whose legislation may not at present be sufficient to deal with the offences contemplated by the two preceding Articles engage to take or to propose to their respective legislatures the necessary steps to punish these offences according to their gravity.

Article 4

The Contracting Parties shall communicate to each other, through the intermediary of the Government of the French Republic, the laws which have already been or may in future be passed in their States relating to the object of the present Convention.

Article 5

The offences contemplated in Articles 1 and 2 shall, from the day on which the present Convention comes into force, be deemed to be lawfully included in the list of offences for which extradition may be granted in accordance with Conventions already existing between the Contracting Parties.

In cases in which the above provision cannot be made effective without amending existing legislation, the Contracting Parties engage to take or to propose to their respective legislatures the necessary measures.

Article 6

The transmission of Letters of Request relating to offences covered by the present Convention shall be effected:

1. Either by direct communication between the judicial authorities;
2. Or through the intermediary of the diplomatic or consular agent of the demanding State in the country to which the demand is addressed. This agent shall forward the Letter of Request direct to the competent judicial authority, and will receive directly from that authority the documents establishing the execution of the Letter of Request; (in these two cases a copy of the Letter of Request shall always be addressed at the same time to the superior authority of the State to which the demand is addressed);
3. Or through the diplomatic channel. Each Contracting Party shall make known, by a communication addressed to each of the other Contracting Parties, the method or methods of transmission which it recognises for Letters of Request emanating from that State.

All difficulties which may arise in connection with transmissions effected in cases 1 and 2 of the present Article shall be settled through the diplomatic channel.

In the absence of any different understanding, the Letter of Request must be drawn up either in the language of the State on whom the demand is made or in the language agreed upon between the two States concerned, or else it must be accompanied by a translation made in one of these two languages and duly certified by a diplomatic or consular agent of the demanding State, or by a sworn translator of the State on whom the demand is made.

The execution of the Letters of Request shall not entail repayment of expenses of any kind whatever.

Article 7

The Contracting Parties undertake to communicate to each other the records of convictions in respect of offences covered by the present Convention where the various acts constituting such offences have been committed in different countries. These documents shall be forwarded direct by the authorities designated in conformity with Article 1 of the Agreement concluded at Paris on 18 May 1904, to the corresponding authorities of the other Contracting States.

Article 8

Non-signatory States may accede to the present Convention. For this purpose they shall notify their intention by a declaration which shall be deposited in the archives of the Government of the French Republic. The latter shall communicate a certified copy thereof through the diplomatic channel to each of the Contracting States, and shall inform them at the same time of the date of such deposit. The laws of the acceding State relative to the object of the present Convention shall also be communicated with the said declaration. Six months after the date of the deposit of the said declaration the Convention shall come into force throughout the extent of the territory of the acceding State, which will thus become a contracting State. Accession to the Convention shall necessarily entail, without special notification, a concomitant accession to the Agreement of 18 May 1904, in its entirety, which shall take effect, on the same date as the Convention itself, throughout the territory of the acceding State.

The preceding stipulation does not, however, derogate from Article 7 of the aforementioned Agreement of 18 May 1904, which remains applicable in cases where a State prefers to accede solely to that Agreement.

Article 9
The present Convention, completed by a Final Protocol which forms an integral part thereof, shall be ratified, and the ratifications shall be deposited at Paris as soon as six of the Contracting States are in a position to do so.

A Protocol recording all deposits of ratifications shall be drawn up, of which a certified copy shall be transmitted through the diplomatic channel to each of the Contracting Parties. The present Convention shall come into force six months after the date of the deposit of the ratifications.

Article 10
In case of one of the Contracting Parties shall denounce the Convention, such denunciation shall only have effect as regards that State.

The denunciation shall be notified by a declaration which shall be deposited in the archives of the Government of the French Republic. The latter shall communicate a certified copy, through the diplomatic channel, to each of the Contracting States, and shall inform them at the same time of the date of deposit.

Twelve months after that date the Convention shall cease to take effect throughout the territory of the State which has denounced it.

The denunciation of the Convention shall not entail as of right a concomitant denunciation of the Agreement of 18 May 1904, unless it should be so expressly mentioned in the declaration; if not, the Contracting State must, in order to denounce the said Agreement, proceed in conformity with Article 8 of that Agreement.

Article 11
If a Contracting State desires the present Convention to come into force in one or more of its colonies, possessions, or consular judicial districts, it shall notify its intention to that effect by a declaration which shall be deposited in the archives of the Government of the French Republic. The latter shall communicate a certified copy thereof, through the diplomatic channel, to each of the Contracting States, and shall inform them at the same time of the date of the deposit.

The said declaration as regards colonies, possessions, or consular judicial districts, shall also communicate the laws which have been therein enacted relative to the object of the present Convention. Laws which may in future be enacted therein shall be equally communicated to the Contracting States in conformity with Article 4.

Six months after the date of deposit of the said declaration, the Convention shall come into force in the colonies, possessions, and consular judicial districts mentioned in such declaration.

The demanding State shall make known, by a communication addressed to each of the other Contracting States, which method or methods of transmission it recognises for Letters of Request destined for those colonies, possessions, or consular judicial districts in respect of which the declaration mentioned in the first paragraph of the present Article shall have been made.

The denunciation of the Convention by one of the Contracting States on behalf of one or more of its colonies, possessions, and consular judicial districts, shall be made under the forms 30 and conditions laid down by the first paragraph of the present Article. Such denunciation shall take effect twelve months after the date of the deposit of the declaration thereof in the archives of the Government of the French Republic.

Accession to the Convention by a Contracting State on behalf of one or more of its colonies, possessions, or consular judicial districts shall entail, as of right and without special notification, a concomitant accession to the Agreement of 18 May 1904 in its entirety. The said Agreement shall come into force therein on the same date as the Convention itself. Nevertheless, the denunciation of the Convention by a Contracting State on behalf of one or more of its colonies, possessions, or consular judicial districts shall not necessarily entail a concomitant denunciation of the Agreement of 18 May 1904, unless it should be so expressly mentioned in the declaration; moreover, the declarations which the Powers signatories of the Agreement of 18 May 1904 have been enabled to make respecting the accession of their colonies to the said Agreement are maintained.

Nevertheless, from and after the date of the coming into force of the present Convention, accessions to and denunciations of that Agreement as regards the colonies, possessions, or consular judicial districts of the Contracting States, shall be made in conformity with the stipulations of the present Article.

Article 12
The present Convention, which shall be dated 4 May 1910, may be signed in Paris up to 31 July following, by the plenipotentiaries of the Powers represented at the second Conference for the Suppression of the "White Slave Traffic".

DONE at Paris, the 4 May 1910, in a single copy, of which a certified copy shall be communicated to each of the Signatory Powers.

Final Protocol

At the moment of proceeding to the signature of the Convention of this day, the undersigned plenipotentiaries deem it expedient to indicate the sense in which Articles 1, 2, and 3 of that Convention are to be understood, and in accordance with which it is desirable that the Contracting States, in the exercise of their legislative sovereignty, should provide for the execution of the stipulations agreed upon or for their extension.

A. The stipulations of Articles 1 and 2 are to be considered as a minimum, seeing that it is self-evident that the Contracting Governments remain entirely free to punish other analogous offences, such, for example, as the procuring of women over age, even where neither fraud nor compulsion may have been exercised.
B. As regards the suppression of the offences provided for in Articles 1 and 2, it is fully understood that the words "woman or girl under age", "woman or girl over age" refer to women or girls under or over twenty completed years of age. A law may, nevertheless, fix a more advanced age for protection, on condition that it is the same for women or girls of every nationality.
C. With a view to the suppression of the same offences the law should decree, in every case, a punishment involving loss of liberty, without prejudice to other penalties, principal, or accessory; it should also take into account, apart from the age of the victim, the various aggravating circumstances which exist in the case, such as those referred to in Article 2, or the fact that the victim has been in effect delivered over to an immoral life.

D. The case of detention, against her will, of a woman or girl in a brothel could not, in spite of its gravity, be dealt with in the present Convention, seeing that it is governed exclusively by internal legislation.

The present Final Protocol shall be considered as forming an integral part of the Convention of this day, and shall have the same force, validity, and duration.

DONE AND SIGNED at Paris in a single copy, the 4 May 1910.

Appendix B: The Questions of the Summary of Reports (1921–1938)

Questions Within the 'Summary of Annual Reports' (Extracted from the 1922 Document)

C. 164. M. 40. 1924. IV.
Geneva, March 1924
League of Nations
Summary of Annual Reports for 1922
Received from Governments
Relating to the traffic in women and children

Question 1.
"Please give the name and address of the Central Authority appointed under Article 1 of the International Agreement of 1904".

Question 2.
"Please give particulars of any new legislative measures taken during the year 1922, which deal directly or indirectly with matters arising out of the traffic and especially with the:

"(a) Licensing of employment agencies (Article 6 of the Agreement of 1904)";
"(b) Repatriation of aliens (Article 3 of the Agreement of 1904)";
"(c) Punishment of offences (Articles 1 and 2 of the Convention of 1910)";
"(d) Extradition (Article 5 of the Convention of 1910)";
"(e) Immigration (Article 7 of the Convention of 1921)"".

Question 3.
"Please give as full information as possible of all cases during the year 1922 in which persons have been discovered committing the offences specified in Articles 1 and 2 of the Convention of 1910, indicating the action taken and the nationality and place of destination of the victim".

Question 4.
"Please give information as to the application of extradition procedure during the year 1922 for this class of offender, giving the names of the countries to which or from which offenders have been extradited.

"Note.—Mention any difficulties which may have arisen in connection with extradition".

Question 5.
"Please give information as to the alien prostitutes who have been deported or repatriated during the year 1922. stating the country of origin, with any information that can be obtained as to the circumstances under which they entered the country from which they have been sent away (Article 3 of the Agreement of 1904)".

Question 6.
"Please give a statement of the work done at railway stations and ports, and, in the case of those Governments which delegate this work to voluntary organisations, mention what organisations are employed".

Question 7.
"Please give information as to experience gained during the year 1922 in connection with employment agencies, mentioning any cases where it is suspected that women have been enticed abroad for immoral purposes through such agencies".

Question 8.
"Please report on the measures taken to protect women and children travelling to and from the country as emigrants".

Question concerning Children.
"If any system of adopting, pawning, or bartering children exists in your country or in any of its colonies, dependencies, or mandated areas, please state what steps have been or are being taken to protect these children from exploitation for immoral purposes".

Questions Within the 'Summary of Annual Reports' (Extracted from the 1932–1933 Document)

Official NO. **C.2.M.2.** 1934. 1V.
Geneva, January 15, 1934

League of Nations

Traffic in Women and Children Committee
Summary of Annual Report for 1932–1933, Prepared by the Secretariat.
Part I. Traffic in Women and Children.

Question 1.
Offences Discovered

"Please give as full information as possible of all cases during the year in which persons have been discovered procuring, enticing or leading away women, or children of either sex for immoral purposes in order to gratify

the passions of another person or attempting to commit these offences. "Please give the age and nationality of the offender and of the victim, the nature of the offence, and the action taken; and distinguish as far as possible between cases relating: (a) wholly to your own country; and (b) partly or mainly to another country, specifying the country".

Question 2.
Communications Between Central Authorities.

"*Please give particulars of any cases during the year in which communications have been sent to or received from other central authorities, giving the name of the central authority*".

Question 3.
Repatriation and Deportation

'*Please give the number, age and nationality of the following classes of persons who have been repatriated or deported during the year:*

"(a) Women and children who have been victims of the offences specified in Question 1";

"(b) Foreign prostitutes not included in (a)";

"(c) Men and women found or believed to be engaged in procuration or living on the earnings of prostitution'".

Question 4.
Employment Agencies.

"Please mention any cases in which it is known or suspected that during the year women or children have been sent abroad for immoral purposes by means of employment agencies, or that any attempt has been made to do so".

Question 5.
Travellers and Migrants

"Please give particulars of any cases in which it is known or suspected that during the year any attempt has been made to exploit for immoral purposes persons travelling in your country, whether as migrants or otherwise".

Question 6.
Children

"In addition to the information given in answer to Question 1, please state whether any cases have come to light during the year in which any attempt has been made to exploit children of either sex for immoral purposes, by any system of adopting, pawning, bartering of children or other method".

Question 7. (Original emphasis)
Legislative, Administrative, and Protective Measures

"(a) Please give an account of any changes during the year in legislative, administrative and protective measures".

"(b) Please give as fully as possible an account of measures, whether official or unofficial, taken during the year to prevent traffic in women and children. This need not include methods described in previous reports".

Index

A

Abolition 93, 153, 155, 234, 279, 296, 324
Abolitionist 16, 106, 111, 118, 173, 174, 217, 255, 298, 325
Adolescent 3, 10, 23, 25–27, 39, 52, 68, 70, 71, 73, 79, 85, 87, 94, 126, 136, 157, 160, 164, 186, 211, 238, 269, 325
African Union (AU) 67
Agency 2, 7, 23, 25–27, 70–76, 79, 83, 86–88, 94, 136, 174, 182, 184, 211, 213, 261, 267, 326
Anti-immigrant 4, 297
Anti-slavery 16, 62, 90, 93, 146, 151, 171, 197, 211, 252, 261, 276, 281, 291, 296, 297, 324
Anti-trafficking 5, 8, 10, 11, 16, 17, 19, 21, 24, 26, 29, 34, 35, 37–40, 51, 56, 62, 68, 90, 93, 94, 106, 110, 114–116, 121, 124, 125, 128, 129, 136, 176, 180, 186, 187, 197, 206, 207, 224, 226–230, 232, 240, 249, 251, 252, 254, 255, 259, 285, 290, 309, 310, 322–326
Anti-trafficking machine 7, 8, 15, 16, 28, 30, 33–35, 37, 56, 61, 68, 84, 87, 93, 209, 224, 229, 230, 240, 250, 255, 296, 297, 310, 311, 323, 325, 326, 328, 329
Archives 6, 30, 31, 38, 60, 106, 107, 115, 152, 213
Argentina 69, 178, 179, 188, 189, 197
Australia 9, 18, 29, 59, 94, 133, 145, 166, 167, 208, 260, 284, 296, 328

347

© The Editor(s) (if applicable) and The Author(s), under exclusive license to Springer Nature Switzerland AG 2023
E. A. Faulkner, *The Trafficking of Children*, Transnational Crime, Crime Control and Security, https://doi.org/10.1007/978-3-031-23566-5

B

Best interests 25, 57, 66, 71, 74, 75, 77, 83, 84, 86, 184, 211, 258, 260, 261, 267, 268, 286, 293, 304

C

Child abuse 167
Child exploitation 163, 164
Childhood 2, 10, 11, 21, 27, 36–38, 51–57, 65–68, 80, 88, 89, 93, 94, 107, 187, 211, 215, 258–260, 321–323
Child labour 11, 12, 15, 18, 28, 55, 58, 69, 133, 148, 153, 163, 167, 211–213, 216, 217, 263, 327
Child pornography 8, 18, 148, 166, 178, 194, 195, 219–221, 266
Child prostitution 8, 18, 20, 24, 28, 55, 68, 126, 148, 178, 186, 194, 195, 219–221, 273
Child protection 6, 53, 60, 72, 83, 193, 259, 273, 274
Children on the move 4, 36, 37, 55, 68, 69, 76–80, 82–84, 86, 88, 89, 91, 94, 292, 308, 327
Children's rights 2, 5, 10, 36, 37, 51, 52, 54, 56, 57, 61–66, 69, 71, 72, 77, 79, 80, 89, 93, 94, 108, 188, 189, 211, 219, 311, 328
Child trafficking 1–3, 5–12, 14–17, 20, 21, 23, 24, 28–34, 36–39, 51–53, 56, 70, 73, 76–78, 86, 88, 91, 105–108, 110, 113, 115, 143, 144, 146, 147, 150, 151, 167, 179, 183, 185–187, 192, 193, 195, 205, 208, 209, 216, 220, 223, 231, 236, 237, 239, 240, 248–250, 258, 268, 269, 271, 273, 274, 279, 283, 285, 289, 292, 300, 301, 310, 311, 321–323, 325, 328
Colonialism 5, 6, 16, 32, 35, 37, 38, 54, 61, 62, 89, 135, 197, 207, 208, 213, 240, 298, 322, 323, 325
Commercial sexual exploitation 1, 27, 51, 74, 163, 192, 195, 219, 223, 255, 278, 285, 289
Consent 22, 26–28, 57, 59, 75, 76, 86, 108, 112, 113, 121, 132, 135, 137, 158, 163, 173, 174, 180, 183, 186, 190, 195, 232, 238, 256, 286, 291, 308, 326, 334
Contemporary slavery 147, 163, 223, 279
Convention on the Elimination of All Forms of Discrimination against Women (CEDAW) 82, 151, 189, 190
Convention on the Rights of the Child (CRC) 2, 7, 10, 22, 36, 39, 51, 52, 56, 60, 63–74, 76, 80, 82, 83, 86, 88, 89, 94, 115, 150, 151, 178, 186, 188–195, 197, 210, 211, 214, 223, 231, 260, 261, 267, 293, 323, 327
Council of Europe (CoE) 40, 232, 247–259, 261, 271, 272, 274, 276, 281, 299–301, 310
Council of Europe Trafficking Convention 2005 300

Court 39, 66, 157, 159, 161, 176, 234–239, 261, 263, 268, 275, 285, 300, 303, 310
Crime 2, 14, 17, 23, 27, 28, 35, 78, 94, 108, 113, 144, 147, 164, 176, 180, 182, 184–186, 207, 210, 230, 232–234, 238, 257, 261, 263, 278, 283, 327
Criminal law 23, 91, 94, 159–161, 176, 177, 231, 232

D
Declaration of Geneva 59
Discrimination 25, 82, 84, 235, 297

E
Economic and Social Council (ECOSOC) 156, 162, 163
Empire 6, 35, 38, 60, 121, 127, 131, 132, 135, 136, 230
End Child Prostitution and Trafficking (ECPAT) 2, 70, 284, 293, 300
EU Directive 248, 252, 268, 281
Eurocentric 7, 115
European Court of Human Rights (ECHR) 3, 22, 40, 88, 157–159, 161, 234, 250, 252, 274, 275, 282, 298, 310
European Union (EU) 40, 72, 182, 247–252, 259, 262–266, 268, 269, 271–274, 280, 281, 290, 310
Exploitation for immoral purposes 5, 131

F
France 108, 110, 111, 114, 115, 127, 152, 157–161, 250, 262, 275

G
General principles 69, 70, 89, 267
Global Estimates of Modern Slavery (GEMS) 8, 127, 143
Group of Experts on Action against Trafficking in Human Beings (GRETA) 254, 259, 261, 272

H
Harm 28, 38, 73, 76, 80, 82, 91, 144, 147, 160, 166, 184, 212, 213, 216, 223, 259, 261, 292, 311, 321, 322, 324, 325, 329
Harmful 22, 86, 91, 134, 166, 209, 323, 328
Hostile environment 3, 226, 282
Human rights 1, 7, 10, 28, 29, 35, 36, 56–58, 60–65, 69, 76, 80, 82, 83, 91, 93, 94, 144, 147, 150, 153, 156, 160, 168–171, 175, 177, 189, 191, 218, 220, 222, 226, 231, 232, 247, 248, 250–252, 254, 256, 260, 267, 281, 322, 327
Human Rights Committee (HRC) 8
Human trafficking 1, 7–9, 11, 13, 15–18, 23–27, 29, 30, 32, 34, 37, 39, 68, 74, 82, 88, 90, 93, 105, 107–109, 112, 113, 126, 136, 137, 143, 144, 147–151, 157, 159, 163, 171–174, 176, 180–182, 196, 197, 205, 206,

210, 211, 217, 218, 220, 222, 224–229, 231, 233, 236, 240, 249–255, 262–267, 269, 270, 275–278, 281–283, 290, 301, 303, 308, 322, 326
Human Trafficking Case Law Database (HTCLD) 39, 206, 236

I

Ideal victims 16, 20, 22, 82, 90, 182, 226, 311
Immoral purposes 7, 38, 110, 112, 116, 128, 131, 133, 134, 150, 322, 332, 334
Imperialism 61, 89, 94, 135, 229, 297, 298
Instrument 7, 12, 26, 37–39, 52, 56, 62, 63, 65, 72, 80, 81, 86, 90, 94, 107, 110, 113, 114, 119, 120, 134, 143, 150, 155, 162, 164, 169–172, 175–179, 182, 195–197, 215, 231, 239, 240, 250, 252, 253, 257, 258, 262–264, 266, 274, 276, 299
International Court of Justice (ICJ) 144
International Covenant on Civil and Political Rights (ICCPR) 62, 74, 81, 150, 170
International Covenant on Economic, Social and Cultural Rights (ICESCR) 62, 81
International Criminal Court (ICC) 39, 155, 230–234
International Labour Organization (ILO) 15, 17, 39, 86, 143, 152, 160, 163, 185, 206, 211, 213, 214, 216, 217, 248, 259, 268, 280, 282
International law 6–8, 12, 18, 26, 29, 30, 35, 36, 39, 51, 52, 62, 64, 68, 73, 74, 76, 79, 81–83, 86, 89–91, 106, 119, 134, 144, 145, 148–151, 167, 169, 171, 176, 180, 182, 183, 186, 188, 191, 211, 226, 231, 260, 293, 296, 321–323, 328

J

Jus cogens 144, 145, 176

L

League of Nations (LoN) 6, 30–33, 37, 38, 51, 56–58, 60, 86, 89, 106–108, 114–119, 121, 125, 126, 130, 150–154, 175, 191, 213, 291
League of Nations Temporary Slavery Commission (TSC) 152, 153, 191, 214
League's Traffic in Women and Children Committee (LNTWC) 31, 38, 106, 116, 121, 125

M

Marriage 7, 15, 18, 24, 55, 126, 146, 150, 162, 163, 166, 183, 209, 212, 268, 281
Migration 7, 10, 11, 25, 26, 28, 29, 54, 55, 78, 79, 82–91, 94, 120, 136, 137, 167, 182, 187, 251, 274, 292, 294, 296, 311, 322, 324, 326–328

Index

Minors 9, 10, 24, 76, 89, 108, 113, 120, 121, 133, 143, 178, 238, 251, 258, 285, 290, 291, 302
Mobility 5, 11, 26, 36, 86–88, 94, 114, 129, 135, 136, 175, 186, 207, 240, 247, 321
Modern slavery 8, 9, 12, 17–19, 28, 29, 34, 35, 38–40, 79, 87, 89–91, 93, 94, 112, 144–151, 156, 158, 197, 205–207, 209–212, 217, 218, 220, 223, 229, 247, 251, 261, 262, 266, 275–287, 289, 291, 293, 296–298, 301, 310, 311, 321, 323, 325, 327, 328
Modern Slavery Act (MSA) 9, 18, 40, 184, 226, 248, 270, 276, 277, 279–286, 300, 301

N

National Crime Agency (NCA) 278, 301
Nationalism 32, 40, 90, 136–138, 240, 260, 262, 291, 311, 325, 328
Non-governmental organisation (NGO) 2, 12, 35, 54, 93, 125, 174, 180, 216, 224, 228, 229, 256, 258, 325
Non-punishment 261, 299–301, 308, 309

O

Optional Protocol to the Convention on the Rights of the Child on a Communication Procedure (OPIC) 69, 187
Optional Protocol to the Convention on the Rights of the Child on the Involvement of Children in Armed Conflict (OPAC) 68, 186, 231
Optional Protocol to the Convention on the Rights of the Child on the Sale of Children, child prostitution and child pornography (OPSC) 68, 69, 150, 186, 188, 189, 194, 195, 221, 231, 269, 271
Organised crime 254, 257, 262, 278
Organization for Security and Co-operation in Europe (OCSE) 248, 261

P

Palermo Protocol 26, 69, 83, 134, 149, 150, 176, 178, 180–183, 185, 186, 197, 222, 251, 255–257, 261, 264–266, 276, 308, 323
Patriarchy 16, 32, 37, 62, 90, 197, 310, 311, 322, 325, 328
Pawned 133, 134
Policy 3, 5–8, 12, 15, 19, 21–23, 25, 26, 28–30, 32, 34, 36–40, 51, 53, 55, 56, 62, 65, 70, 75, 78–80, 83, 86–88, 90, 91, 93, 105, 118, 134, 146, 149, 176, 182, 193, 197, 207, 211, 222, 224, 226, 233, 247, 248, 251, 255, 265, 273, 280, 281, 287, 295, 299, 300, 321, 323–326,

Politics 5, 36, 94, 115, 153, 169, 325
Powers attaching to the right of ownership 157, 233, 234
Practices similar to slavery 150, 162, 163, 165, 256
Protection 21, 22, 27, 29, 37, 52, 53, 56–60, 63, 64, 69, 71, 72, 74, 78, 80–86, 89–91, 93, 111, 120, 121, 126, 135–137, 144, 153, 159, 169, 170, 174, 175, 177, 178, 184, 192–194, 210, 213, 220, 225, 237, 238, 249, 253, 256–258, 261, 265, 268–271, 283, 292, 293, 296, 297, 299, 308–310, 321, 326, 331, 339

R

Race 6, 16, 21, 37, 38, 59, 62, 69, 90, 107, 109–111, 115, 129, 134, 135, 138, 172, 187, 197, 208, 226, 262, 274, 290, 294, 309, 310, 325
Rescue 2, 7, 16, 21, 24, 54, 76, 82, 83, 87, 89, 126, 135–137, 173, 174, 182, 211, 212, 215, 240, 258, 279, 289, 296, 321, 324, 326–328

S

Sale of children 8, 18, 68, 148, 194, 210, 219–221
Servitude 3, 133, 145, 150, 157–163, 167, 170, 171, 226, 248, 256, 281–283

Sex 11, 12, 17, 19, 22–24, 27, 28, 107, 118, 121, 168, 172, 174, 187, 194, 210, 213, 219, 229, 255, 275, 276, 281
Sex trafficking 13, 16, 23, 227
Sexual exploitation 1, 2, 7, 18, 20, 21, 24, 39, 56, 108–110, 134, 144, 147, 150, 172, 175, 180, 189–192, 194, 195, 209, 217, 219, 220, 227, 238, 248, 252, 253, 255, 256, 262–264, 266, 273, 285, 289–291, 322
Sex work 255
Siliadin v. France 157, 158, 161
1926 Slavery Convention 152–155, 157, 159, 162–164, 171, 232, 282
Slave trade 93, 145, 150, 162, 170, 171, 237, 261
Sold 8, 20, 110, 132, 173, 255
Special rapporteur 8, 20, 39, 85, 143, 194, 206, 209, 217–222, 272, 284, 286
Statistical Office of the European Union (EUROSTAT) 8, 9
Sustainable Development Goals (SDGs) 39, 143, 205, 208, 209, 211, 212, 217, 274

T

The 1956 Supplementary Slavery Convention 165
The US Trafficking in Persons Report (TIP report) 227–229, 301
Third World Approaches to International Law (TWAIL) 30, 33, 35, 36, 169, 170, 323

Index

Trafficked child 7, 9, 16, 20, 21, 27, 28, 51, 61, 72, 89, 94, 193, 259, 269, 274, 285, 286, 311, 327, 328
Trafficking in Persons Report 8, 9, 13, 18, 79, 228
Trafficking in persons (TIP) 12, 18, 20, 39, 84, 85, 93, 150, 174, 177, 179–181, 217, 222, 226–228, 233, 237, 238, 247, 248, 251, 257, 272
Trafficking Protocol 12, 14, 15, 19, 22, 27, 68, 73, 81, 86, 110, 113, 172, 173, 176–178, 181, 185, 187–189, 195, 205, 231, 232, 238, 240, 253, 263, 264, 267, 281, 308, 322
Trafficking Victims Protection Act (TVPA) 13, 224–227, 258, 269, 271, 276, 292, 297, 299, 309, 328
Transnational Organised Crime 177, 195
Treaty(ies) 10, 60, 62, 64, 66, 69, 70, 76, 77, 80–82, 118, 119, 150, 153, 170, 171, 173, 177, 188, 189, 234, 250, 256, 274

U

United Kingdom 2, 10, 16–18, 22, 31, 39, 40, 72, 106, 108, 109, 145, 148, 157, 166, 184, 219, 226, 247, 248, 262, 270, 274, 276, 279, 281, 287, 298, 299, 302–307, 310, 328
United Nations Children's Fund (UNICEF) 12, 39, 79, 163, 185, 192, 206, 216, 223, 224, 248, 259, 268, 285, 300
United Nations Convention against Transnational Organised Crime (UNCTOC) 177
United Nations High Commissioner for Refugees (UNHCR) 68, 78, 268
United Nations Office on Drugs and Crime (UNODC) 8, 21, 39, 79, 143, 190, 205, 236, 268, 285, 290
United Nations (UN) 2, 6, 9, 18–20, 22, 31, 32, 35, 37, 39, 51, 52, 56, 57, 60, 61, 63, 64, 67–69, 71, 73, 76, 79, 81, 82, 85, 86, 94, 110, 115, 143, 148, 151, 154, 157, 162, 166, 168, 169, 171, 172, 175–177, 180, 183–186, 189, 191, 193, 194, 197, 205, 206, 208, 209, 213, 216, 219, 221–223, 231–233, 240, 248–250, 257, 268, 272, 280, 284, 286, 293, 296, 322
United States of America 9, 11, 23, 118, 178, 179, 224, 328
Universal Declaration of Human Rights (UDHR) 60–62, 86, 150, 155, 162, 168, 170, 171, 252, 274

V

V.C.L and A.N. v United Kingdom 3, 40, 157
Victim 3, 4, 14, 16, 17, 21–26, 28, 36, 40, 53, 61, 71, 79, 82, 83, 85, 86, 88–92, 94, 106, 111,

113, 126, 131–133, 135, 136, 144, 151, 157, 158, 170, 173, 174, 177, 178, 183–185, 210, 218–220, 222, 224, 226, 232, 235, 237, 239, 249, 252–254, 256–259, 261, 263–271, 273, 281, 283–287, 289–291, 293, 297–300, 302–304, 308–311, 323–328, 332, 339
victimhood 4, 88
Victims of crime 186
Vienna Convention on the Law of Treaties (VCLT) 171
Violence 13, 25, 89, 109, 113, 136, 181, 193, 209, 210, 217, 218, 232, 284, 296, 308, 334
Vulnerability 15, 25, 28, 36, 52, 57, 63, 74, 80, 82, 83, 134, 183, 184, 212, 256, 259, 260, 265, 267, 271, 273, 276, 297, 326

W

White slavery 4, 6, 20, 21, 30, 31, 90, 111–113, 119–121, 126, 127, 129, 130, 136, 226, 289, 291, 322, 323, 327
White supremacy 37, 135, 230, 310, 322, 325
Women 2, 4–6, 12, 17, 20, 22, 39, 57, 58, 74, 82, 85, 88–90, 106–108, 110–116, 118–121, 126, 127, 129, 130, 132, 135, 136, 145, 151, 172–180, 182, 189, 209, 213, 217, 218, 222, 223, 226, 227, 230, 233, 237, 252, 254–256, 263, 264, 267, 268, 272, 281, 291, 322, 326, 331–333, 339
Worst Forms of Child Labour 15, 29, 160, 163, 210, 211, 214–216, 282
Worst Forms of Child Labour Convention no.182 (WFCL) 15, 214, 215, 231

Printed and bound by CPI Group (UK) Ltd, Croydon, CR0 4YY
03/12/2024
01799310-0001